Dear Bill.

Letters of WWII wartime adventures

By William "Bill" Alderson & William "Bill" Burling

TURNER PUBLISHING COMPANY

Turner Publishing Company Staff:
Chief Editor: Robert J. Martin
Designer: Shelley R. Brown

Library of Congress Catalog Card No.
97-60749
ISBN: 978-1-68162-274-3

Limited Edition. Additional copies may be purchased
directly from the publisher.

Cover photo: (l-r) Front: Earl J. Norris, Ford B. Rogers, Robert B.
McGlasson, William H. Alderson. Back: Harry A. Ehlers, Carl E.
Duncan, Louis S. Lazenby, Frank S. Tietz, George E. Sloan.

Table of Contents

About The Authors - Bill Alderson 6
                  - Bill Burling 6
Author's Acknowledgment 7
Synopsis of Manuscript 8
Publisher's Message 9
Prologue 10

Letter Date	**Open**	**Close**	
14 Mar '43	Dear Bill	Box Car Bill	11
15 Mar	Dear Bill	Baggy Eyed Bill	12
21 Mar	Dear Box Car Bill	Snowbird Bill	13
24 Mar	Dear Baggy Eyed Bill	Much Better Now Bill	14
16 Mar	Dear Bill	Truly Sorry Bill	15
18 Mar	Dear Bill	Outhouse Bill	16
27 Mar	Outhouse Bill	The Lowest Midshipman	17
21 Mar	Dear Bill	Bacillus Bill	18
24 Mar	Dear Bill, AKA Albert E.	Grand Prix Bill	19
30 Mar	Dear Bacillus & Grand Prix	Weary Bill	20
27 Mar	Dear Weary Will	Tinker Bill	21
8 Apr	Dear Tinker Bill	Pooped Bill	22
17 Apr	Dear Begonia Bill	Anxious Bill	23
1 Apr	Dear Pooped	Begonia Bill	24
12 Apr	Dear Beat Up	Hog Wallow Bill	25
3 May	Dear Hog Wallow Bill	On The Move Bill	27
26 Apr	Dear Movable	Bridegroom Bill	28
29 May	Dear Bridegroom Bill	Paroled Bill	29
21 May	Dear Parolee	Titillated In Texas	30
29 Jun	Dear Titillated	Ignoramus Bill	31
24 Jun	Dear Deck Officer	Bull's Eye Bill	32
5 Aug	Dear Bull's Eye Bill	Rubbery Knees Bill	34
30 Jul	Dear Rubber Kneed	Beau Brummel Bill	36
28 Sep	Dear Beau Brummel Bill	Older & Wiser Bill	38
18 Sep	Dear Older & Wiser	Poppa Bear	40
21 Nov	Dear Poppa Bear	Over Drilled Bill	42
12 Dec	Dear Wm.	Getting Nervous Bill	44
8 Nov	Dear Over Drilled	The Snapshooter	45
12 Jan '44	Dear Snapshooter	Busy Bill	47
2 Jan	Dear Bill	Philosopher Bill	49
20 Jan	Dear Nervous	Ripcord Bill	50
24 Jan	Dear Ripcord Bill	Aloha Bill	51
14 Feb	Dear Bombardier	Somewhat Sober Bill	52
17 Jan	Dear Busy B.	Brimstone Bill	54
1 Mar	Dear Bomber Bill	Really Sorry Now Bill	56
1 Mar	Dear Aloha	The Replacement	58
15 Mar	Dear Bill	Bronco Bill	60
28 Mar	Dear Brimstone Bill	Nervous Bill	61
22 Mar	Dear Jolly Tar	Bereaved Bill	63

7 Apr	Dear Somewhat	The Traumatized Toggler	65
14 Apr	Dear Bombardier Bill	Snakesbelly Bill	67
11 Apr	Dear Really Sorry	Cheers . . . Wino Will	69
20 Apr	Dear Nervous	Mayday Bill	71
7 May	Dear Bereaved Bill	Extremely Sorry Now Bill	74
17 May	Dear Pub Crawler	Tired Of It All Bill	76
12 May	Dear Bill	Take Good Care - Magellan	78
23 May	Dear Snakesbelly	Bereaved Again In Britain	81
?? Jun	Dear Traumatized Toggeleer	Enough Of This Bill	84
29 May	Dear Extremely, Etc.	Sitting Bill	86
17 Jun	Dear Bomber Bill	Becalmed Bill	89
14 Jun	Dear Bill	Quick Draw Bill	91
23 Jun	Dear Wino Bill	Expendable Bill	94
24 Jun	Dear Tired Of It All	Believing Bill	96
2 Jul	Dear Enough Of This	Buzzard Bill	99
12 Jul	Dear Tired & Had Enough	Biting The Bullet Bill	102
20 Jul	Dear Guns	Cliff Hanger Bill	106
26 Jul	Dear Wherever You Are	Bemedaled And Bemused Bill	108
5 Aug	Dear Fore And Aft	Barnacle Bill	110
17 Aug	Dear Paradise Islander	Pensive & Proud Bill	112
1 Sep	Dear Slocum	Bill Of The Squared Circle	115
5 Sep	Dear Permanently Pacific	In Hog Heaven Bill	116
16 Aug	Dear Bereaved Magellan	Worn Out Bill	117
16 Sep	Dear Worn Out	Basking In Bounty Bill	119
30 Sep	Dear Sitting Bill	Disposable Bill	121
27 Sep	Dear Disposable	Bug-Eyed Bill	123
15 Oct	Dear Surviving	Rear Echelon Bill	124
7 Oct	Dear Quick Draw Bill	The Seagoing Guinea Pig	125
21 Oct	Dear Guinea Pig	Baron Bill	127
24 Nov	Dear Bomber Man	Shadow Bill	129
1 Jan '45	Dear Shadow	Running In Place Bill	131
27 Dec	Dear Believing Bill	Filipino Bill	132
2 Feb	Dear Filipino	Kittyhawk "45"	134
23 Jan	Dear Buzzard Bill	Homesick Bill	136
2 Mar	Dear Homesick	Ace Alderson	138
3 Feb	Dear Homeward Bound Bill	Student Of The Philippines	140
4 Apr	Dear Filipino Student	Regards, Kangaroo Bill	142
1 Mar	Dear Wild Blue Bill	Blue Bill	144
14 Mar	Dear Chicago Resident	Scared Silly Bill	146
30 Apr	Dear Wild Blue Boy	White Haired Bill	148
1 May	Dear Scared Silly & Blue	Baron Bill	150
2 May	Dear Homebody	I Want To Go Home Bill	151
7 May	Dear Bombardier	Anxiety Bill	152
10 May	Dear Cliffhanger Bill	Anxious Bill	154
14 May		Happy For You Bill	156
17 May	Dear Barnacle, Etc., Bill	Short Fingernail Bill	158
20 May	Dear Hog Heaven Bill	Gung-No Bill	160
23 May	Dear Kittyhawk Bill	End Of The Rope Bill	162
2 Jun	Dear White Locks, Anxiety	Loopy Bill	164
26 Jun	Dear Ace, Kangaroo, Baron	Urgent Civilian Bill	166
1 Jul	Dear Anxious	Straight And Level Bill	168
17 Jul	Dear Loopy Bill	Exterior Decorator Bill	169
24 Jul	Dear Airborne Acrobat	Barnacle Bill	171
2 Aug	Dear Short Fingernails	Former Flying Fool Bill	172

14 Aug	Dear Straight And Level	Survivor Bill	174
29 Aug	Dear Former Flying Fool	Banzai Bill	175
31 Aug	Dear Gung-No	Wondering William	177
21 Sep	Dear Urgent Decorator	Job Hunter Bill	179
9 Oct	Dear Wondering William	Reluctant Wanderer Bill	181
22 Oct	Dear Barnacle Bill Burling	The Housemaid's Knee	183
17 Nov	Dear Job Hunter Bill	Inching Along Home Bill	184
23 Nov	Dear Domesticated Bill	Wayfaring Stranger Bill	186
1 Dec	Dear Banzai Bill	Blowout Bill	187
21 Dec	Dear Reluctant Wanderer	Tote That Bale Bill	188
23 Dec	Dear Returnee Bill	Choked Up Bill	189
27 Dec	Dear Housemaid's Knee	Homeward Bound Bill	190
1 Jan '46	Dear Inchworm	Scrivener Bill	191
7 Jan	Dear Tote That Bale Bill	Frisco Derelict Bill	192
12 Jan	Dear Choked Up Wayfarer	Welcome Wagon William	194
17 Jan	Dear Welcome Wagon Bill	Reluctant Seafarer Bill	195
12 Apr	Dear Bill	Soon A Civilian Bill	197
17 Apr	Dear Soon	Bacchus Bill	198

After Word - 10 April 1990 199
After Word - 20 June 1995 199
Epilogue 200

ABOUT THE AUTHORS

WILLIAM H. "BILL" ALDERSON

Bill Alderson was born 9 February 1922 in Pittsburgh, Pennsylvania, and raised in Chicago, Illinois. Married 6 June 1942 to Shirley R. Russell.

Alderson attended Illinois Wesleyan University, Bloomington, Illinois, where he met William "Bill" Burling who became a fraternity brother, enduring friend, fellow hunter, fisherman and correspondent.

Alderson served as bombardier-navigator aboard B-24s during World War II and aboard B-26s during the Korean conflict.

Alderson has four children, six grandchildren and two great grandchildren and lives on the shore of Lake Michigan in New Buffalo, Michigan.

WILLIAM S. "BILL" BURLING

Bill Burling was born in 1922 in Bloomington, Illinois, and was raised there attending public schools and Illinois Wesleyan University.

Burling entered the Navy shortly after Pearl Harbor and qualified for Officer's training.

At Illinois Wesleyan University, Burling met Bill Alderson, a fellow pheasant hunter and fraternity brother. Their friendship spanned the war years and many subsequent forays into field and forest.

Burling served as deck Officer aboard a Landing Ship Tank (LST) in the Pacific. His ship participated in a score of landings against Japanese forces dug in on atolls and islands. Burling returned home in May of 1946, after the decommissioning of his ship on the East Coast.

Bill Burling lives near Howe, Indiana, on a small lake. He is married to Dorothy, and they have four children and two granddaughters.

"DEAR BILL:"

The authors wish to thank the following for their valuable contributions to the completion of this book.

Brian Rzepczynski
Woodbridge, Illinois

Bill Alderson, Jr.
St. Simons Island, Georgia

Al Aplin
Bettendorf, Iowa

Beverly Albright
Decatur, Indiana

SYNOPSIS

The radio announcement of the attack on Pearl Harbor effectively subdued a group of carefree young men gathered for Sunday dinner at their fraternity house in Bloomington, Illinois. For them, it began a long hiatus from campus life and classroom studies. The learning process, however, continued on a much accelerated level with an entirely different curriculum in unusual and often very dangerous surroundings. The wartime lives and times of two of those naive midwesterners, Bill Alderson and Bill Burling, and their metamorphosis from students to combat veterans has, at long last, been assembled (over 50 years hence) to answer the proverbial family question, "What did you do in the war, Daddy?".

The letters passing back and forth between these two "Bills" trace their day-by-day wartime adventures (and occasional misadventures). The fear and uncertainty. The loss of friends and comrades. The longing for stateside family and friends. The hope that the two would "see the elephant" and live to tell about it.

"Dear Bill:"

A true accounting of the experiences and thoughts of two young midwesterners and their metamorphosis from students to combat Officers during World War II.

In a series of letters, the "Bills" trace their leap from civilian life to Midshipman and Aviation Cadet . . . and, finally, to deck Officer on a Landing Ship Tank (LST) in the Pacific and bombardier-navigator aboard a B-24 Liberator over Germany.

The letters, to a kindred spirit, bolstered their determination to return home with body, mind and psyche intact. The "Bills" find humor, cynicism and courage (or the lack of it) in their journey from naive volunteer to the sights and sounds of vicious combat on the sea and in the air.

Two average guys, now much older and a tad wiser, still proud to be Americans and numbered among our combat veterans.

Sunday
14 March 1943

DEAR BILL—-

        S.A.A.C.C.! To the uninitiated this stands for San Antonio Aviation Cadet Center, Texas. Currently I am on board a train headed for I know not what with a bunch of other guys who know not what. Judging by the appearance and countenance of my "fellow travelers" the V for Victory symbol is woefully premature. The Third Reich may go on an extra 1,000 years at a full gallop.

        The Army, in it's infinite wisdom, has commandeered rolling stock that civilians (in their infinite wisdom) quit riding on at the turn of the century. The prevailing weather conditions locally are the prevailing weather conditions inside. The bleachers at Soldier Field are much more comfortable to the weary rump than the seats on board. Three hours out of the 8th Street Station in Chicago, cigarettes, cigars, arm pits and someone who had sauerkraut or brussel sprouts for dinner nearly ended my budding career in the air. Opening a window was out due to the prevailing local weather conditions.

        Judging by the frequent stops at sidings to allow V.I.P. express trains to pass, and our blistering pace when we are moving, we may be two or three days en route. This, of course, means attempting to sleep on our thundering Iron Horse and standing in line to visit a tiny cubicle labeled "women" on our end of the car. First time for me in a ladies john. No surprises . . . but after a thousand sorties by the volunteers, no woman alive would hoist her skirt in our less than tidy facility. I shudder to think of conditions in the one labeled "Men" . . . or after breakfast tomorrow in either cubicle.

        Another siding stop and a mail box within sight. Should we be permitted a five minute leg stretcher, I'll drop this in for delivery. Perhaps we can correspond during the upcoming unpleasantness and keep track of one another and whatever happens along the way . . . or just to reminisce. The next communique from the Red Baron will come with a return address. I am sure by that time there will be further reasons for seeking employment in a deferred occupation. Perhaps the political arena is the answer. They only get shot at, and deservedly so, by sadly disillusioned constituents and not whole armies of Germans or Japs screaming Banzai or Heil Hitler or whatever.

BEST REGARDS—BOX CAR BILL

P.S. When you write, don't worry about having your letters miss me. Even the Army P. O. can't screw up forwarding.

Monday
15 March 1943

DEAR BILL——

The Postal box in which I had hoped to drop my letter of Sunday was there . . . but no one was allowed to detrain, even for such an important document. The plan now is to mail in New Orleans this evening. Neophyte that I am, even I can see that the Army will change its collective mind and the Postmark might read Ellis Island . . . or even Chicago, from whence we came. A truly inspired thought, that one.

We are in Mississippi at the moment, thundering along as usual, and viewing a lot of red earth, tin and tar paper shacks . . . and "Whites Only" signs nailed on everything. I don't think the South will rise again, as some Rebs predict, until they adjust some of their thinking.

My misgivings about food and sleep have not entirely come to pass. The food has been pretty good, and the railroad people try to prepare and present it in an appetizing manner. Some of the two hundred guys sharing this governmental largess have not been accustomed to more than one eating utensil. To them, cups and saucers and tablecloths are foreign objects . . . so there is a great deal of slurpings, gnashings and knives garnished with mashed potatoes and peas. The head waiter often has an expression on his face like a basset hound crapping Coke bottle caps.

Getting to sleep on this bucket was not difficult. The clickety clack of the wheels hitting the rail joints has a soporific beat like counting sheep, only a lot faster. Staying asleep is the problem. The Fourth of July celebration we have at every crossing or small town would wake a hibernating grizzly bear. Whistles, hootings, bells bonging and flashing red lights add up to about fifteen minutes of clickety clacking sleep at a time. Having a wonderful time . . . wish I was home.

Listen up, y'all . . . Noo Orleeens in sight. Will write again concerning the further misadventures of——

BAGGY EYED BILL

21 March, '43

DEAR BOX CAR BILL—-

It is good to hear from you. Let's keep the letters coming. You'll note that I am in Plattsburg, NY, which is somewhere this side of the North Pole.

It seems years since we were college boys and Pearl Harbor was a neat Naval base. I am now called (among other things) a Midshipman, which is the lowest form of life in the navy.

I joined the Navy in Sept. '42, and was promised Officer's training if I could make it. I had to go back to High School for some math and physics and Jim Welch went with me. We continued at IWU and were told to finish out the year. With going to both High School and IWU, plus working, I found it left very little spare time.

My job at the theater provided some excitement when four hoodlums tried to crash the gate and started a fight. Without thinking I joined in and pinned one of the social misfits to the floor. One or two of his accomplices circled me, all the while hitting me in the face and kicking me. We were soon joined by other employees and the fight was under control. Police arrived and we found that our opponents had criminal records and one or two were on parole. I had a very sore nose and blew chunks of meat out of it for a few days.

As soon as school ended in early June, I took a job at Tipp City, Ohio, which is near Dayton. The pay was good and the work was monotonous. I was on an assembly line making parachute flares. These items are filled with white phosphorous which burns at an alarming rate. I soldered the caps on . . . very carefully. I worked a little fast for the older people on the line and was put in a room full of women making wiring harnesses. That was very educational considering the shortage of men.

The job didn't last very long and I quit so as to have two weeks before going to the Navy in August. I went home and began disposing of my personal wealth. Most of it went into a can in the alley and my trusty shotgun went to an ex-neighbor who will keep it while I'm gone. My beautiful 1931 Ford touring car was sold to a friend with the understanding I can have it back for the same price, $50.00, when I return. I then walked everywhere and soon told my girlfriend goodbye and boarded a train such as you've described with the destination being Mt. Pleasant, Michigan, and a teacher's college.

We made the 6-hour trip in only two days with the usual stops to let modern trains go by. The days were very warm and the nights cool and it was very crowded.

Upon arrival at Central Michigan College of Education, we quickly learned they weren't ready for us. The housing was fine, but uniforms were issued one item at a time . . . the food was good, but sparse. The students in the girls dorms complained of the noise we made while marching at 6 A.M. It seemed that they feared we might be carrying some sort of plague. Within a short time, the classes picked up steam, the uniforms arrived (and almost fit) and the guy in charge of the food was caught selling food stamps. We then got enough to eat. The classes were tough but the teachers were good. Some fell by the wayside, either because of the schedule or voluntarily to escape the monotony of the routine. It was run everywhere, calisthenics, study, run again. Lights out!

So, in late December, we were divided and I drew the short straw and came to Plattsburg, NY. Another beautiful ride in an antique wagon with square railroad-type wheels.

I often think of our college days and the hunting trips and walking all day at a brisk pace. Your fording of streams always afforded a good deal of levity and, of course, your shooting ability was a study in total frustration for you . . . and comedy for me. I'm sure we both remember moving toward home in our jointly owned $40.00 car when you fell asleep and tried to bulldoze a culvert. Poor George Sweeney bore the brunt of the sudden stop and bent his shotgun over his knees. We were very lucky that day and the loss of the car was not all that bad. It was beautiful with the shades on the back windows and the vases for flowers and the reclining front seat. It would have been more valuable if the damned thing would start without pushing. Ah, memories.

The guard says "lights out." Will write again later.

SNOWBIRD BILL

DEAR BAGGY-EYED BILL—

Here you are touring the sunny south and eating fancy meals . . . and I am sweating out the last days of school here at good old Plattsburg. It's no wonder they held the Winter Olympics here . . . they could do it in August. Your train ride is much longer than either of mine. I personally think a 400-mile ride could be accomplished in less than three days. Perhaps you've already thought of that!

My last epistle was cut short by one of the guards here. I cannot fully describe my feelings upon my arrival here. The sky was black and snow fell thick and fast. We hadn't eaten since a bare breakfast and it was about 1600 when the train thankfully stopped. We had about an hour of daylight left . . . it seemed very dark already. We stumbled from the train in the middle of nowhere and noted that it wasn't any colder outside than inside. The air smelled funny without all that coal dust. Just before we froze in our tracks, a guy in uniform came along from a car and said, "follow me". As we moved along the tracks, we gathered more bewildered people and I'd guess there were about 500 of us finally. Another walk, just far enough to fill the shoes with snow and ice and freeze gobs of white stuff on the eyebrows . . . and Camp McDonough came into view. This was a World War I Army camp they apparently couldn't sell. The two-story barracks have a nice coal stove in the middle of each large room. We lined up, counted off and were divided and I found that my home was barracks #7, and that I was in Company B. The guy in charge pointed through the snowstorm to our barracks and advised that we could get coal from a pile on the parade ground . . . if we wanted heat. He further shouted that when we had heat, we could report back to him and he'd see if he could get water turned on. My fellow inmates and I found the building and dropped our luggage and carried coal back in a cloth bag. We started a fire and raised the temperature at least 2 degrees and then trudged back to get the water turned on. We were also wondering about food. Of course the man in charge was gone and in his place was an old boatswain's mate who didn't cotton to young officer trainees. He felt we were reasonably intelligent to start the fire, but he knew nothing about water. He implied we had been living the life of Riley and that it was now over. Perhaps if we wanted water, we could melt snow. His attitude was such that we hated to ask about food, but it was approaching 1900 and it had been a long day. After awhile, he became somewhat human and I believe he almost smiled at one point. He said to go "home" and that coffee and sandwiches were "on the way". We not only got food, but also water and two blankets to place on our canvas cots. Pure luxury!

Since that horrible day, things have improved somewhat, but if you are going to a place like this, I hope you are still on the train!

I think (when I have time to think) of Mt. Pleasant, Michigan, and how it almost became "home", even after a poor arrival. It was snowy there when winter came, but there were some good times. The Navy people in charge of us were either enlisted men who had tested into the program or Junior Officers who were teachers or unfit for other duty. We hated the civilian ex-coaches who tried to kill us with running and calisthenics, but the day came when we outdid them. The civilian students were more or less separate in every way and there was little time to fraternize. Bay City was beautiful until winter came and Saginaw was great at any time . . . beer gardens, friendly girls, we were treated well. I miss that. I was there with a guy from Bloomington and I believe he fell in love. As usual, I guarded my innocence at any cost.

I now see the reason for some of the math and physics we were subjected to. The teachers were good . . . very helpful. We've lost some people along the way and will probably lose some more.

Must sleep. Hope you get some time in New Orleans. It's one of my favorite places.

Hang in there. When the war is over, maybe we can buy one of these railroad cars and raise chickens.

MUCH BETTER NOW BILL

Tuesday-Wednesday
16-17 March 1943

DEAR BILL——

No night on the town in New Orleans. No nothing in New Orleans!

I had visions of wrought iron balconies, Cajun beauties, long black hair, eyelashes fluttering up and down like window shades, vintage wines, French cuisine and a delicate, manicured forefinger beckoning me to shinny up her wrought iron trellis. So much for Air Corps P.R. Ten minutes to stretch, mail letters and back on the train for dinner (not cuisine) as we once again began ambling down the tracks toward whatever.

Tuesday morning, we stopped and had breakfast at Brenham, Texas, at the Hotel St. Anthony (100 Rooms, cafe, laundry, bus terminal all under one roof). Our dining cars had disappeared sometime during the night. Breakfast was quite good as well as plentiful . . . and, aside from some gooky mush they called "grits" and trying to understand Texanese, it was an enjoyable interlude for us weary troops. We also proved our loyalty and devotion to our duty . . . no one pillaged and no one deserted. Of course, there was nothing to pillage and nowhere to go if you did desert.

Arrived at San Antone about 5:30 P.M., and stumbled off the train with our meager belongings to be greeted by some mean looking guys wearing stripes and screaming bloody murder. The cuss words between what I thought were orders were more understandable than the orders. "Tenhut" eluded me for quite awhile until one of them spelled it out for me loud and clear . . . and six inches from my face. He had very bad breath. "Harch" is march, so we "tenhutted" and then "harched" to a supply building where sheets, blankets and pillows were issued, and we then "harched" to our barracks and were assigned bunks. More screaming and "harching" to and from the mess hall. Then, thankfully, lights out at 10:00 P.M.

Sgt. Halitosis frightened us out of the "sack" (bed) at 5:15 this morning and we spent the day standing in line and "harching" hither and yon . . . as well as freezing to death. Warm weather was the expectation for Texas, so the bulk of the Cadets were unprepared for the rain and cold. Uniforms will be issued soon and, in the meantime, we wear a thin, one-piece overall laughingly called a flight suit. So, who's flying?

There are all kinds of groups (a.k.a. "formations") "harching" around here and all those raggedy ass bald headed guys keep yelling, "You'll be sorry" as they "harch" past our virginal bunch. Hey, I'm sorry already. Could this get worse? Food has been good and all you can eat, but the rule is don't take more than you can eat. This has been a learning process for those who grab simply because it's there. I grab because I'm starving . . . my aluminum pan is a mirror when I'm finished.

The long lines end up at various desks with various snotty personnel filling out forms for insurance, next of kin, allotments, educational background, etc. We were furnished with a mimeographed form with our return address which I hope you will find useful.

a/c Wm. H. Alderson
Cadet Squadron 113-Flight G
Army Air Force Classification Center
San Antonio Aviation Cadet Center
San Antonio, Texas

There must be a way to abbreviate all that, otherwise I suspect that my volume of mail will be on the light side.

Speaking of light, ours will be going out in a minute or two so I will close on this happy note for the future. I know it can't get any worse.

TRULY SORRY BILL

Thurs.-Fri.-Sat.
18-19-20 March, 1943

DEAR BILL—-

The last lines in my letter to you of 16-17 March had to do with the future and how things couldn't get worse. As a prognosticator of happy days, apple pie, etc., I have been shot down in flames. Into my traitorous crystal ball I shall now drill three holes and, in the future, use it for bowling. Worse does not adequately describe what has befallen this would-be warrior of the skies.

Montezuma has his "revenge" on the Yankees . . . the Army has "the G.I.s", the "green apple two-step" and the "latrine lover's lope" for its fledgling flyers. The great grand daddy of them all came to visit me during the 5:30 A.M. formation. Every time I coughed, sneezed, or blew my nose I had to pull on the pucker string so hard my circulation must have stopped . . . to no avail. The Sgt. was downwind and was able to recognize a true emergency almost immediately. He dismissed me just before I decorated his bemedaled chest with last night's dinner. I added a new dimension to the already sickly green color of issue shorts, socks, shoes . . . and I, and they, showered all together.

This A.M. (Friday), I made roll-call, even though my get-up-and-go remained kaput in the sack. More uniforms were issued early this A.M. . . . including six uniforms, an overcoat and some accessories. Except for the overcoat, most of my dashing wardrobe fits. The overcoat is about ankle length and weighs twenty-five pounds, dry. Should I get caught in the rain, it will soak up water like a humpback camel and weigh a ton.

This P.M., began taking tests headlined by a six-part dandy called "Psycho-Motor". This is a "hand-is-quicker-than-the-eye" type thing testing reflexes, nerves and coordination. The thing is festooned with buttons, bells, lights and levers and turned out to be difficult, but fun.

Testing continued today (Saturday) after barracks inspection. Barracks inspection brings out the chicken shit (another new expression for my expanding vocabulary) lurking behind the shiny new bars and heavily starched shorts of our tactical officer. He's a 2nd Lt., old for that rank, and I think he hails from La-La Land. He wears white gloves with which he searches for dust on windows, doors, lockers, beds, etc. The only place he has missed so far is where the sun don't shine. One speck anywhere and we do the whole thing over and also risk guard duty or K.P.

Tomorrow we get a day off . . . but as we are confined to the base I'll spend the time writing to my bride, perhaps you, take in a movie and try and recover from the mounds of C.S. (abbreviated new vocabulary) from which they hope to fashion an Air Armada.

HANGING IN THERE—OUTHOUSE BILL

DEAR OUTHOUSE BILL—-

I have yours of March 16-17 and 18-19-20. I'm having some temporary problems keeping up, but things will settle down soon, I hope!

Sorry you missed some nights in New Orleans. One of my very favorite spots. You'd think they could let a guy have a little fun now and then. I note you had a train with a dining car. Good God! I also note you are eating well. How do I go about getting a transfer? Isn't "harching" fun? Waiting in line, also. I'm surprised you are freezing, but guess it won't be long and you'll be warm enough. I note that you say it can't get any worse. Now THAT'S an optimist! In your latest letter, you advise that it had gotten worse. So much for optimism.

Sorry to hear of your bout with Montezuma's revenge. It's so difficult to hide. All that, plus tests and inspections, might cause one to wish for life as a civilian. I dare say that, no matter what branch of service a person joins, it's bad news. Your thoughts are the same as mine . . . and your experiences very similar. When they divided up the bastards to be in charge, they sent you some and me some. I have been close to violence a couple of times but I don't want to flunk out of this outfit now that I've come this far.

I think my last letter covered my arrival here; it was unbelievable. We all got straightened around in about three or four days and we actually got some much needed rest. Somebody screwed up pretty badly, but I guess it's just another experience. We're doing fine and the school classes are interesting. How the big guns are made, how ships are built, navigation, Morse code and blinker lights, seamanship, Naval courtesy and, of course, rules and regulations. I find some of it interesting. Meanwhile, a bunch of civilian ex-jocks or coaches is trying to see what our bodies will stand in the way of exercise. I don't mind that, either. We have had one weekend per month off, except if someone screwed up. We've lost two weekends off base because somebody was caught doing something wrong. It's the Navy's way of making the wrongdoer feel bad . . . it works because we'd strangle them if we knew who they were.

Anyway, I took one trip on the ferryboat down Lake Champlain to Burlington, Vermont. A very pretty town, but a bit stuffy. Three of us went and were able to buy a fifth of whiskey at the state-owned store. We then took a hotel room and ran into some girls whom we invited to our party. The party was progressing rather well, I thought, when the house detective almost broke the door and ordered the girls out. He remarked that we could be put under arrest according to this or that ordinance. An attempt at a bribe by one of my friends threw the detective into a real fit and I believe he would have arrested all of us if he hadn't feared for his own well-being. The upshot of it was that the girls left and we went to bed. I haven't been back.

The real place to go has been Montreal. It is a short train trip (on a much better train) and the city is beautiful . . . and alive with females. The Canadians don't serve overseas against their will, so the only ones remaining are those who refuse to go. They are not looked upon in a kindly way. Good food, good booze and good companionship. Unfortunately, that's all over. The English and the French have been fighting each other and it's now off limits.

I trust your lot will improve. Must don my apron for K.P. (24 hours).

REGARDS—THE LOWEST MIDSHIPMAN

Sun.Mon.Tues.
21-22-23 March 1943

DEAR BILL——

Sunday, as anticipated, was a day off. The troops all needed a respite from the bizarre methods the Air Corps employ to change civilians into soldiers. All things considered, it hasn't been all that bad. However, latrine rumors persist that upon leaving the classification center, the discipline will be based on writings by the Marquis de Sade and classroom studies on the theory of relativity.

During the ride down here behind the little engine that couldn't, I tossed my glasses down the chute in the cubicle labeled "Ladies". Some poor track walker is in for a shock when he sees a pile of doo staring glassy-eyed back at him from between the ties. That amounted to burning my bridges with regard to the eye exam. Well, in for a penny, in for a pound. Today, Monday, passed said exam with only a little struggle with depth perception. Eureka! 20-20!

Along with the eye thing, there was a blood test, urinalysis, X-rays, vaccination and a chat with a scraggly bearded psychiatrist who wore horn rims with lenses like magnifying glasses. He looked a great deal like the owl on our fraternity crest. His main line of questioning had to do with the frequency of intercourse (and whether I enjoyed it), masturbation, window peeping and homosexual acts. My parents have failed me . . . none of these goodies was mentioned in our birds and the bees discussions. The guy made me nervous. One of his eyes kept straying to my crotch, maybe hoping to get a rise out of me. Well, just in case, I crossed my legs, put my hat in my lap and lied enough to pass.

Tuesday didn't amount to much. We "harched" around a lot and viewed a couple of training films on military courtesy and discipline. Just in time. My courtesy is getting frayed around the edges. The vaccination they insisted on administering looks as if I should be hospitalized immediately. And feels even worse. All the loud protests I made about already having had a vaccination and showing the scar to prove it went for naught, so today I watch the bubbling blisters and pray for courtesy and discipline to see me through this assault on my immunity.

TAKE CARE—BACILLUS BILL

Wed.-Thurs.-Fri.
24-25-26 March 1943

DEAR BILL . . . A.K.A. ALBERT E.—-

Tucked in with all the letters from Shirley and the family that miraculously appeared today was yours of 03-24-43. To say the very least, it was just great to hear from everybody. The news from the home front was all good with a liberal dosage of suggestions on how best to survive and prosper in a military environment. Mother suggests I see the General regarding the Sergeant's vile language. Dad recommends going man-to-man behind the barracks with that (expletive deleted) 2nd Lt. My wife warns me that I will face a firing squad when I get home if I so much as peek at a Southern Belle. The family appears to be a great deal more war-like than the enemy.

The return to high school and algebra, geometry, etc., must have come as a shock to your Naval and academic self-image. I'm real proud of your grades and that, even being surrounded by all those toothsome young coeds, you and your libido continue to march to the tune of "Anchors Aweigh". Should your libido double-cross you, the alternative tune most likely to be heard would be "If I Had the Wings of an Angel".

Your smart-assed remarks about my deadly marksmanship were just pangs of jealousy, so I will forgive you. And on the occasion of our next romp down the corn rows, I will instruct you on how to accurately and efficiently use your ancient pump gun. I refer here to your Winchester only. Destroying our jointly-owned automobile against an unforgiving culvert was indeed my error, but there were extenuating circumstances . . . the hot sun through the windshield, carbon monoxide poisoning and several high speed foot chases after the wily pheasant. I merely joined the three of you for a nap. Sweeney didn't get hurt badly when he got thrown out of the car, just broke his shotgun over his knee. All's well that ends well . . . what the hell!

More training films concerning military courtesy and discipline. The Sergeants should be required to attend as they are notably short on courtesy. Physical Ed. (P.T.) is due to begin shortly. We Cadets were required to buy our own gear . . . $8.94 for shoes, pants, shirts, socks, etc. There was a great deal of P.M. (pissing and moaning) about this blatant robbery of indigent troops. Testing is now completed after a four-hour number today, Friday. I am quite sure my passing numbers were all pretty good, so I hope to get my choice of the three . . . either pilot, bombardier or navigator (a somewhat rare opportunity I am told). If I do have a choice, I intend to devote some serious thinking on which route to take.

Keep me posted about your further trials and tribulations in academia, the job market and rumble seats.

GRAND PRIX BILL

30 March, 1943

DEAR BACILLUS BILL AND GRAND PRIX—

It sounds as through things have picked up a bit for you. Glad to hear that you passed your eye test, even sans glasses, and that your academic classes have gone well. We haven't, to my knowledge, been examined by a psychiatrist, but I suppose they are confident that we are all unhinged because we volunteered for this. I see you have been the recipient of double shots and vaccinations because of a records foul up. So far, I've been lucky in that respect.

Just got two letters from you dated 21, 22 and 23 March, and then 24, 25 and 26 March. Very nice to get letters. I have expanded my list of correspondents as much as possible, so I have a pretty good mail call. I am trying to write some females and drum up a little pen pal thing in case I ever find myself alone and lonely.

In your recent epistles you mention my return to high school for some needed math and physics. That now seems a long time ago and . . . of course, I went to study and was not aware of any female classmates.

I see the tests continue for you, too. One would think they would run out of tests. The Navy has a scheduling problem with its films about the horrors of sex and the various diseases said to sometimes follow. They show these miserable films before breakfast, which does ruin breakfast . . . and the message is forgotten by the weekend.

It is clear, however, that there is no sex here. Fathers usher their daughters into the house at the approach of a sailor, and the local watering holes will not serve a drink to anyone not seated. No singing or loud conversation in general . . . the locals seem to just wish we would go away. Very shortly we will do just that!

Since we can no longer go to Montreal, I have some time on my hands . . . time to study and think. I was recently thinking about my pre-war existence and the tight schedule consisting of school and my various jobs. I think I remember telling you some of it. I worked nights (after my theater job), delivering for a package liquor store. I also delivered booze on Saturday mornings to a few select spots. One of the "select" spots was "Bea's Colored House Of Pleasure". Bea was a fine older woman who learned the business as a much younger person, and we got along just fine. Saturday A.M. was the time for the girls to rest and for the booze to be replenished (Bea sold a lot of beer and booze) . . . it made her girls look better to the customers. On an ordinary Saturday I would carry in twelve to twenty cases of beer plus assorted booze. The unusual part was that several of Bea's girls would be bathing in wash tubs in the living room area, and some would taunt me as I carried my heavy burdens to the back room. It was my job to keep my eyes on my path and to ignore the various suggestions from the girls. Happily, I fought off evil and maintained my innocence.

So it is that the end of my time at this place is near . . . only the Lord knows what's next. Leaving here will not draw many tears, but it depends a lot on what the next place is like. I am sick and tired of study and training, and I sure don't want a desk job anywhere. I hope for some sea duty and a brief view of what is going on in the war. That should not be hard to get. Keep writing!

WEARY BILL

DEAR WEARY WILL—-

       Received your letter of March 30. Mail call of late has been quite rewarding and kudos are due the Postal people as well as to my faithful and numerous correspondents. All news, any news, from back yonder gives me a shot in the arm. That is a very unfortunate choice of words . . . but administered by a pen instead of the harpoons they use here, it is a real boost for my sagging morale.

       Your pre-war schedule would, undoubtedly send a lesser man to his happy hunting ground. Obviously, you recovered enough to make it to the induction center. Perhaps you can create a logo featuring naked whores rampant in the wash tubs. That, in vibrant colors, along with your business name, "Burling's Express: Serving Beer And Booze To Brothels", in large letters on the sides of your '31 Ford touring car (provided you get back after all of this is over) should be a real crowd stopper.

       Comparatively speaking, my last few days have been humdrum at best. With P.T. soon to be a big item in our daily schedule I'm trying to jump start the old bones by running a mile every day and doing the obstacle course as well. A couple of days ago I drew K.P. The designation "Police" after the word Kitchen is not a true job description, but merely a play on words by the Army to disguise the mean, menial and miserable work. They assigned me to the kitchen. The only thing that resembled a cop was a fat guy who worked as head hog for the Inquisition and was reincarnated as a five-stripe mess Sergeant.

       My assignment was pots and pans. Such pots and pans you wouldn't believe . . . I still don't. Picture, if you will, horse troughs for mashed potatoes, vats for vintage gravy and three foot by five foot warming trays for greasy pork chops. Everything stuck to everything, including your future flyer. After scraping (using a chore boy the size of a catcher's mitt), rinsing, drying and then polishing, I was wearing enough of the menu to feed a Russian regiment.

       This was a twelve-hour shift (2:30 P.M. to 2:30 A.M.). At 1:00 P.M., just before reporting to K.P. duty, we all were treated to typhoid and tetanus shots. After the dinner hour, and during the pot and pan deluge, my arm began hurting so badly it made me dizzy, particularly if anything touched the arm. My inquisitor laughed like a mad monk and piled on more horse troughs. Everyone in the flight had bad nights, many of them yelling in pain if they rolled over and bumped their arms. About the time I surrendered my detail to the next poor soul I was feeling better, but bitter.

       Keep all your ducks in a row!

TINKER BILL

DEAR TINKER BILL—

Thank you for yours of 27 March to 3 April. I dare say your lifestyle is affecting you in some strange ways. You seem not to be happy with K.P., which is designed as a breather to take you away from a mundane existence, and to make you happy to return to said mundane existence. The grease, the steam and the stench are all designed to aid you in a more pleasant life. The shots do, indeed, bring about pain . . . but you must admit, you feel better when the pain goes away! One must find a way to enjoy these things. If you discover a way to do that, PLEASE send instructions.

It is noted that you are preparing for the various physical fitness exercises devised over the centuries by military misfits. Good luck! The trick is to make damn sure you are not last in any event because there is always a "prize" worth foregoing. I have had pretty good luck with all the physical tortures introduced so far, but have learned that running fast is not my strong suite. I may, as time goes by, need to resort to tripping someone so as to avoid the "prize".

Life here (if you call it life) is much the same. Nobody seems to know what goes on in these accelerated programs and it seems that we are somewhat ahead of schedule. I could have told them that. At least things have slowed a bit and we are enjoying it. We will soon be out of here (if exams are passed) and I feel they'll be glad to be rid of us. The weather is better, but not yet good, and there is nothing to do when we have time off. Nowhere to go since Montreal is off limits. We are not really welcome in the town of Plattsburg; too many of us and too small a town. We have learned to drink warm ale here, and in Montreal, and I actually like it. At first, I thought it was concocted to induce vomiting, but with a shortage of everything else . . . one comes around.

Meanwhile, we are just sweating it out and hoping to become Ensigns . . . the lowest form of Navy life. I hope I can make it, but if I don't, there will be other opportunities to have my dignity stolen and myself placed in jeopardy. In reviewing my Navy days so far, I am not any more impressed with the Navy than it is with me. I am not fond of spit and polish, petty rank-pulling or browbeating. I wonder if any of this has crossed your mind.

Here in the far north, we see signs of spring. The snow has melted to the point where the roofs of abandoned cars are beginning to be visible. The ice on the parade ground has slush on top and, as it fills the Navy oxfords, we know it will be another night by the coal stove to dry the shoes . . . and another hour to polish them. The temperature in the obsolete barracks no longer freezes the Civil War plumbing, and one is now accustomed to a quick shower before the "hot" water runs out. Some say that within a month or so, the geese will fly north again. Geese are not especially bright birds.

Hope you can excuse the wandering thoughts. Keep 'em coming.

POOPED BILL

17 April, 1943

DEAR BEGONIA BILL—

I have yours of 1 to 11 April, and now have a short time to answer. We are going in spurts here; slow for a while and then catch up. It's as though they don't know exactly what is next.

It is with tears in my eyes that I learn of your various indignities and, also, your quickly learned gardening skills. I'm sure the WWI stories from your father and Shirley's Uncle helped your morale. Indeed, it can get worse!

Congratulations on your good grades and your choice of the upcoming jobs in the Air Corps. Your reasoning for choosing to be a bombardier seems logical, and we both hope it works out that way. I thank the Lord you'll not be a gunner, but I suppose if the enemy crashed in a fit of hysterical laughter, the end result would be laudable.

Your gardening appears to have some perks. I hope you were able to enjoy San Antonio and that your various hoped for passes in the future will allow more scenic travel.

Guard duty is real fun. I feel for you in that heat. I've only drawn guard duty once, and that was back in February. This old base has a chain link fence around it and I drew what seemed like an endless stretch to guard. There was a wood stove at a guardhouse and we walked a beat from there. The snow was new and rather deep and they could tell whether we walked the beat or not. I figured I'd be tested, to I made sure I did it right. It was so cold that nobody checked on me. I could have stayed by the fire.

I can read your excitement regarding Shirley's arrival, and I hope it is soon. It would sure ease things a bit. I'm happy for you. We are not allowed to be married, but one guy here in my company is. He's about 31 years old and is having a hell of a time with the physical fitness routine. We envy him when his wife visits, but she never brings a friend. For everyone else it's been a long, dry spell.

My routine is just that; run, run, run everywhere . . . and then wait. Classes are not so bad, but there is a lot to remember. Naval courtesy sounds pretty painful and I hope I can avoid some spit and polish assignments. I'll sure try.

There are hints that Spring may really arrive here. The natives say they do have a Spring, and that it is overdue. It will be most welcome. I'm so used to arctic temperatures and snow that they'll surely send me to the Pacific.

It's winding down here and, assuming I pass some exams, I will be declared an Ensign, the lowest form of Navy personnel. We don't know exactly when it will all be over, and are afraid to ask. I'll send my new address when I know it.

Hope Shirley joins you soon and that all goes well with your gardening. Wish we had some gardens here. There is nothing to do on our one weekend off per month.

ANXIOUS BILL

Thurs. Thru Sunday
1 to 11 April, 1943

DEAR POOPED—

You may take heart as I recount some of the sinister indignities I have endured over the past few days. The chant, "you'll be sorry", echoes over the barren landscape of Texas and I am sure, over the "Bounding Main" as well. I have heard from Shirley's Uncle Joe and my father, both survivors of duty overseas during WWI. They spoke of such things as cleaning honey pots, popping lice and eating cold beans three times a day. Uncle Joe drove an ambulance during the big allied offensives at Argonne, Chateaux Thierry and the Somme. His reluctant remembrances of those days were horrifying. My dad was sitting on a park bench in Paris and got hit by shrapnel from Germany's super cannon, "Big Bertha". He was only scratched, but enough to spoil his enthusiasm for the Eiffel Tower, the Rues Piagalle and LaBelle Francais. With the advent of modern plumbing, DDT and Sterno, we can perhaps serve our nation without being knee deep in doo and bugs and musical fruit. A day or two ago, I returned to the barber shop for a trim. Actually, it was a repair job more than anything else. The original that Pierre created left me looking like a molting canary. Now that it has grown back a little, the humidity causes it to curl and I now appear to have just returned from the beauty parlor with a marcel. My ears look like jug handles, particularly when my oversized hat is perched on them. I peek out from under the brim, seeing nothing but the ground.

Early this week, I was introduced to gardening, even after explaining at great length that I was a "city feller" and without horticultural expertise. I was rudely informed that a green thumb was not a prerequisite for the job, only muscle to move rocks and break up the concrete that passes for ground here. With my pick and shovel, I gardened.

During this pastoral period in my Army learning experience, I was reinjected with the venom to shoot down typhoid and tetanus, and said venom promptly shot down both arms. Picking and shoveling became a real test of the inner man.

The following day, I was ordered to appear before the Lieutenant "ASAP" (which is Army for instantaneously). He informed me that the test results were in and that the results, and I quote, "were quite exceptional". Therefore, he said, I could select the school of my choice. He briefed me on the curriculum, length and various stages and venues of each program. He expected an immediate decision, and I chose bombardier (although I am well aware that a pilot is the fair-haired boy in the Air Corps and is more apt to get preferred assignments and promotions). I had a gut hunch that I could survive the war as a bombardier, so I opted for M.O.S. #1035 (Air Corps Job Number). Hopefully, my crystal ball is tuned in to my devout desire to survive.

The Lieutenant also informed me that he was delighted by my efforts in his garden, although he would have liked to have seen deeper furrows, straighter furrows and fewer lumps. Further, and with a devout look in his eye, he rewarded me with the privilege of planting the seeds and tending them 'til blossom time. He also tossed in an eight-hour pass to San Antonio. That boy is out in the sun too much.

After a tour of the Alamo and its historic environs, I returned to the base and found my name on the bulletin board, again. This time, it is guard duty from 4:00 P.M. to 6:00 A.M. The guard detail required memorizing all the various maneuvers with a rifle: shoulder arms, port arms, present arms, etc., along with the litany that goes with guardsmanship ("Halt! Who goes there", "Advance and be recognized", etc.). By the time you could get through all the rigormorole, the bad guys would have advanced and killed you before they were recognized.

Shirley is determined on becoming a camp follower and will make arrangements to arrive at wherever I end up as soon as she can. I have tried to dissuade her, but she's a mite strong-willed and I'm a pushover for a nifty "figger". How the hell we are going to manage on the $75.00 per month, which includes flying time and overtime, I'll never know. Her confidence is overwhelming and based on the following truisms . . . her truisms:

FIRST, I get free room and board and that I will give to her. But, it is a rather shitty thing to say, considering what I'm enduring in order to qualify.

SECOND, she can get a job wherever the fickle finger sends aspiring birdmen (that is only a weak excuse maybe because being a Yankee in the Gobi desert populated by unforgiving Rebels is not job conducive).

THIRD (and the most devastating), she can't get pregnant under the existing conditions. Why did I let Pappy sign me away? My mind dwells on more likely scenarios . . . the public dole, bank robbery or becoming a eunuch. Ah well, in for a penny, in for a pound. And I have another hunch. We'll work it out . . . and have some fun trying.

Y'all come down and I'll show you my bloomers.

BEGONIA BILL

Mon. thru Sun.
12 to 25 April, 1943

DEAR BEAT UP—-

 The round-by-round account of your heroic attempt to become the new white hope of the squared circle has arrived here (Ellington Field), after a circuitous journey from San Antone.

 The latrine rumors finally became fact and we have moved and will remain here for approximately nine weeks for pre-flight training. Ellington is about 20 miles from Houston. Should you be able to spare the time from your Spartan training as lightweight contender, I can be reached at the following address: a/c W.H.A., Group 21, Sqdn A, Flt I, AAFPS Ellington Fld, Texas.

 I, too, am a contender . . . not for such a lofty and lusty crown as you aspire to, but as Air Corps gardener of the Texas outback. If the troops would only quit calling in cadence, "Daisy Mae", as they march by my petunia patch, I would be more inclined to be enthusiastic.

 Quite seriously, that was indeed a nasty little brouhaha with those not-so-young hooligans. I trust you paid particular attention to your eyes until you were sure there was no ongoing damage. I hate to think your piercing baby blues weren't up to snuff when you once again stalk the corn rows striking terror amongst the pheasant hordes. As far as your nose is concerned . . . fear not, for a little bump, a little bend, a little scar tissue, will give you the savage visage you will need when shouting, "Belay" and "Avast" at the terrified swabbies of your command.

 The last week at San Antone pitted the Cadet corps against the Army slave drivers in a series of non-title bouts. Needless to say, the fix was in and for whom the bell tolled (and frequently) was the Cadet corps. Monday, we were to gas warfare and how to operate and survive with the issue gas mask. All went well in the gas chamber (very depressing nomenclature) with the mask living up to its billing . . . and then they were pulled off. Fifteen seconds later, we were out in the fresh air (Texas style) hanging on the ropes and cussing tear gas, the Air Corps and draft boards. Red-rimmed and teary-eyed, we then doubletimed to the phys.ed. arena for an hour , then "harched" for an hour, lunched for an hour and "harched" again for an hour. Two o'clock came and off we "harched" to the cinder track and a track meet, of all things.

 The track was a quarter mile and I was thinking, "piece of cake" . . . then the word came down to do four laps. Then I was thinking, "Oh, shit!" Out of a field of eleven, I was seeded eleventh. The other ten guys were a foot taller than me and skinny looking runner-types. My shrill and panicky suggestion to move the venue to the swimming pool fell on deaf ears and away we scampered. The oddsmakers took a real bath . . . I came in fifth. Retreat finally sounded and we dined and retired to the barracks for a well-deserved rest . . . in a pig's eye. The bell didn't toll, but some sadist with a bugle blew fire drill, which nobody recognized . . . and confusion once again raced through the Cadet corps. The Lt. saved the day by running up and down the street screaming, "Fire! Fire!", and nearly got stomped to death by the thundering herd that erupted out of the several barracks. The last idiot out was me . . . lugging the friggen fire extinguisher . . . which, oddly enough, was assigned to the orderly room during a fire.

 During the balance of the week, I managed to get to San Antone, shot a roll or two of film and ogled the dusky local maidens promenading along the river's banks. The Alamo and The Mission San Juan de Capistrano (built 1731) were truly impressive. Rumors are thick like kernels on a cob as to when and where we will be shipped. Rumors not withstanding, I caught K.P. again . . . by mistake . . . but the error was not discovered until I had gone 15 rounds with the pots and pans. This does not inspire confidence in one's leaders, nor does it cause the intrepid Boche to tremble in his flying boots. Friday found me with the all day detail of HQ runner. My superior effort on K.P. has apparently gone unobserved and unappreciated, as usual. An entire day spent running all over the post, popping in and out of attention . . . and saluting everything wearing sunglasses and looking satisfied.

 Summer uniforms (sun tans) were issued, but before I could hang them up (much less put them on), the Lt. called me back to the petunia patch putting pretty pansies and poppies in peat. I think a couple of shingles just blew off my roof. Send for the shrink. A fifteen mile hike was suddenly announced, and I just as suddenly fell madly in love with my beautiful bloomers and their desperate need for nurturing. After a sales pitch to the Lt. far superior than that given to Eve by Adam, I was left in my patch frantically weeding and watering as the troops "harched" off under the hot sun. I ain't lost all my shingles.

 The night of the 20th, we boarded a Pullman (wisely left behind by the Union Army), our destination unknown . . . and took off for pre-flight school. About 7:00 A.M., the train shuddered to a stop and a big sign welcomed us to Ellington Field. Great food here and a large selection to choose from. Eat all you want, but take only what you can eat at your peril. We can leave at will here instead of leaving en masse in formation. Classes begin Friday and include math, physics, code, aircraft I.D., navigation and others. There is no K.P., guard duty or gardening. Saturdays off from 2:00 P.M. to 3:00 A.M., and

Sundays all day until 12:30 A.M. Monday. We are in hog heaven. Shirley saw the above schedule and is packing her bags, regardless of the wolf slavering at our heels. We don't have a doorstep, so he will have to salivate at our flying feet instead.

The first day of classes was scheduled for Friday and we were anticipating the academics as a real leap forward . . . and away from the menial C.S. we had been enduring so far. Lo and behold, VIPs are expected. Not just any old VIPs, but the number one and two VIPs, Roosevelt and Arnold. This touched off a veritable storm of orders and counter-orders from the paddlefeet (ground personnel). The entire Cadet contingent set to work washing streets, barracks inside and out (unbelievable), whitewashing rocks and cutting grass (already suffering mortally from sun-stroke) . . . while 2,000 officers and their henchman stood around slurping up Cokes, smoking cigarettes and urging the cadets onward and upward with thinly veiled threats featuring firing squads and iron maidens. An heroic effort by all concerned to bring the axis closer to unconditional surrender. Hog heaven is turning ugly.

Up and at 'em Saturday. Shine the brass, tidy up the barracks, brush the teeth and line the roads standing at parade rest . . . which is a tiny bit less tiring than attention. After a couple of hours in the hot sun, the ranks began to thin out a little as guys passed out and were carted away. In some places, the formation looked like a picket fence missing a slat here and there. Salvation from this delightful day in the sun was sponsored by the VIPs themselves, they didn't show up. Eleanor might have come down with the megrims. The Air Corps, noted far and wide for frugality in its expenditure of time and effort, immediately sent us off for a battery of tests . . . testing our individual speed, dexterity and coordination of hand and eye and hoping, I'm sure, that all that egg-on-face was not noticeable.

Sunday we were given a day off; perhaps to quiet the treasonable mutterings of the elite Cadet corps.

REPORTING FROM THE HOG WALLOW — BILL

3 May, '43

DEAR HOG WALLOW BILL—

        Yours of 12 to 25 April has arrived and I note that you are now in cool environs near Houston. I will very soon join you in the warmer climes.

        Your last week before moving sounds rather busy. I note you kept your gas mask on in the gas chamber. That was probably an intelligence test. Congratulations! I have never been tested for gas, but we have fought some large oil fires both in a pool and on the parade ground.

        Got a kick out of your running ability. I'm in the greatest shape I've ever been. I believe I could run all day . . . at a slow pace. However, I cannot run fast and I don't know why. Several of our P.T. instructors are ex track coaches and they love running. The guy who finishes last always gets a prize, which means more running. Thanks to one pink cheeked fat boy, I have never been last.

        I see that, once again, your garden paid off in avoiding the 15-mile hike. Good for you.

        Ellington Field sounds like a real country club . . . hope it continues that way. The mishap regarding the visiting VIPs must have been a lot of work, but it's nice they didn't show. VIPs do not visit this place . . . and are not missed. I'm not sure the Navy knows about this place.

        Sounds as though Shirley is virtually on her way (hope so). Living with all these characters is interesting, but not a complete existence. I trust that when she arrives, you will be given a month off on per diem at one of the better hotels.

        It has been a hurried and harried existence for what seems like a long time. Several have dropped by the wayside and some more will go in the next few days. I plan <u>not</u> to be among them. I'm reasonably relaxed and feel I can pass the exams. I'm anxious to move on.

        Talked yesterday with about 4 psychologists who inquired as to my wishes for the future. They were a friendly lot and I told them I wanted the hell out of snow and ice and that I wanted to see a bit of action so I could tell my kids what I did in the great war. I told them I'd like a small ship without a lot of spit and polish. I was excused, but called to the Executive Officer's office about 4 hours later . . . and he advised that, assuming I passed the final exams, I would be assigned immediately to an LST (that stands for "Landing Ship Tank", but is commonly called a "Large Stationary Target"). I wanted to ask if I could try it for a week or so, but thought it might enrage him. He indicated that the ship would likely be scheduled for Pacific duty. He wished me well in a way that frightened me!

        So, everyone is packing what can be packed and getting ready to go. Some will do hazardous duty in Washington, D.C., and some will live on destroyers or carriers. Everyone will leave here with a few good memories . . . and a lot of bad ones.

        I'll let you know where I am as soon as I can.

ON THE MOVE BILL

Mon. 26 April 1943 to
Thurs. 20 May 1943

DEAR MOVABLE—

Yours of 5 April and 17 April are in my hot little hand and, as you so succinctly point out, our correspondence is indeed in a state of snafu. With your lengthy service as an old salt, I am sure I do not have to decode snafu for you. I am equally sure this situation prevails in the Navy as well, as in our nation's Air Arm. Come to think of it . . . our duly elected blustering, brave and bloodthirsty civilian legislators in our nation's Capitol are mired to the arm pits in said snafu on a daily basis. Your eagle-eye and shrewd analysis has immediately discerned the difficulty; I concur and will adjust. Mail deliveries being what they are, and my haste to fatten both our mail calls, is causing my return letters to reflect some history as well as current events. Incidentally, I hadn't noticed before your eagle-eye or shrewd analysis of flight patterns when pheasants exploded out of the corn within spitting distance of you and your trusty 12 bore. The Navy must be force-feeding you carrots.

Has "Anchors Aweigh", "Old Glory", Sousa's Marches, Mom's Apple Pie, and a Thirteen Button Fly caused your elevator to stop a couple of floors short? Asking the psychologist for a "bit of action" so you can tell largely exaggerated war stories to a passel of progeny is tantamount to writing your own epitaph. You have been at death's door often enough by just stepping down the corn rows with Barrage Bill to trust your luck much farther. Riding an LST (large stationary target) as you so aptly put it, can be viewed as stretching a rubber band a mite too far . . . or adding the last straw to a humper's back. My branch of the service provides parachutes in the unlikely event that someone on the opposing side gets lucky. They don't expect us to swim through miles of sharks, mine fields and pissed off barracudas. On the brighter side, you might wash ashore on a tropical isle and become the panjandrum of grass skirts and heavenly hooters.

Packing, particularly in our line of business, surely does (as you point out), bring forth memories good and bad . . . and a great deal of speculation as to what's going to happen next, mixed with equal parts of optimism, anxiety and determination. We, however, are survivors, Willum. Keep that thought uppermost in your musings.

A tentative date of 22 May has been set for Shirley's arrival here. I have been doing some bird-dogging for suitable quarters and got lucky. The wife of one of the Kdets (Clark Barritt) arrived a day or two ago and has a nice room in a private residence with kitchen privileges and bath/laundry facilities for $20.00 monthly. Apartments are non-existent and rooms as scarce as VD in a monastery. Helen (the Kdet wife) rented the room next to her for Shirley. This . . . as I have so often done in the field . . . kills two birds with one shot. Shirley will have a Cadet wife for company . . . and we will renew our marriage vows in a private and comfortable double bed, instead of on a bench in the railroad waiting room. I shall dine on oysters and rhinoceros horns until that happy day arrives.

Along, or close to along, the above lines is a guy in a bunk adjacent to mine from some tiny village in the Appalachians who wakes up every morning with a spectacular erection. He is quite proud of this throbbing evidence of his masculinity and talks hillbilly to it on his way to the shower room. You would think that modesty is not one of his most endearing traits . . . but you would be mistaken. He hangs his Garrison hat on "down ole Tobe, down boy" on his march to the cold water.

Classes continue here to fortify us with skills to face the implacable Boche or Japs or whatever. Physics, math, code, map reading and other timely topics such as VD and VD and VD. The rhinoceros horns may fail me at the critical moment if they keep scaring me to death with these horror stories brought to the screen in living color. Physical training continues to eat up a couple of hours a day and we are all looking and feeling like the robust and handsome men that any mother would trust with her young and naive daughter. One exception, however, is our Appalachian Adonis and his awesome appendage.

Hopefully the Post Office and the exigencies (ain't that a dandy?) of the service will cooperate in our effort to maintain a more datewise line of communication as our further service to the President, his minions and the republic we defend continues.

In the meantime, I remain for the second time in one year—

BRIDEGROOM BILL

29 May, '43

DEAR BRIDEGROOM BILL—

I'm happy for you that you can look forward to a precise date that Shirley will arrive. I assume that her arrival will somewhat hamper your correspondence and, perhaps, your general inattention to learning how to be a flyboy. I shall be patient, and when you recover and can again pick up a pen . . . we'll carry on with our correspondence.

Your letter dated 26 April to 20 May has arrived, which is a pleasant surprise. They actually did not lose my forwarding address. You will note I am now a resident of New Orleans and will be for a short time. I am actually residing, at the request of the Navy, at Algiers, which is an island . . . New Orleans is a short ferryboat ride away. I love New Orleans, but this may be the time to complain of chronic seasickness on the ferryboat in order to seek a desk job in Washington, D.C.

I note a snide remark about your imagined remembrance of me missing a pheasant and blaming it on my eyesight. It's time the truth was known . . . I am basically a conservationist, and there is the very real desire not to embarrass my companions.

I am now aware that I was somewhat brash (or disoriented) when I asked for sea duty. I have seen two freighters in New Orleans that were simply carrying coffee and were torpedoed in the Caribbean. I was much impressed by the size of the holes . . . and their ability to float and get here. It appears the enemy is using live ammunition and this seems a rather serious issue. I wonder if it's too late to study for the ministry!

In rereading your letter, I discover Shirley may be there now. Tell her hello for me. You have my utmost envy. Living off-base (forever) is now one of my prime desires and I wish you luck.

Your tales of the continuing education remind me that I have finished with all that, thank the Lord! A good deal of very practical learning lies ahead and I welcome it because it spells "survival".

News from here is rather short and I hardly remember what my last letter may have contained. Somehow I did pass the various tests and Congress confirmed upon me the rank of Ensign. I, at first, believed that apprentice seaman was the lowest form of life, but it is now clear that Ensign is. My brand new uniforms (that don't fit well), my boyish appearance and the shiny braid and emblems arc a cross to bear.

I came here alone with the last leg of the trip being aboard a civilian train with round wheels, a dining car and seats that were both padded . . . and covered with some form of material that holds the coal dust, all the while penetrating and pricking the posterior. Progress? The trip was only 18 hours (the last leg), so we got coach and a pillow. To show that our Navy is all heart I was given three days delay en route from upper New York . . . so I had time to play. I did see my mother and my girlfriend . . . both of whom seem to think I have about a week to live. It was depressing because I feel certain I will live three months.

My ship is not yet here. It is en route from the Chicago Bridge and Iron Works and further assembly will be done here. Meanwhile, I have unheard of freedom and enough money to use it. I must report in at Algiers every morning at 0800 and then I am free. I can sleep and eat here or do as I please, but I cannot leave town. This must be what parole is like . . . except that it won't last long, even if I behave myself. I have no intention of behaving myself.

The ferryboat docks at the foot of Canal St. and a short walk takes me to the Roosevelt Hotel. Rates are reasonable for such a good hotel and in the evening Johnny Long and his orchestra play in the ballroom. A smaller ballroom has the music of Candy Candido and his Latin rhythms. I love to watch the Cubans dance. Actor Robert Taylor is a Navy flyboy stationed here and he is a nightly visitor to hear Johnny Long. The women seem to prefer him over me, but I am hanging in there hoping for one of his culls.

The food is excellent everywhere and I eat about five times per day at Gropp's, Antoine's, the Court of Two Sisters and others. I am trying to learn how to drink some of these exotic southern drinks. All I have to do is catch the ferryboat at 0700.

Must get dressed and away from Algiers.

PAROLED BILL

Friday 21 May to
Wed. 23 June 1943

DEAR PAROLEE—

Congratulations, Willum!!! Please accept my literary hand salute in lieu of a face-to-face brace. My apologies for not addressing you as "Sir Parolee". At the moment, I'm happy to be in Texas whilst you are screwing off on the Gulf of Mexico with Robert Taylor's culls. I have no wish to carry your sea bag, polish your brass or field strip your 12 gauge Winchester scatter gun. I am harassed enough by the Air Corps Sergeants and 90-day wonders.

So, Chicago Bridge & Iron is mailing you the parts for your ship. When all that stuff gets there, do you lay the parts out on the dock and follow steps one through five hundred? Sounds like something you put together Christmas Eve under the tree. I hope the parts that are left over are not crucial to the flotation of your version of Noah's Ark. Beware, you enemy dreadnaughts, Burling is about to embark and your days are numbered.

Dining at Antoines' and The Court of Two Sisters, plus what amounts to permanent shore leave, hobnobbing with movie stars (and their entourages) makes me want to belt my tactical officer right in his aviator sun glasses. Is this just a Navy tradition or can I expect a similar vacation when I pin on my golden bars? Maybe the Navy is setting you up with this uncharacteristic display of good fellowship. A paraphrase of some famous lines come to mind, reminding me of your oft spoken desire to "see a little action". "My cup of exotic southern drinks runneth over and I shall dwell in the Navy's LST house forever." Onward and upward, Wm.

Shirley left Chicago on Friday the 21st on her first solo long-distance train trip. Changed trains at St. Louis and spent the night in the same coach you and I rode in to our rendezvous with destiny. Switched trains again Saturday at Palestine, Texas, and arrived in Houston around 6:00 P.M. . . . an even older coach this time. Her landlady and across-the-hall roommate met her and we both arrived at the house about the same time. She was plumb worn out, very grimy and pissed off at the railroad, the Air Corps and FDR . . . in that order. All that aside, she still looked like a keeper to me.

All in all, our reunion was great and only marred by duty calling . . . back to the post before 3:00 A.M. Unlike naval ensigns, we get passes (shore leave in Navy vernacular) on Saturday and Sunday only and must return each night for bed check. There is a certain amount of shenanigans attached to bed check . . . and some crafty and horny Cadets have been known to bamboozle the checker, whilst the checkee is elsewhere enjoying the forbidden fruits of his chicanery.

Hind sight being what it is, I can now see that I nearly blew the reunion out of the water before it got fairly started. I was informed, in no uncertain terms and tones, that I embarrassed her to tears by trying to forcibly drag her into our room while mumbling about mattresses and springs and forget the damned shower for now! This, of course, in front of Mrs. Franciso (landlady) and Helen and Clark Barritt (our co-tenants). By way of an excuse for my primitive behavior . . . it has been a long separation and our first anniversary comes up on the sixth of June. I feel I am entitled to some premature and lusty foreplay.

The days seem to be flying by and the cadets still aren't. A move to advanced school and the wild blue yonder is imminent, however. I am looking forward to this enthusiastically, but I have to admit to wondering from time to time why the hell I'm enthusiastic about jumping into a rickety airplane with some 20 year old pilot who got out of flight school two or three weeks ago.

Shirley has made friends with a number of other Cadet wives and is enjoying her first separation from Kimbark Ave. She got a job a couple days after arriving here working for a detective as a watcher in a large store. She quit after two days because (I think) she didn't like turning in the shoplifters she caught in the act. A couple of days later, she began a new job as a comptometer operator running payrolls and inventory. This is her skill and the position is permanent while she is here. During the week, the wives go out on the town in the evenings . . . movies, the drug store for sundaes and card games at their different rooming houses. The guys get in weekends and we generally find something to do in groups (not what you are thinking).

Saturday, the 19th, there was a class dance at the Rice Hotel in Houston. We all got rooms and stayed the night. Great time was had by all. Shirley found a piano and played a little classical . . . . then yielded to Johnny Albanese, who played good popular tunes. This about signifies the end of Ellington Field. When next I write, I'll have a new address where I will continue my quest to be anointed a 2nd Lt. by Congressional decree.

Be sure that you get that bucket properly glued, tattooed and bolted together so that shot and shell and new Ensigns cannot sink her.

Take good care, Sir—

TITILLATED IN TEXAS

29 June, '43

DEAR TITILLATED—

I have yours of 21 May to 23 June and have spent some time thinking about your animal behavior and the embarrassment to your child bride. There is probably some of that ugly sex going on here too, but I have been able to maintain my wholesome, shy demeanor.

Sorry to hear of your harassment by the Air Corps people. Sweat it out and you too can be a 2nd Lt. . . . which means harassment by an entirely different group!

Glad to hear Shirley has made some friends and found work. It sounds like a pretty good arrangement for all concerned. Perhaps with your new wealth you can buy a Captain's Commission! It's good to hear that your days are flying by. When I hear of your continued parties, dances and weekends in an apartment, it makes me wonder why the Navy doesn't participate in some of this lusty entertainment.

The Chicago Bridge & Iron Works has delivered its most recent product to Algiers. I boned up on all the various salutes, courtesies and phrases necessary to board ship and was greeted by a Chief Quartermaster who couldn't care less. He has about 16 years in the USN and is apparently being punished for some oversight by his assignment to an LST. You'll note on my new address that it's now LST 628. A lucky number, I'm sure! A guy I went to Midshipman's school with showed up soon afterward, so we have two greenhorn officers and a Chief Petty Officer. We also have numerous Navy people from the shipyard who come and go and look at charts and scratch their heads. Thankfully, there is no saluting and I can't tell if some of the sailors are our crew members or technicians from the yard. At this point, I have a place to sleep and coffee to drink, but no place to eat. You guessed it . . . I must climb on the ferryboat to New Orleans to eat. I am hungry several times per day.

I did notice that some of the welders and inspectors are females. Some are quite pretty and some are even friendly. They work 3 shifts, around the clock.

The mast went up with its various antennas, stays, and shrouds, and they are now welding on some guns. Twin 40 mms fore and aft and several 20 mms along each side on each deck. Each gun has bent pipe welded around so we can not shoot each other. A novel idea. I find this contraption very interesting and wander around constantly trying to figure out what everything is. The decks are crowded with huge coils of steel cable. This coffin is 328 feet long and 50 feet wide and we'll be standing sea watches 52 feet above the waterline. My bunk is on the starboard side and just ahead of my one porthole is the exhaust vent for the starboard engine. If the wind is just right, or nonexistent, I am able to sleep while enveloped in diesel exhaust. I am thinking of complaining to the first Chaplain I see.

The crew has grown. My friend from school and I are supernumeraries, which means we are to keep the hell out of the way while learning. At first, I was assigned to the supply officer, although I wanted gunnery or desk force. Some changes have been made and I am now the assistant 1st Lt. (or deck officer) . . . in charge of construction and repair. My friend is now the supply underling. I am now learning to drop the bow anchor and stern anchor, launch and recover our two boats, keep everything clean and greased . . . and am studying blue prints so I know where frame #14 is, etc. I think I need another 3 years of school, but things are progressing rapidly here. My boss is an old Navy boatswain's mate who really knows his job. He works hard and plays hard and I've learned not to go ashore with him. He mainly wants someone to carry him home. In view of the fact that he's in charge of the boats, we now avoid the ferry sometimes.

Every morning at 0800, each division officer inspects his division and assigns work. He also bitches about long hair, dirty bodies, unkempt clothing, late arrivals, etc. My boss says the trick is to work yourself into a rage beforehand and chew them out every third day or so, whether they deserve it or not. Now I'm beginning to understand the Navy.

Hate to bore you will all this B.S.. Especially the Navy lingo, which seems silly. I realize it's tradition, but the story goes that "here" everybody calls things by the same name. We have some Cajuns, some New Jersey Italians and a little sprinkling of all kinds of Americans, so we must communicate properly. I am embarrassed at the age of 20 to be giving orders to men aged 40 (or less). The new ones out of boot camp think an Ensign is important. The experienced ones put up with me. In general, I keep quiet . . . but my boss tells me to shout what I want done-and mean it. He's right.

Much to tell, but little time. It's time for shrimp creole at Gropps, and then to the Roosevelt Hotel and perhaps a drink or three. Tomorrow, I'll have to walk around in the hot sun and pretend to know something.

Let me know your next address. Say hello to Shirley.

Best regards—

IGNORAMUS BILL

Thursday 24 June to
Thursday 29 July 1943

DEAR DECK OFFICER—-

After reading your last letter of 29 June 1943, I could not in good conscience address you as you had signed off in that letter. On the contrary, you seem to be absorbing nautical know-how like a deep sea sponge. The mass of detail you must learn is awesome . . . coupled with the tricky business of a command posture, this leads me to think of you as a modern-day Captain Nemo.

The learning experience from this multitude of things, Naval and mechanical, must surely be fascinating and fun, as well as practical and demanding. Are you to be known as a plank owner when #628 is commissioned? If so, you may be able to foist off your diesel fuming bunk on some unwary newcomer. Use a maneuver similar to the one that left your fellow Ensign folding towels in the bowels of #628 whilst you prowl around the wide-open spaces of the promenade deck.

The installation of the 40 and 20 mm cannon should prompt your thoughts on how serious this war is becoming, as well as a feeling of confidence in that you can throw something at the bad guys besides your middle finger. Should you be aiming or firing those guns . . . please remember that if it has wings, makes a lot of nasty noises, and has red spots on it . . . it ain't a duck. It is a real bad guy, for Pete's sake . . . shoot him!

The overall size of your ship surprised me quite a bit. That 328 feet is longer than a football field. It must take a large, well-trained crew to run the ship and fight it at the same time. When you consider my only experience has been in boats propelled by oars, paddles and 10 H.P. outboards, my surprise is understandable.

Now that you have transport to New Orleans in your private barge and are a V.I.P. at Gropps', Francois' and the Roosevelt Hotel, you must surely cut a wide swath through the bevies of Rosie Riveters currently infesting your ship. There are those of us, however, who are not wallowing in shrimp Creole and comely riveters . . . but are eating Texas dust and being ever-alert for scorpions in our shoes, and sidewinders and tarantulas on the obstacle course. Were it not for the fickle finger, I, too, could be leaping on barges and comely riveters. Such are the fortunes of war.

After a train ride featuring, of course, the usual deluxe amenities, I have arrived at Midland, Texas. This is one of the advanced training schools for bombardiers, and my address is a/c W.H.A.-Squadron #1, Class 43-13, AAFBS, Midland, Texas. The barracks are liveable and roomy, and the food, as usual, is good . . . although not on a par with that to which you have become accustomed to in the French quarter. Ground school, formation marching and phys. ed. . . . in fact everything . . . has been intensified. The formation "harching" has now become a contest between flights, squadrons and classes. I have "harched" 5,000 miles and have yet to see an airplane.

The Norden Bombsight is an intricate machine, and the bombardier is required to protect the thing, at whatever cost. I don't care for that "whatever" at all, but we have learned a lot about its innards and how it works. The downward flight of the bombs and their ballistic co-efficiency also are featured . . . which facts I will take home to civilian life and wonder forever how I got myself in a mess like this. After three weeks or so, we practice bombing on top of a 10 foot high, wheeled platform. The platform, directed by a cadet and his bombsight, chase a little bug around the floor and drop electronic bombs at its target area. Hitting the bull's eye is called a "shack". Nobody in Texas will sleep nights if I do as well in an airplane as I do with this thing.

On the 20th, at long last, your war correspondent, along with a couple of other Cadets, became airborne in an AT-11 (a twin-engine trainer) for our orientation flight. We were all gussied up in flight coveralls, parachutes and helmets ... the picture of intrepid birdmen thirsting for action. We got action in capital letters. At about 6,000 feet, the heat and the strange movements of the airplane disagreed violently with the pork chops and gravy we had for lunch. I was feeling pretty rocky, but hung onto my chops . . . the other two guys couldn't. One of them heaved in his helmet, which made the other poor soul puke in sympathy. This wiseass didn't want to foul up his helmet, so he tossed his cookies out the bomb bay doors. The slipstream blew it all back through the camera hatch and we all ended up wearing his barf. The two officers driving got very, very upset. After a very hasty landing, and a truly inspired chewing out, we were allowed to wash down the inside of that hot and treacherous machine.

Shirley arrived near here on the 1st of July, followed by her luggage two days later. She got a nice room with privileges in Odessa for five bucks a week. Living accomodations are scarce as can be for the Cadet wives. She got really lucky a couple of weeks later when she and another gal found a 5-room furnished house in Midland. Bill and Donna Behrens are our housemates and, strangely enough, Bill is a Phi Gam from Minnesota. We Fijis are everywhere. Flying pay (upchucking for money) pays the rent, so we manage fairly well. Shirley and the other wives can visit the post and use the pool, PX, theater, snack bar and other facilities. The Cadet cadre has a lot of off-post freedom, unless you get on bad paper with the TAC officer. All in all, a giant step forward.

Some events I have not covered, due to the length of this letter . . . and to keep your attention span at a fever pitch. I am looking forward to further word on the outfitting of your ship and your unswerving march toward flag rank.

REGARDS . . . BULLS EYE BILL

DEAR BULLS EYE BILL——

I suppose one might paraphrase your most recent title to Bullshit Bill, but I'd be the last to suggest it. I now have yours of 24 June to 29 July and note that, since Shirley arrived, your letters take longer to write. We long suffering singles who are deprived nevertheless understand.

It is noted that you are now a citizen of Midland, Texas, and are involved in advanced Bombardier learning, along with advanced marching. I trust that your complete understanding of the Norden bombsight, along with superlative training, will truly change you to "Bullseye Bill". It goes without saying that when the current problem is over, you should be able to kill or wound a pheasant by dropping bombs. Thank the Lord you are not a gunner!

Apparently your first airplane ride in the AT-11 resulted in a safe landing, which I've always considered a rudimentary necessity. I don't know what an AT-11 is and must admit to a complete lack of interest in finding out. I hold to the belief that when the Good Lord wants me to fly, He'll give me wings of my own. At this point, I hope He holds off about 70 years. Glad you retained your usual composure and I have a sympathy for those who lost their lunches. I trust they will get another chance . . . before lunch.

It sounds as though you and Shirley have again done well with a job, housing, and pleasant people. I envy you all the theater, PX, snack bar and all the other privileges extended to Air Corps people. We of the poor branches of service envy you!

My lot has changed somewhat . . . but is bearable and even interesting at times. We have a full crew and many of the shipyard workers have moved onto other ships. Truck loads of supplies arrive day and night and we now must bring it all aboard and store it in its proper place. We have technicians aboard involved with the compasses, radios, radar and even gun sights. Our Captain has implied that we should stand watches (24 hours) to prevent theft and brawls . . . as the crew returns from liberty in high spirits and high alcohol content. This, of course, conflicts with my social life. War is truly hell!

Sometime back, our intrepid Navy went to Martinique and took control of a small French carrier and its crew. The ship was brought here and the crew has total freedom in the city. I don't understand the politics of all this, but it seems the crew claims neutrality and will, therefore, fight the war in New Orleans. Obviously, they are smarter than you or me.

It was a recent pleasure trip to nearby Shell Beach that brought about a little more reality to this 90-day wonder. I took the whole crew on some of the first buses ever manufactured on a trip through jungles and roads designed to test vehicle springs and human sacroiliacs. New Orleans is both hot and humid and we arrived at Shell Beach hoping for a shower and a nap . . . only to learn that we were to submit to gunnery school. The school is the same for every crew, so the crew of a small boat still learns to fire everything from the .45 auto to an 8" gun. They recognized my inborn talents immediately and I had some fear they'd send me to sniper's school. Of course, the small arms had to be disassembled and assembled quickly while blindfolded. Each man then fired about two rounds on each. When we got to the big guns we were issued ear plugs, which helped a little. The 8" gun has a fairly short barrel, and the muzzle blast is something to behold. It pops out the ear plugs and causes sharp pain in the ear drums. Just before dark, it was back to the antique buses and a long ride to the ferry and "home".

More recently, we took a pilot aboard and went upriver over 100 miles to fuel and ammo. It was a truly beautiful trip and I envied the people on the shore and on the houseboats as they got together and roasted corn and fried catfish. The trip was uneventful and, although we stood watches for experience, the pilot was in charge. We changed pilots often as they each knew different stretches of river, not a bad job. All old men. No openings!

The crew wonders where we're going and nobody knows. The fact that our camouflage paint job is in jungle colors rather than the zigzag grey and black, should give a clue. I, therefore, believe that we will soon be in warm water with sunshine, naked beauties, shining beaches and sharks . . . also (I guess) Japs, who so far have proven to be excellent sailors and marksmen. I must check to see about openings in Chaplain's school!

It's amazing all the things necessary to get a ship ready for duty. We've been degaussed, so we are not electrified and we have "swung ship" to check the compasses . . . and we have checked our navigational instruments for accuracy. All this has kept me away from the food and pleasures of the city. Very shortly, we will go on a short "U-shake down cruise" to see if the ship floats and if it cannot only go out to sea . . . but make it back. I am anxious to start. I am trying to learn my own job and at least something about everyone else's jobs. I want to know all the skills of the seamen and all about the guns. Frankly, it is too much to crowd in, but I still have time. At night, I usually have to time to think and that is not necessarily good. It wasn't very long ago that we were college boys sweating out an education and swimming and drinking beer . . . knowing everybody around us. I feel that growing up this fast has robbed me of part of my youth, and I have a great deal of growing to do. I wonder where all our friends are and what they're doing and how many of us will ever get back to "normal". I guess we'll just wait and see.

The thing that really impresses me is the amount of work . . . and the lack of sleep. Work goes on 'round the clock, and there are watches to stand when not working. All this and we're in New Orleans! My college days trained me to operate on little sleep and constant work, but this is worse. I'm learning who the goof-offs are . . . and when things get dangerous, they'll be a real worry. Maybe they'll straighten up.

I wish you the very best of luck with your advanced training. Keep your parachute in good condition and don't ride in airplanes that don't hit on all cylinders. Tell Shirley hello. I'll write again when I can.

RUBBERY KNEES BILL

Friday 30 July to
Friday 17 Sept. 1943

DEAR RUBBER KNEED—

"Now hear this," as you swabbies are frequently heard to say, yours of 5 August '43, has arrived where the sign over the mess hall door reads "Through These Portals Pass the Most Dangerous Men in the World." If that refers to our bombing scores . . . it is most abysmally overstated, but is right on target as a description of the way some of these guys savage their vittles with the tableware. The ground pounder who created that hyperbole never got out of an AT-11 wearing a couple of pork chop lunches.

Your crew must be a very exceptional bunch to withstand the rigors of a trek to and from the gunnery school in a vintage bus and still learn to field strip small arms and become proficient marksmen after two rounds of firing. Tossing in the 8" gun as well fairly boggles the mind. Your leadership and vast experience with weaponry undoubtedly worked miracles with these raw recruits. Snipery lost a seagoing Sgt. York when you elected to stay with ole #628.

The cruise up river for fuel and ammo servicing must have been a real treat after being parked in one spot for so long a period of time. Did your pilots hang over the side tossing the lead and calling out "by the Mark, Twain?" Your short cruise probably helped coordinate the many functions of the ship and crew in preparation for the shake down cruise. Nothing should come as a complete surprise now, but that's probably pie in the sky. Don't worry about putting out to sea . . . just make sure of getting back. That might be a mite more difficult. Learning other jobs as well as your own certainly makes sense to me and might sometime become the difference between sailing on the sea or swimming in it. Hang in there, knees and all . . . knowledge is survival.

The work load you describe is a great deal more demanding than what we are required to perform, at least at this time. Learning the innards and operation of an entire ship plus the role of each man has to be a 24-hour a day job. I suspect that when you depart for wherever it is that you are going, that you will have the additional time you need to become a journeyman in your trade. You made mention that the good Lord didn't provide you with feathers and wings. Well, He didn't issue me webbed feet or fins and I am happy to be soaring on gossamer wings above the tempestuous typhoons that you are facing in your birch bark canoe.

The past six weeks or so, we have been flying at least once a day (lunches intact) and chasing the bug around the hangar floor when not airborne. Classes on a variety of subjects continue to be held. Instructions on how to properly use a parachute when bailing out of a disabled aircraft received the undivided attention of all the junior birdsmen. We even tried some dry runs off a tower. The shock to the family jewels can be horrendous, but the alternative bears no thinking at all. "Not to worry" the riggers tell us. "If it don't work, bring it back and we'll fix it or give you a new one".

Shirley and many of the other wives are daily visitors to the post and have access to the PX, snack shops and the movie theater. They also make use of the swimming pool. When the formations "harch" by the pool and a gaggle of these babes are sunbathing on the pool deck, guys meander out of line, step on other guys' heels and come up with some pretty imaginative whistles and suggestions. We have had some of the single cadets, as well as marrieds, to the house for dinner on a Saturday or Sunday. A real house, real kitchen and a female cook break the monotony for all participants. Shirley and four other gals took an overnighter to Carlsbad Caverns and met two new 2nd Lt. pilots. These throttle jockeys had a yellow rag top Chrysler and provided the cute quintette with transport around the area. The philandering five have declined to comment about this phase of their trip, except for some subdued tittering and eyebrows making like window shades.

The AT-11s we fly have two engines, which is a comforting thought if one quits. On the other hand, if they both quit, what then? Our fearless throttle men assure us that they can glide to a perfect landing any ole place. The problem is that Texas is completely covered with oil derricks, cows and millionaires driving limousines, which doesn't leave a lot of room to land any ole place. The bombsight is a tricky little number to operate. It has a high speed gyro that stabilizes the sight in flight. You stick your eye in the sight and try to get the crosshairs to remain fixed on the target. The two knobs we adjust have inner and outer knobs to kill drift and determine the time and place in space, according to the ground speed that the bombs are released. If the crosshairs don't move, you can't miss and you have scored a shack. Needless to say, this is not always the case. Incidentally, we drop 100 lb. practice bombs with a small powder charge which is visible and photographed through the camera hatch. To graduate, you need a circle of error of less than 100 feet.

In a combat situation after the turn on the bomb run, the airplane (bombing platform) must fly straight and level for several minutes. The control surfaces of the ship are connected by servos to the bombsight . . . so, in effect, the bombardier flies the airplane down the bomb run. This is not a fun time. The flak gunners on the ground know your altitude, speed and heading, and I am told really unload both barrels, the kitchen sink and the overalls from Mrs. Murphy's chowder. I am also told the fighters are much worse. How does one get out of a mess like this without appearing to be yellow to the core? Advise at your earliest.

Tuesday, the 14th, a party was held in Odessa for the graduating class. Unfortunately, Bill Behrens, our house mate, washed out and will be sent to radio school. He and Donna are disappointed, but fate is strange and this may be the saving of him. Wed. P.M.., the entire cadet contingent marched in parade at retreat, complete with the marching band and flags . . . the whole ball of wax. The Cadet Corps, to the astonishment of the viewers and participants alike, "harched" as if they were career men. An impressive final retreat.

Back to the parade ground on Thurs. to receive our gold bars and wings. The wives, mothers and/or girlfriends were rewarded for their inspiration, support and weeks of discomfort by getting to pin the wings on their fledgling bombardiers. Incidentally, an honor well deserved by a lot of young ladies who endured a great deal of worry and primitive conditions to be with their men folk. The balance of Thursday was spent clearing the post for me and packing and saying goodbye for Shirley. Our only regret is the concern we have for what lies ahead for all these wonderful kids . . . and for us as well.

My orders are to report to Salt Lake City for crew and airplane assignments with a ten-day delay en route. Shirley and I will embark once again on what the railroad insists on calling luxury coaches for the trip to Chicago later today or tomorrow. Use this address until I can get back to you with something more permanent. Two quick thoughts before I close. First, you outrank me by virtue of the date of your commission. Think not of popping me into a brace . . . or the world will know about your drooping tail surfaces slowly sliding down a sapling in the middle of a swift-moving stream. Second, in my tailor-made sun tans, I am the epitome of the young, virile, handsome and courageous aviator about to answer his country's call to arms.

ONWARD AND UPWARD

DEAR BEAU BRUMMEL BILL—

I have yours of 17 Sept. Congratulations on your commission and graduation, et al. I shall await your new address in Salt Lake City and am in true envy of your trip to Chicago en route. It sounds as though you are leaving some close friends and a pretty good life, but I know you've had some hard work and tough schedules. Hope your future is better still. You should be happy that you are one of the "most dangerous men in the world". I hope you learned the use of a parachute well and that you are friendly to the man who rigs it. It would seem to me that the parachute rigger is in a position of paramount blackmail. Are there any openings?

Your bombsight has some similarities to our gyro sight on our 20 mm guns. If operated correctly, they are deadly. The problem is the short-range effectiveness. I hate to see an enemy plane approach that close. Our gunners are great!

Your description of the bomb run is a little unsettling. Perhaps you can contact headquarters and bring about a method whereby you resort to violent antics during the run so as to throw off the gunners on the ground. Tell them it just doesn't seem fair! Your description makes sharks seem better all the time. Perhaps you could resort to bed wetting or violent outbursts and be transferred to a desk in Washington.

I am happy to report that I have returned from one of the worst shakedown cruises ever visited upon a red-blooded American coward. I felt as though I was going to miss the war in its entirety. A pilot took us through the long, confusing Delta area and happily gave us a new course as he swung down to the pilot boat and returned to his post, a shower, a good meal and a few more drinks. The sky was black with a yellow pallor and the sea began to grow angry. I suggested we turn back and try it another day . . . and they thought a little humor was a good thing. They can't tell humor from stark fear! Some of the men were sick immediately and we had to run around and secure everything that was loose. We had already done that before getting under way, but we soon found things breaking loose and some of them were heavy and dangerous to be around. We strung "life lines" everywhere so a man could hold on rather than go over the side. Torrential rains blew horizontally over the heavy seas and the salt in the eyes soon turned them red. We had to change course to approach our goal, Panama City, Fla., and, when we did, we really rolled. The ship would roll over so the deck was awash and then hang there as if to decide whether to go clear over or not. Thus came the news that we were taking on water in our lower "tank" deck. This aroused my total interest and I joined my boss and the chief engineer in pouring over blueprints to discover what to do. It was correctly decided that I wasn't needed in the blueprint area and I was assigned to rouse sick sailors from their racks and form a bucket brigade. We could bucket the water into the laundry room where it could be pumped overboard. The sick sailors greeted me with some disdain. Their attitude was that sinking was no worse than dying from their illness in bed. After what seemed like ages, the problem was solved . . . but the whole night was lost and now everyone was pooped. Another day and another night and the hurricane moved away. We had no idea where we were and largely didn't think much about anything except that we weren't rolling anymore, and the sun might even shine. In short, we sighted land and sent a boat to stop someone on the highway to ask where we were. We then moved into Panama City and fell asleep. One more lesson was learned. "Capitol" ships tie up at docks and crews walk ashore while "throw away" ships anchor out in the boondocks and take their boats ashore. We were anchored in the discharge of a paper mill and the brown froth smelled of tannic-acid (I guess) . . . and it was a long way to anywhere.

Our return trip to New Orleans was pleasant and uneventful. We are now tied alongside five other ships, so there is continual traffic over all the ships to get to the dock.

The Natives I met last night in the French Quarter and at the Roosevelt Hotel say the storm was of a minor nature. Good God!

I have observed that of all the fouled up messes aboard ship, the worst is communication . . . radios go out, radar goes out and messengers stop for coffee, and then forget the message. Intercoms short out. A radio technician is a guy who comes aboard with a suitcase full of test equipment and, if the radio doesn't work when he kicks it, it has to be replaced. I'm glad I didn't end up in that division.

So, now we have a short period of time to make some repairs and take on more supplies and collect our thoughts before a sightseeing tour of the Panama Canal and beyond begins. New Orleans almost seems like home now and I'll dislike the leaving. Except for a few battles, the war has not been going well in the Pacific. I still want to see a bit, but I'm a good deal less enthusiastic than a few months ago. Wonder if I'm getting smarter or if the bravado is wearing away!

We get ashore every other night. We can leave at 1600 and must be back aboard by 0800. When we are aboard at night, it is a real problem handling the drunks as they return. Some of these guys can't handle two beers, but they keep trying. I will say that they have been decent enough with me no matter how drunk they are. We have several who were told by a judge that they could go to the service or to jail. That is their secret, and mine, but some of them are very unhappy, mixed-up people.

It seems that you and I are progressing at about the same rate. I don't hear from very many of our friends and wonder where they are and what they're doing. I do hear from some acquaintances of the female gender, but they are all a long way away. I looked up a girl from my high school days on the base here. She was uncomfortable with me in her office and it is verboten to be with her on the outside, poor girl seems lost away from home.

I do hope Salt Lake City is a great experience for you. It will be tough to be without Shirley, or is she going with you? Hope she can. Meanwhile, sweat it out, and we'll meet again somewhere somehow. If you don't mind bombing Japs, we may again swim together.

Best of luck.

OLDER & WISER BILL

Sat. 18 Sept. to
Sun. 7 Nov. 1943

DEAR OLDER & WISER—-

Apparently the most understated and ambiguous words in the Naval lexicon are "shake down cruise". In your best interests, and the diminishing hopes that you may have for future progeny to tell your war stories to, find a way to get off that iron tank hauler, and pronto. Do not think for one minute that that hurricane was an act of God . . . it wasn't. The Navy put it there on purpose. Beware, too, of the Navy that gives you buckets to empty your flooding lower deck. There are such things as pumps and they should, at least, let you know where they hid them. Another thing, no matter where you park them whilst enjoying the sinful pleasures of Panama City and New Orleans, the term "throw away ships" should raise some suspicion concerning the motives of the capital ship Admirals in the far away (and safe) Pentagon. The guys on the bounty had it much easier and Bligh ended up rowing to Honolulu or some such place. Should you happen close by Pitcairn on your next shakedown, keep that in mind, Ensign Christian.

On a serious note, that must have been a frightening initiation into the rites of the deep sea sailor. I can well imagine the chaos and danger on the decks with heavy equipment on the loose and looking for someone to squish. The antics of the ship and the sea in those enormous winds must have been terrifying to neophyte sailors. The pucker strings of all aboard must have been cinched to the max. Having had some small experience with vomitus, its cause and effects, I can sympathize with your efforts to rally the crew for the bucket brigade. I can visualize the crew quarters awash in the stuff while guys are heaving in their hats, shoes and on one another from the top bunk down. I can also visualize the fastidious Ensign Burling sliding around the slippery bucking deck and wishing without hope for a gas mask or separation from the service. I'm sure the experiences you have had thus far . . . from outfitting for sea, the trial runs and finally that mad shakedown cruise . . . will build esprit de corps, as well as confidence in the ship and the job skills of the officers and crew.

Shirley and I arrived Sat. the 18th at Fort Worth and retrained for Kansas City on the Rock Island Rocket . . . the first and only comfortable trains either of us has ridden since induction. From K.C. to Chicago was a fourteen-hour disaster. Square wheels, standing room only, sliceable air and the constant murmuring of hot, hungry and pissed off passengers. Found out a few days later that the baggage car caught fire and our gear got damaged. I shall file a claim which will set all future standards for fraud. After being force-fed for days by a variety of family kitchens, I took off for Salt Lake City on the 29th. Lucked in with a Pullman and two fellow graduates, Albanese and Abmyer. No quarters here, but our luck held and we rented a garret room in a vintage hotel . . . three of us, one bed and a toilet took some getting used to. About the time we learned to turn over at the same time, we left S.L.C for Kearns, about twenty miles away. At Kearns, we got quarters with individual beds and long-delayed and much needed showers.

Here at Kearns, we will be assigned to a combat crew and to a combat training airfield. While we await these awesome events, we wile away our time in a rather difficult dead reckoning navigational course, among others of lesser degrees of difficulty. Shirley once again hit the rails on the 7th and met a Midland wife on the train. The train broke down a couple of times, but they arrived at S.L.C. on the 9th and were met by another wife (Janet Bailey) and directed to the Hotel Semloh. These ladies look after one another as if they were sisters . . . and, in a way, I suspect they are for the duration and perhaps later on.

Living in a hotel and eating out every day keeps us on the edge of poverty constantly. My $327.00 doesn't quite last the month, but Shirley again got a job and the wolf retreated from the door step to the front yard where he slavers away waiting for the other shoe to drop. Crew assignments have been made and I have met the nine men who will share with me whatever the fickle finger has in store for this crew. Incidentally, we will be flying B-24 Liberators. I had hoped for B-17s, but our pilots tell me the B-24 is faster. I am a B-24 booster. More on the crew and airplane in a later letter.

On the 2nd of November, we received orders to report to Casper, Wyoming, for combat crew training. The crews went by troop train, which was a wise move on the part of the Air Corps. Left on our own, now that we are down near the nitty and the gritty, half the contingent might have looked for a hidey hole in the nearby mountains. Shirley and most of the other wives traveled by bus and reached Casper on the 4th of November and have rooms in the Wyatt Hotel (ten bucks a week and share the bath). Officers and men were restricted to the base until the 6th when I managed to get to town and view the new quarters. We began looking for something less frontier-like immediately. Another feature of the Wyatt is the slot machines in the lobby . . . and our meager exchequer cannot handle

Shirley's yen to hit the jackpot. Her eyes begin to resemble cherries and plumbs, plus a nervous tic in her right arm.

Betty D. (our toilet and tub-sharing fellow sufferer) and Shirley have announced that they are with child. Nobody told me something like this could happen while riding those insufferable trains. I may be reached by mail or in person at the 463rd Bomb Sqdn., Crew #18, A.A.B., Casper, Wyoming.

POPPA BEAR

DEAR POPPA BEAR—

Good to hear from you and to learn your new address. The US Postal Service is doing a great job, but it's obvious that there will likely be some big gaps in our correspondence. How they can deliver mail to ships with APO or FPO addresses beats me.

I'm glad to hear you and Shirley experienced a decent train ride, although a short one, followed by the usual cattle cars. What do you suppose happened to all the decent trains we rode as civilians?! My guess is they are reserved for Congressmen and people in the military who rank somewhat higher than you or me. They must have emptied every museum in the country to move "our boys". Sounds like one long ride for you all the way to Salt Lake City. I note that two of your acquaintances, due to the alphabet, moved with you. That helps somewhat. I have one such friend aboard this vessel . . . we were at Plattsburg together.

My God, but you make a lot of money! Obviously, the Air Corps is overpaid, but I suppose some of it has to do with a wife and off-base living. I am drawing a magnificent 10% for sea pay and have a place to sleep and three meals per day, plus the added privilege of buying uniforms (when available) at less than retail . . . also free medical attention (when available).

Somehow your assignment to a combat crew in B-24s is somewhat foreboding. Training crew would sound better . . . in Piper Cubs. Is it too late to switch to aircraft designing or perhaps the ministry? Perhaps you and your nine cohorts could someday bail out into the wilderness on one of your training flights now that you are in Wyoming. You could build a cabin in Jackson Hole and live off the land. If so, take plenty of frozen food along so you won't have to depend on your shooting skill for food.

Congratulations to you and Shirley regarding her pregnant condition. I doubt this is a result of riding trains and suggest you buy a book which may reveal the cause of this condition. A little more training and less time off might be the answer.

My life has been busy, but a bit monotonous since I last wrote. I have been trying to burn the candle at both ends because things are obviously better for me than they are going to be. I am going to be somewhat limited from now on in my details because of censorship. Ship movements are of real interest to the enemy, although I can't imagine that the whereabouts of this particular ship will be of any great interest. I like to think they wouldn't waste an expensive torpedo on this hulk, with its green crew of lovers (not fighters). It consoles me somewhat on those dark nights all alone.

My last days in New Orleans were spent eating, and I also drank some of the very fine concoctions served at the various watering holes. I heard some great dixieland music and watched the Cubans dance. They make it look about as close to foreplay as the law allows. I took in some rather bawdy floor shows and, in general, enjoyed myself. It was a distinct misfortune to see a couple of freighters at the New Orleans docks that had been torpedoed just offshore. How they made it in, I'll never know. One could drive a truck through the holes in their sides. It's clear that there is no place to hide and one must trust to luck. I have bought twelve rabbit feet!

We have been to sea a few days now and it's a pleasant trip. Calm seas, beautiful nights and warm days with a good breeze. We move at about 10 knots and are all alone. We have some .22 rifles and pistols and some Springfields. I have also been issued a .45 caliber pistol. My 45 A & P was made by Remington Rand and is new, and it works. We have had a chance to shoot at flying fish, debris in the water or anything visible.

We have also been involved in firing at towed targets . . . everyday for several hours. I swear we have the best gunners in the Navy. The crews towing the targets have the target and the cable shot away within seconds and have to rig a new one. When not firing on towed targets, we have drills, night and day . . . general quarters, fire, abandon ship, collision, etc. The signals for each drill sound different and it takes awhile to differentiate. We also launch and recover boats while underway, which is very dangerous. Also drills for dropping or picking up the anchors and for docking. All this means is that I must assign men for each drill and see that they get on station . . . fast. They (and I) are so tired of the repetitive drills that it's hard to maintain any interest. I have to be an example and I keep telling them the purpose is survival. We need sleep. Some men are sleeping near their posts so they don't have to run in the dark. Trouble is they never know what drill is next, so they'll have to move anyway. A guy could wear his clothes out just taking them off and putting them back on.

In our "off time" from drills, and during the day, we have hausers to splice and boat lines to make up as spares . . . and there is always something that needs welding or fixing. We have made up pipe frames for some awnings to shade some areas from a very penetrating and hot sun.

Still, I like it. I stand at least one watch at night. A signalman and a messenger are with me on the conning tower, 52 feet above the water. Below in the wheelhouse are the helmsman, a radio operator, a radar man and another standing by the engine room messenger. There is a lookout on the bow and another on the stern. They must all be kept awake and that's not easy. It is quiet and peaceful and beautiful . . . and a little exciting. I believe I could love being a sailor in different circumstances.

My boss was a boatswain's mate before the war and got a commission early in the war. He saw the early part, which was one loss after another . . . and when he speaks, I listen. I asked him how long we'd likely be out and he said we'd come back either in a box or when the war ends. I choose the part about the when the war ends.

In a few days, we arrive at Coco Solo in Panama on the east coast. We'll go through when there are no important ships wanting through. My boss tells me some tales about Coco Solo that are hard to believe. If he's correct, the sex pools around Peoria and Indiana Harbor are like church socials. We shall see.

I trust that you and your nine accomplices can stretch out your training until an armistice is arranged. What happens if you can't do anything right? Take care of yourself and Shirley.

I'll write again when these damned drills end!

OVER DRILLED BILL

12 December, '43

DEAR WM.—

Haven't heard from you in awhile, but realize the Postal Service may be confused as to my whereabouts. Trust that all is well and that you are somehow in charge of training recruits for the rest of the war.

My last letter, I believe, was written as we approached Panama. It was a peaceful, if not restful, trip. The various drills were incessant, but I can see that our crew now knows the shortest and quickest way to the various posts for the various drills. All of us have advised the Captain that he has reached his goal and that the drills have achieved the point of diminishing returns.

We reached Coco Solo about 0800 and anchored offshore while some important ships entered the Canal. If you don't already know, Coco Solo is on the east (or Atlantic) side, but is actually west of Panama City, which is on the west side of the Pacific. Either of the cities, and the whole Canal Zone, is well-versed in how to entertain (and fleece) sailors of the world. My boss arranged for him and me to test one of our boats while we were at anchor . . . we went to Coco Solo to see if we could more or less act as chaperons. My God! This place is unbelievable. I saw my first bonafide transvestites and viewed various girls in the cribs on the street where they are more or less confined . . . little kids on the sidewalks selling their sisters for a pittance. Some of the "sisters" looked more like grandmothers and some were very young. The first drink at every bar is strong enough that one can't tell the second one is cheap bar whiskey. A real carnival of carnal delights and general debauchery. As soon as we discovered we could not reform the town, we found our way back to the boat and then the ship. My boss made it up the Jacob's ladder, and so did I.

The following morning, we entered the Canal and went through without incident. Everything looks just like the pictures in my grade school geography book. The Gatun locks and Gatun Lake. Hot, humid and not much to do.

We pretty much followed the coastline up to San Diego. I got off watch at midnight on a clear, starry night. A gentle breeze was blowing and it was beautiful. I no sooner got to sleep, when I was awakened by a severe rolling of the ship. Everything in the room that was loose was crashing from side to side and we were in those rolls where the ship dips one side into the water and hangs there awhile and then violently back onto the other side. I couldn't image what had gone wrong in only a few minutes, so I quickly donned my life jacket and made my way outside the deck house. This is no mean task. When one reaches a door, he first becomes enmeshed in a very heavy canvas set of drapes (treated to be fire retardant). There are two of these things and they overlap. When one finds the center and wrestles his way through, he is then at the door. The drapes have heavy weights at the bottom to keep them in place and their purpose is to allow use of the door at night without showing any light. So, while fumbling for the dog (latch) and the 100 lb. door, the drapes swing away and hit one from behind. The door is too heavy to open until the ship rolls toward the side the door is on. At that point, a skillful sailor opens the door and falls out with it as it opens. When the ship rolls back the other way, the door slams shut and must be latched immediately. I hate to bore you with all this, but a guy could be badly hurt just trying to get through a door! I must invent something better! The gist of the problem was that we were off the gulf of Tehuantepec, which is notorious for sudden, violent storms. I noted that the whole crew was up and about in their skivvies and I pretended to be totally casual and just looking for a cup of coffee. It was still clear and now moonlit and I casually slipped back to my rack and to sleep. The seas calmed in a few hours. Next day, we passed close offshore at Acapulco. Beautiful! A steep, tall bank with a long waterfall and a shorter one.

We have seen about four old three and four masted schooners. I couldn't believe my eyes and thought I was seeing something from the previous century. They are carrying lumber up and down the coast. I wonder how they made out at Tehuantepec. Surely, I will be one of the last to see these old ships.

So, now I am a short-term resident of San Diego and, from here, who knows! We are at a dock and taking on supplies and loading both decks as tightly as possible. Loading and unloading is my job and it must be done right. Everyone waves to me as they leave for liberty and the fun ashore. Loading goes on night and day.

I'll try and get you another letter, whether I hear from you or not, before I leave here. I'm guessing we'll have about a week here.

GETTING NERVOUS BILL

DEAR OVER DRILLED—-

The Postal Service, as you have pointed out on occasion, has indeed been doing a great job. Your letter of 21 November was eagerly being read on the 6th of December. Also, as you and I suspected, the time lag between posting and receiving will soon increase quite substantially. We seem to be heading in totally different directions . . . your "large stationary target" to the Pacific and, as rumor has it, our "thin skinned" bombing platform headed for Europe. Our most devout prayers are for the 15th Air Force in Italy, as opposed to the 8th Air Force in England. The losses air crews are taking in that theater are terrifying, and I terrify easily. Wherever we end up will be a permanent base, and this might help the mail. But on the bounding main, you may be hard to locate.

You were entitled to your last days of debauchery and dixieland in New Orleans, judging by the 24-hour days of brutal drill-drill and watch-watch that greeted your return from Liberty to the war. This Coco Solo you mentioned sounds like a place your frail physique and slim wallet should avoid like the plague (and there surely is some of that lurking around the Naval tourist traps of Loco Coco Solo). To my utter despair for life, limb and sanity, you tell me that you are beginning to enjoy the life of a junior executive aboard that iron maiden. Take your sextant in hand, plot the coordinates of Pitcarin and prepare to abandon ship. Regardless of my hurrahing, I'm real happy for your rigorous training schedule, for it will surely reflect in crew response when the bad times come . . . as they most probably will. We try to get in one another's pockets for the same reasons and, with nowhere to go in one of our lumbering limos, it can definitely spell the difference in longevity.

Here in the land of howling winds, freezing temperatures and horizontally driven snow, our room in the Wyatt Hotel was beginning to test our recently recited vows (as well as my misbegotten pledge to defend the US of A against all enemies, foreign and domestic). The damned bed squeaked if I tossed my hat on it, much less anything heavier or more athletically inclined than my hat. Shirley felt as if we were in an acoustical fish bowl, what with the cardboard walls and the badly sprung bathroom door. We were privy to the most intimate functions of our neighbors' lives, from morning ablutions to nighttime frolicking . . . and we were reduced to whispering and trying not to make splashing noises when using the john. These Eunuchian conditions led us on a frantic search for a place where brushing, flushing, burping and baring are home grown. Lo and behold, through a referral by a Marine Shirley met on the bus from Kearns, we finally got a nifty furnished four-room apartment at 614 E. 5th St. for $22.00 a month. The flying Eunuch has landed.

Flying both day and night, along with the bomb trainer, classwork, small arms and some plinking with the 50 calibers makes for some long days and nights.

Takeoffs and landings in these big airplanes are the critical moments, and the navigator (E. J. Norris) and I generally ride in our glass house in the nose. There is no getting accustomed to that at all. With the cement runway zipping along five feet underneath, and the mountains coming closer by the second, you try and lift that sucker off the ground by sheer force of will power. Landing, with the airplane deliberately diving at the concrete strip, and nothing between you and it but a pane of glass, you put on imaginary brakes with your feet and horse back on an imaginary stick with both hands and pray a whole bunch. It's like being the head pin in a bowling alley and hoping the guy throws a gutter ball. Without the confidence I now have in our pilots (Robert McGlasson and Jack Airey), my heart, and the laundry bills, would have killed me by now. One of our friends has been grounded because he loses three to four pounds every time he flies. He (Ed Dumas) barely makes a shadow anymore.

A few more notes of possible interest. When not flying, attending class or playing poker (Black Jack), I spend a lot of time at the skeet range. Combat crews have unlimited access to the range and I get in an hour or two daily. The range is equipped with model 12 Winchester pumps, and my well known and documented deadly skill as a snap shooter is being honed to a razor's edge. I mention this only to spare you undue embarrassment when next we trudge the corn rows and the birds begin to fall before my unerring patterns.

Thanksgiving came and went, and we enjoyed peanut butter sandwiches and ice water as our salute to the bounty provided by the Pilgrim fathers. Fortuitously, the next day a precooked chicken dinner arrived from my folks and a large package of assorted goodies came from Shirley's mother. The two bucks we have left until payday can now be spent recklessly. This infusion of food foiled the ever-present wolf once again.

The weather has been very cold, and aggravated by a howling wind. Shirley likes to hang the laundry out on the roof because it smells so fresh and springlike, but trying to maneuver a frozen sheet the size of a frigate's sail through a doorway in a "sou-wester" without becoming airborne is a risky proposition. Shirts, skirts and undies are also frozen and appear to be occupied by very thin people. The weather also gave me a cold and a bit of fever. I trotted over to the dispensary for some pills, but was, instead, incarcerated in the hospital. No amount of extremely bad manners and vulgar language with which I assaulted the staff got me released. I will never again visit the dispensary, at least under my own power. I can't remember ever being that angry before in my life. Shirley thinks the whole thing is funny . . . very funny . . . which pisses me off still further. These people never heard of thermometers that take temperatures orally . . . they do everything ass-backwards. The doctor was running around with his fly open, and when loudly informed that his caduceus was hanging out, he ordered the nurse to give me a shot. I suspect he had just given her one in the linen closet and was annoyed at being caught. In any event, that ripped it and I was given the heave-ho, including a verbal autopsy that left no doubt about our future doctor-patient relationship.

Christmas Day, Shirley cooked her first turkey . . . with some doubts as to what the end product would look and taste like. The lady downstairs loaned her a big pan and told her to toss the bird in, add a gallon of water and let it rip. Miraculously, it was a beautiful sight to see, as well as eat. We had six guests: McGlasson, Blythe and Jack Airey, a friend of theirs, Betty and Ed (Skinny) Dumas. The hostess was extravagantly praised to her great surprise and pleasure. Jack Airey, our co-pilot, will be leaving us to become a first pilot with another crew. We will miss him . . . and Blythe as well, she is a Smith graduate and a consummate lady from fingers to toes.

New Year's Eve there was a party and dance at the post officer's club which was attended by all off-duty personnel. Shirley had a new black silk dress and looked terrific, even before the cocktails. There were a few sober celebrants left as the evening wore on and became 1944. The line at the ladies' room became so long that one small group, unable to stand the pressure and despite the snow and wind effects, dashed outside and attempted to write their names in the snow. A truly heroic effort, considering the weather and their party attire. To my astonishment, I found out later that my bashful, blushing bride not only was a leading participant, but also the only one who could dot the "I".

All in all, and despite the dangerous nature of our work and the usual foul-ups, the duty here at Casper has been good duty. We lost a 24 and a crew a few days ago when the drove into a mountain shortly after take off. This sort of thing happens on occasion and we feel these losses deeply, but of necessity have to put it out of our minds and get on with the serious business of learning enough skills to stay alive . . . not only now, but when people start shooting and the cheese really begins to bind. It is quite likely that I will be here in Casper for another month or so before collecting our own airplane somewhere and leaving for somewhere else. In the interim, I intend to keep my head out and soak up as much flying time and book larnin' as is available.

I will continue to write, even though your replies will be dictated by the exigencies of the service and the cooperation of the Postal people. Write when you can, and as often as possible . . . I can't worry about you and the Luftwaffe at the same time and still hit a high deflection shot with my trusty 50 caliber.

THE SNAPSHOOTER

12 January, '44

DEAR SNAPSHOOTER—

I will comment only in that I'm glad you didn't say sharpshooter. Frankly, bullshooter might be appropriate.

Our correspondence is not doing too badly, considering the distance and circumstances. I now have yours of 8 Nov. '43, to Jan. '44. In the meantime, I sent you a letter from San Diego sometime back. Wish I were there!

In a way, I envy your possibility of going to Europe. At least I do if my information is correct. I do not envy your choice of service because I have no yen to fly. I guess it's the thought of such a long fall that bothers me. Keep your parachute at the ready. I hope you do get Italy, and I shall be on pins and needles till I hear of the fine hotels, beautiful scenery and fine food and wine.

Meanwhile, I shrink from your description of howling winds and freezing temperatures. Snow, too! We suffer the monotony of clear skies, gentle breezes and 85-degree temps . . . endlessly. I would dwell on this for a while, but time is limited!

You appear to have been less than pleased with the Wyatt Hotel. I have been in some like it and understand your disgust. All that, plus having Shirley there, could result in a certain amount of abstinence. We at least have abstinence without temptation, except for the ever-present imagination.

You sound very busy with all the flying, plus classes and gunnery exercises. Your position in the nose and near the runway doesn't sound like anything but pure excitement. Couldn't you have them redesign that aircraft so that your office would be safer and more comfortable? Try asking. I feel for the poor guy who loses three or four lbs. each flight. I believe I would be like him.

Keep practicing on the skeet range. I do sincerely hope you improve so that when we get home I can see you hit something. I suggest some improvement in your 100 yd. dash so you can, if need be, catch the cripples.

Thanksgiving! I had forgotten it. Glad you had a belated decent meal. My congrats to Shirley and her preparation of the feast.

Sorry to hear of your hospital stay and I hope you avoid the activities that reduce your ability to fight disease. Your experience at the hospital sounds terrible, and not unexpected.

Your Christmas sounds great. I laughed at the girls "writing" their names in the snow when the local restroom had a long line. I witnessed a similar, but different situation recently . . . but I digress.

I'm glad Caspar has been basically good. Sorry to hear of the loss of a plane and I suppose you knew the crew. These things, unfortunately, do come along and it seems such a waste of our best young people. My boss, who has been there, says to be friendly, but don't become good friends because it hurts a little less when they're gone. I'm developing that attitude, but don't like it.

I believe I last wrote from San Diego and it has been busy since then. It seems that everything is hurry-up . . . and we never stop for long. Loading and unloading is a lot of work and time and, of course, I am trying to learn how to unload in a hurry!

I got ashore just before leaving San Diego and three of us visited Tijuana to see if we could learn anything new. The people of Tijuana seem to have little interest in the war, but love sailors . . . and money. We wined and dined and then wined some more. We met some very pretty, intellectual-type girls who took us here and there, and we laughed and joked and wined quite awhile. It was at our last watering hole that the men's john was out of service . . . and it was necessary to enter the alley and "write" one's name on the fence or in the sand. The intellectual-type girls joined in the fun . . . and so it was that "Paul" was perfectly written in the sand . . . but it was Rosa's handwriting. Of course, we congratulated them both, and that was just before the gendarmes arrived. There were two of them and three of us . . . and we quickly discussed whether we were going to sea tomorrow or spend the war in a Tijuana hotel for the morally deprived. We unwisely decided we would resist incarceration. In short, I will forever hold the Tijuana police in high regard. They reminded us of some sort of a curfew, the gate and announced we were well overdue. I guess the curfew was midnight or so, and the police pointed to the rising sun. We had a fast ride to the gate at the border and the police talked with a surly, no-nonsense character at the window. Shortly, a cab arrived from the USA and we made it to the dock. We had time to shave and drink some coffee, and then we took in our lines and got underway. It was a little after Christmas. For Christmas, we had frozen turkey (partially thawed) and real potatoes. Then it was back to work.

The trip from San Diego was pleasant and uneventful. We don't move too fast . . . about 240 miles a day. From Panama on it has been no lights at night and we have been alone at sea. I like it, but admit to some fear of the future. My childish idea that I could swim forever has been somewhat diminished by reality. Some of the ships limping home for major repairs are not a pretty sight, and talking to their crews has convinced me that I should have asked for duty in Washington, D.C. It now seems a bit late.

So now I am residing in Pearl Harbor, briefly. Everyone wants to know where we're going and I can only say it won't be San Diego. There is some debris and clutter here, but it's mainly cleaned up and humming with activity. Can't say much. Honolulu is the "crossroads of the world", but I haven't met any old friends. We have an early curfew, no lights at night and night life is nonexistent. There are two hotels on the beach at Waikiki, the Moana and the Royal Hawaiian. The Royal Hawaiian is pretty well reserved for Air Corps personnel. I have watched the swimmers and sunbathers from under the banyan tree at the Moana Hotel, but drinks are expensive and the man who pays the Navy has not been around. Hawaii is a disappointment. Again we've unloaded and reloaded and will leave soon. Wonder if you've left Caspar. Hope you went to Italy . . . or better yet . . . Chicago. All mail is censored now. I might slip something by, but I want as few risks as possible. Where we're going must remain secret, but I can tell where we've been.

It's embarrassing to censor the mail of the men in my division. Their letters to wives or girlfriends (or both) are none of my business. Some of them raise hell about me and I let that go, but they cannot mention the ships they see or the damage or where we're going. I hope they learn the rules pretty soon. Their letters home are truly sad . . . and I guess I'm lucky to look upon all this as an adventure, although with diminishing zeal.

In my eagerness to receive mail, I am writing several people from high school, or anywhere else. They're writing back and I guess that's being encouraged at home.

I trust I'll have time to write at my next stop. Keep them coming, and I'll do the same. This place is a killer, but I've learned to hate being in port . . . at sea is fine.

BUSY BILL

Bill (top row, far right) and some members of the crew of LST 628, Tijuana, Mexico, December, '43.

Sunday 2 Jan. 1944 to
Sunday 16 Jan. 1944

DEAR BILL—-

Happy New Year wherever you happen to be on the calm and serene Pacific. Although I have not as yet received a reply to mine of 1 Jan. '44, I thought I would keep you abreast of what cooks in the wild and wooly skies of Wyoming. Posting and receiving mail on your "Eagle of the Sea" is probably a very chancy thing, so I will write more often in the hope that your mail calls will always provide you with something to read from another trembling patriot. You can now pass your Sears catalog along to the ward room so everyone can enjoy the sexy women in the bra and girdle ads.

Since our arrival at Caspar and a semi-permanent base, the wives have been introduced to the caste system which separates the officer corps from the enlisted personnel. Shirley and the other new officer's wives attended a tea hosted by the wives of the permanent officer cadre. Those ladies wear their husband's rank by some form of osmosis peculiar to the military. I assume this to be true in all the service branches. The new ladies were taken aback by the superior and condescending attitude of the regulars, particularly with the dos and don'ts of deportment and grooming. Fraternizing with enlisted personnel or their spouses is a "no-no". Standing up for and addressing the higher ranks as ma'am is a "yes-yes". Some hints on makeup, attire and social graces were also featured at this happy gathering. The reservist ladies found all of this to be as unacceptable as dog doo in the finger bowls and have no plans to attend future teas or surrender their civilian identities. I will not offend your view of the gentler sex by repeating some of their remarks upon returning home.

The services are going to have to adjust some of their pre-war thinking in order to cope with the huge influx of new officers, NCOs and their wives. The air arms in particular are getting people who are educated, motivated and not interested in playing military politics in order to get promoted or a safe seat in the bleachers. There are exceptions, of course. I'm all for strict military posture while on duty, but off the job is another matter altogether. The ladies of the crews, although from different backgrounds and locales, have much in common and, as a group, are supportive and sympathetic of one another. The worries about the future, as well as the daily frustrations of limited financing, awkward accommodations and gypsy-like constant moving are shared by the group . . . a great morale-booster for the crews and their camp followers, and a big plus for the services. There are six NCOs and four officers on a B-24 and, if it goes down, they all share the same ride. This is a new kind of warfare, so traditional thinking should be modified a little in some areas.

You have just been saved from the further boredom of my philosophical attempts to restructure the hidebound military Juggernaught. Your letter posted from San Diego on 12 December 1943, has arrived. It seems we both had the same idea about dropping a line or two before receiving a reply to our previous lines or two and not a response to your next letter, which is not yet in my hot little hand, and to which I will reply with more than a line or two. Now that I am completely lost somewhere between your line or two, and my line or two and the onset of senility . . . I'll try to get off a line or two . . . oh shit, here goes!

PHILOSOPHER BILL

20 Jan. 44

DEAR NERVOUS—

Regarding Coco Solo, forewarned should have been forearmed. You should take more heed of my warnings about the perils of shore leave in towns hard by Naval anchorages. In the future, you should learn to control your raging thirst and hyper hormones with harder work, longer hours, less food and colder showers. As chaperons, you and your boss were like a pair of randy foxes in a pheasant roost. I hope that, blinded by booze and passion, you guys did not believe for a minute the kid who assured you that his grandma had never been touched. On a more serious note, I think we are both naive and Midwestern enough to be astounded, not only by the women the kids and the skullduggery in the bars, but a little sad for the buyers and sellers alike.

The descriptive prose you used to describe the canal, sunny days, calm seas, Acapulco and, most of all, the three and four-masted schooners almost convinced me that you have it made. Azure seas with clipper ships ghosting along on the horizon, that did it, and I was mentally submitting a request for immediate transfer. You then sailed serenely into Tehuantepec and spent a whole night getting the stuffing kicked out of your life jackets. Next, you spend days and nights making that bucket heavier and heavier with the floating characteristics of an anvil. As far as I am now concerned, you guys can remain our first line of defense while I peer down at your warlike activities from 20,000 feet and gratefully count my flying pay.

Both of us are afflicted with sensitive nerves . . . which is not too surprising, considering how the poor things have been abused night and day for the past several months. After reacting to our daily thrillers with such enthusiasm, I hope when the shooting starts, they are numb enough so that we can conduct ourselves in a seemly manner. A seemly manner, of course, includes anything short of shrieking and jumping ship.

More to follow—

RIPCORD BILL

24 Jan. '44

DEAR RIPCORD BILL—-

     Surprisingly, your letter of 2 Jan. to 16 Jan. got to me in pretty good time. A belated Happy New Year to you and Shirley!

     I am somewhat surprised at the caste system you mention. That would be hard to take and I'm glad the women are resisting. I have long ago noted that some wives tend to take on the importance (real or imagined) of their husband's rank, and I'm sure you've noticed that the guy who got there a day ahead of you is an "old hand". We cannot fraternize with enlisted personnel, and I suppose I would run into the same problem if I were assigned to a base. I have always been en route somewhere, so have escaped the attitudes of the higher ranks . . . or the "regular" Navy. I agree that "they" will have to change attitudes . . . there are many more of us and we're the ones headed out where it is less pleasant.

     Your snide remarks about my attempts to reform the people of Coco Solo are noted. You are correct that it is sad. I agree that we probably are somewhat naive . . . it will be difficult to stay that way.

     My tales of warm breezes, blue water and moonlit nights may sound pretty good in Caspar. At the risk of causing you some envy, I must report that our leaving Pearl Harbor has been delayed by some alterations to the ship. There has been some spare time, and I have been able to get around a bit. I believe I told you the Royal Hawaiian Hotel was pretty well reserved for Air Corps personnel. Nevertheless, a friend and I visited a couple of times for a drink in the afternoon. Most Air Corps people were friendly and either coming or going somewhere else. The Moana Hotel is my favorite because of the big banyan tree on the patio . . . and the view of the beach and Diamond Head. A trip around the island was nice, but not too impressive. A trip to "big" island, Hawaii and its town of Hilo, was impressive. It is beautiful. Perfect climate and good food and drink . . . and very expensive. Anything that would provide a feeling of normalcy is either closed or off limits. At night, it's lights out and off the streets. There are damned few bona fide Hawaiians here. They are mixed with various Asiatics, and who knows what. Not many beauty contest winners here . . . and not enough females to go around. Still, I'd give my right arm to sit out the war here and learn to like it better.

     Perhaps later I can relate more about Pearl Harbor, but not now. I've talked with several people on the way home and there is some bitterness here and there. It seems that we all are like poor cousins in the big picture and are going to be operating on a shoe string. I note very little interservice rivalry, and everyone from the different branches of service feels respect, or envy, for the others. Marines and soldiers are not fond of LSTs because they ride a little roughly and venture close to shore batteries. I could very easily do without some of this information! One way to get back here is to have one's ship badly damaged or be seriously wounded. There must be a better way! I must have been out of my mind to look for adventure.

     On our way here from San Diego, we had a few more drills just to keep us on our toes. We had more target practice with towed targets off San Diego, and again as we approached Pearl Harbor. I can't boast enough about the skill of our gunners and it's a good feeling.

     We came out here short of uniforms and we're told that it only gets worse. We are working in pants and long-sleeved shirts and army shoes or boots. For "formal" attire, we put on a jacket and Navy shoes, but there is little use for formal gear, except at the hotel.

     I trust that you are learning your job well and taking good care of your parachute. I'm betting that when you get where you're going, the formalities and rank-pulling will ease considerably. We have virtually no saluting and are working as a team. Of course there are a few who are troublesome, but their shipmates keep them under pretty good control.

     Just learned the honeymoon is over. No more afternoons at the hotels. No idea where we're going, but will mail this now. Good luck!

ALOHA BILL

14 Feb. '44

DEAR BOMBARDIER—-

At last I have a little time on my hands, but can't write much. All hell is breaking loose out here, and I wonder if the news gets home or not. Surely not much of the details get back home. We have had no news from the outside world and can only surmise that it still exists.

Some of the crew came up with a turntable and it is hooked, sometimes, to the P.A. system. We have one record (probably purloined) with Guy Lombardo playing "Drifting and Dreaming". Nice song, sort of Hawaiian. However, hearing it all day for weeks on end, one begins to use the Navy earplugs designed for retaining one's hearing near the guns. It is my fond hope we can trade that record to another ship or, better still, destroy it and find another. When the ship rolls a little, the needle slides all the way across the record. The end result is listening to loud static with a musical background. But it's our only toy!

We are nearing the end of a long trip, and it has been beautiful. Perfect weather and gentle seas and, as far as we know, no real danger. I doubt the Japs would waste a torpedo on us.

We are in a convoy with some nondescript freighters and Liberty ships. All are loaded to the gills, and my division stays busy just tightening the turnbuckles on the chains holding the deck load, hopefully, in place. Up at the bow, we have barrels of 100 octane gas stashed on slanting racks and held in place by small chains and secured with pelican hooks. Pelican hooks are someone's brainstorm and they can be released from a distance by pulling on a chain. I am not happy with the gasoline, which is near ammunition storage, but I was not consulted about the floor plan or the cargo.

Below decks, we have heavy equipment and miscellaneous supplies, including Army rations. The canned cheese and chocolate bars are delicious. We have the equipment operators and truck drivers aboard, and it is their first trip on an LST. They seem to think it moves around too much.

Watches now must be all business ... although they always have been. We're 500 yards behind the ship ahead and 500 yards from the ships on either side of us. We must memorize the size of the ships, through binoculars, so that we can keep station at night. We are sometimes, but not always, forewarned of an upcoming emergency turn, which is always 45 degrees right or left, and the sudden signal is someone screaming on the radio, "Turn emerg, or emerg turn". We learn before the convoy forms that "Turn emerg" may mean either a right or left turn. Sometimes it is changed during the trip, so all we have to do is get it right and either add or subtract 45 degrees from the course. It ain't always easy! The purpose is usually zigzagging or an emergency. So far, we have always received a short warning, so we have time to think. A wrong turn means a collision, because we have no brakes! I hate to bore you with all this, but I must dispel any notion that we spend all our time in joyful pursuits.

It is hard to imagine how quickly cheap steel rusts in the salt spray. A sailor's life could be spent chipping and painting. It is monotonous, dirty and noisy. I personally saw a bin of paint scrapers, chipping hammers and wire brushes that would supply the Navy for a year or so ... I thought. Lo and behold, most of them have "fallen" over the side. So, no more paint chipping for a while. I am told it was ever thus. Each man is now issued a scraper and must turn it in at the end of the job. Now the records get lost. One wonders if the Japanese have this problem.

The sea at night is beautiful. As the ship moves, there is a wake at the bow, and the water is full of phosphorescence (no dictionary) that travels along both sides most of the way. We leave a short trail of this behind us ... not always, but sometimes. Most nights have been quiet, and there isn't much to do but keep on station and see to it that no one is sneaking cigarettes. They look like a searchlight in the total darkness. Unfortunately, the nights are a chance to think or talk with the signalman or the messenger. Once one has heard the life stories (and dreams) of everyone else, there is a lot of silence. I find thinking, or rather remembering, to be both sweet and rather sad. I'm sure that all the minds that think in the quiet darkness probably think the same things. I'd rather be at the Polar Grille or my girlfriend's or in a duck blind. It would even be a pleasure to walk with you through the corn fields and watch you waste shells as you frighten the wily pheasant!

We have had our first Captain's Mast, the lowest form of criminal justice in the Navy. One man accused another of the theft of a mattress cover. Each man has his name stenciled on all his personal belongings, so it was a battle of wits to tell if there was a theft and, if so, by whom. Both men were in my division, so my boss was the lawyer for the accused. The alleged thief got a few hours of extra duty and some friendships went down the drain.

I hesitate to describe this crew because you may feel we are out to provide aid and comfort to the enemy. If the Japanese find this letter, they'll believe they've already won. Actually, I'm very proud of these guys . . . who learned so much so quickly. But we do have some odd balls, and it is sometimes difficult to see the humor in it all. We have one man who is in his 40s who is so fat that he can't fit through a deck hatch. He suffers from claustrophobia and can hardly go below decks. I sent him to the engine room one day and he had to be carried out. Don't know what to do with him. Another "old" man didn't seem to fit anywhere, but proved to be a fair mechanic and now is in charge of gas-driven portable pumps that seldom start. He checks four to six of them each day. We have a few sullen young men who were told by some judge to choose between jail and service . . . and we got them. They do their work and may snap out of it. We have a few that are quiet and hard to figure out. We have one who just will not work and he is an expert at disappearing. No punishment will cause him to work.

Fun time is over. Hope you're still in Caspar enjoying the winter sports. Hope you stay as an instructor. I must say I'd rather be here than flying in those damned airplanes!

We are approaching a fairly quiet place, so I should be in touch. I'll write whenever I can and hope you'll do the same.

SOMEWHAT SOBER BILL

Monday 17 Jan. 1944 to
Tuesday 29 Feb. 1944

DEAR BUSY B.——

Mail call on the 4th of February yielded your letter from Pearl Harbor dated the 12th of January. Not bad, considering the distance and current state of the Union. After your recent forays into the sordid depths of Coco Solo, San Diego and now Tijuana, you should not consider Hawaii as a disappointment, but rather a refuge where you can rest, seek guidance from the Good Book . . . and feed your abused liver some milk and cookies. A word of warning if I may. Do not consider returning to the November cornfields of Illinois on our annual pheasant stalk with an arrow piercing a heart and Tijuana Rose tattooed on the cheeks of your ass. The temptation would be more than I could bear . . . my 12 gauge might go off accidentally.

My mathematical mind has deduced that at 240 miles per day, you are hurtling along at 10mph, somewhat less than that in knots. The label "large stationary target" now becomes alarmingly clear. Would your Captain be open to some suggestions? A rapid increase in your RPMs, dumping the cargo, higher octane fuel oil . . . or a battleship escort. This has to be worth a shot, even if promotion is denied to you in the foreseeable future. You again mention being a tad uncertain about the future, and at the same time, feeling an adventurous tingle. My feelings are about the same as yours, but my fat ole heavier than air machine is looking better to me by the minute. The precarious grip I have on the pucker string wouldn't last one night aboard your war canoe. You guys got nerves of steel and the balls to match, while I, on the other hand, would view passage on your ship like running a gauntlet with Lizzie Borden and Ghengis Khan at the finish line.

Loading hither and unloading yon appears to be the primary mission of your ship. You have written at some length on how demanding on physical stamina and staying in the time frame is on man and machine. I can see some time in the days ahead where off-loading with bad guys in the neighborhood can become a really hairy operation. Perhaps it would be necessary to evacuate casualties, which would mean prolonged exposure to the nasties. Getting from hither to yon is also likely to get as adventuresome as you could want. For Pete's sake, Wm., lift that barge, tote that bale and keep your head out.

And now to the sub-zero skies over Wyoming, blowing snow on the runways, peanut butter sandwiches by lantern light and my bride bundled up in her most impenetrable flannel pajamas and quilted robe. Do not misunderstand. I love every frozen minute and every inch of altitude. It sure beats an unpredictable ocean inhabited by the equally unpredictable denizens thereof.

Flying is number one on the agenda here, both day and night. Our new co-pilot (Lt. Ford B. Rogers) has arrived and has been dubbed, as you already guessed, "Buck". He is also referred to as "Longcoat" . . . a little shot at his calf length overcoat. The rest of us wear hip-length coats and freeze our fashionable asses off. When not in the air, we all attend classes and hands-on training with the tools of our various trades. I have been introduced to the Sperry bombsight, a large square box that is structured internally like a Norden, but is a wee bit easier to operate. Another gadget was unveiled and amounts to a couple of wires on a stick. At very low levels, you squint down this thing, toggle the bombs out and hope you hit Wyoming. The pilots train for instrument flying in the windowless link trainer. The trainer is a mockup of a B-24 cockpit and simulates a plane in flight. The pace is picking up noticeably.

The two grandmothers to be, undaunted by the horror stories about war time travel, took their thin suitcases and fat picnic baskets aboard a train bound for the wild west and a visit with their progeny. Fortunately, they both have a good sense of humor and, as it turned out, they needed their funny bones. The rolling stock on the R.R. has deteriorated even further since last I was a victim of their hospitality. Their coach had the usual iron-hard, upright straw seats. A large pot-bellied stove occupied the middle of the car and, operating at full blast, provided heat for nearby seats and only the illusion of warmth for those sitting further to the front and rear. A pair of G.I.s surrendered their seats to the ladies and, as a reward, got to share the contents of their portable pantries. The ancient engine pooped out at Sheridan, Wyoming, and they remained overnight while emergency first aid was trying to resuscitate their stricken Loco. Quarters for our daring damsels were provided for in a hotel that probably served the mountain men during their spring rendezvous. They dined on something large, tough and burnt . . . then retired to a double bed located in a room over the bar. The uproar from the sheep, cattle and train herders below . . . and their use of adjectives and verbs heretofore unknown to the ladies . . . kept them awake, I think, for fear of missing something. They arrived at Caspar the next evening around 6:30 (31 Jan.), bleary-eyed and saddle-sore. Shirley and I moved back to the Wyatt Hotel so they could build up strength for the trip back home. Our apartment will be quieter and more comfortable and, I hope, won't bore them to death after their recent trek west.

Orders came down on the 5th of Feb. suggesting we report to Topeka on the 6th to pick up an airplane and await orders for overseas assignment. My mother left for Chicago and her job in a carbine assembly plant. Shirley and her mother will take off for Chicago on the 7th, leaving our excess household gear with a couple of couples who will remain in Caspar. Upon arriving at Topeka, I discovered that the crew will be here for a while because of slow delivery of the airplanes. Shirley repacked her bags and hopped on another of the RRds earlier models and, accompanied by my sister Beverly, who will act as lady in waiting to the pregnant Mrs. A., arrived in Topeka on the 10th.

The Throop Hotel in Topeka, our latest abode, has ceilings so high that a light fog is always drifting around the ornate molding that, separates ceilings and walls. We have two rooms that are comfortable, although the spoor of thousands of previous guests lingers on visibly to the eye and mysteriously to the nose. Sgt. Tietz and his wife Willard (Shirley's buddy) occupy a room down the hall. Others who won't say goodbye until the last hurrah are here and in accommodations elsewhere in town. Shirley met the parents of Earl Norris on the train . . . and Buck's parents, Dr. and Mrs. Rogers, are also in residence here somewhere.

Just now, it occurred to me that my leaps to and from the different tenses (present, past and future) could be very confusing. Ours, we, us and I also might get screwed up as a result. By way of explanation . . . I write these things over a period of time, so what is actually current sometimes becomes past and future, sometimes, is already past. After putting this down, it would be a miracle if you weren't confused. I'm not even sure what I was talking about.

During the next two weeks, military duty was minimal . . . merely checking daily for the arrival of our airplane. After some disappointing and unusual dining and entertainment experiences in Topeka, everyone opted for the facilities on the base. The Officer's and NCO clubs offered pretty good meals, while the Post Theater showed fairly current films. We did attend one movie in town, but had to sit like Hindus with our feet in our laps because of rats. These critters ran down the aisles, under the seats and across the stage. When they passed in front of the screen, their shadows looked like miniature dinosaurs. The eeks and shrieks of the audience drowned out the sound track of the movie. Popcorn eaters could see beady red eyes under the seats, waiting for the next kernel to fall. We left real early, feeling squirmy as hell.

The most popular spots on the base were the snack shop and the PX. The snack shop served huge malts, sundaes and banana splits for 15 cents per, along with other goodies that are becoming extinct in civilian life. We gobbled away at this stuff with no regard at all for the war effort or our waistlines. The PX yielded cartons or cigarettes for $1.00 and the large-size Hershey bars. The wives' homeward bound suitcases were crammed with this booty, while nonessentials (like clothing) were shoved into old barracks bags.

Our airplane arrived on the 25th, and the following night and day we spent test hopping the ship, boxing the compass and checking out all the equipment. The afternoon of the 27th, we, the officers, met the families at the O Club for a farewell visit and Shirley, Beverly and I returned to the Tietz's room until train time. The 9:25 train left at 10:55 for Chicago, a long delay in the rain and cold making our efforts at stiff upper lips even more difficult. We did manage to wave and force a sickly smile or two as the train pulled away.

A couple of days of bad weather kept us grounded, but off we go tomorrow, the 1st of March. Florida will be our first of many stops on our way to the 8th Air Force in England. So much for wishful thinking. I'll try and keep you up to date on events as they occur and send them off to you from time to time. Our mail calls will be sporadic at best, but keep writing. I can hardly wait to hear about the further derring-do of Ensign Burling and the intrepid crew of the target, "Ole 628".

My next letter will contain what I hope will be a permanent APO address so, with heart in mouth and a tight grip on the string, I shall mount my winged charger and beard the beastly Boche in his own bailiwick.

BRIMSTONE BILL

1 March, '44

DEAR BOMBER BILL—

I don't know how well outgoing mail moves, but it's damned slow coming in. I suppose (and hope) you are about to greet Spring in beautiful Caspar and trust you have somehow become an instructor on your way to Chicago.

It seems like eons since I last wrote and we have been on the move. I guess I can say where we've been because we are again on the move. It is work, night and day, amid unpleasant circumstances . . . and we are tired. If it isn't loading or unloading, it's bringing supplies aboard and making repairs and improvements. The Chicago Bridge & Iron Works overlooked some of the finer things when they built this ship, but it still floats!

When I last wrote, we had passed the Marshall Islands with no problems. Kwajelain and Rai were being invaded. We missed it. We stopped for a scenic tour of the Solomans and Russells. There's a lot of history there, and a lot of destruction and grief. It was hot with a couple of rains per day (at least). The rain is a bit different in that the clouds just lose it all at once. It's as though a giant emptied a huge bucket overhead. I stared with awe at the shattered palm trees and sunken ships . . . some beached and some that didn't get that far. Most of the small debris has been cleaned up, and Guadalcanal is fairly neat. The Japs removed their surviving troops long ago, but nearby islands contain Japs by the thousands. They have been bypassed. The "slot," a waterway between Florida Island and Guadalcanal, is a graveyard of ships . . . mostly ours. Having long prepared for war, the Japs have been very skillful thus far. Their fanaticism and barbaric tactics, along with their skills, make them formidable indeed. We are told how their prisoners are treated and have learned they do not surrender. They'll crawl a mile to kill one man, even if it is sure suicide. I plan on a visit to our Admiral, whoever he is, and see if we can't change the rules a bit. I would much prefer a more genteel hostility.

One sunny (what else) afternoon, three or four of us came upon some medical alcohol and conceived the idea of a picnic ashore. We found some sweet grape juice in cans and sat down on the Guadalcanal beach drinking "Purple Ladies." Unfortunately, we ran out of grape juice before alcohol, so we opened a couple of coconuts and used the milk. Neither of these mixtures will ever take the place of any mixed drink . . . but by then, who cared! I remember leaving the group to wade in the water and then I remember waking up on a small carrier the next morning, just in time for lunch. A fine track man we knew at Wesleyan, Harold Wimberly, had been on shore patrol and had brought me to his ship. I was fed and my ship was notified and our boat took me "home". I was slightly embarrassed, but no one said a word. We toured the general area, which is sizable, taking this here and that there. Lunga, Tulagi Island, Florida, Rendova and Vella Lavella are all small places that are known to those of us here, and probably no one else.

The local feminine beauties are even worse than I had been led to expect. Small, bare-breasted, potbellied, grass skirts, their bodies covered with yaws and insect bites . . . and dirty. The term for physical romance is pom-pom or push-push, and there is absolutely no need to warn the sailors about whatever God-awful diseases lurk under those grass skirts. The men are less charming in appearance, but they are friendly and can almost understand the pidgin English they've learned from the British. They did not like the Japanese.

Not too far away is a fair-sized Jap base, Rabaul, on New Britain. We have been introduced to "piss-call Charlie", who is anybody in an airplane flying around in the middle of the night with one small bomb to drop. He (or they) awakens everyone at the moment of the very best sleep and, after fooling around a short time, drops his bomb and goes home. They stay out of range of our guns and avoid destroyers. The Army shines searchlights on them, and they circle and play in their limelight. The Army has some 3-inch guns with a barrel about 50 feet long, and when they can, they'll fire a shot or two. I dare say, it's the Army's least dangerous weapon and "piss-call Charlie" thinks so, too.

No close calls, but a reminder that the bombs shake things up when they land. You showed a tremendous wisdom in choosing to drop them, rather than catch them.

Most aircraft we see are from carriers. There are still some operating from the islands, but all are easy to identify . . . P-47s, B-25s, Hellcats and an occasional B-17 bringing mail. A lot of TBFs and some PBYs. The M1 Garand and the carbine are showing up, and the general feeling is that we're going to win eventually. Considering the attitude of the Japanese, and with a look at the map, it doesn't look like it will be tomorrow.

On our way out of there, we passed close by Bougainville, which bears a bad reputation. They've bypassed it pretty well, but have raided it to keep it quiet. It is supposed to contain thousands of Japs. They are forgotten by their country, but are fanatical. It is a big island covered with thick, dark jungle and looks foreboding.

We are on atabrine, a substitute for quinine (which is unavailable). It will, hopefully, forestall malaria. The skin turns yellow, and the whites of the eyes turn yellow. All this, plus the weight we've lost, and we look like candidates for a complete overhaul. I weighed 172 lbs. in New York and probably gained some more in New Orleans because of the gastronomical delights. I would guess I might depress a scale to about 150 lbs. now. Oh well, the uniform never really fit anyway.

There is absolutely no news of the outside world. Our information comes from sailors or troops that we meet, and you know how scuttlebutt goes. The Army suffers from boredom, and one can see several men riding a road grader at 2 mph and fail to realize they are only taking a ride somewhere. They have pet monkeys and parrots, and they play cards or sew their torn fatigues or shave now and then. They ask us what's happening, and we don't know. The food is not great, but no use bitching. Hydraulic potatoes, fish on Friday, roast beef (Navy type) now and then and canned vegetables. Nothing to complain about, and the Army has it worse.

I bought some fine Havana cigars at Panama. Some almost a dollar a piece and packed in glass cases (I had been paid). I discovered them about a week ago and shared them with my fellow expendables. Some kind of a worm had invaded the cigars, so we had to put fingers over all the worm holes in order to get any smoke. It was a weird looking group, but they were good, if a bit dry.

If one approaches these islands from downwind, the air is filled with the perfume of the flowers. Orchids are like dandelions, and the smell is beautiful. The perfume can be noticed 80 to 100 miles away . . . and it arouses one to think he is about to visit a beautiful south sea island populated by the likes of Dorothy Lamour. One quickly learns that if he expects nothing, he is seldom disappointed. On shore, the smell of rotten, shattered palm trees, the buzz of insects, the hot black sand, along with the clattering of monkeys and parrots is only part of the problem. The mangroves in the swamps and shores, the souvenir that might be booby-trapped, the reptiles, the overpowering and energy-sapping heat, and the growth overnight of heavy mildew all combine to convince me this area will not likely become a tourist center. If I could buy the whole group of islands for a dollar, I would fiendishly bequeath it to my worst enemy.

But enough tales of the good life in the magnificent south seas. I'm guessing I will soon rank those islands with New York and New Orleans. It is one hell of a long way from home.

One of these days, I hope to hear from you, but I will keep writing. I also want to hear from the girls I've been writing, but I can't really bare my soul to them or they'd stop writing!

I trust that you now are an expert in B-24 routine and that you are skilled in dropping bombs with enough accuracy to hit a continent. I do not see any B-24s yet, but the ones I've seen look well-fortified, stable and durable. It is to be hoped that you will refuse to fly in one with some of the lewd painted figures I've seen on the noses of B-17s. You Air Corps people must have dirty minds!

My narrative mishmash must be concluded. My person is requested on the next watch. As usual, my watch will begin as the large black clouds gather to dump water by the ton. We stand watch in the open and four hours while sopping wet passes slowly.

Even though you didn't ask, my advice to you is to feign insanity and request a straight jacket. A padded cell will be pure heaven! Meanwhile, check your parachute and have a little fun at every opportunity.   Best Regards—

REALLY SORRY NOW BILL

Wed. 1 March 1944 to
Tues. 14 March 1944

DEAR ALOHA—

The final stop I made when clearing the post at Topeka on 28 Feb. was the base Post Office. Your letter from 'neath the banyan tree and the view of Diamond Head was there, apparently forwarded from Caspar. I had just concluded my reply to yours of 12 Jan., so dropped that one in the slot shortly before taking off. Unfortunately, it is not permitted to bomb the politicos and draft dodgers cavorting about beneath our bomb bays and pointing single fingers skyward . . . so my duties as a mere passenger afford me the time to reply (or begin to) to your latest of 24 Jan., rather than wait until we arrive and reply on memory. I'll write daily from my aerial crow's nest during our eight to ten hour flights and pop the batch into the mail as soon as I arrive in England and have a new A. P. O. number.

You asked if I was taking good care of my parachute, and the answer is a resounding affirmative. The problem is restraining myself from a premature test over a virgin forest where I could await the end of hostilities safely . . . whilst chasing virgins amongst the flora and fauna. "You Jane, me Bill". The progress your gunners are making must be very heartening to your anxiety about deeper probes into Japanese waters. I would hope that you are encouraging them to even higher levels of accuracy with all the means at your disposal. May I suggest you recount to them the many occasions you have been a witness to a born deflection shooter, and coach them in my smooth, but deadly style.

I, too, would have enjoyed your visit to Hilo on the big island, and am happy you enjoyed the food, drinks, scenery and weather. Keep those things in mind because the honeymoon, as you so euphorically put it, appears to be over for both of us bewildered pacifists. The rumors you have heard about you guys being low on the totem pole for men, machines and ordnance are probably true. What I hear suggests that the brass figure we can handle Japan after we deal with the Germans. The Jerries, at this time, are one hell of a handful. Their U-boats, Luftwaffe and armor are everywhere, like horse apples. They are a tough bunch, and their innovative technology could be a nasty little rascal in the woodpile. Beneath those coal scuttle hats are some devious and clever fighters. Meanwhile, feed your gunners carrots.

The wheels just clunked down and the pilots suggested I wake up and come upstairs for the landing at Morrison Field, West Palm Beach, Fla. Today, the 2nd, we languished at the end of one line after another in order to satisfy the unhealthy lust the Army has for paperwork. The paper pushers look at the combat crews like we wuz a hint the door when brains wuz dished out. Sort of smirky . . . I'd be forever embarrassed if someone else did my share of the fighting, not withstanding my lifelong aversion to pain and its causes.

Back in the saddle again on the 3rd. Another day of perfect flying weather, with unusual scenery passing beneath the wings. After a long day in the air, we landed in hot and humid Trinidad . . . alive with all kinds of creeping, crawling and flying critters, all looking for a free lunch. We have been issued atabrine tablets to delay the symptoms of malaria. If you become a victim of this disease after you get home, you are not supposed to remember it's service connected. Censorship of the mail has begun and the crews censor their own mail (which shoots down the whole theory of the thing). We are not privy to F. D. R.s innermost thoughts, anyway.

Belem accepted our call for permission to land, and we did so after our navigator once again hit our E.T.A. and destination smack dab. All day we flew over endless miles of rain forest, truly awe-inspiring. The Lord, indeed, moves in mysterious ways. There are a couple of ships long overdue and feared to be down somewhere in those forests. Air searches and native trackers have been sent to locate the missing crews. I am told they are usually successful and I certainly hope they are. Surviving a landing in the tree tops would be pretty iffy to begin with, and then to be afoot in those jungles would add new meaning to survival training.

Seven hours in the air on the 5th put us into Natal, Brazil. Rumor has it that we will be here for a day or two. Another mile of red tape was laid on by the ground pounders, followed by directions to the mess tent and our comfy quarters. After eating, I atabrined, then sprayed the quarters, the airplane and myself, hoping to wipe out the Anopholese before they launched a mass attack. A native orderly awoke us at 7:00 A.M., and we tore over to the mess tent hoping to get there before they ran out of edible stuff. Didn't make it . . . so we ate the inedible stuff. Went down to the beach and were swarmed over by Brazilian con artists of both sexes. Buck bought a jug of bathtub gin and I had a sip or two to my infinite regret. If the firewater you have been guzzling all over the Pacific is at all like this brew, you'll erode everything from your Adam's apple to your ass. Be temperate, William. The Brazilian army appeared in a column of stragglers . . . no two men wearing the same uniform . . . and took up a position on a bluff overlooking the beach. They then began firing their flintlocks at the ocean and occasionally racked up a lucky hit.

Remaining on the beach became a kind of Russian Roulette, so we wrung out our shorts, put on our pants and beat a tactical retreat.

Today, the 7th, I visited the PX with Buck (The Big Hangover), who is afflicted with the shakes and the lingering taste of Guano in his mouth. Bought some Gaucho boots, which will cause hysterics amongst the brass conformists of military attire. Around midnight, we went to the flight line to ready the ship for an ocean crossing.

Two o'clock A.M. (8 March), took off on our "Short Snorter" hop across the Atlantic . . . destination, Dakar in North Africa. The weather again stayed in our corner with visibility to the horizon, but only water forever and ever. Twenty ears fine-tuned into those engines the whole, wet way. A submarine lookout was supposed to be kept, but no member of the wolf pack made an appearance. What difference? They couldn't very well torpedo us, and all we had to drop on them were bologna sandwiches from our cardboard lunch boxes. A perfect landfall, again. E. J. Must have paid attention in class, and here we are in Dakar, reading a sign at base HQ which says, "Around here, we shave, bathe, wear ties and dress for dinner". This show of teeth by the rear echelon was ignored for the most part, although I was forced to shower. Some poor soul, loaded to the gills, mistook my sack for the john last night and peed over the end closet to the aisle . . . fortunately, the foot end.

Left Dakar far behind this morning, the 9th, which restored morale, but only briefly. We made Marrakech in the afternoon after an uneventful flight. Early Aboriginal best describes our new quarters, and the food defies description at all. I would not choose this place to retire to in my old age, if I have one at all after the next meal or two, that is.

Sgt. Tietz and the crew are pulling a 50-hour inspection on the ship, so we'll be here a day or two at the mercy of the innkeeper and his cohort, the chef. I briefly visited the town today (the 10th). The locals are a shifty-looking bunch wearing KKK outfits and curved pig stickers. The little Arab kids fight tooth and toenail for discarded cigarette butts wherever they land. Considering the number of camels, goats and dogs wandering around, plus people squatting over the gutters, the proverbial hits the fan each time the mob dives for a butt. A little of this, along with the vendors grabbing your arms, goes a long way in a hurry . . . I beat a retreat to the base.

Back to town again today, chaperoning our curious co-pilot. He was hustled by a 12-year-old who was pimping for his sister and his mother . . . a virgin, never been touched. Surprisingly, this kid had endorsements in writing from a couple of previous customers. The irony of the thing is that the kids can't read, and the endorsements luridly describe the ladies' medical and physical conditions. Some of their ailments I have never heard of and, if true, a plague is surely going to sweep through the allied armies . . . devouring people, one piece of anatomy at a time. The important appendage first. We ran into a retired British officer and spent a couple of hours with him God saving the King and our own forty-eight. There are some highly-touted shows featuring naked French ladies, donkeys and dogs. The Britisher told us to stay real clear of such entertainment because of some recent killings. Some transients, retaliating for what he didn't know, shot up the area to a fare thee well. An arduous day . . . will now atabrine and hit the sack. I could now spit in a swamp and kill every mosquito within range.

The 12th was spent checking all the equipment and the airplane. I took down all the side arms, cleaned and loaded them so we all now sport hawg laigs on our hips or in a shoulder holster. All of these warlike preparations are in anticipation of tonight's over the water flight to England. The possibility of German night fighters roosting on our probable routes and shooting cannons inspires little confidence in our trusty hawg laigs. The brass has laid another egg, which we devoutly hope will not become an omelette. Sticking a pistol out the window at night, aiming at something you can't see while traveling at 300 MPH strikes me as being insanely optimistic. To bolster our plunging morale, they begrudgingly provided us with 500 rounds for the fifty calibers . . . which amounts to a one-second burst from each of our ten guns. A rotten time to pinch pennies.

We departed the land of camel crap about 9:00 P.M., lifting slowly into the air due to the heavy load of ammo on board. We sighted no night fighters, but couldn't have, even if they flew on our wing tip. Sighted England about 8:00 A.M. on the 13th, after a great job of celestial navigation (eleven hours over water . . . and at night) by our intrepid trapper and guide, E. J. We flew inland a ways and had the opportunity to view the patchwork quilt of varying shades of green that is the English landscape. Quite beautiful.

Today, the 14th, we arrived at Stoke on Trent, where, I am informed, we will wait for assignment to a bomb group. We are now classified as a replacement crew . . . a rather ominous way to describe what happens when you open your big mouth and volunteer for the glamorous life of a smart-ass aviator.

I have no permanent address as yet, but I'll get this off in order to keep you posted on the various stages of shock I am going through. More to follow as things continue to unravel, and I become a shadow of my former self.

THE REPLACEMENT

Wed. 15 March '44 to
Tues. 21 March '44

DEAR BILL—-

Arrived today, the 21st, at our permanent base and will make this a brief synopsis of the last few days in order to provide you with my new address as promptly as possible.

Lt. W.H.A.   0-691628
93rd Bomb GP., 330TH TA Bomb Sqdn.
APO # 558   c/o Postmaster
New York, New York

The 93rd participated in the first raid on the Ploesti oil fields in Rumania and is justly famous for that action. I, now even more than ever, understand what replacement crew signifies.

Going back a few days to our arrival at Stone, Stoke on Trent, the combat crews were assigned to various details . . . presumably to keep us from laying waste to the surrounding countryside and the pubs and women therein. The real reason lurks in the devious minds of the permanent staff. They need longer lunches, coffee breaks and cocktail hours, as well as time for emergency aid for paper cuts. Norris and I drew four days of censorship duty and, for the most part, the guys were conscientious about not revealing operative military information. On the other hand, if we had deleted all the four letter words and steamy prose regarding reunions with their women folk, nothing would have remained but the names of the addressees and the senders' signatures. I should have taken notes and written a "How To" book after the war with 1,001 different ways and places to dip your wick.

One evening, after a cold shower brought on by my vicarious snooping, went to town and sampled English brew, which I found to be quite good, but served warm. No matter, when in Rome. From the pub, I was directed to the local dance hall and found the English to be very cordial and likable, although some of the men were muttering about the Yanks being overpaid, over sexed and over <u>here</u>. I really can't fault them, some of our guys come on like plantation overseers. The following afternoon, I abandoned my post, and the traumas of celibacy, and took to the byways on an English bike. Most of the homes had open doors and windows . . . and that, along with the bicycle seat, convinced me that the Britons are a very hardy bunch. I got back to the base with a runny nose, saddle sores and a tendency to walk bowlegged due to other sensitive areas of pain. English saddles have no sympathy for the more amptly endowed American fanny.

To be continued, and take good care . . .

BRONCO BILL

28 March, '44

DEAR BRIMSTONE BILL——

Yours of 17 Jan. To 29 Feb. has arrived in my hot little hands, along with letters from some girls I've been writing. I won't say which one I read last. I wonder if you got my last letter, which I mailed at Guadalcanal. This doesn't seem like great mail service, but I'm told it can, and will, get worse.

Your snide remarks about my efforts to teach the gospel in Coco Solo shall not be legitimized by a comment. There will be no tattoos because of my distaste for needles, and Tijuana Rose was Paul's friend, briefly.

The idea you stated about a battleship escort for us expendables was a good one. I'm working on it, but I seldom rub shoulders with anyone higher than full LT.

Can you believe that your blowing snow sounds good? Not for long, you understand, but once in a while. Sounds as though you are flying a lot, along with classes and individual practice. Busy, isn't it?! One cannot be too skillful, and it's nice to concentrate on something when the noise begins.

It's nice to hear that the two grandmothers made the visit, and I'm sorry to hear that Shirley left for home. She's a good, strong girl.

Sorry to hear that Topeka was not more of an enjoyable stay. Seems that a lot of cities have been pressed into service and either don't like it, or haven't handled it very well. All that, plus the shortage of apartments, makes it pretty tough to move about. Glad the officer's club was somewhat better. The malts, sundaes and banana splits sound great. It seems I'm hungry most of the time.

So you are on your way (in your letter) and are certainly now in Florida, or have moved out. I wish you the best. It's a long way to England and I wonder why you don't take a different route. Guess that's why I'm here instead of at headquarters. Keep the letters coming.

Since my last letter, we went into the Admiralty Islands . . . another dismal set of islands. It seems like only yesterday we went into Manus Island and, later, Green Island. Manus had an airstrip called Lorengaw near the town of Lorengaw, and I suppose we went there so we could own the airstrip. Why the hell we went into Green will forever be a mystery to me. Both were relatively small invasions and were over fairly soon . . . and will probably never be heard about ever again.

I learned a lot. I now know that no matter how small the invasion is, the noise, smoke and intense fear take a toll. We carried Army and tanks and were aground offshore and had to wait for a bulldozer to build a ramp out to us. The Japs are very skillful with a variety of mortars, and we couldn't unload or get off the reef until the next high tide. Our important ships fired their big guns over our heads and, I thought, a little closer than necessary. The shells going over sound like a P-47 in a dive with the engine shut down. We got a Zero, which is one fine fighter, but not durable. They sound like a washing machine engine, and the pilots are crazy. Again, the smell of shattered coconut trees and other trees, plus the smoke and noise, is enough to make one wish he were delivering memos in Washington, D.C. In a day or so, the smell of swollen bodies wafted our way. We visited Los Negros, which was quiet, but an ammunition ship had blown up the day before. Debris was everywhere, and the graves crews were in boats picking up arms and legs with gaff hooks. That night, I had the midnight to 4:00 A.M. watch and had one man who truly disliked his watch at our bow doors. There were some body parts, including the hairy part of a skull, bloating at the beach by our bow ramp. That, plus the fear of a small infantry attack, made for a scary night. The Japs have sometimes allowed the Army to overrun them, and they then pick and choose their own targets. The nights are filled with jungle noises . . . birds screaming and God knows what else. One can imagine Jap soldiers copying those sounds in a code all their own. I want to go home!

We are close to Rabaul, and just north of New Guinea. About everywhere we look is enemy territory with airstrips, and though the strips are bombed often, they are also repaired often . . . they're working. With loading and unloading and the adrenaline cascading through one's body, we are tired. Several air raid warnings day and night, and most of them don't come about. The ones that do are small, but it only takes one bomb or one strafing. It is my fervent prayer to be hit real good (if it must be) rather than a severe wounding. My choice, of course, is to get the hell out of here and eat a big steak before visiting my girlfriend . . . at home.

When our radio tells us "all clear" after an air raid, everyone pretty well collapses at his post because the next warning will be along soon. I don't know why, but I can't seem to sleep during the bad nights. I have a real thing about surviving and don't want to be caught napping. Foolish, because there's no place to hide. This pace must end soon, or we'll all be in a loony bin.

I'm now somewhere else and a mail boat is due shortly, and I'll send this off. Things have quieted somewhat, and we are back to meals rather than sandwiches and coffee . . . also sleep now and then.

I look at the crews of the LSTs that were with us . . . and they have yellow skin and eyes, and their eyes are like saucers. The shirts hang on bony bodies and the pants won't stay up without a rope for a belt. I wonder if we look that bad . . . and we are supposed to be winning!

With all this, I've got to hand it to you and those damned airplanes. I'm afraid I just could not be strapped in that aluminum box without dying of fright, either at take off or landing. I really have decided that my real calling would have been as a recruiter on a college campus . . . or better still, a civilian aide to a Congressman.

My wish right now would be to get my hands on the throats of those Hollywood characters who gave us the marvelous movies about the South Sea Islands. The mangrove snarls, the swamps, mosquitos, hot and humid air, black sand and noisy birds and animals all remind one of nothing but hell itself.

Some idiot is playing our record "Drifting & Dreaming" by Guy Lombardo again. Ludicrous!

We've been short of water for a while (drinking only). We gave some to the Army and were apparently over generous. The bread has weevils baked in, so we do get a little meat with our bread. After all, they look a little like caraway seeds, but don't have much taste.

A lot of soldiers lost it all in the Admiralties. They look like the guy next door. We came out in great shape and have no real legitimate complaints. It does help to bitch a little.

Good luck wherever you are. Perhaps news of your arrival on the scene will cause the Germans to cave in. I hope so, because maybe then they'll send us some equipment and some air cover. Drop your bombs with accuracy, and write when you can.

NERVOUS BILL

Wed. 22 March 1944 to
Thurs. 6 April 1944

DEAR JOLLY TAR—-

Greetings from Nisson Hut #4, to which Buck and I are assigned together with seven other roomies currently in residence. The mail now has a chance to catch up to me, and if you can prevail upon your Captain to park your cruise ship near a mail box, we will be in business. Against the possibility that he may decline to be a nice guy, I will continue my on-the-spot reporting of our efforts to piss off Adolph and his cronies and hope for early delivery.

The Nisson huts are small, half-round structures made of corrugated steel. A bomb shelter is located conveniently (Thank God!) just outside our door and, if scared enough . . . I can make it in six seconds . . . maybe less . . . we'll see. Showers and tubs are located in a nearby building. When hygiene finally overcomes fear of the frigid air and the water, which frequently is colder than the air, we bathe . . . quickly. Each of the huts is equipped with a pot-bellied stove, which provides heat depending upon how close you are, and also serves as a hot plate for sundry foods. Compared to the infantry, we've got it pretty darn good. I feel for those guys and what they have to endure.

Orientation classes covering a variety of subjects are SOP for the new crews. Guns, navigation, evasive action, bombing and parachuting are of particular importance. The mission veterans in the hut are a good source for things that only experience teaches and, on occasion, will advise us nervous nellies. Every word has my devout attention. Oh yes, we had our P.O.W. pictures taken for the fake IDs we carry on missions for use in the event of an untimely landing in occupied territory. All this chit chat about guns, parachuting and P.O.W. pics tends to put me on the edge of my seat. Incidentally, if I ever have to spring that picture on anyone, I'd be in the pokey on suspicion alone. It looks like Jack the Ripper on one of his good days.

My first air raid came and went to my utter embarrassment. The siren was still sounding as I outdistanced everyone to the shelter with a burst of speed seldom seen outside the Olympic arena. As my breathing slowly returned to normal, I discovered that I was the sole occupant of the place. The old-timers were all standing on the roof watching Jerry bomb Norwich, which is safely distant from our field. Very unobtrusively, I weaseled my way to the rear of the group and watched the searchlights and listened to the thump of the bombs. The unsynchronized beat of the engines makes the German planes easy to identify if you fail to notice the bombs.

I have joined the ranks of the short order cooks huddled around the stove and have been made privy to the methods used to maintain our supplies. The demand for bread, butter, eggs and stray hunks of meat always exceeds the supply on hand. There is an espionage system dedicated to foiling the mess Sgt. and his stingy minions. The kitchen and commissary are constantly under surveillance for our quick and timely raids. The Sgt. has a counter network equally determined to protect his goods . . . but we manage, by hook or crook, to keep the cupboard supplied. Another source of supply is the Officer of the Day detail. About every ten days, one of us is O.D., and a case of K-rations finds its way into the O.D.'s jeep. The Ks contain candy, gum, fruit bars, canned stuff and cigarettes . . . and these are highly regarded as trading items with the local people. We especially like eggs . . real ones. To give the Army credit, the food here is good and reasonably prepared, but we always seem to have room for more. I again think of the infantry and their combat conditions and count my blessings.

Back to the real business. We flew practice missions in our new ship and are delighted with the airplane and confident it will be a good one. McGlasson had a gal wearing a swimsuit painted on the nose and named it "Ever-Lovin'-Gal". I don't know if the reference is to the airplane or to a real girl, but judging by her pair of hooters, it ain't the airplane. Norris boxed the compasses and the rest of us fine-toothed all the equipment . . . everything worked on the familiarization flights around the local area. "Oles" and "bravos" to the people in the assembly lines at Willow Run or wherever.

Our hutmates have all been flying missions and reflying them when they get back around the stove. The things that happen on these missions set my teeth on edge, yet they describe those moments as if they had just returned from a walk around the park. It seems to me that this casual attitude is a veneer covering some ragged nerve endings. The veneer keeps them glued together enough to climb on board 25 times with a little guarantee of survival on any of the 25. This serves to remind me that I had better get to work on some veneer of my own. The stories they tell have my hair standing on end. After 25 missions, if I have even one hair left, it will be standing at attention alone in a barren wasteland of scalp. I am praying for veneer. A bald pate is acceptable . . . but please, no screaming meemies.

Today is the 28th of March. Yesterday I was joking (a little) about losing my hair and acquiring veneer. Today I have egg on my face and badly need some veneer. Earl Norris went out as replacement navigator on a mission this morning and was killed. His B-24 and a B-17 collided in the overcast at about 12,000 feet. No one aboard either airplane got out. The planes crashed a short distance from our field and I heard that a group of passing soldiers went over to extricate the living, if any. Some bombs blew, killing some of them as well. I have mentioned the overcast to you before and how dangerous it is with so many airfields and airplanes occupying a limited amount of space. The missions have to be flown, and overcast doesn't disappear to accommodate the war effort . . . so you cross fingers and sweat it until you break out. McGlasson, as airplane commander, will write Earl's folks for the crew. I have thought long and hard about writing also, but am afraid of adding to their misery, so decided to pass. A feeling persists inside me that this may come back to haunt me. Shirley will write, but, oh shit. To add further grief to his stricken family, some rear echelon son-of-a-bitch stole his rings, watch and bracelet. E.J. is resting in an American cemetery here in England.

Following the loss of E.J., I was assigned to navigational school preparatory to assume his duties, as well as my own. Celestial navigation is not included in the course, but I'll be given thorough, but speedy training in the basics. We will now be flying as a nine-man crew on our baptismal flight and, presumably, thereafter.

We were scheduled for two missions, but they were scrubbed due to bad weather over the target area. This on-again/off-again stuff gives me the willies. I wish they would do it or get off the pot. When they do, I'll take the pot with me . . . I'll probably find a use for it. Our group did fly a mission (we were standby) and were rather badly mauled over the target. One of the lads in our hut took a 20-mm cannon shell in the shoulder, fortunately it didn't explode. His crew doused him with morphine and got him home in fair shape. A doctor and an armament man operated and removed the shell. I wonder what thoughts were going through their heads as they fished around for that thing. In any event, out it came and armament found a burr on the firing pin. Speculation has it that a forced laborer may have deliberately sabotaged the shell. The Lt. will return to flying status. Could my veneer and I handle that?

The first mail from home arrived today, the 6th of April, but nothing from the wide, blue Pacific as yet. As you have found, the letters we get about everyday routines . . . and even disasters . . . from our families and friends makes it a little easier to accommodate yourself to the unusual lives we have been living lately . . . particularly now when it is down to put up or shut up. With this thought in mind, I'll get this off to you and start another to keep you up on what rattles my chain next.

BEREAVED BILL

Friday 7 April 1944 to
Monday 10 April 1944

DEAR SOMEWHAT—

An envelope showing the battle scars of land, sea and air travel of about 18,000 miles arrived today, the 7th, in less than pristine condition, but, nonetheless, it is here. Your letter is dated the 14th of Feb. and, considering our worldwide movements during this period, I can find no fault with P.O. Department. Perhaps a mighty Huzzah would encourage them to even swifter completion of their appointed rounds. So, Huzzah!!! Keep the cards and letters coming.

Sailing into combat situations to the dulcet strains of Guy Lombardo's "Drifting & Dreaming" is not going to make the enemy's blood curdle, his knees knock or, for that matter, inflame your crew to a fighting frenzy. More than likely, they will choose up partners and dance. Surely you can steal or trade your "only toy" for something more martial . . . at least have the Bos'n tweet some Sousa over the P.A. system with his whistle. Whilst drifting and dreaming, you must have been delighted to have good visibility and gentle seas while zigging and zagging in the midst of that convoy of merchantmen. In bad weather, the watch officer must go bonkers trying to maintain position without getting plowed under by one or more of those hippos. I'm sure none of you can stop or turn on a dime, so keep on your tippy toes. You sure don't want one of those guys nudging the 100 octane barrels. I also note that you have found your cargo of Army rations to be delicious, particularly the canned cheese and chocolate bars. Methinks that, somehow, some cases were damaged, lost at sea, eaten by rats or just plain vanished at the hands of the Almighty. We Air Force gentlemen would never stoop to such unlawful tactics. By the way . . . if that fat sailor of yours gets into the goodies, your plot could be exposed when the ship tilts in his direction.

Chipping and painting sounds like work for slave labor or chain gang prisoners. I can well understand why your inventory of scrapers, brushes and chipping hammers has bottomed out. That is definitely not my cup of grog. It is, however, along with submarines, typhoon and torpedo juice cocktails, one more reason to be content with the wild blue yonder. You know, in order to inspire the fat guy and his merry men, you could take chisel and scraper in hand, kneel on the deck and show them how much fun it is to tidy up "Ole #628".

For a couple of days, I have been flying the bomb trainer and attending the last few navigation classes. Both my bombing and dead reckoning navigation have shown marked improvement. The imminence of putting them in use over Germany, where our butts will be hanging out, has certainly worked wonders for my job skills. Speak of the devil . . . we have just been invited to join the group tomorrow for a jaunt over Germany. I am apprehensive, of course, but my bones tell me that this crew will return tomorrow and 24 more times. With this happy thought in mind, I will finish this letter following tomorrow's Baptismal.

My bones were right, Bill, and we have returned after losing our virginity the hard way. The Baptismal waters turned nasty and damned near drowned us all. My confidence has not gone down for the third time, but I am hoping the Lord tosses me a life preserver . . . luck.

The mission got off on the right foot. We didn't get creamed in the overcast, and continued nicely until we were south of Denmark over the Baltic Sea. We had been congratulating ourselves about the milk run and hooraying the storytellers in the huts when things suddenly began going down hill. The Luftwaffe arrived. The first one I saw (an FW 190) came boring in at us from out of the sun about 10:00 high with red lights blinking at us from the leading edges of the wings. I tried to become invisible behind a sixteenth of an inch of aluminum fuselage, hoping to revive my comatose confidence. Duncan, in the front turret (new model 24) froze. Buck was trying to dig a fox hole between the rudder pedals. No one on board fired a shot and, by the grace of God, we only got a few holes in non-strategic places.

This all happened in seconds. The closing rate between the two planes was over 500 MPH. It is amazing what you can think and do in that short period of time. Looking forward out of my port window, I could see 15 or 20 FWs forming up for another go at us (they got one 24 on the first pass). Then, suddenly, two P-47s (Thunderbolts) tore into those guys from above and to their rear. They broke up the German formation and the last I could see was airplanes wheeling all over the sky. Our fighter jocks showed guts beyond the call and, no doubt, saved others of us in our formation. I sure hope those fellas made it back to base. Drinks are on us wherever you are.

From that point on, we had fighters off and on all the way to the target. We were in a flight of four on the far left of the group, and were a little vulnerable to further attack. After surviving the surprise and paralysis of that first fighter pass (pure luck alone), we began to fight back and watch the whole sky . . . up, down and sideways. No one in this crew will ever get caught again with their mental drawers down around their ankles. We sustained no further damage en route to the target, although we were doing some shooting. McGlasson called out a fighter at 9 o'clock and then hollered that he had been hit. He discovered, upon feeling no pain, that his sunglasses had fogged and frozen over. When he had yelled "fighter", his oxygen mask slipped a little and his warm breath hit his glasses. Instant blindness. The temperature up here is about 30 degrees below. Shortly thereafter, the top turret began to turn and shoot erratically. The radio operator found Sgt. Tietz's oxygen hose disconnected, plugged it back in and our punch engineer returned from Never Never Land to fight again.

Approaching the target, we could see flakbursts before we got there. Once on the bomb run, we saw a whole bunch more and right amongst us. On the bomb run, we fly straight and level for several minutes while the boys on the ground get to play fish in a barrel. First off, you see red flash, then a ball of black smoke. Next, you hear the crack of the explosion . . . and then (much too often), shrapnel hitting the ship. Our luck held and we were still in the air after I dropped the bombs . . . well, all but the two that got hung up in the rear bay. The guys in ground school said it was a cinch to trot back there and toss them out. They failed to mention that you had to remove your chute, that the catwalk between the bays is ten inches wide, that it's 30 degrees below in a 165-MPH slipstream, that you have to carry a walk-around oxygen bottle . . . and, further, that you would be scared shitless. So much for ground school academics.

En route to the rear bay (and those two friggin' bombs), the slipstream snatched my oxygen bottle (not possible, says ground school) and, at 23,500 feet, this is not so good. I thought I could hold my breath long enough to do the job, and did manage to trip them out. On the way back, I was hurting. I slipped a couple of times, the last time grabbing the inside bulkhead of the ship. Most of me was hanging out over Germany and no git up and go was left when Lou (radio) hauled me in and gave me his mask. In a couple of minutes I was OK. I remember thinking when I was hanging out over the bomb bays with nothing between me and German terra firma, "I hope I land on a flak gunner and drive the S.O.B. into the ground". We lumbered home without further misadventures to inflict on your credulity.

Today, the 10th, I finished this letter and also sent out my laundry. Do not make a vulgar connection between that mission and my laundry going out. My undies remained unsullied, and that was the most surprising and successful part of the whole damned mission.

THE TRAUMATIZED TOGGELEER

14 April, '44

DEAR BOMBARDIER BILL—-

I thought that I'd get some mail at our last stop, but not so. The whole crew shows disappointment. Some of the men have brothers all over the globe and, of course, wives and girlfriends, and they want to know that all are OK. I suppose it is worse for wives and girlfriends who read and hear the news and wonder. What a ridiculous way to live!

So . . . things have slowed temporarily, and I have time to write, but can't say much. I am still in the general area I wrote about in my last letter. It is much like the Solomons' and Russells' . . . same type of natives and the same tangled jungles. We've made repeat trips to the recent invasions and the repeat trips are sometimes worse than the D-day. In between these trips, we need supplies of our own and it seems that everything is in short supply. We expendables, of course, are at the end of every line, and what is left is divided among us. The supply people have an attitude that all we need is enough for the next trip because we might not come back . . . and why waste all those supplies? I've given some thought to carrying some of those bastards aboard for our next trip so they could understand our anger. Actually, I'm sure they're doing the best they can, but it is frustrating. I believe we're angry because of what we've seen and been through, and these guys are bitching about heat, mosquitos and boredom. It appears that boredom results, at least, in longevity.

I'm trying to perk up my attitude by thinking of the "good old days", or at least something pleasant. I don't believe I told you of my first (and only) experience on shore patrol. It was in Panama at Coco Solo, and I was in charge of four of our men. We all donned S.P. bands and the men carried clubs and I wore the trusty .45 Colt. We assembled downtown and were divided, with two men going with me to the Club Florida for the all night duty. It turned out that the Club Florida was an old hotel with a lively bar on the ground floor and a three-story whorehouse above. We were to stop fights, see that drunks got back to their ships, direct revelers to the nearest Pro station and, in general, throw a wet blanket on anyone having fun beyond acceptable limits. One of my men was an older motor machinist of Italian background, and a sincere family man. The other man was a young weight-lifter of Polish origin and he was a mountain of muscles. We were lucky to have a relatively quiet night, but it was an eye-opener. I traversed the hallways of the girl's quarters and found it to be a slow night for them. I suppose the presence of the Shore Patrol kept business to a minimum. The girls spent a lot of time and effort trying to seduce the Shore Patrol (without success), and there was much laughing and joking. They removed their flimsy costumes and danced and posed, and told us, in their faulty English, how great they were in the sack. It was kind of sad, but fun.

All that seems like a long time ago, and I wonder if the same girls are in the same place now.

We took on some fresh water recently from a pool on an island. We carried a hose up a hill and through the jungle and pumped the water into our tanks. One had to keep the hose under the algae and floating debris. The chief engineer then treated the water, probably with Clorox and the end result has been sickness . . mostly diahhrea. I believe we've built a resistance to whatever the bug was and are now reasonably well and drinking the same water.

The "rear" areas here are basically islands where the Japs were driven beyond an airstrip and the island was called "secured". Supplies were collected and our aircraft operates from the strips, but the Japs are there in the hills . . . and one never knows when they might mount an attack. An attack is suicidal for them, but the point is that they don't care. They steal food and anything else they need and, as long as they behave in that way, nobody bothers them. A strange situation. It is an eerie feeling to realize they are probably watching our every move. I doubt that we have any secrets from them, but don't know if they are capable of passing information along.

It's no secret we are now attached to the 7th Fleet . . . and the man in charge is dugout Doug MacArthur. A strange and highly unusual situation. MacArthur is generally disliked and apparently feels he is more godly than mortal. My mother thinks he is the most handsome man on the planet . . . and he agrees. This strange linkup between our Army General in charge of a Navy is noteworthy only in that it gives us and the Japs a clue as to our future. It is depressing.

The natives here are friendly and keep to themselves. They live in their villages and walk around scrounging what they can. They dislike Japanese and, at the moment, like us because we leave them alone or pay them when they work. It's the same old grass skirts, yaws and an appearance that makes abstinence easy.

I have visited some of the caves the Japs built when they owned these islands, and their existence was most unpleasant. The entrance to a typical cave is about 18" square and one can barely squeeze through. Actually, it is a palm log structure, partly underground with dirt piled on top. We found two bodies in our last "cave" and both had blown the tops of their heads off. I picked up a few worthless souvenirs, along with a small flag from one of the suicides.

It is disturbing to realize what this has done to both sides. The Japs are brutal, savage and inhumane in their treatment of prisoners. They are great soldiers and gladly lose it all in a hopeless fashion. On the other hand, the bodies I see have the teeth knocked out and many a gold tooth collection will go home with our soldiers or sailors. I imagine the natives wonder who in the hell is the civilized bunch. Actually, I guess everyone is joining in the reality of the situation with little hope of survival at this point.

We have made some repairs and have built some awning frames to provide a little shade at sea. We built a boat boom to secure our boats alongside when it's rough. I am supposed to invent a method of holding our bow ramp down in heavy seas while unloading. So far, my mind is a blank.

Now we're beached and loading again. This time it is combat equipment, and the crews will board us when loading is completed. There seems to be no hurry and, for once, we can put things in such a way that they'll go off easily and quickly. Can't help but wonder where it is this time . . . and what it will be like. Are there really unlucky numbers? Is #3 or #7 unlucky? For the answer to these important questions, stay tuned to the Postal Department. Only one thing is known . . . it won't be good.

I must change my outlook somehow. I wonder where you are now and what you are doing. We have no news from the real world. Navy radio messages are not thrilling and we don't have access to any other radios. The Army knows even less and we do not see new people in our midst. The Air Corps can tell us about the parties in Australia and that a bottle of whiskey is $20.00 . . . but that's about it.

Time's up! Take care of yourself. Say hello to Shirley. I'll write when I can.

SNAKESBELLY BILL

Tues. 11 April 1944 to
Wed. 19 April 1944

DEAR REALLY SORRY—

Since last writing to you on the 10th of April, I have been taking notes daily in order to remember all the happens that might be of interest to you. When one of your letters arrives, I won't have to rely on memory alone. My memory, due to aging 50 years in the past few days, has taken a giant step toward senility. Just a minute now, where was I? Oh, yeah, your letter from the invasion fronts arrived here the 17th of April, bearing the date of March 1st. You make mention, therein, about news being very thin on the ground for you wandering gypsies. I am sure you are waiting with bated breath to read another installment in the saga of your Air Corps, its men and its machines. But before consulting my notes and doing so, some thoughts on your news from the verdant atolls.

With the exception of major engagements, news here about your life and times in the south seas is equally sparse. We do have BBC (British broadcasting) and the *Stars And Stripes* who concern themselves, primarily, with Europe and its environs . . . so your letters are timely (relatively speaking) and fascinating. They are alarming, as well. I think we can both feel a modest amount of pride in having worked hard and continuing to survive under some very dangerous conditions. To tell the truth, I get a little embarrassed to even feel modestly proud when I consider the Army and Marines on the islands, the tankers and infantry in Africa (soon to be on the continent), and the submariners. The environment and conditions they live in, and fight under, are beyond my comprehension. I often wonder if I could cope with any such things.

Somehow, I wandered away from the pithy contents of your letter. The sunken ships (mostly ours), blasted palm trees, brutal labor in oppressive heat, deluges, "Piss Call Charlie" and other indignities too numerous to mention, have again confirmed my allegiance to Wilbur and Orville's invention. They probably didn't imagine flak and fighters . . . but, hell, this is progress. Your fall from grace on the occasion of that picnic on the beach comes under the heading of R & R (rest and recuperation), to which you were more than entitled. "Purple Ladies" and "Coconut Coolers", however, do not qualify as either rest or recuperation. Debauchery would be a more apt description. If you had stuck with coconut milk, sans firewater, you would not have awakened on a strange ship with your mouth as tasty as a buzzard's butt and your head hurting like a hot nail in the nuts. Remember, also, being rescued from a grisly fate in the pincers of legions of land crabs by a friend from college is not very likely to happen again. Eschew the demon rum and bite your nails instead.

Since arriving here, I usually hit the officer's club after dinner and have discovered a marvelous potion, port wine. Prior to the first mission, it was my custom to sip a glass as an aid to digestion and sleep. Since then, although my digestion is still humpin' along, I find it takes three or four glasses to induce peaceful dreams. We are going to have to liberate the French vineyards soon before my growing thirst empties the British wine cellars. Confronted by my growing addiction, I feel I may have been a little harsh in my critique of your beach party. So, cheers, skoal (?), here's to you and let your nails grow . . . the buzzard has landed.

Incidentally, did you and your fellow expendables pick those little critters out of your cigars (like weevils out of a biscuit), or leave them in their hidey holes to add an exotic flavor to the smoke?

Regarding censorship once again, as you point out, having once been somewhere, it then follows that the enemy is not unaware of that fact, and in our case, it is particularly evident. Therefore, if I get a little more specific, the rules of censorship will not be busted out of shape, nor will the Boche invade New York. If my perfidy is discovered, I will refuse the blindfold, but accept instead a final tot of port.

We flew our second mission on the 11th, and dropped six 1,000-pounders on a target inside Germany. On the first mission, we dropped ten 500s. The target dictates the bomb load we carry, but no matter what we drop, it must be hell to be on the receiving end of this hardware. Word the brass gets from inside Germany is that the townsfolk are not at all happy about inadvertent hits in their midst and have taken to stringing up some of our people who bailed out over the target area. Damned if it ain't one thing, it's another. Surrendering to the first uniform you see is not heroic, but it beats hell out of the alternative. This mission there were only a few fighters hanging around on the lookout for stragglers. The flak batteries were quite impressive and we took a few hits, nothing vital, but enough to encourage a new growth of gray hair. Most of us worry about catching a flak burst in the family jewels, so we sit on the flak jackets and leave the rest of our vulnerable bods to chance. Progeny and posterity are being preserved in the flak-ridden skies as we protect that which will produce them. The production procedure itself is high on our hit parade. This mission found us pretty well settled down and about as calm as can be expected under the circumstances. We still get scared, but not all that worried. Does that make any sense?

Arose at the usual 4:00 A.M. a couple of times, briefed and saddled up with the fans turning, only to get scrubbed due to weather over the target. Another day, we broke out of the overcast and were unable to find our group, so we were forced to abort. Much ado about nothing, but very hard on already sensitive nerves. We finally got off on our third mission and pasted the target with 52 100-pounders. The target was a Dornier (airplanes) factory at Oberpoffenhoffen . . . try that after a couple of "Purple Ladies". A few fighters showed up hunting for strays, again, and the flak was moderate. We only got dinged a couple of times. My God, am I becoming immune to this chaos? Three or four days ago, I would have needed artificial respiration.

My turn arrived for duty as Officer Of The Day, a 24-hour tour extending from one day to the next. I was equipped with an armband, a .45 automatic and a jeep. The .45 and the armband were merely accouterments of the office, but the jeep is for moving contraband K-rations to the hut . . . and an occasional sortie past the guard posts. Toss another log on the fire, mother, sustenance is here.

Inasmuch as your mail calls tend to be thin, I'll write more often, hoping to fatten them up a bit. Do not feel you have to reply to each letter individually. Depending on when they arrive, answer as many as you wish at one time.

Once again, I admonish you to ignore the sun over the yardarm and take the pledge.

CHEERS . . . WINO WILL

Thurs. 20 April 1944 to
Thurs. 11 May 1944

DEAR NERVOUS—

Aren't we all? Yours of 28 March reached here on the 10th of May. Speaking of being nervous, I have an ambivalent feeling toward this combat crap and wonder if it is the same with you? Before a mission, I have a feeling of excitement and almost anticipation of whatever will soon be happening. During the shooting, I'm hoping like hell not to get killed, but I'm not really scared out of my socks. That comes then it's all over and we're parking the airplane, and I wonder where the hell that irrational feeling of excitement came from. Maybe a shingle or two has been blown off my roof. Maybe we are all like that and that keeps us climbing back into those things when the odds are so unfavorable. Fatalism? Faith? Confidence? Must be something. Tell me, oh great prophet.

Congratulations for splashing the Jap zero! That is no mean feat, as we well know, and you are entitled to paint a rising sun on the side of your bridge . . . both sides. It pays to advertise. So far, I think we scared a few Jerries a little, but not enough to have them consider a truce or abject surrender. When you speak of body parts floating past your bow ramp, mortars bracketing "Ole #628" and screeching and howling at nights from the jingles, I'm glad I can't see or hear what happens to life and limb when our bombs impact the ground. You must feel terribly exposed as you go about loading and unloading in that bloody bedlam. I can also imagine that exposed feeling escalating right off the charts when you found yourself aground on a reef and sweatin' out a life saving tide. Methinks it is a similar thing to what I feel on our predictable bomb run through a flak barrage. You are indeed right in that, no matter how small the invasion (or mission), it only takes one round out of the thousands being fired to stop your clock. Think lucky . . . we need all we can get.

We flew another mission on the 20th of April to the Pas de Calais region in La Belle Francais. It was rough as a cob. Usually we have a barrage type flak and just drive through, hoping we don't get hit real bad. The stuff we ran into this time got real personal. The three gun batteries on the ground picked out a single airplane and followed it with aimed rounds. We were singled out of our three-ship flight, and our pilot had to predetermine each evasive action in order to cross up the guys who were trying to pick us off. The 88s take about 25 seconds between bursts to reach us, so about every 17 seconds Mac would slide us to one side or the other and hoped he picked the right direction. No sooner than we would level off, three bursts would blossom out about where we would have been. Several times, the bursts would rock the ship, some no more than 20 feet away, but fortunately none directly beneath the bomb bays. We did get dinged several times, but nothing was structurally serious. On the bomb run, I could feel St. Pete blowing his cold breath down my long johns, but to my infinite relief, the flak battery shifted to the group of three behind us . . . and promptly blew one out of the sky. We were lucky to get home in one contiguous piece. McGlasson's skill and aplomb made most of our luck.

One of my jobs is to keep just as accurate account as possible of the airplanes, friend or foe, and the parachutes that go down. The intelligence people compare all these sightings, I suppose, to get some idea of the number of people who may turn up as POWs, in the underground or K.I.A.

Parachuting is not what it appears to be on the silver (tarnished) screen. The guys pile out of burning or out of control ships, and the first thought is yank the rip cord. Their rate of fall and the forward speed of the airplane whoas them up with a 150-MPH jerk. I get sympathetic throbbing in my groin when I see them almost horizontal when the chute pops. Another danger is pulling the cord too quickly in the presence of so many airplanes charging around in just a little airspace. Mac has almost thrown our 24 on its back to avoid a chutist. A wing tip can cut a man in half, and a prop just raises particular hell.

When I see these things happen, I feel real sorrow for those men and, at the same time, real deep relief that it isn't me. I feel somewhat guilty for thinking that way, and hope it is instinctive with everyone and not an aberration singular to me.

After your frequent comments about the oppressive heat and humidity, I can only suggest that you get a nice tan, drink lots of water (if available) with salt tablets and be content.

The only time we see the sun is after breaking out of the overcast that seems to be permanently attached to England. At our altitude, the sun does not provide heat, only German fighters who hide in the glare and pounce on us as we lumber eastward. Bright sunlight, blue skies and visibility to where the Earth curves downward . . . it's beautiful, and cold enough to freeze the balls off a brass monkey. The large waist windows are open throughout the mission and our gunners (one each, port and starboard) stand there for several hours in 20 and 30 degree below zero temperatures in a continual blast of wind. We have heated suits and boots which frequently short out, causing "hot foots" (and foul language). We are all cold, but not like the waist gunners. I have to work barehanded, so my hands are near frostbite all the time. Some people have lost feet or hands to the cold. When fingers or toes get critical, our home remedy is to stick them between another man's legs next to the skin. This is a great comfort to the freezing digits, but causes another digit to shrink out of sight. No matter, it ain't doing anything anyway. If it weren't for Japs, mortars, bugs, dysentery, artillery, zeros, weevils, swamps and back-bustin' work, I'd be tempted to give up these cool breezes for a deck recliner and a "Purple Lady" on sunny "Ole #628".

Someone must have screwed up; our crew was issued a long expected (and often denied) three-day pass. All of us hopped a train for London and were enjoying the ride, and the absence of warlike airplanes, until a B-17 buzzed the train twice at an altitude of about 30 feet. Not only did he scare the hell out of everyone, but his bomb-nav in the greenhouse added insult to injury by giving us the finger on each pass. About the time our tuning forks quit vibrating, we arrived in London and hired a little square taxi for the ride to the Regent Palace Hotel. God save the King, and He would have had to if the King had ridden with us in that cab. The guy driving was in his sixties and seemed to drive at a speed equal to or exceeding his age. We tore through London, escaping death by inches from buses, other madmen driving cabs, light poles and other large, freestanding objects. All this on the wrong side of the road. That old fart must work for the other side.

Mac and I roomed together, while Buck soloed one floor below. The hotel was loaded with Air Corps people, so many that I wondered if anyone was back home minding the store and flying missions. We split up after a wartime meal in the dining room. I retired to the downstairs bar until closing time and then hit the sack. Sometime during the night, a tap on my shoulder awoke me and a naked lady inquired as to the time. One thinks of many things in a situation such as this. Am I dreaming? Do I (equally as naked) leap out of bed and introduce myself, tumescence not withstanding? Is the house dick hiding in the closet with a camera? Have I, on the other hand, struck the mother lode of all fantasies? None of the above became reality. She was up again at 6:00 A.M., quite unabashedly peed in the sink, had a sponge bath and got dressed. It seems that Mac had arrangements to bunk elsewhere and loaned her his bed. I trust you will consider the foregoing as a top secret communique. Although innocent of anything but visual stimulation, explaining this to Shirley might stretch her credence a tad further than is prudent for my health.

Buck and I did the whole town. Buckingham Palace, Westminster, Windsor, Madame Toussaud's . . . the works. We walked until we darn near dropped. The subways are far below street level and serve as sleeping quarters for as many people as can crowd into them. Damp, cold and drafty. I feel sorry for these folks, but (for the most part) they show good spirits, the phlegmatic Britisher at his best. The blackouts are black to where, quite literally, it is hard to see your hand in front of your face. The Bobbies chased us into Air Raid shelters a time or two, where we spent most of the time apologizing for bumping into, and stepping on, people. The tourism took a heavy toll on my feet, and the midnight ride of Paul Revere a further toll on my vows of celibacy, so I was not too unhappy to return to base to prosecute the war effort against the Nazi.

Prosecuting began at 4:00 A.M., about eight hours after returning to base, with a tap on my shoulder. This time, however, the tapper wore Corporal's stripes, thus ending a dream which was just beginning to show real progress. The fighters were everywhere to and from the target today, and more aggressive than usual. We were shooting on and off for a couple of hours, taking some hits in the wings and fuselage. On the bomb run we dropped 52 100-pounders on Augsberg, and the flak gunners reciprocated by shooting out our #4 engine. The pilots fortunately were able to feather the engine (turning the blade sides into the wind) to reduce drag, thus making it more likely we could maintain our position within the formation and the protection of their guns. Becoming a straggler in this business is usually curtains and, even in a formation, one engine out entitles you to special attention from the fighters. Under the best of circumstances, these big airplanes take skill and muscle to fly in formation . . . with an engine gone, it's a real bear. Mac and Buck sweated pounds and, despite the Luftwaffe, we hung in close to the other ships and their firepower . . . a super exhibition of skill and training by our pilots. The crew deserved credit as well for calm and disciplined reactions under these stressful conditions. Touched down at the base at 6:30 P.M.; older, wiser and grateful for the Salvation Army and their coffee and doughnuts.

The C.Q. got us up again, this time at 2:00 A.M., long before the cock crew (or crowed, or whatever), and it was into the overcast again. This time to Mannheim, which has a nasty reputation for flak and fighters. When the target was unveiled (a window shade is run up, exposing the bad news beneath), the moans and groans could be heard for miles. Each mission we are briefed in a general way about weather, flak, fighters, fighter cover, etc., with all crews attending. Occasionally, the briefers are right. After the general brief, we go to specialty briefings for each job on the plane. We pay very close attention. Today, when we reached the target, there was 10/10 cloud cover over the area, so we were unable to drop. There was a huge pall of black smoke from flak bursts over the target, and all of us were happy to pass this one by. We did have fighter opposition, but they did not press very hard.

Hit the sack early the same night and, as we were dropping into sleep, some pervert ran the length of our corrugated tin house with a brick in his hand. Nine guys hit the cement floor, running balls-out for the bomb shelter, wondering how we survived the strafing and bombing. After a minute or two of freezing in the shelter in our underwear, we realized that we had been had. There are plots thicker than flies on road apples for a revenge adequate enough to restore our dignity. As the plots thicken, I will keep you advised.

Up and at 'em again this A.M. Today, it was an invasion practice mission, wherein we were to support ground troops storming a beach. The beach is on the southern tip of England, and as we approached at a very low altitude, we saw countless numbers of invasion craft scurrying around the ocean like so many water beetles on a pond. We were to drop (100 pounders) ahead of the troops, who were hitting the beach, but my reckoning put us too close to the forward skirmish line. Mac called the lead ship and so informed the Colonel who replied, rather tersely, drop or it's your ass. I delayed my drop a little anyway. To add to my concern about where the bombs impacted, four of mine hung up in the bomb bays. Thinking back to a previous unforgettable incident, I opted to leave those suckers decide for themselves . . . two of them fell, electing to bomb England to the further detriment of Anglo-American good will. I saw them slide by our nose, headed for a farmer and his horse plowing a field. The farmer looked up as we roared overhead and dove into a ditch. The horse stood fast, probably assuming no one could possibly be dumb enough to bomb his own side. To make a long story short, the bombs overshot the field and the farmer crawled out of the ditch, apparently unhurt. Dobbin was not to be seen. He, no doubt, decided Yanks were capable of being that dumb, and fled the scene in order to be available for the next day's chores. We still had two bombs aboard, which was a bit worrisome when the time came to land. But Mac greased it in and we walked away from another one.

Both of us are in deep doo, and the only alternatives I can think of for a way out of this mess are as perilous as staying in place. We could shoot ourselves in the foot, but that would hurt like hell (or, in all likelihood, we would miss and embarrass ourselves to death). Neither a swim through 30 miles of shark-infested waters, nor parachuting into a maddened mob of bombing survivors with ropes, would be without some risk. Think of something viable and reply ASAP. In the meantime, I'll begin another report . . . and let's be ever mindful of the slings and arrows of outrageous Japs and Jerries.

MAYDAY BILL

7 May, '44

DEAR BEREAVED BILL—

Happy day! We got a ton of mail a day or so ago and I have three letters from you. Better still, I have time to answer and shall do so in the order you wrote. I have no watches to stand tonight and all is quiet. I love it!

Your letter dated 1 March to 14 March passes the word that you are still a resident of Jolly old England . . . it sounds good. Frankly, you may be sorry you didn't bail out over the forests somewhere so that you could live off the land and meditate.

Your trip must have been designed to confuse the Germans. It sure confuses me. You indeed took the scenic route and perhaps, if I can find a map, it will all make sense. I'm sure you'll agree that visiting all these places while tied to an airfield (or dock) does not give one the perspective of the average tourist. Perhaps your C.O. will allow a few days, or weeks, so that you can investigate along the way. Glad you survived Brazil and I wonder where in hell you'll wear the gaucho boots.

It sounds as though your various stops are arranged to make England look like heaven itself. Your description of your stops leaves the impression that you don't especially like those places.

I feel it to be an absolute certainty that your safe trip from Africa to England had to have resulted from the German high command learning that you were armed . . . with a loaded .45 pistol. Any German pilot would quake in his boots at the thought of pursuing into your range. Pure luck they didn't arm you with a shotgun, which would cause levity amongst the Hun flyers. Glad you made it!

Your letter of 15 March to 21 March is now in my sweaty palms. Thanks for your new address. "Replacement crew" could just as well have been called something else. Perhaps "Homeward Bound Crew", "Bomb Shelter Guards" or "Female Pleasure Crew" would have had a calming effect. I believe I'm in the wrong business, and perhaps you've thought of that, too.

I see that you, too, are learning about the personal desires of lonely men through the censorship route. Sometimes the desires and dreams are the only part of the letters that can go through. You keep notes, and I will too, and I hope to try some of these stunts some day.

The warm beer you mention requires a little time and effort. I first experienced it in Montreal (ages ago) and stuck with it until I liked it. Warm ale was another minor problem, but it too became downright tasty. One didn't dare complain. I note that your bicycle ride revealed some tenderness in some areas, and I trust you recover soon.

Your letter of 22 March to 6 April is the last of my booty, except for the uncounted epistles from females who are doing what they can to keep our boys' morales up. Wish they were here. My morale could stand an injection.

I see that you are now ensconced in a Nisson Hut and that you have found your way to the bathroom and the bomb shelter. That's probably all you need to know! It sounds as though you are well furnished and equipped.

It is noteworthy that you won the race to the bomb shelter. The hardened veterans who watch the raid from up top will likely be gone before long. It is a bit hard to appear calm and detached with urine streaking the front of one's jeans and the teeth chattering until the silver amalgam is crushed. I never claimed to be fearless.

Your crew seems enterprising enough in "requisitioning" food supplies, and this is a sign of pure survivors. I dare say our crew is of the same sort and we now own a jeep all our own. The idea of having a real egg makes the mouth water.

Glad you're happy with your airplane and that everything works. That, of course, is elementary and my desire would be for one guaranteed durable.

Sorry about the loss of Earl Norris . . . and sorry that you had to know about it in the way it came about. When one thinks about all the machines, ammo of all kinds and a bunch of reluctant civilians among all this, it's a wonder there aren't more accidents. It is a supreme struggle to learn the job and stay alert . . . and that's about all that can be done. Still, it is depressing (and frightening) to see or hear frequently about someone you know dropping out. So, hang tough and be smart. I want to see you after this hell is over and see if the Army taught you how to shoot a shotgun!

Can't remember exactly when I last wrote, but we are back at Manus and licking our wounds and repairing and provisioning. Next comes loading again. We have returned from Hollandia in New Guinea . . . another garden spot, and a relatively soft invasion. Hollandia is on the north side of New Guinea and toward the west. The Dutch own the western part, and we have seen a few Dutch vessels around here. New Guinea is very close to Australia and the Aussies have been considerably worried. Most of their men are elsewhere and they figured the Japs were coming soon. Some of the Aussy troops have walked northwest along the coast, along with some Americans. They have taken Lae and Finchaven and other well known spots and Hollandia. Will probably complete the action there. We were at the foot of "Pancake Hill" on D-day and the troops we carried made good headway immediately. Before we left, it got tougher, but the resistance was spotty. New Guinea is largely uncharted and unexplored. The coast has been colonized for years, but the interior is said to still be native only, including some Headhunters. Having heard these reports, I believe the coast is all we want . . . and the airstrip.

Saw a P-38, and it looked great. They're supposed to be night fighters, and they go like the wind. Other than that, it's still P-47s and B-17s now and then. We got a Jap Betty Bomber and it was beautiful. It's a twin-engine bomber, and it came over us at twilight. We hit it and set it afire and could see it lose altitude until it hit the top of the jungle. It mowed a path through the tree tops for a long way, exploding and losing parts as it went. One more out of the way. The hit was exciting (even more so than seeing you hit a pheasant). Our gunners are still the greatest and they didn't waste much ammo, either.

When I have time to think, I reflect upon the idea that you are seeing London and Liverpool, etc., and your targets may be Bremen, Hamburg, Berlin, or maybe Paris, Brussels, or Ploesti. I'm telling you about Banika, Manus, Los Negros, Santa Cruz, Lae, Fenchhaven and Hollandia. Another garden spot is Emirou and who knows what next. I wonder what my kids (if I ever have any) will tell me when I tell them I was at Aitape. They'll think I was out of my mind . . . and I certainly agree.

Our biggest problems, so far, are mortars. The Japs must have had one hell of a class in Mortars 101. They have small ones and big ones and they are accurate. They drop those damned things on the beaches and walk them left or right and in or out . . . and when you're grounded and see them walking toward you, it is a real sensation. I'm in plain sight of everyone and am supposed to be the fearless leader, and the legs turn to jelly. The Army wonders where the hell you hide on "this thing" and the fact is you just stand and pray a lot. The other problem is sneaky aircraft. One to three Zeroes coming in out of the sun or at night and bombing and strafing the beach. They are quiet at slow speed, but their sound is unmistakable. They are not very accurate, but we are side by side and they would have to struggle to miss all of us. A ship that catches fire then becomes target #1 and can expect special attention. If you don't see them coming, they're gone before you can fire on them . . . and at night we can't see much.

At times, the Japs will load a torpedo or a bomb into a small boat and ram a ship at night. We have men on guard at night with some Thompsons and 03A3s, or even Jap rifles . . . and the orders are to fire at any approaching boat. The word has been passed that no boats are to be out at night, but some are. We stopped one a week ago (or so), with its occupants screaming "Americans, Americans" and they're lucky to be alive.

Can't help but think . . . what in hell am I doing here?! I'm not mad at anybody. I asked for a little action, but I've had that and I want to go home. My girlfriend needs me. The Polar Grille needs me. I should be studying economics. What possible need have they for cowardly lovers? Nobody listens!

Understand that I would not trade my fate for yours under any circumstances. I'm not fond of flying or flak or takeoffs or landings or cold weather in aluminum boxes with wings. I hate to admit it, but I am tired of being in a state of near panic. A little rest is beginning to cure that.

I don't believe it's any secret we're going back to Hollandia, and sometimes the return trip is worse than D-day. With Dugout Doug in charge, it's easy to guess what our future is, but some of these areas have to be cleaned out. We've bypassed some strongholds of the enemy, but we can't tolerate their aircraft, even though they inflict "minor damage". Hey, that "minor damage" might be me!

Thanks for the letters. I know you need them, too, and I'll do my best. Say hello to Shirley.

EXTREMELY SORRY NOW BILL

17 May, '44

DEAR PUB CRAWLER—

Got a chance to write and will take it. It's hot as hades, and one of our several rains per day just quit. I believe the food, water, atabrine and lack of contact with acceptable females have affected my memory. I know I wrote you recently, but I don't remember where we were or when I wrote. Among our shortages are calendars. I have to walk the length of the ship to find a calendar, and it is one of those with pictures of deformed women in the buff. The women are all very attractive (who isn't?), with large lungs and small sterns. Unusual, as I remember! More and more I feel the need to know what day it is.

Anyway, we're at Hollandia again, and it is now pretty quiet. Perhaps the Japs that ran into the interior have been killed by natives, and the Army tells us it is nearly all quiet. The word "nearly" is disturbing, but the executive officer and I took a boat and a lunch and went up a river recently . . . a picnic so to speak. The river is small one . . . about the size you have tried (unsuccessfully) to jump while hunting. We explored some Jap caves and dugouts and passed through (or under) a native village. The bamboo houses are on stilts above the water, and the natives here are stark naked . . . and ugly. I suppose we went a mile or so and ate our baloney sandwiches before meeting four buxom young ladies. They giggled and chattered and gestured . . . and we had no idea what was on their minds. I noticed that, sans clothing, girls are different from boys. I also noticed the various open sores all over the black bodies and a goodly amount of dust above the waist with white mud below the waist. I believe they had been fishing . . . at least they smelled like fish. Our meeting was short, and they went away. We then took a fork in the river and came upon four or five sailors panning for gold. They were only barely civil, but loosened up a bit and showed us how they got the gold. They were living in a canvas covered large assault boat from an APA, and had a good supply of C-rations and canned goods. They also had some fruit cocktail fermenting, and it was good. Black clouds gathered, and we left while we could still see. It has crossed my mind that maybe these guys are AWOL and we may have been shot. I would rather have been taken prisoner because they seemed to have a good pocketful of little yellow nuggets.

Back on the ship, nothing was going on and no orders to leave. The executive officer is a good friend, and he has an interest in girls. Somehow in his travels on the beach, he came upon the rumor there are nurses here. He wondered if I cared to join him to see if the rumor was true. After careful and deliberate thought, I said I would go, but (with any number of nurses, and considering some 35,000 men on the island) it seemed to me the odds were not good. We took our trusty Marine Corps jeep, now painted navy blue, and set off for a tourist guide. We didn't really believe anyone was going to tell us the whereabouts of nurses, but one can't just work all the time. In asking questions, all we did was to magnify the rumor, and we got no information. Just about the time we had to return to the ship, we saw a ragtag group of GIs in fatigues lining up for chow and, on close observation, we made the discovery that these were bona fide white nurses from the USA. We could only talk with the ones at the tail-end of the line because a female officer with a no-nonsense look was chaperoning the head of the line. The pretty girls were not at the tail-end of the line, but they were gorgeous. Perhaps a bit disheveled, maybe a bit plump, possibly not totally clean . . . but with their hair combed, and a dress on, they surely were real, genuine, bona fide girls. I must admit, I let down all my usual barriers as I talked with one sweet young thing named Ruth. My friend chose another close by and explained that it had been awhile since we conversed with genuine females and that we'd like to pursue the matter on the morrow. To our surprise, these two said they'd meet us at the gate to their compound the following evening. We then moved because the female officer with the permanent scowl was approaching.

I'll continue this drivel even though you are probably already asleep. You must realize that seeing a white woman out here is an unbelievable miracle. Anyway, the next day went very slowly, and the executive officer and I saw to it that we had fresh green undershorts, ironed pants and shirts, and a close shave. We put on some smelly aftershave lotion and stuffed two blankets in a ditty bag to take ashore. We had all the necessary accessories, which we left in the jeep so as to not allow the girls to guess our motives. They were at the gate on time and got in the jeep, and we then asked if there was a cocktail lounge, dance hall or opera in the vicinity. The answer was, of course, "NO" . . . so there. There was nothing to do but drive down the beach further than the protective officer was willing to walk and spread the blankets. The girls insisted that we stay close and announced that they had a bed check soon. Ruth was a very nice, smart, loveable girl who was willing to partake of some conversation, but was saving herself for the future. She hoped she never saw us in her hospital, and we agreed. I believe it was about 10 minutes later that some MPs advised that we get the hell off the beach.

You'll be green with envy as I tell you we've been to Surabaya, Wewak and Salamau. Got another Jap Zero that just missed us as he hit the water. They don't float long. It is total relief to see them come down.

Now we are in a "rear area" and loading combat equipment and, later, troops. We have taken on fresh water from our favorite algae-covered pool, and everyone has the same old diarrhea. To add insult to injury, we (yesterday) took shots for Black Plague. They were large shots and are guaranteed to make us sick in a few days. The work goes on and the arms hurt.

The "rear area" here is part of an island among several others which are Jap-held and have been bypassed. Some are close enough that the Japs can swim the distance, and they are good at hiding small airstrips from which to send Piss-Call Charlies frequently. Charlie seldom hits anything with one bomb, but he nevertheless gets our attention and ruins the little sleep we get between watches. The Army just pretty well sleeps through it all, except for the operators of their "Long Tom" 3-inch guns, which have to be the most worthless AA gun in existence.

Barring a lot of luck, we won't be getting mail for a while. I think of you often and wonder how it goes. I do hope you do all you can to avoid silly accidents and foolish actions. I note that, after a while, a lot of these guys just trust to luck . . . and I believe one can do more than that. Keeping alert takes a lot of energy and sleep loss, but it just might get us back home.

I can't really imagine taking off in one of those big bombers and spending all the necessary time getting to the place where they shoot at you. I am not especially fond of airplanes anyway, and they seem a bit flimsy to the uninitiated. I suggest you talk with your C.O. and advise him of your many skills and talents. You could teach shotgun shooting to recruits or running the 100-yard dash while shooting . . . or fording streams even though falling in the water. Surely, if they learn you are about to become a father, there will be some stateside desk job available. With all these accomplishments, it is truly a shame to have you dropping bombs through the countryside and injuring cows, pigs and maybe a farmer.

We gathered around a radio yesterday (Army radio) and learned that you and your cohorts are doing a hell of a job on the Germans. The news from other fronts is good, and I feel much better now. It's a long road ahead for us, but we're getting stronger and we're on the move. Keep up the good work!

We have some new replacements and are fitting them in. We've lost some fine young men (some due to psychiatric interviews), and we'll be at full strength for the next one.

Loading continues, and we'll be underway in a few days. Is this one a lucky number? Watch your mail to find out!

TIRED OF IT ALL BILL

Fri. May 12, 1944 to
Mon. May 22, 1944

DEAR BILL—

As has become customary now, I am starting my report of current events here before receiving your next letter. Should I get lucky, I'll change my salutation to your latest Nom-de-Plume.

Current events here, as I report them, or as you do, will not resemble in any way the pontifical poop put out by the newscasters in their swivel chairs. As we both know now, you can't describe it unless you have done it. As a change of pace, I would like to dandle a comely and willing secretary on my lap while swiveling merrily around the newsroom . . . but I would always wonder thereafter if I would have been able to measure up.

Now, as I look ahead at the number of missions yet to be flown, I feel like I'm looking down a telescope the wrong way. The light at the end of that tunnel is a mere flicker. That is much too negative an analogy, so I will concentrate on the doughnut instead of the friggin' hole. Measuring up, no matter how you look at it, sure does take some doin'.

We flew a nice, short mission to France a few days ago. That is a little misleading . . . the only thing nice about it was its brevity, 3-1/2 hours. As usual, flak alley lit up with gusto as we approached, and the boys on the ground had lost none of their old skills. If anything, the amount of practice we are providing for them has improved their accuracy and enthusiasm to a fearsome degree. Cloud cover obscured the target, so we were forced to return with our bomb loads and face a hairy landing. This is always a big disappointment, to run all the inherent risks from engine start to shut down and not leave our calling cards. The mission was rescheduled for later on that day, but was scrubbed because darkness set in. We had been sitting around the airplane all afternoon, contemplating the doughnut, so nightfall came as a relief to us, if not to our planners.

Another horror story evolved from this unconsummated drop. A 24 crashed on landing this afternoon, and the impact of the crash dislodged the upper turret from its mounts, and it fell on the radio operator. The poor guy was pinned under several hundred pounds of turret. The remaining fuel ignited and efforts to free him were futile. The pilot heard his shrieking and couldn't bear his agony and went into that furnace and shot him. That took real courage, and I hope the review board looks at it the same as us rank and filers. Flak had hit them in the target area. This occurred at a base adjacent to ours.

Mac received a reply to his condolence letter to Mrs. Norris, E.J.'s mother. Any reply he chooses to make to her letter is going to be very, very difficult to compose. Perhaps I was right in not attempting a condolence letter of my own, but right or wrong, this keeps niggling my conscience a bit.

In the midst of our frequent journeys over the fatherland and its environs, plans for vengeance upon those who bricked our corrugations have been bubbling on the back burner. A final retaliatory stroke was adopted, and we drew straws to select the hitman, boosted him atop the target hut, where he dropped six 50 calibers (minus the slugs) down their smokestack. The results more than exceeded our modest expectations. Soot, cinders, smoke and half-naked guys bailed out the front door as if Lucifer was in hot pursuit. A peace treaty has now been negotiated, with all parties agreeing that we have more than enough nervous prostrations just flying to warrant any further feuding.

Quite surprisingly, mail call yielded a bonanza of 15 letters and a large package a day or two ago. Not too surprisingly, my box of goodies was decimated almost instantaneously by the savages I live with. One guy even made some sort of an omelet out of the stray crumbs. The letters I kept to myself, although a couple of the moochers considered that to be downright selfish. There was nothing from the South Pacific, to my regret.

Bicycled to Norwich one afternoon with considerably less pain than on the previous journeys. It is still like straddling a 2 x 4, which has not gotten any softer, so it must follow that my butt has become numb . . . one more unsung casualty of the war. Buck was with me, and we fished, chipped, aled, bittered and spent a couple of expensive hours with a couple of RAF pilots. They fly twin-engine mosquito bombers . . . a somewhat chancy occupation. The British airmen have, and are, taking heavy casualties and have every right to be proud of themselves and their service.

Back in the saddle again . . . this time, my abused butt riding a flak suit. We flew a practice mission, followed by the real thing, over Pas de Calais again, and I feel more and more like a clay bird on the skeet range. Those three gun batteries are murder, and we took some close bursts that rocked the boat, some causing minor damage. Cloud cover forced us to return with our load, and no credit allowed for the mission. Here again, the unhappy fact that you can get killed just as dead on one that doesn't count as well as on one that does. What am I fussin' about? It wouldn't matter anyway in that event.

A case in point . . . one of our 24s nosed over on takeoff today, just before becoming airborne, and blew up. Our ship was coming back high over the runway, en route to forming up, and we got tossed upwards 100 feet or so by the blast. Five men got out of that ship before she blew, and I have no idea how they managed to escape. A couple of their bombs that didn't go off in a sympathetic explosion were detonated later, and the noise was horrific. How people can handle air raids and hundreds of these things going off all around them is beyond me. That is one more thing you can't dwell on or you couldn't effectively do your job.

The mission today was completed in darkness, and the large number of ships in the area made for another bad half an hour. We had two very near misses, but our pilots, bless their instant reaction time, kept us intact once again.

Orders have come down, directing me to attend a regular navigational school eight hours a day until I am capable of finding our way to the target. More importantly to our crew, finding our way home from the target will also be included, and I assure you no stone will be left unturned in that regard. Although this does make some sense (rare as it is in the military), it is a bitter pill to swallow for me. I have a dread of flying with another crew and can only hope they don't get too far ahead of me. Will you recognize me with snow white hair?

For several days, my I.Q. rose in a direct ratio with my sinking spirits. My lead pencil and E6B computer waged a fierce campaign against time and my ineptitude for things mathematical, until I finally prevailed. A colorful sheepskin from the 8th Air Force testifies to my skill as a D.R. navigator. This diploma, I think, is a ruse to give the crew confidence in their substitute navigator. The crew, incidentally, is only two missions ahead of me, which is not as bad as I had imagined. I will now postpone thinking about riding with someone else until that time comes, and then I'll be hysterical.

During this period of cerebral overkill, I visited the O.C. nightly and engaged in a few games of poker and won enough to pay for the imminent arrival of our first born (I hope). I told Shirley to be sure the doctor understands and appreciates what I'm going through to get his fee.

Up and at 'em about 4:00 A.M., as usual, and took off for Germany. We were recalled around 8:30 A.M., a discouraging business after having once again survived the overcast. I really shouldn't complain . . . there might have been something out there today with our name on it. My maiden flight as a navigator (and a bombardier) was eminently successful. I followed the lead ship. Returned to the ship in the afternoon and did some cosmetic repairs on the gal adorning our nose section. She was beginning to look like an accident victim after the rough treatment the Aryan gents have been lavishing on her. Some of the other ships have some really inspired artwork and names on their noses. Plastered Bastard, Ruptured Duck and Impatient Virgin, to name a few. The virgin was naked as a jay bird and a joy to behold, but the Colonel, in a fit of plebeian modesty, ordered her clothed. This did not brighten the Colonel's image in the eyes of the crews, or probably the Luftwaffe as well.

The group flew a real long mission against the marshaling yards in Mulhouse, France. Eight and a half hours in the air, seven and a half of it on oxygen. The cold was unusually penetrating, and the whole front of my gear was covered with ice formed by the vapor that escapes from the oxygen mask. The skies were very clear, and when I dropped, I followed the bombs down with the binoculars and watched the mushroom heads of the strikes walk along the yards. Good bombing today. The Jerries are going to be busy getting that yard running again . . . but they will.

Rumor has it that the much-talked-about invasion of Fortress Europe will be happening very soon. Our group will be a mustard gas retaliatory force, should the Germans resort to that nasty business. We are equipped with gas masks for use when we get near the stuff. The Colonel (he of clothe that woman fame) is also running base defense practice alerts. We all dash about, festooned in full field gear, pistol, canteen, web belts, the works. I rather doubt that hordes of German parachutists, according to rumor, will in fact appear. Should they show up, I will surrender to the first guy I see in a coal skuttle hat. This will be much safer than having the headquarters people behind me waving .45 autos. You can also bet they, indeed, will be far behind.

More good weather today . . . and another long, hard and cold haul like yesterday. We missed the target, which was near Leipzig in Germany, and of course, were disappointed to be at risk like that and accomplish little or nothing. There was a large gaggle of enemy fighters in the target area, and they worked us over to a fare-thee-well. I saw two or three of them going down in flames, hopefully there were more. The flak was intensive and damaged almost every ship in the formation, and we lost some ships. The flak today came in a variety of colors: red, green, blue and the regular elongated puff ball stuff. They even sent up some bursts that simulated parachutists or burning bombers, presumably to confuse our intelligence people. It all only looks like flak to me.

Landing today kept the ambulances and fire trucks busy. Engines out, landing gear up and crew members wounded or worse. Mostly everyone got down all right, considering the damage to planes and crews. A testament to young civilians in Army uniforms.

Every so often, I find myself wanting to cold cock some of our ground personnel. Some smart ass always manages to ask if it was "rough out there today", with a silly smirk on his face . . . while the sirens on the emergency vehicles still are wailing. I don't refer here to our maintenance crews who work long, cold, miserable nights getting these birds back into combat readiness, and then sweat out their crew and their airplane while the mission is ongoing . . . and then meet it on the hardstand.

After a night's sleep (3 hours), we took off on our 10th mission. I don't feel too bad about counting them now that they are beginning to amount to something. On the other hand, 20 more (they raised it five) is enough to ruin your day if you consider what you are likely to go through to reach that happy plateau. Tutow was again the target and, unlike that first trip, we comported ourselves like the veterans we seem to be becoming. We got some attention from fighters, and a modest (one can kill you) amount of flak, but breezed through without damage or injury. About 50 American and German fighters mixed it up in a whale of a dog fight a short distance from our formation. Quite a thrilling thing to witness, and doubly so, because our little brothers were keeping those 109s and 110s off our backs. Things for us would have been real iffy had our fighters not been present. Love those crazy fighter jocks.

We must have really pissed the Jerries off today because they followed us home and worked us over in the landing pattern and on the runways. Our ship had just touched down when the first JU-88 started bouncing rifle balls "off 'n our punkin haids". There were three of these guys (JU-88s are twin-engine fighter bombers), and they made three passes squirting 20-mm cannon shells and 30-calibers all over the place. Most of our ships, if not all of them, didn't fire a return shot as we had pulled the gunners out of the turrets for landing. Base defense, however, went bananas (after a long pause to check their aircraft I.D. book) and filled the air with shot and shell, missing the Germans and holing two or three B-24s. Well, at any rate, nothing got hurt, except the Laundry Lady's Feelings.

I suspect we will be riding the turrets right onto the hardstands in the future, prepared to defend ourselves against base defense.

Some of the events I described in this letter actually took place in April. My last letter got so long, and I wanted to get something going to you, that I temporarily held them back. My daily notes helped. The good weather here has made for increased sorties, and the upcoming invasion has made time of the essence. This mounting pressure against Germany reflects on my time to write.

I expect something from you to show up any day now, and then I can use your latest signature . . . and fire off an answer forthwith.

TAKE GOOD CARE—MAGELLAN

Tues. 23 May 44 to
Sun. 28 May 44

DEAR SNAKESBELLY—

In the closing remarks of my last letter, I mentioned that I expected a letter from you momentarily. The day after I mailed that letter, yours of 14 April appeared . . . almost as if the P.O. Dept. had been reading my mail.

Snakesbelly? I presume you mean "lower than" and not that you have been slithering through the jungles injecting venom into unwary Japanese buttocks. Nipping a nip as you might say. Should you discover a way to shanghai some of your rear echelon heroes for an eye-and-a-bowel-opening trip to an invasion, please advise. There are some smirky paddle feet around here that need to share some of the thrills of warfare in the skies. But short of shooting them, I don't see how to get even one on board. Unlike your situation, we seem to get all the supplies and where-with-all it takes to fly the thousands (?) of sorties that are put up. Should the invasion prove to be successful, your problem may continue for some time to come.

Your remarks about Genl. MacArthur raise some doubts in my mind also. I wonder about the frustrations this must cause in the upper levels of the Navy . . . and the mistakes in judgment this could cause. Those errors mean casualties to front line troops. I'm not sure but that the loss of face means more to Annapolis and West Point than the loss of us expendables. The General, hereabouts, is usually referred to as "Dugout Doug", but I find that connotation very hard to believe. Let us hope that horse sense prevails and some day history buffs can tell us what the hell was really going on.

The experiences you are having convince me that you are a lot more attuned to the more down and dirty realities of this war than I am, or maybe the reality is where you are and what you're doing. In any event, decomposing bodies, caves, gold teeth, searing heat, snipers, lousy food, bad water, etc., etc., are a far cry from an English airfield. We do share one thing in common . . . the feeling of expendability. Perish the thought. Let's concentrate on a cornfield with pheasants as thick as ME 110s after a straggler. Nuts, there I go again! Well, without the 110s . . . you get the idea. Think positively, all this will pass.

With the rash of good weather here, we have been scheduled to fly every day for quite a while, but due to one thing or another, many missions have been scrubbed. When the Brass scrubs a mission, they must feel that idle hands and minds might foment a mutiny, so they invent things to occupy our susceptible minds. Practice missions, classrooms and V.D. movies are their favorites.

Things pop into my mind, besides thoughts of mutiny, so knowing your thirst for everything but the water on ole 628, I will put them down and hope they read better than your menu for dinner.

My father continues to offer his services to the military, and I keep telling him that WWI was enough and that he couldn't handle having to salute me. He feels that in my case, this would not be necessary. He is wrong.

The Salvation Army ladies (mostly British) are at the entrance to the briefing building after every mission. They dispense coffee, doughnuts and smiles to all of the crews as they trudge in to attend the briefing. I hope they know how thankful we all are, particularly for the smiles. In the briefings, we recount our tales of woe to an intelligence officer, and he and the others of his kind compile our information with other groups, wings and squadrons to come up with a composite picture of weather, flak, fighters, parachutes, 24s down and claims for enemy fighters shot down. To get confirmation on an enemy fighter, you need witnesses . . . so claims are always outnumbering confirms.

The Salvation Army brings to mind the American Red Cross . . . and comparing the two leaves the Red Cross looking pretty bad. The Red Cross charges us for everything, including cigarettes marked "a gift from the American people to their service men". That really gets my nanny goat and will reflect on my spirit of generosity when donations are being sought in the future. Another thing that bothers the troops is the Red Cross girls hobnobbing with officers, usually Majors and above. I know that pisses off the E.M. and some 2nd Lts. as well.

The schedule for tomorrow was just posted and we are on as I had expected. What I didn't expect was George Sloan, our ball turret gunner, being slated to ride with another crew whose waist gunner was killed. To me, with this thing I have about riding with another crew, this has an ominous feel. We did all we could to get him back and failed.

Enough for now; I shall return from tomorrow's flight and continue this chronicle of life and times in the ETO.

Much better we should have stayed in bed. We flew a real piss-cutter of a mission today to a wagon works in the middle of the town of Brunswick in Germany.   Take off and forming up the squadrons, groups and wings was accomplished without incident and turned out to be the only ray of sunshine all day. We flew across the Channel, as usual, and over the Dummer Lake flak installations. There are flak batteries concentrated over this entire area because we use Dummer Lake as a point of departure for many of the prime targets in Germany. We got peppered for about 20 minutes . . . lost two ships and a couple more were damaged, and had to abort for home. Incidentally, there is a lot of action going on out of my line of sight.

Our intelligence had briefed us to expect the possibility of 200 fighters and 300 flak guns in the immediate vicinity of the target. Most unfortunately, their prognostications were close to the mark today. After plowing through the lake barrage, we began to encounter Herr Goering's own yellow-nosed fighters as we approached the target. These guys are real tough, and when they rip through a formation, they frequently put a 24 down. At this point, our interphone was going hog wild, calling out fighters coming in from all directions. I spotted an ME-109 at our 9 o'clock, flying level with us, and I called to Sgt. Tietz in the top turret to watch him. He paced us for a minute or two and then turned in toward us and Tietz and the waist window got on him with a no deflection shot. We usually shoot short bursts to preserve ammo and gun barrels, but the guys held the triggers down for this ME, and he flew right into a torrent of 50 caliber armor piercing slugs. I could see the hits and he began to wobble and come apart. His canopy came off, and the pilot caught some of the 50s in his face and chest. He passed no more than ten feet below us and Frank picked him up again on the other side. The airplane began to break up . . . not blow up, just kind of disintegrated into small parts. I'll never know what that guy was thinking, probably to ram us or maybe he got sick of the whole damned war. He was sure a mess when he passed below us.

Everyone seemed to be shooting. The sky was full of vapor trails and smoke from burning airplanes. I saw a 24 blow up and others going down, burning. A 24 is hard to get out of when it's going down and seldom, if ever, do you see ten chutes open up. Five, maybe six, is usually tops. Today I saw few chutes.

At the I.P., we turned on the bomb run and flew straight and level, bomb bay doors open, then flak started. They were shooting barrage style. There was no need to pick out flights of four, just shoot, and someone in that mob of bombers was bound to get hit. We were about to drop when a huge cumulus cloud drifted over the target, obscuring it completely, and we were unable to drop. The Colonel ordered us to shut the doors and to go around for another attempt. It took about twenty minutes to hit the I.P. again with the bandits all over us . . . and it was almost a relief to straighten out on the bomb run, catch the flak and watch the fighters peel away. Just before bomb release, a formation of B-17s flew beneath us on their bomb run, and once again we could not drop. Our going around had screwed up the timing. Out of the flak and into the valley of fighters again rode the 600.

Once again our Colonel gave the order for another pass and got an earful of blue language from the pilots on the command set. The Colonel, however, was not to be denied. Ships were still going down, and to make matters worse, our escort had to leave because of fuel shortage. We must have looked like free lunch to the Jerries, who had been able to land, refuel and return to the fight.

We began our circle again with everyone screeching for fighter cover. Some fellahs in P-47s answered, asked our location and assured us they would be right along to chase the bad guys away. The 47s showed up and began to mix it up with a large disadvantage in numbers, and smoke trails began falling out of the squirming melee of fighters. I hope our guys got out of that mess alive . . . no one can tell me that the age of chivalry has died. We managed to get through and finally dumped the damned bombs. Just as we departed the target, an 88 went close to my starboard window. Luckily, the bulk of the flak was expended upwards, so we only got a few holes punched in the nose. One hunk that came in took the hide off the knuckles of my right hand.

George Sloan was riding a 24 off to our right a ways and they took a burst of flak in their starboard engines. They began lagging behind and losing altitude; and no one could go down and ride herd on them. The integrity of the defensive formation is more important than a single ship in trouble; a hard rule for many of us to live with. Two fighters jumped them as they began the last thirty miles or so before safety, over the channel. We were all yelling encouragement to them over the radios when they burst into flames and went down. Three chutes got out, but landed in the freezing water out of range for air-sea rescue. I don't know whether George got out or not, but it didn't make any difference anyway. George was the baby on the crew and this will devastate his mother. She lives in Pritchett, Colorado, and Shirley corresponds with her frequently. My feelings about riding with some other crew become a full-blown phobia. E.J. and now George. Damn, damn, damn!

Got back to base, out of gas and a lot worse for the wear and tear. After briefing, went to the mess hall, but could only handle coffee. A letter from my sister, Beverly, awaited me with news that Shirley is doing just fine and that we have a daughter, Dawn Marie. The Lord moves in mysterious ways, doesn't He?

This is the day after and no mission scheduled, so I used this free time to finish this letter to you and to reflect on yesterday. What were the Germans thinking as they saw those bombers come back again and again, disregarding those that were burning, falling or blowing up? Surely their fighter pilots must be aware that the Third Reich is not going to last 1,000 years and that Adolph has conned them into a no-win situation. I'm sure a lot of other Germans think this is no way to run a train, but I'm also sure a big bunch of them will continue to believe in the master race. I fear we are going to lose a lot more of our people before this is over . . . and I also fear we are going to have to lay waste to them before they holler "uncle."

I used to have a twinge or two of conscience when I dropped a load; no more. The quicker we destroy them, the better for all concerned. Germans will never be my favorite people.

I have been running off at the mouth a little too much here, so will cease burdening you with the inner man. We got another pass to London, went and returned to base the next day. Somehow, I couldn't get into a holiday mood. I did take in a production of "Panama Hattie", but it wasn't so hot. The girl sitting next to me was, so I watched her instead of Hattie.

Word has come down that our crew is being transferred to the 15th Air Force in Italy. Until I get further word on this, I'll get this off even though it only covers a few days. For the sake of our return to the happy hunting grounds on Sweeny's farm, keep your head out and your gun crew awake.

BEREAVED AGAIN IN BRITAIN

DEAR TRAUMATIZED TOGGELEER BILL—

I have your letter of 7 April to 10 April in my hot little hands and will answer piecemeal as time permits. I note that you had just received my letter of 14 Feb., so there are some letters lost or en route somewhere.

The German High Command is probably a group of nervous Nellies since you arrived on the scene, and now you say your bombing accuracy and dead reckoning have improved even more. Of the two skills, I suggest all possible energy applied to the dead reckoning. It's the thing that gets you home. If you're off a bit and merely circle England, at least you are still practicing!

So, your first mission was a success. Congratulations! It matters not if you destroyed the entire German fighter inventory or if you merely wounded some farmer's chicken. The important part is coming back . . . and I'm happy you made it because I need all the mail I can get.

The reaction of you and your crew seems perfectly logical to me. To see an FW190 (or anything else) approaching head-on and firing brings on a high level of emotion. When they say the legs turn to rubber . . . they've been there. I bet the P-47s looked like the answer to several prayers. That airplane seems to go on and on in spite of its age. I'm happy that your first brush awakened everyone to the idea that being alert and reacting is a lifesaver. I note that they, too, are scared.

It is noted that you successfully dropped most of your bombs, but that kicking out the last two was somewhat nerve-wracking. My God! I suggest you invite the ground crew personnel (who says it's easy?) to handle the bombs that hang up. Your tale of kicking them out sends shivers up and down my spine. Glad I'm not a fly boy! Please don't do it again.

I believe I last wrote following our second trip to Hollandia in New Guinea. Then it was back to the Admiraltys and Manus for loading and crew replacement. I believe I told you about the usual bad water and the resulting diarrhea . . . plus the shots for Black Plague. Anyway, the shots were very large and made the arm hurt . . . and then everyone got really sick. All this at a time when we continued losing sleep and had to reload combat equipment. This kind of a load has to be done in accordance with the wishes of the Army, so they get off what they want first. Meanwhile, a bulldozer does its best to keep the sand ramp out to the ship in good enough shape to be useful. Much of this is done at night in the dark, and a tank or heavy truck has to be backed up quite a distance on the sand ramp to the ship. Inevitably, one goes about half in the drink and then we wait until they can pull it out and start over. Tanks are placed on top of dunnage (mahogany planks from a sawmill ashore). Otherwise, they slide on the deck. Amongst all this, we took on our own supplies, which is hard work. Doing all this with diarrhea and a slight case of the Black Plague made me think seriously about my telling the Navy (about a century ago) that I wanted to see a little action. In any future interviews, I shall tape my mouth shut . . . unless it has to do with when I'd like to go home.

When loaded, we took off early one foggy morning and formed up with a small convoy for a trip of about a week. I noted that our convoy did not contain any great firepower and that is always unsettling. These small invasions seem to be carried out by us expendables . . . and I suppose if we don't make it, they'll try again. About 27 May, we arrived at that garden spot, a jewel of the Pacific called Biak. You may remember from your geography lessons that it ranks somewhat less in importance than New York, London, Berlin or Tokyo. It is a miserable, forbidding piece of sand and palms off the northwest coast of New Guinea. We took people in from the 41st division (Army), and it was not an easy one from our position. It was another case, in my opinion, of doing too damned much with too little. I believe every Jap on the island was killed (or killed himself), and the end was never in doubt. Still, very costly for a small group. We had some destroyers and some aircraft soften it up . . . and they continued with firing or bombing and strafing, as requested by the Army. It was hectic, and none of us felt very well, and hadn't for a couple of weeks. We unloaded without difficulty and made the return trip with a couple of other LSTs . . . unescorted. All is OK, except for the nerves. Our trip back to the "rear area" was ruined by the Japanese Air Force. They have airstrips all over the area, and it's hard to tell where they come from. They did little damage, but they sure do keep one on his toes.

The gunners in my division helped keep our guns clean, but no other work was done . . . save standing watches. These men look terrible, and I suppose I do, too. We are worn out, and I am constantly urging them to stay alert. Some don't seem to care anymore.

Now we're at anchor in an unprotected area and have to watch so the anchor doesn't drag. The water is deep and there are ships all around. It takes awhile to start and warm the engines and if the anchor does drag it gets a little hairy. We're pretty free to go ashore, but there's nothing to do but play checkers or cards. The novelty of watching the natives is pretty well old hat, but it is interesting how they live. The women have long, flat breasts and it seems that most of them over 12 years old have a baby on their backs. If the baby is hungry, the woman flips a breast over her shoulder and goes on working or walking. They hang around the Army, hoping to be given something valuable . . . and sometimes they bring bananas or other fruit to barter. We have the "bumboats" all around us, and the fresh fruit is most welcome . . . spiders and all. The army here has rigged a windmill with a Jap truck transmission for gears. On the bottom of the long shaft is a plunger in an oil drum. It is a washing machine. It takes awhile, but it works. The men put the clothes on wet. They'd be wet in a few minutes anyway. All this contributes to "Jungle Rot," which everyone has. Uncomfortable, but not life-threatening.

I'm aware from my other correspondents that Jim Welch and Jack Zweng are out here. Chuck Correll and Bob Campbell are in the merchant marine, and Chuck has been (lately) on the Murmansk run. Ugh! Would like to see any or all of them, but don't know how to locate them. I have lost at least four friends from my high school days. All of us are scattered all over the globe, and it will take a long time to talk it over when we meet again. I intend to be there!

We're unloading the trash we brought out of Biak and must clean up. In three days, we load again. Good God! What I'd give for a genuine sleep of over four hours.

The Navy (or MacArthur) reserves the right to change things. We are underway, empty, to load at another place. Suits me. Every day we waste in these "rear areas" means another day to recoup the attitude. Before we left, I visited a paint barge in a little bay and discovered the duty I'll request soon. An old chief boatswain's mate and two sailors lived on a barge about 60 feet long . . . loaded with paint and scrapers and chipping hammers, etc. We took what was available and brought it back in our boat. I personally saw to it that it all went under lock and key. We have some rust spots on our main deck that need attention. Now we're at our loading place, but will have a few more days of catch up before that takes place. These islands (around here) are pretty much the same. Here the girls wear grass skirts, and I think they'd look still better in long coats. The stark naked ones in New Guinea and elsewhere would do well to cover up and create a little mystery. How in hell the boys and girls get close to each other, I'll never know!

It's pretty hard to tell what happens to me next. I couldn't tell you if I knew, but we usually learn where we're going the day or so before we get underway. We all agree we should get a little break in the schedule if possible, but the guys running this show are not as tired as we are. Some of the men are practically out on their feet and look like zombies. I'd rather be home!

I'm thinking of writing Hitler and advising him of your shooting prowess . . . if I could send him some identification of your airplanes. I'm sure he'd order his boys to avoid you. After all . . . all's fair in love and war.

So send identification . . . it may shorten your war. Meanwhile, stay alert and drop your bombs only on the enemy.

ENOUGH OF THIS BILL

DEAR EXTREMELY, ETC.—

The last thing I did before leaving our base here was to stop by the mail room. Your further tales from the Palmetto patches, dated 7 May, 1944, were there, but I only had time to skim through before leaving. In the meantime, I'll keep a running commentary of things as they happen and answer your letter in depth when time permits.

As you are well aware, the volume of paper involved in a change of station is enormous. Turned into tissue and put on rolls, it could easily serve 10,000 butts during an epidemic of Montezuma's Revenge. Our lucky airplane will remain here, hopefully, to be as lucky for the next crew that flies her as she proved to be for us. We turned in all the equipment we had been issued and signed chits for what had disappeared. The Air Corps did not sign a chit for the hair, weight and shattered nerves that we are leaving with them. Two new men have joined our crew to replace E.J. and George Sloan . . . Lt. Leo Garrity Jr., a navigator from my own neighborhood in Chicago, and S/Sgt. George Clark from Boston. Clark pronounces his "A"s as if he had a tongue depressor in his mouth . . . unmistakably a Bostonian.

Lts. Cool and Sykes flew us down to St. Mawgum in southern England, and we checked into a seaside resort hotel, which featured fine beds, good food, comely waitresses and a friendly chambermaid. Eat your heart out, Wm.! Had lunch, processed again, had dinner and flaked out. The chambermaid appeared in the morning, fluffed the pillows, straightened the quilts and served us breakfast in bed. Four minds had but a single thought. She, to the contrary, went to the door, and using the English expression to have courage, "Keep your pecker up, Yanks", departed, unaware that that was, in our case, an imposing reality. We concluded processing and made arrangements for transport to Italy by air, and then adjourned to the beach. There were people in that frigid water, presumably having fun . . . they had to be part of the lunatic fringe, masochists at the least. A large cave under the cliffs served as a ladies bathhouse while the tide was out. We lurked around there until the tide came in. Around 11 o'clock P.M., we boarded a C88 (ATC designation for a B-24 converted for passenger service) and took off for Italy. The night flight cut down the possibility of interception by Jerry fighters. The converted 24 has none of the character or charisma of a combat-rigged ship. Box cars with wings.

Casablanca was our first stop after a long, cold night in the air. We landed, refueled while eating lunch and took off again . . . passing over the meeting place of F.D.R. and Churchill. This ATC plane operates like a milk train at home; stopping here and there for passengers or light cargo.

At Oran, we almost did a touch and go . . . just picking up a V.I.P. with a briefcase chained to his wrist . . . and immediately into the air again heading for Tunis. En route to Tunis, the hot sun and bumpy ride brought out the worst in the V.I.P. . . . he lost his lunch and what appeared to be last night's dinner all over his spiffy uniform, the briefcase and the seats adjacent to his. Long after he was helped out of the ship, his memory lingered on and on and on. Tunis had other sights to see besides the Ashen-faced upchucker. Hundreds of fighter aircraft (P-47s, P-38s, P-51s and Spitfires) literally covered everything but the runways. Jerry is in deep doo doo. Now, maybe the Pacific Theater will begin to get some needed armament.

Algiers showed up after darkness had set in, and the friendly flight crew from ATC dumped us out on the hardstand with the problem of finding the mess hall and barracks in the dark. Lugging our large and heavy B-4 bags, we located the mess hall, navigating by nose . . . the spoor reminiscent of that left behind by the V.I.P. Chow was an unmitigated disaster. Supply issued us cots (unassembled), blankets (of questionable vintage and use) and candles (one inch in length). Along with our B-4 bags, this made for quite a load. The barracks were still under construction, so locating an empty room was hazardous and slow due to the feeble glow from the candles. We finally located a room and assembled the cots by the light from our Zippos . . . the candles having sputtered out. We fell into an exhausted sleep, which was short-lived. A scream, right from the dungeons of the inquisition, snatched us from sleep and, by Zippo light, we saw Buck slashing and stabbing at a couple of large rats with the fourteen-inch shiv he carries in a shoulder sheath. He looked like King Arthur in jockey shorts. The rats escaped, but his blanket and cot sustained mortal damage. Dawn found him asleep in the wreckage.

In the A.M., I was unable to identify the chef's offerings, so settled for a couple of pieces of bread with peanut butter. We hopped a Gooney Bird (C-47) for the trip across the Mediterranean Sea destined for Naples. Clark was sick the whole way over, undoubtably a victim of the mess hall at Algiers. Upon arriving at Naples, Mac decided to stay a day or two before reporting to our new base. Our transportation was "as available" so, for the moment, H.Q. only knew we were en route somewhere. Good thinking by our pilot for not leaping into the breech once again until absolutely necessary.

After some finagling (and an understanding billeting corporal), we got quarters in a downtown hotel with running water and a view of the harbor. Garrity and I made a quick tour of Naples in what remained of the afternoon. Any preconceived pictures in my mind about romantic beautiful Napoli vanished. Feces were everywhere. The bank of Naples had a fresco of the stuff adorning their impressive entranceway. The harbor was full of cruisers, destroyers, and a host of smaller craft all pumping waste. The rocky perimeter of the harbor was a scenic outhouse with an Italian perched on every other rock, straining and grunting and waving to the swimmers in the water below. Truly sad to see.

Woke up about 8:00 A.M. and was propositioned by the linen maid before I could get my pants past my knees. Her three assistants were working the rest of the room and got one taker . . . a Texican who, ignoring the audience, jumped her bones. I am pathetically naive. Buck and I walked around most of the day peering into off-limit areas, sampling Vino and fending off hustlers of all ages and sexes. Early on, we learned not to get caught in a narrow street without store fronts or doorways. Army 6x6s tear through the streets, slowing down for no one or nothing. Word has it that many a pedestrian has gone to the "Big Pizza in the Sky" under their wheels. Combat will probably seem like child's play after surviving the action on these streets. After all, the Jerries don't jump out their planes, stiff you for your wallet, give you V.D., run you over with a truck and then give you the finger.

We returned in time to eat in the Army mess hall close to our quarters. For a wonder, it was pretty darn good, and we had a menu to choose from . . . limited, of course, but still a menu. Bringing up the rear has advantages completely unheard of by the front line dog faces. Hit the sack early, between clean sheets, of all things. Another dog-face dream.

Arose early and went out early before another dog-and-pony show got started. A blond (chemically acquired) Italian girl (English speaking) struck up a conversation with me and, at once, began to extol the superior fighting and frolicking qualities of the Italian and German soldiery. The Americans, of course, can't fight, frolic poorly and, furthermore, are depraved, disgusting and demented. Pappy told me never to strike a woman, even an Italian bimbo . . . so I beat an ignominious retreat and spent the balance of the day with the crew.

At 5:00 A.M., breakfasted at the air field, hopped aboard another C-47 and headed for Bari. En route, we circled over Vesuvius, a very handy gadget to have at a weeny roast. At Bari, another round or two with the processing people, and final assignment to a new group and squadron. My new address—

Lt. W.H. Alderson
449 Bb. G.P.— 719 Bb. Sqdn.
APO # 520 c/o PM —NYC, NY

From Bari, we journeyed by truck to Grottaglia, a six-hour trip over roads that were unaware that the wheel had been invented several hundred years ago. All ten of us and our luggage were tossed into the bed of a regular Army 6 x 6. The only way we avoided serious injury was to sit on or burrow into the B-4s and barracks bags, which were as lumpy as the road. The QM Sgt. at the 449th issued us cots and blankets and assigned tents, one for the officers and one for the E.M. We are located 150 yards north of the crew, so we're still neighbors.

The remainder of the day was spent housekeeping and getting the poop from group. It seems that 50 missions are needed here to complete a combat tour. They have a system of single and double credit missions flown, depending on distance and the intensity of the defense. We are to get double credit for all of our 8th Air Force missions, so 22 from 50 leaves 28. One does not have to be a Rhodes Scholar to realize that one is going backward faster than one is proceeding ahead. This equation, on top of being at the mercy of Italian roads in an Army 6 x 6, driven by a Brooklyn cab driver, left me feeling that this had not been one of my better days.

Things continued downhill . . . our permanent quarters is a tepee previously inhabited by Sitting Bull and his menage. Four cots and two packing cases just barely fit in, allowing no room on the dirt floor to roll around on buffalo robes with dusky Indian maidens. There is a 60-watt light bulb hanging from our lodge pole, providing far less heat and illumination than did Sitting Bull's camp fire. I am now going to get in the sack, draw the mosquito netting and hope that the creeping and crawling critters don't penetrate my perimeter and perform tribal rituals on my suffering body. I shall also, by light of yonder 60-watter, attempt to read and answer your letter as I had promised earlier on.

You and your gunners should be relieved of duty out there and returned stateside as instructors in Air Corps gunnery schools. I'll put a word in with Dugout in your behalf. By my count, that is the third enemy aircraft you have killed . . . and a Betty at that. I note that as you watched that sucker begin to burn and then explode as it hit the jungle, you had a feeling of excitement and satisfaction. I had the same reaction when we put down that ME-110, and often when I've dropped a load of bombs. To tell the truth, when a pheasant falls my feeling for the bird are a good deal more charitable than those I have for the Germans.

Those Jap mortars you describe remind me of the flak batteries at Pas de Calais. I sometimes think those 88 shells have eyes. Your predicament is undoubtably worse for being immobile as you are . . . and hearing and seeing them walk toward you relentlessly must chill you to the bone. If exposing yourself during these attacks comes with the territory . . . for God's sake, don't invite further scrutiny by making obscene gestures or shouting foul suggestions about their mothers. Let us not overdo this "Fearless Fosdick" stuff, the roosters are multiplying like mad in the north forty and awaiting our return with our trusty smoothbores.

For the most part, we get to sleep peacefully (if only briefly) at night. Such things as torpedo attacks and Banzai charges are thin on the ground around here and you guys are welcome to them. We are getting high temperatures here during the day, as has been your lot for so long. However, we lack the humidity that is so pervasive around the jungles. Our problem is to adjust to plus 100 degrees on the ground and minus 30 or 40 in the air. One extreme to the other.

I was feeling pretty proud about our covert supply requisitioning until your operatives liberated a jeep. Did you lift the jeep in one fell swoop, or did you do it the hard way by putting it together from scratch with purloined parts? Your crew is indeed one to sail with!

The home front is agog with the presence of the new baby. I am slowly adjusting to this fatherhood thing and thinking in terms of begetting a boy . . . should Shirley and the Germans cooperate. Fathering by heresay is surely not the same as hands-on experience, and I'm looking forward to giving it a shot.

I remain here camping on the old campground amongst chameleons, olives, Vino, snails and jackasses (rear echelon is everywhere). Take care.

SITTING BILL

DEAR BOMBER BILL—-

I just wrote a week or so ago . . . but we are still goofing around and getting some rest. It appears there has been a change of plans, and I don't know when we're leaving.

We now have the news of the invasion at Normandy and, even though details are sketchy, it appears to be going well. We're told the campaign in Italy is virtually over. It sure is great to hear good news. I hope you haven't been too busy and that all is OK. Now that you are on the move, then maybe we can get this miserable situation over. Our information comes from Army radio. We also heard some bombastic (and partly true) reports from Dugout Doug MacArthur, who is attempting to write the history of the Pacific War. Guess who the hero is? Quick victories due to phenomenal strategic planning . . . few or no casualties, and on and on. Methinks he is a pathological liar.

The thing that really amazes me is how absolutely isolated we are here. We've always had bits and pieces of local news . . . but a lot of it is mere scuttlebutt and we take it with a grain of salt. It seems that the world could come to an end and we'd be the last to know. If the war ends, will they tell us about it? We are here among stone-age people and living a cut above that. Logically, we are limited in our radio reception, and it is reserved for fleet exercises and orders. I guess we have just been on the move enough that we haven't talked with anyone who knew anything.

It would appear that you and your B-24s will be taxed to the limit with ground troops in France. Hope you get some airfields there so you can get better fighter protection. I'm anxious to hear from you and learn how it's going.

Heard that John Rodino is in Italy. Hope he's safe and sound. I wonder if they ever send anyone home.

Not much to report from here. We are moving around Manus, the Admiralty Islands and New Guinea. The distances are pretty great for a slow ship, and our average jaunt is five to nine days. We all agree that the days and nights at sea are pure heaven, compared to the time in "port". "Port" usually means some miserable beach, and we nose up on the sand and are stuck there . . . and work begins and doesn't end until we hit the road again. We laughed when we came in here. There were two pretty long bamboo piers or docks . . . the first we've seen since God knows when. They were built for fishing and for fishing boats by the local unskilled carpenters. Anyway, they certainly served the purpose until we came in. There was a pretty strong cross current, and one LST wiped out a whole dock. We didn't hit the other, but we didn't get very close either. The piers were worthless for our purposes. One is now worthless for any purposes! We see the same ships and the same islands endlessly, but seldom have a chance to talk with anyone but the Army. We did, awhile back, carry a couple of piper cubs (I think) and their pilots, and they were interesting. They were spotters and circled at slow speed and low altitude, directing fire from ships or artillery. They look like they could be brought down by the average BB gun . . . or perhaps even your shotgun. It brings to mind that few of us are happy with our lot, but the other guy's job doesn't look very good either.

All of which brings my rattled mind to food. I think both you and I agree that everyone bitches about food. When I first entered the Navy, I heard guys complaining about food that was perfectly good . . . and I wondered if these people were accustomed to three meals per day at the Waldorf. I am not especially choosy, but it seems that for months now we are having a great deal of mutton from Australia. It tastes like wet wool smells and is not particularly tender. A meal of this with hydraulic potatoes and maybe some canned green things known as vegetables doesn't always hit the spot. Another I would never dream about is liver. I can't eat it. You guessed it . . . we have a corner on the liver market, and the cook seems to like it. I have spoken pointedly to our supply officer, who says he takes what is available. I have grown to tolerate the weevils in the bread (much protein they say), and I eat the powdered eggs with the green tinge on them, and I swallow my atabrine regularly. I also do not complain . . . others have it worse, and it must be a hell of a job getting it to us. At another time, I'll devote an entire letter to my opinion of Spam as a steady diet. Obviously, it's a Japanese invention furnished free to any enemy. In jolly old England, you may have some fare that is a little different, too, but please don't tell me about your gourmet dining at the fine hotels. While on this mundane subject, I should mention that we get some canned stewed chickens that are pretty well shredded in broth, and it is delicious. Even makes the potatoes taste like potatoes. A real delicacy is canned fruit cocktail, and that takes me to my next paragraph.

When we're at sea, I keep good track of the course and distance to the nearest land . . . I'm a pessimist. How I'd ever get there is beside the point. We have several life rafts and two Higgins boats. I have a life jacket and can swim. The life rafts have fishing equipment, medical supplies and wood water casks. It dawned on me recently that the water in the casks might be pretty stale, and even our water purification pills might not handle it. We had good fresh water aboard, so I inspected the water casks. I found that most of our missing fruit cocktail was fermenting in the wood casks, and there was no water on the life rafts. The brew was like a fine liquor. And I wondered, if we sank, whether this might be better than water. Some nosy individual passed the word, and we dumped all the booze and refilled with water. Still, it is exceptionally good tasting water. It took me a couple of days to learn that one of our older sailors from Kentucky is the brewer and is experienced . . . and, I think, extremely talented. I had a talk with him and learned it had been going on quite awhile and that only a few knew about it. He confessed that another batch was brewing in the chain locker . . . a very difficult place to enter. The moonshiner feared a stretch in the Brig, but we worked out a compromise wherein he remains unknown, but must submit his brew to the taster when it's done. I am the taster.

Yesterday, I took a leisurely ride along the shore with some of the Army. Several of us hung precariously on a road grader and traversed the black sand and exclaimed at the beauty of the mangrove thickets and colorful parrots. Our driver was pretty quiet, but on the way back, he told everyone to hang on as he moved the throttle to full speed. We raced back at a good honest 3 mph, with the wind in our hair and the sweat evaporating from our clothes. Wonderful . . . good to get away from home now and then. Good God . . . I really mean it!

I am giving some thought to becoming listless and inefficient, with the idea they might transfer me to Washington, D.C. We are a pretty close-knit group, and the Captain ruined my idea. Apparently, it's his plan, too, and I am placed near the end of the line. Pretty soon, the Germans will learn that you are flying over them and they'll give up. I doubt the Japs will ever give up. They certainly aren't around here. An Army Captain who has questioned some of the few Jap prisoners, says they like the food, but fear ever returning home because they will be marked for life as one who surrendered.

We're seeing more Hellcats now, and it's a good feeling. I'm told there is a big new bomber in the region . . . B-29. We don't see many bombers, but B-17s bring the mail. I think they are all busy working over airfields, but I must say the airfields are repaired pretty quickly.

Another day in limbo. Not much to do but sit and wait. I guess this is what I prayed for a week ago, but it is monotonous. Time to think isn't always good.

Take good care of yourself and give 'em hell. I guess we're both making progress toward the end of this thing, but it does seem slow and costly. If I had a beer, I'd drink a toast to the 8th air force.

Do write!

BECALMED BILL

Tues. 14 June 1944 to
Fri. 23 June 1944

DEAR BILL—-

The quick change of station I just made has, no doubt, slowed the mail down even more than usual, so I'll send this off probably before I get your next letter.

Bailed out of the sack at 6:30 A.M. for one reason only . . . no breakfast served after 7:00 A.M. We approached the mess hall from down wind and knew then that getting up had been a mistake. After viewing the source of the ill wind (the sausage), I settled for bread, butter and coffee. Not only was that stuff offensive to the nose, but in appearance it could have been the discards in Lovers Lane after the senior prom.

Later on, Mac got directions to the equipment graveyard, and we collected some odds and ends to make the Wickiup more tolerable. A discarded five gallon oxygen bottle became our water tower, and some old fuel line tubing connected the bottle to our packing case wash stand. A couple of helmets serve as basins. We whacked some nails into the lodge pole to hold clothing, gas masks, pistols, etc., and . . . Voila, a home in the suburban wastelands. Our crew stole lumber for their floor and, with other exotic carpentry, made our efforts look pretty barbaric . . . proving us chiefs don't know home remodeling from buffalo chips.

Temperatures run in the nineties here most of the time, which is a welcome relief after freezing our butts off in the air. The ground is as hard as cement with long, bottomless cracks running hither and yon. Little lizards dash back and forth from crack to crack. Snails are everywhere, and they shinny up ropes, tents, cots and mosquito netting, leaving a shiny trail of mucous behind them. The rest of the wild life is airborne, solo and in formations . . . and enthusiastically attacks any exposed skin.

You will be thrilled to learn that we have our own private outhouse, without the house. It is a splintery one-hole packing case located 100 feet to the east of the tent and 50 feet south of a narrow gauge R.R. commuter line. Big on ventilation, small on privacy.

Several of the men from surrounding tents stopped by to introduce themselves and to check out the new kids on the block. They don't appear to be too friendly and seem to think we see ourselves as prima donnas having migrated south from the 8th Air Force. The 8th gets most of the publicity, and these guys resent the implication that their war here is an easy one. The single and double credit system for missions do nothing to diminish that appearance. We assured them that the only prestige we wanted was to end up in one piece with a ticket for home. After all, when you climb into a 24 and start down the runway, any one of a hundred Gremlins can kill you, no matter where you are . . . even at home. The Germans just make it a lot iffier.

I had occasion to use our commode today (something devoutly wished for before flying and once again testing the reliability of your sphincter muscle) and was perched thereon when I heard a train approaching. Looking up, I saw what is best described as a Toonerville Trolley. It snorted down the tracks at an impressive 10 m.p.h., humanity jamming the inside of the car and an equal bunch festooning the sides and roof. I hustled into my pants, forgetting hygiene for modesty's sake, but apparently too late. Every wench on that thing had a remark to make . . . all in Italian of course. Well, maybe they were compliments and I was unnecessarily modest. It does pay to advertise.

Our second wedding anniversary came and went with no resemblance whatever to the first. I had sent money to my father for flowers and an explicit reminder of the date. Otherwise he might have sent them on the day I enlisted . . the dates are very close. Shirley would have viewed that much the same as discovering a buffalo chip in the punch bowl.

Lately, I have been having some nasty chest pains . . . and this morning walking and breathing got too tough to handle. Mac and Buck lugged me down to the dispensary, where the doctor advised me that I might have Pleurisy, gave me some pills and advised me to go bask in the sun. So much for 10 years of schooling. The pilots lugged me back to the tent and dropped me on my cot in the sun. The next day, barely ambulatory, I reeled down to the doc and ended up in an ambulance bound for Manduria, 15th A.F. H.Q. Stood in line two or three hours waiting for processing and X-rays. Fortunately, I was not bleeding arterially or I would have cashed in before reaching the head of the line. The X-rays showed me to be healthy as can be . . . and the Major in charge suggested it was all in my head and that I was malingering. One thing led to another and the Major became quite inflamed over my shouted remarks about his physique, his family tree and his heroics far from the combat arena. Two M.P.s conducted me to a returning ambulance, along with a hot letter to my C.O. . . . who, in turn, had me repeat my conversation with the Major, verbatim. The C.O. then got off a letter to the Major's C.O., indicating that no C.S. paddle foot was going to accuse one of his men of malingering. Much, much ado about nothing.

Sun bathing does help, and I am once again my formidable self. Sgt. Tietz, out on a scrounging mission, came upon a sack of onions that fortuitously fell off a parked supply truck. Clark sweet talked some K.P.s into providing bread and butter, so the crew invited us down for a feast. We all sat around hogging onion sandwiches and hoping we would not fly the next day. Onions talk back at 20,000 feet.

It figures, the next A.M. at 2:30, the wake-up Corporal came by and we briefed for a mission to Trieste. Our target was a tank farm and oil refinery, and we dropped a mixture of 500 pounders and gasoline-rubber fire bombs. They were very effective because we could see a towering column of smoke for 70 or 80 miles after leaving the target. The flak was light, and only two timid fighters showed and did not choose to contest the formation. This amounted to a milk run by 8th Air Force standards. Our crew was concerned about the loose formation flying and inattention of the gunners. In the 8th, if the Jerries didn't get you for that, the Colonel would. Mac complained about it at the post-mission briefing. We landed early on in the afternoon and were greeted by some pretty girls (American) who served us fruit juice and doughnuts. This was more than welcome to our crew because of the residual antics of our onion binge. The girls were Red Cross and, unbelievable as it may sound, the goodies were for free.

On a non-scheduled day, we took the opportunity to visit Grottaglia. It is small and not very neat or clean. Most of the homes are kind of a 1-1/2 storied building, with the livestock occupying the street level and the household plunder and family the upper area. Herds of goats roam the streets, with the goatherd bringing up the rear. Goat milk is sold on the hoof, and when a customer appears, he (the goatherd) chases down a likely looking female and drains her crankcase right on the spot. The kids (people kids) are a sorry-looking lot by our standards. Many of them are afflicted with running sores, probably due to the lack of personal hygiene and medical attention. Determining the sex of the children up to about 10 years of age is easy . . . they don't wear pants. I'm not knocking these people, but for an accident of birth, there go I.

For a real change of pace, we hopped a truck to the beach and enjoyed ourselves immensely. The Mediterranean was as blue as pictured in the travel brochures, and warm and calm enough to make swimming quite pleasurable. The sea was bordered by a wide beach of gold-colored sand, perfect for fun in the sun. Except for the roar of B-24s passing by overhead, the war could have been on another planet.

The same snotty wake-up Corporal came by in time for us to attend the briefing for a strike against Munich. Better we should have stayed in bed.

We flew at 21,000 feet with a bomb load of twelve 500 pounders. As we approached the target, we stirred up a nest of fighters and fought them off with no casualties within the scope of my vision. They were not as aggressive as Herman's yellow-nosed 109s . . . almost tentative. The flak at the target was extremely heavy, with the largest bursts I have yet seen. One burst went off fifty feet in front of us, and when we hit the pall of black smoke, it turned day into night for an instance. The blast effects from close bursts would rattle every loose piece of equipment and bounce the airplane and its unhappy occupants. The splinters that found their way into our ship were all long, ragged jobs weighing perhaps six ounces or more. I am not an artilleryman, but those guns must have been 155 mm or 205 mm stuff if I have my sizes right.

The flak was concentrated in a horseshoe-shaped configuration, with the bend in the shoe to the north . . . and our briefed course took us up and around the bend. The lead ship dropped his load, and we all followed suit and then continued on our predetermined course . . . which the Germans had also predetermined. We were taking a hell of a shellacking in the middle of the horseshoe bend when Mac came on interphone and said we were going to get the hell out of this mess forthwith. He dropped the nose, banked about 45 degrees to the left and descended about 5,000 feet at red-lined airspeed. I thought we were alone, but looked back a couple minutes later and saw the rest of the group barreling ass, right behind us. The Major in command continued on the briefed course with eight or ten other ships, losing one. Mac had his fanny chewed out when we got back, but it was not a real spirited reaming . . . probably because of the loss of a ship on the prescribed course.

After the mission, people from the other crews dropped by our tent to visit; a backhanded way to compliment our pilot, Mac, who said, "I made a prudent change in our flight plan, mainly because I was scared shitless". It would appear that we are accepted here, at least by some who want to get home in one piece, flight plan or not.

Up and at 'em on a relatively easy mission to Osijek in Yugoslavia. Trips like this one tend to make me feel as if 50 missions might be attainable. The bombing was very good today, and we bracketed the target with twelve 500 pounders from each airplane. We left the target area burning fiercely, and the only opposition encountered was light flak over the target. Even amongst light flak, it only takes one, so what am I happy about?

Intelligence cautions us to be sure to avoid landing or bailing out over territory controlled by Tito and his merry men. It seems that nothing pleasures them more than shooting Americans. All of our charts have these areas marked, and we are to go to any lengths to avoid coming down in those places. Should your luck run out and you end up in such a spot, we have been advised (by the rear echelon) to shoot anyone with a red star on his hat before he shoots you . . . the idea (rear echelon) is to get as many of them as you can before they get you.

We all fly armed to the teeth now. I carry my own .32, as well as the issue .45, and some guys carry trench knives or bayonets. I think we are all kidding ourselves. Beyond 20 feet, I don't think any of us could hit Yugoslavia, much less a guy with Mayhem in his eye . . . or, for that matter, stick a knife in a guy when he's totin' a rifle and pissed off at you for waving a shiv at him. The rear echelon must be smoking Chinese water pipes in the local chop suey joint.

We have been briefed from time to time for a mission to Ploesti, and it has been canceled each time. There must be a wild hair running amok in H.Q.'s collective shorts about Ploesti. Rumor has it that the next time, it will be a go. Should rumor become reality soon, I'll post this now so we can both sweat out that particular trip and the action it portends.

Onward and upward! Be careful—-

QUICK DRAW BILL

23 June, '44

DEAR WINO BILL—

Happy Day! I've got mail . . . including yours of 11 April to 19 April. I don't keep track of when I start or finish a letter. Sometimes, weeks go by and I write a little when I can. I am handicapped by what can be told and I know you are, too. It seems to me that the Postal Service is doing a great job, but it does help us to go to a "rear area" to get it.

I am not surprised that you get little in the way of news from out here. Of course, being in England might be part of it, but I just feel we are more or less the forgotten ones. There has been a lot of action north of us, but I suppose that our smaller invasions are not very newsworthy. Then, too, Dugout Doug's communiques dwell mostly on his stellar planning and quick conquests without casualties . . . so why worry?! I can't help but feel for those who lose someone on these forgotten, rotten islands . . . and can't even find it on a map.

Yes, my overindulgence at the Guadalcanal picnic was poor planning. Straight alcohol acts rather quickly and is not very tasty. Wish I were back there now.

I note that your visits to the officer's club after dinner have introduced you to the Port wine. I tried it once or twice and especially liked Tawny Port. No doubt it is perfect for your medicinal use, and it should calm the nerves if you take enough of it.

Our worm-infested cigars were smoked without attempting to remove the stowaways. The result was a nutty flavor that might become a best seller to the uninitiated who knew not from where the flavor came. Perhaps a good business opportunity when this unpleasantness concludes.

I can't imagine that I would be filled with joy in your lifestyle. Between the flak, the fighters and the cold, plus the mistrust I have for the flying boxes, I would rather just go home. All this, plus getting lost or separated from the others, would give me fits. Sorry to hear that parachuters are not always treated well . . . perhaps you can arrange for some insignia suggesting you are a chaplain. It might be possible for you to obtain a piece of heavy steel to sit on . . . and wear a metal boxer's cup in your jock strap. You might have to leave one bomb at home, and you might fly with a slight list, but at least the family jewels would be preserved. I'm sure the 8th Air Force would understand. I would also suggest some armor plate wrapped around your office in the aluminum box.

You are correct that dropping those bombs is nicer than catching them. The 4th of July aspect is OK at a distance, but when they fall close, they shake hell out of everything. I doubt I've ever heard a large bomb, but the little ones are scary. When they hit a ship, they absolutely mutilate all the bystanders. There's no place to hide, and they are going to either get you, or they aren't.

I note that you, too, arrange to "requisition" various comfort items not issued to the peasants. I am happy to learn we are not the only thieves. The barter system works like a charm here, and one man's junk is another's treasure. One's wants are so simple as to be laughable sometimes.

Things are looking up a bit here. We unloaded our combat load at a quiet place and have returned to a fairly quiet place. I can't remember where I was when I last wrote and cannot say where I am now, but we have had some time on our hands. I must be nuts, but I would like to get on with it and get it over. I know it's coming, but I don't like the limbo of this existence.

Another R & R opportunity recently . . . a whole afternoon ashore with games and liquid refreshments. Every man was allowed two warm beers, and I was able to negotiate a deal with some of our nondrinkers. My attitude is that they should not start drinking now, but it would be a shame not to use the beer. I'm happy to report that our crew won the baseball game and, more importantly, the fight afterward. Actually, the fight started slightly before the game ended, but we were ahead at the time. A crew member from another LST complained about being hit by a wild pitch, and it went from there. Our boatswain's mate, who has boxed in college and professionally, was a standout at the fight, but is only so-so at baseball. I noted that no one tried to stop the fight, and the fighters were hoping someone would. When they all got tired, they just quit. I did not participate in the fisticuffs, partly because I was unofficially a chaperon and partly because I had to protect my beer. I feared someone might fall on it, and I would have only warm foam. As the sun sank in the west, I led my boys to the boats, and the tattered, bruised and bandaged bodies found their ways to the chow line or their rack. I was proud of them. They are a team and they think they are the best and toughest crew in the Navy. I believe they may be right.

We are beginning to see F4U Corsairs now, and we hear of B-29s in the area north of us. This is good news. The Corsairs look great, and we're hoping for more . . . and more. Nobody seems to know where the Jap Navy is, but I'm sure they'll come out someday, and they are good. I have wondered how a small nation could muster such an Army and Navy as to be all the way from China to near Australia and Alaska. Many of their soldiers are rotting on several of these islands. It is unsettling to realize that we "own" strips of beach, and perhaps an airstrip, and that thousands of Japs are in the jungle watching our every move. They won't give up and usually choose not to attack, but we don't dare go inland, either. I have spent some evenings with the Army and must say that Yankee ingenuity is alive.

As night falls, sentries are placed out on the perimeter, and the rest of the men sleep or gather to talk or play cards. They have portable generators and rig lights in tents covered with tarps or in trucks. No lights can show, and they are good about not smoking because a cigarette is a beautiful target at night. The weather has been good and, except for bugs, the nights are pleasant enough. The sentries have a hell of a watch with all the jungle noises, and they are alone and must stay alert. It is nerve-wracking, and trying to approach a nervous sentry to relieve the watch is life-threatening. They sometimes have radio contact, but you probably know by now how much you can depend on radios. We listen to Tokyo Rose, who can tell us where we've been and where we're going . . . she's often correct. Good to hear a woman's voice. I remember!

Remember the square wheeled trains and the sandwiches seasoned with coal dust? Remember the long lines for uniforms, chow . . . short-arm inspection? How about the lack of freedom to get off the base? Or finding that your favorite spot is now off limits? All that was pure heaven, and we should have enjoyed every minute of it. I almost dare not think of the years before all that.

"Piss Call Charlie" hit an ammo dump the other night, and several soldiers were wiped out. Everything blew, and debris was everywhere. It was close enough to bring on that kind of fear one is ashamed of. Every ship opened up on Charlie, but nobody hit him. Those among us who have been sleeping through Charlie's night time fun are reminded that every now and then he hits something.

The following night, I awoke to the general quarters alarm and assumed Charlie was back. When we are on the beach, we have a stern anchor out. It is on a big cable rather than a chain. We had some pretty good rollers coming in at our stern and lifting it. As it lifted, the anchor cable came out of the water, and it looked to our stern watch like a torpedo wake. No matter that the wake moved away rather than toward us. It was worth the excitement and loss of sleep to know the guy on watch was awake . . . and nervous.

Going to sea tomorrow . . . thank the Lord! Times in port are hectic and unpredictable. This time, we'll learn where we're going after a convoy forms up. In my dreams, the convoy will consist of us and 50 battleships and 100 carriers . . . and the course will be set for San Diego. I dream very well! I am numb. I have no emotion. I wonder if all this will end soon enough that I can be a civilian again and walk the streets of a real city with real people. Do you ever feel like this?

This must go in the mail bag. We are all buttoned down and ready to go . . if we can get off the beach!

Take good care of yourself and try and hit something with your bombs. Learn to speak German and how to make soft landings sans plane.

EXPENDABLE BILL

Sat. 24 June 1944 to
Fri. 30 June 1944

DEAR TIRED OF IT ALL—

Yours of 17 May, '44, arrived here today, the 24th of June. I skimmed through your letter to make sure your health remains robust and will answer with my comments about your further adventures and misadventures as soon as time and my trembling fingers permit. Meanwhile, I'll fill you in our efforts to bring the axis to its collective knees.

Today, the 24th, at 3:00 A.M., we went through the rigamorole of briefing and then waiting for the green flare from the control tower to send us once again into the wide blue yonder. After sitting in the airplane for two or three hours, ready to start engines, we were scrubbed. I no longer complain about cancellations, feeling that our number may very well have come up, and kind Providence has stepped in and saved our bacon. To calm our abused ganglion, Buck and I went to town and made the acquaintance of an elderly wine merchant. He sells his ambrosia directly out of a large cask on his donkey-drawn two-wheel cart. We bought a round for ourselves and our vintage bartender at a nickel a cup. That red vino is a fooler. It is clear-looking and slightly sour to the taste. The first cup makes you think you could drink the stuff all day, but the second cup ambushes you. My gums shrank away from my teeth, and my larynx became paralyzed. For two bits, you could be on a boat headed for home in the D.T. ward with a medical discharge. There were two public urinals in downtown Grottaglia. The bulkheads start at the knees and end about shoulder high on a short man. The gents stand inside, tipping their hats to passing ladies, while their specimens cascade down the bulkheads and into the gutter where small boys are sailing their paper boats.

On the 25th, we hit Bradislava in Yugoslavia. The mission took us over four countries: Yugoslavia, Germany, Hungary and Czechoslovakia. The target was an oil refinery, and our 400 bombers gave the enemy a pretty good lickin'! Black, oily smoke pillared up to 17,000 feet as we were leaving the target and later strike photos showed great amounts of destruction.

Flak at the target was moderate, but well aimed, and we took some light damage. The fighters, on the other hand, were out in force and intensely aggressive. Most of the bandits were JU-88s with a sprinkling of Italian fighters. The JUs are twin-engine planes and do not have the capability for speed and agility that the FWs and MEs are cursed with. We fly diamond-down four ship elements with three ships in an arrow shape and the slot plane below the others (behind leader) and far enough down to avoid the turbulence from the #1 ship.

We were flying slot today, and a JU-88 had been dogging us for a while, lobbing cannon shells at our rear end . . . hoping for a lucky hit. Jake Jacobczek, in our rear turret, would give him a burst now and then to keep him at a respectable distance, but was getting pissed off at the cat and mouse game . . . Jake being the mouse. We could see some of those 20 mms zipping past us, and there was no joy in Mudville, for Casey could strike out.

Our intrepid gunner then came up with an idea on how to bell the cat. He let his twin 50s point upwards, as if he or the turret had been hit and was out of action. The Jerry watched for a while and then began to sneak up on us to administer the coup-de-grace. Jake was talking to us through the interphone, as this little game unfolded . . . a real nail-biter. The Jerry got to about 500 yards out and Jake brought his guns down and really poured it to him, a no-deflection shot. The German got a mess of 50s in both engines and the cockpit area. He wobbled a bit, began to burn, and then blew up in a nifty ball of flame and smoke. The kill was confirmed, and our crafty Sgt. Jake was duly credited.

The formation flying here is still too loose, and someone is going to pay the price one of these days. Double credit on that one, twenty more to survive.

Ploesti, or "Ploeski" as Mac calls it, is still appearing regularly on the board, and as regularly is being put off, weather apparently not cooperating. This Ploesti thing has a real ominous sound to it. The first mission there was a disaster, and losses were enormous . . . I have heard 80%. The 93rd, our group in England, was on that one shortly before we joined them and suffered <u>heavy</u> casualties. I am glad for these delays, but there will come a day, I am sure. The delays allow for sunning, and I am now the same color as Sitting Bull and will be known as Sitting Bill as long as my tan holds up. I believe I signed off that way in a previous letter.

Someone popped a chute by accident and discovered that the canopy was riddled with holes, as if a giant moth had been nibbling away. All chutes were turned in for repacking and others were found to be damaged. Speculation has it somebody stuck a hypodermic containing acid of some kind into the innards of the chutes. This is not inspirational in any way. Bailing out is chancy enough without having to worry about a colander on strings jumping out when you yank the cord. If it ain't one thing, it's always something else, in spades.

The monotony of scrubs was finally broken, and we flew a mission to northern Italy on the 28th. The lead navigator and bombardier snafued the whole thing and home we came, bombs and all . . . and no credit, of course. We ran all the risks and struck out. Sitting Bill is tired of playing with his pemmican and would like to go on the warpath again. Lord, please make it a small warpath.

Ploesti, this time, we managed to take off and get about 50 miles from the base before being recalled, not without loss, however. The Germans have a neat little trick they use to interdict our lines of entry and departure. Flak trains. These batteries are mounted on flat cars, and they move them around to bisect our routes. For the most part, they are ineffectual, but today they got lucky. One of the 24s a flight or two in front took a burst and started down in flames. Nine chutes got out before it blew, and then fate took a hand.

One lad pulled his rip cord too soon after exiting the aircraft. His chute deployed OK, and he began to descend in good order. When the ship blew, a flaming bit of the wreckage hit his chute and started it afire. As the fire devoured more and more of his chute, the faster he fell. In no time at all, he was making a free-fall. What in God's name was he thinking about as he watched his canopy disappear? He had a long, long way to fall. I'll tell you, Bill, that one really bothered me.

On the 30th, we finally did get to "Ploeski." Some nutty Air Corps photographer accompanied us, breathing fire and brimstone and in a perfect sweat to film flak and fighters . . . particularly fighters. I'm sure this twit didn't have the foggiest notion about what his thirst for combat footage would get him into . . . his cup may very well runneth over. Duncan and Clark got him rigged up and put him in the waist where he could see everything, while the cool -30 degree breeze fanned his fevered brow. When they took him through the parachute drill, they added some gloomy and exaggerated stories about hypodermic injections. The guy's cup was half-full . . . and we were still on the ground!

Ploesti is a long flight, and we were about an hour from the target before encountering opposition. Enemy fighters showed up then and were with us the rest of the way to the target and for a while afterwards. Clark told me later that the Photog had been hopping from one window to the other, doing his thing until one ME bounced some 30 calibers off our left wing. He then tried to dig a fox hole in the deck. While the Photog burrowed, Tietz in the top turret, Duncan in the waist, and Jake in the rear, all took a pop at him. Jake claimed we damaged him as he left trailing a little smoke. We got in a few more licks at others, but no damage to either side.

That was the only real bad moment until we reached the oil fields, and the flak began in no uncertain terms. We had been aware of the black pall over the target long before we got there. Once into it, the sky was black and blue with bursts and hundreds of red flashes announcing the arrival of more. I had thought I had built up an uneasy tolerance for flak, but nothing I had seen before came close to this . . . it was damned scary. We chugged through it for several minutes with a lot of near misses. We must have actually rocked from concussions fifty times. The Photog came out from under the flak suits, took a few shots and, like the groundhog, returned to his burrow.

We emerged from the maelstrom alive and with only a few dings . . . a lucky happenstance, which minutes before I would have given long odds against. Some of the others were not as fortunate and went down, usually burning, with very few chutes to be seen. In that mess, a parachute is no guarantee either.

The three other ships in our box of four must have thought we were on a training mission. None of them saw the first ME that bounced us, and on one ship, I didn't see the guns move during the whole trip. The formation was loose and sloppy and, unless they tighten up, they are going to kill somebody else as well as themselves. The formations are designed to provide maximum protection for all the ships, and one sloppy guy endangers all. The Germans are trying enough to kill us without any help from assholes like that. Mac and Buck raised hell at the post- mission briefing, to what avail is highly questionable.

When we parked and shut things down at the base, the fire-eating member of the fourth estate took off without so much as a thank you for his entertainment. I'll bet he concocts a story that will make him the toast of bars, boudoirs and brothels on an international scale. I took a shower, shaved and felt pretty frisky about walking away from that one. By the way, we try and shave every day because whiskers in the oxygen mask drive you goofy, particularly if ice forms in the mask.

Eureka!!! A day off . . . no flying, not even a scrub. Before I reply to your 17th of May, a few comments on some of the contents of my letters. I am sure you will not infer from my funnin' around that this is anything other than a flat out serious business over here. Trying to see the humorous side of things in an otherwise very unfunny war is my way to avoid the white coat and rubber walls. I notice that you, too, seem to use a similar life preserver. I would not want anything I say to detract from the accolades the combat crews deserve. That applies equally as well to your guys and all the rest who are doing the real fighting, and to some limited extent, the much maligned rear echelon. The aplomb with which the combat troops (air, sea and land) face hours and days of cruel discomfort and mortal danger, is extraordinary. They are a credit to themselves, as well as to their flag. Writing back and forth as we do, with a view to the lighter side, helps keep the other aspects of the job from grinding me down to the nub.

You mention having memory lapses, yet you can trot the length of the ship with elephantine accuracy to the hidey hole where the calendar girl wantonly displays her bare bottom. All is not yet lost . . . you don't need a memory when your hormones respond instantly as they do to the slightest stimulus, be it real (Nurse Ruth), or mere calendar art. Someday, after this period of enforced celibacy, you will return home prepared hormonally to restore your memory bank as you sweep through sorority row leaving shrieks of gratitude in your wake. My memory, too, is becoming just a memory. My hormones also bubble away just beneath my outwardly placid self, and I'm afraid Shirley won't get off the front porch before I restore our mutual memory banks . . . as well as providing the neighborhood the spectacle of my hormones in their finest hour.

Glad to hear you are getting a little time off in Hollandia, away from Mortars, Zeros and the like. Picnicking up a lazy river sounds like the perfect way to soothe one's nerves and put the war behind one . . . if only for a few hours. You, however, find enemy caves, AWOL still operators with guns panning for gold, and unclothed women dropping out of stilt houses giggling and making obscene gestures. So much for soothing one's nerves. Off you go the next day, picnicking this time on a sandy beach with Nurse Ruth and her companion, Florence Nightingale. Be a little understanding about striking out . . . not withstanding your clean undies and the pint of aftershave lotion. Nurse Ruth probably knew about the harsh abrasiveness of sand, should hormones get out of control. My suggestion would be to return to the chow line and invite the scowling officer in charge to join you on the beach. She sounds mean enough to love abrasion.

Back to the more mundane side of life on "Ole 628." You and your crew splashed another Zero, and that is four by my reckoning . . . one more and you will be aces. Come fly with me. It is nice to see your frustrations from abortive picnicking being put to such good use.

As you load up men and equipment prior to getting under way, don't wonder if it will be a lucky number. Believe it . . . believing will make it so. I await your next letter. I hope like hell you get another from me (just a little play on words).

BELIEVING BILL

Sun. 2 July 1944 to
Tues. 11 July 1944

DEAR ENOUGH OF THIS——

The Post Office and, probably, lucky happenstance on mail flights combined to get another letter to me in what was record time. Yours of 11 June made its appearance here on 4 July, a day in my former life as a civilian that was celebrated by shooting loud and colorful pyrotechnics into the sky. The Germans here try real hard to make us feel right at home in that regard. It will be unnecessary for you to identify our airplane to Adolf; we are trying to be anonymous, and calling his attention to our deadly skill with gun and bomb might prove to be counterproductive. Knowing the Navy's affinity for paint and its enthusiastic application of the stuff on every visible surface, I thought you might have some that would render us invisible. If so, skip the note to Adolf and send the paint.

That shot you got to ward off the Black Plague sounds like the one we got at San Antonio, or some such place. Our arms hurt unbelievably for two days. I note that, during this immunizing period, you continued to load combat gear, stand watches, etc. I don't know how you guys could stand that. That's worse than being shot at. The shooting comes and goes, but that pain doesn't let up for a minute. It drives me nuts.

My geography lessons provided no clues whatever about Biak, and I'm sure the guys who were killed there were similarly uninformed. That little battle probably will never even get a mention in the news anywhere. What an epitaph! Killed on an unknown island by an unknown Jap who was, likewise, unaware of where he was, and none of the protagonists knowing why that little fly speck was important enough to die for. There must be something to be learned from all this, but the word expendable keeps creeping into my thoughts and I would prefer to face up to that reality, S.N.A.F.U.

About the only word I have on any of the fellas we know is that Harry Anderson is an infantry Lt. in Italy somewhere, and that Ernie Yarke survived the sinking of the carrier he was on . . . burned a bit, but recovering nicely.

In my little sector of the war, I don't have the problem of exhaustive physical labor, bad food and the Jungle Miasma with its creepy crawlies that you face daily. I can well understand guys looking emaciated and acting strung out from those things alone, much less tossing in invasions and the friggin' Japs. I can barely handle riding around in an airplane.

Speaking of which, we rode around in one on the 2nd and hit an aircraft factory at Schweicat in Austria. This town is fairly close to Vienna and is well guarded by flak batteries on the ground, with our unfriendly chaperones buzzing about in the air. The fighters, again today, were tentative with their approaches, but the flak barrage was anything but tentative. We sustained some minor damage to the ship and, as usual, major damage to the nerves.

One B-24 took a blast right beneath the bomb bays, and it flipped the ship right over on its back. The airplane fell about 10,000 feet, with the two pilots fighting it tooth and nail through the violent antics the ship was going through. To the wonderment of all, they managed to regain control and rejoined the formation. The inside of that airplane must have been like marbles in a Mixmaster. Half the crew is not buckled to a seat. The pilots are to receive the DFC for their efforts, and probably deserve more. As we bore down on the target, a couple of fool pilots were exchanging information about their altitudes, airspeed and heading. That takes the rag right off the bush!

We got the green flare again this A.M. and started out for Budapest, but turned aside about 70 miles short of our primary target and hit the secondary at Brod in Yugoslavia. Four or five ships in the formation hit the assigned target, marshaling yards, while the rest of us dropped our loads of fifty-two 100-pounders right into the town. Somebody in the lead somewhere screwed up. My load walked down a neat row of bungalows which, at our altitude of 12,500 feet, were clearly visible all the way down. These kinds of strikes are accidental, but that means nothing to those who get hit. I'm glad I'm not down there to see and hear what these things do to people and places. Thinking too much about it is a ticket to the funny farm, so I drop 'em and hope the war is shortened a little each time I open the bomb bays.

Back at the base, I did my dry cleaning by dumping everything in 100 octane gasoline, which does a good job . . . but tends to make you careful lighting cigarettes until you get aired out.

A package from home arrived today. I use the word "package" because, in its original state, it was one. It now looks like road kill. The contents, wrapped individually by loving hands originally, have become a cookie, cake, fudge and strawberry jam goulash which, when eaten with a spoon, proved to be delicious.

Briefed a mission in the A.M. and it was scrubbed. Sixteen more to go, eight if they are double credits. It is very difficult not to keep this diminishing figure from perching on my subconscious like a damned buzzard. The smaller the number gets, the more often and uglier the buzzard appears. On the way back to the tent from the flight line, Buck and I stopped at the mess hall for breakfast. I knew from approaching downwind that sausages were not being featured today, so went in and had pancakes with syrup and scrambled eggs. I rather enjoyed the meal until I got back to the tent and tried to brush my teeth. My gums had disappeared. Never, repeat, never brush your roots with a stiff toothbrush. The syrup must have been laced with an astringent strong enough to shrink rocks. Maybe this has something to do with preventing V.D. Buck had dined on some sort of hash and was stricken with a violent case of the trots. He got to our one-holer one step ahead of disaster, clad only in his hat and boots. Fate then stepped in, interrupting his noisesome meditations. The Toonerville Trolley appeared with its usual overload of excitable commuters, all shouting and pointing fingers at our stranded aviator. Sacrificing his modesty for the sake of harmonious relations with the Italians, he stood up and tossed them a salute. The Italian ladies responded with piercing shrieks of "Bono, multi Bono", and some lewd gestures as well. The Trolley meandered out of sight, with captivated ladies still shrieking their approval, and Buck returning to his meditation.

Later on, a must movie for all personnel was shown to a mandatory full house. This epic was filmed in color and ran for about an hour and a half. The subject matter was V.D. and covered the conquest of a dedicated fornicator from his last orgasmic shudder to the day he began pissing through a flute. The various stages of the infection, from gonorrhea and syphilis, were shown for both male and female genitalia. The audience began barfing in their hats when a vagina, in glorious color, was spread open to show the ravages of syphilis in its final stage. Needless to say, the sound of panic buttons being pressed could be heard throughout the hall, and a long line appeared in front of the dispensary . . . even before the final curtain.

Took a run over the Visecit Airdrome at Budapest (Hungary) this A.M. We carried fragmentation bombs today, which are tricky little devils to handle . . . or even have just lying around. The hot sun makes them a little unstable, and once the little propeller on the front spins off, any contact with the business end sets them off. When we dropped, a stack of six of them got hung up in the bomb bays and, as unwilling as I was to go through that again, we couldn't risk not getting rid of them . . . so back I went. I got them out okay, but with trying to avoid falling off the catwalk during our evasive actions (no chutes) and thinking about the consequences of one of those things bumping into the side of the ship, my day turned irrevocably to shit. The strike results, however, were good. The frag bombs are like hand grenades, only bigger. They landed all over the airfield, and I'm sure caused extensive damage to planes, equipment and people. A couple of strings hit an officer's barracks and I wonder if we caught the boys at home.

During the run on the target, a couple of pilots (who have a nasty habit of flying sloppy formation) slid over the top of us on the bomb run with their bomb bays open, and completely oblivious to the flight of four B-24s 100 feet beneath them. You can't imagine how frightening it was to look and see open bomb bays with frag bombs hanging there with the release point just seconds away. Mac got us out just in time. After the mission, he had a long chat with those two jerks, along with Sgt. Tietz (who mans the upper turret). Mac ordered Tietz to shoot them down if they ever came close again and Tietz told the pilots that he was looking forward to doing just that . . . and with real pleasure to boot.

It is no wonder those scrawny-necked buzzards keep my subconscious in a tizzy. This was not a day for the faint of heart.

Leo Garrity (our navigator) finished his tour today and got tossed into the showers. The water was like ice, and I could only wish I was in there with him. After Garrity's shower, we returned to the tent to discover that we had been looted. The suspect is an Italian M.P. who stands guard to prevent looting. He has a sentry box, much like the old outhouse, 100 feet or so from our tent and he is usually asleep. We will be watching this guy.

Up, up again . . . a double credit run to Giugiu in Romania. Twelve more to go. I wonder what the buzzard has in store next for your reluctant bomb dispenser. Today we got banged around some, but were luckier than some of the others. I saw two or three ships go down, and a lot of chutes blossomed out for a change. The Germans, unbelievably, began shooting at the chutes. I can't imagine, and don't want to, what those big shells do to a man swinging around on shroud lines. The concussion alone, discounting the shrapnel, tosses a 24 around it it's close. Again today, I saw another crewman accelerating out of sight under a burning canopy. Some of our fighters heard the uproar over the radio and dropped down on the deck and strafed the area. I hope they got some of the triggermen. Whatever few reservations I had about dropping bombs disappeared in those flak bursts today. Let 'em fall on whoever, whatever and wherever the fickle finger points. Screw 'em all!

No air activity for our group today, although other groups were busy and the skies were full of their ships and the roar of their engines. On the way back from the mess hall at noon (peanut butter sandwiches), I stopped by the garden spot of the base, the community latrine. About fifteen 55-gallon drums, with lids, are perched over a nice deep slit trench surrounded by a five-foot high modesty panel (tarpaulin). The trench is cleaned by pouring 100 octane gas into it, and then lighting it off. After burning, the lids are replaced and it's then business as usual. From time to time, accumulated fumes will cook off in the hot sun and blow the lids off. Unaware that the weekly cleaning had just been completed, I picked a seat and got nice and comfy when the fumes reached the point of no return. "Great Balls of Fire", the immortal words of a cartoon character, came immediately to mind. Back to our one-holer and Trolley voyeurs.

Heaved my charred cheeks aboard our 24 the next day and dropped 500-pounders on the sub pens at Toulon. I don't think we could hurt the pens with 500-pounders, but we did have scare value and maybe knocked off a few unwary bird watchers. This was the worst trip ever for me. I spent most of the time curled up on the floor of the radio compartment, fighting for breath. That pleurisy thing was sending agonized jolts of pain through my chest and sides, and I got up just once to drop bombs. When we landed, the rest of the crew went to the post-mission briefing, and I started the 400-yard trek to the tent. It took me an hour, some of the time on my hands and knees. I thought a passerby might offer to help, but I guess you have to leave a trail of blood behind you to get a second glance. I won't go to the dispensary because they will ground me and, at this time, up with that I cannot put. What I need is a stand down or two to bake in the sun.

Somebody up there loves me. We got a couple of days off, and I laid in front of the tent, naked as a jaybird, soaking up the heat. I am once again my chipper self, breathing with some difficulty, but nothing I can't deal with.

Ten 500-pounders to Ploeski, as Mac continues to say in his Oklahoma drawl. The mission was pretty much a milk run until we got to the target, then the flak batteries began pouring it on to a fare-thee-well. The barrage was very heavy, but we slithered through with minor lacerations to the ship . . . and major abrasions to the nerves.

After bomb release, we turned for home feeling euphoric after another stay of execution when we caught a burst dead center in the #2 engine. It was just one hell of a jolt. My first though was that we would have to jump, but Mac and Buck kept us in the air and reasonably straight and level.

I have been watching airplanes in similar straights, mission after mission, and empathizing with them. But I now know what those guys were feeling. When crippled, keeping within the protective cover of the formation is almost impossible. And alone, you're dead meat for the fighters. There is also the specter of fire, loss of altitude, fuel loss or controls damage. Strangely enough, I don't think any of us were afraid for our lives, at least after the initial hit. When we realized that we were still flying, confidence became the norm . . . intercom conversations were almost laconic; business as usual.

We were losing gas and altitude, so Mac dove 5,000 feet or so, hoping to escape notice by a fighter (and to build up air speed). We limped along, losing gas and altitude, until we reached the Adriatic Sea, no fighter interference (praise the Lord) en route. We were hanging on to 500 feet of altitude with our fingernails, and Mac was seriously considering ditching, when we spotted the Italian coast and picked up a marker beam at an emergency landing field. We sent out the Mayday calls and, with only 200 feet of air under us, we spotted the field and fired red flares to alert the ground crews to the imminent possibility of a crash landing. Fuel gauges at zero means an airplane stops flying right now, and gravity becomes boss. The meat wagons and fire equipment came out, prepared to give assistance, but were not needed. Mac greased it in and, as we turned off the runway onto a taxi strip, the engine quit. Sgt. Tietz had been monitoring our fuel and assuring us we could just barely hack it, but he must have had some doubts because he was patting the dials and looking upward with his lips moving.

A truck was sent for us and picked us up three hours later, and after a four hour beating on the back of the 6-by, we got to Grottaglia. Valhalla couldn't have looked any better.

After I get glued together again, I will begin my next letter, hoping that you, too, are still glued together and smiting the wily Jap, hip and thigh.

BUZZARD BILL

Wed. 12 July '44 to
Friday 19 July '44

DEAR TIRED AND HAD ENOUGH—

An outstanding effort by the Army and Navy Post Office people has brought me the very welcome tidings that you are OK and carrying the war forward to its inevitable conclusion. Quite seriously, Bill, glad to hear from you. Two letters arrived here, one dated 17 May '44, and the other 11 June '44. The state of your health worries me and, at the same time, I am glad to know you're OK . . . aside from being exhausted (not unexpectedly) and catching the Plague, the rot, fleas, beriberi or whatever. Those small invasions sound dangerous as hell with those little enclaves loaded with little mean guys who don't know how to surrender. Your gun crew must be an exceedingly sharp-eyed group . . . I'm beginning to lose track of the number of Zeros you have splashed.

The names of the large islands and small atolls, Hollandia, Truk, Guadal Canal, Wewak, Surabaya, Salamaua, Manus, Admiraltys, Biak, etc., come as a surprise to me. I was aware, of course, of the larger Islands, but all those little ones really surprised me when you describe the mini-invasions on so many of them. News we get speaks only of the big ones. The little ones (a bunch as I now know) are just as mean and life threatening as the big ones the press reports to the public. For Pete's sake, keep your tin hat on and be careful. Shall I liberate a flak jacket and send it to you?

You may be pooped and praying, but you still manage to discover a well-turned ankle or two. Maybe I worry about you too much. The nurses sounded like a very welcome sight after the blandishments the native pin-up girls wasted on you stalwart, clean-cut Yankee lads. The lady officer must have seen something in your eagle eye and starched pants that rang her panic button, or maybe she was just frustrated herself.

You mentioned some of the other Phi Gams, and it would appear we are all right out in front, where it's either fish or cut bait. Correll is on the Murmansk runs. I always thought he had a wild hair somewhere. Those convoys are widow makers. I'm pretty sure the whole bunch of us have ended up in situations as far from our expectations when we signed on as it is possible to get. Be grateful for all the luck you can find, but keep your head out of your butt.

Incidentally, keep your Pinocchio nose out of Jap dugouts, avoid souvenir collecting and ransacking Jap supplies. I understand they booby trap a lot of those interesting items. One other thing . . . those four or five sailors panning for gold, brewing torpedo juice and camped out in the boonies in an assault boat were not Clementine with herring boxes without topses for sandals. Those were very bad forty niners. Am I going to have to come out there and save you from yourself as I once did as we stalked the wily pheasant?! I think you lucked out in walking away from that one. Those guys were as unpredictable as werewolves. I got enough on my plate without your scaring me to death as well.

Off to the Riviera today, unfortunately not as a tourist. We bombed a river bridge at Var in LaBelle Francais. Each airplane carried five 1,000 pound bombs, and the bombing appeared to be quite accurate today. Only a small number of ships participated in this raid, but with 1,000 pounders, it doesn't take the whole Air Force to cream a target . . . that is, if you manage to hit it. Opposition was light, but it only takes one to ruin your day. I rode nose turret with another crew today. They were short a gunner and the bombardier and I were too damned chicken to ask why. Had to hop out of the turret on the run to drop the bombs. It was comforting to have those twin fifties in my hands to use on the fighters instead of my usual armament of pencil and E6B computer. Fortunately for us, my uncanny dove, quail and pheasant snap shooting skills were not put to the test.

When I got this assignment to fly with a strange crew, the specter of E.J. and George floated out of my memory and roosted like a damned buzzard on my back. Climbing into the airplane carrying that buzzard piggyback was like having a final cigarette and refusing the blindfold. After eight hours to and from the target, particularly with light opposition, I finally got the buzzard to float away and peer down at some other superstitious panty waist.

Speaking of panty waists, I have developed an ailment . . . not to be likened to your yaws, scabs and fatigue that mark the combat officer. I have a hemorrhoidal condition that, although not painful, is aggravating and embarrassing when it itches like hell and one must absolutely scratch like mad wherever you may be at the moment. I don't know whether to blame it on the freezing ammo cans I sit on in the air, the mess sergeant or the ever present fickle finger . . . or could it have been the shot I got from our community volcano as I perched there for a few seconds. Shirley thinks I deserve the Purple Heart and a discharge.

Leo Garrity left today for Naples and transport to the States. We tossed him into the showers again and loaded him down with messages to all the kinfolk back home. I hope he visits Shirley . . . we live only a few blocks from one another on the southeast side of Chicago. We are all delighted that he has escaped this mess in one piece and, at the same time, we all wish we were wet from the same shower.

About seven this A.M., it began to rain . . . rain like you describe out in the Pacific. I haven't seen rain since arriving here, but today was the kind of rain that prompted Noah to think of a quick career in shipbuilding. One minute it was hot and dry, and the next minute we were letting the sides of the tent down against a solid wall of water. This didn't do much good at all on account of the holes we cut in the roof to hang the netting. The water coming in the roof was nothing compared to the rapids roaring through on the ground. We got into our cots, no lifeboats handy, and then to our horror found that we were slowly but surely sinking into the morass beneath us. When our fannies hit the mud, we abandoned ship and set sail for the mess hall to wait out what looked like forty days. The mud was knee-deep, and forward movement was all that kept us from oozing out of sight like our shoes and boots. A couple of hours later, we returned to the tent and dug out our gear, put it out in the sun and, soon, no sign of flood was evident.

This afternoon, an Italian woman came by with her young son in tow. While she was trying to sell us on the idea of a gang bang, the kid was ransacking Mac's luggage. He got caught red-handed, was upended and shaken loose of his plunder. Buck began honing his Bowie, and our matronly hooker and her pint-sized shoplifter took off. We got some stuff that did not come from Mac's luggage.

We fly tomorrow. No one would dare shoot us on Mom's birthday. They wouldn't dare. Happy Birthday, Mom!

This was a big mission for McGlasson and Lou Lazenby. They finished their missions and were forthwith dunked in the showers when we got home. We are all genuinely happy for them and hope they understand the deep regret we feel at losing their companionship, and the fortitude and skills they have shown over the last many months. McGlasson on more than one occasion saved our collective butts singlehandedly. Lazenby pulled me up into the ship when I was hanging by my fingernails over Germany on our first mission. I owe these men, and I can't come up with what to say to them which would be comfortable for them to hear or for me to say. I usually manage to put my foot in my mouth, so I'll leave this one be and hope we are all feeling the same way.

Backing up a little, the last mission for our graduates was not a walk in the park. We went to Budapest, where we encountered heavy and accurate flak and a mixed bag of enemy fighters. One burst of flak underneath our tail position and the tail turret cut one of Jake's new boots in half. He, fortunately, was not wearing them. They were for use in the event of a hasty exit and a long walk. Luftwaffe, beware! Our sanitary engineer from New York is now really pissed off.

I mentioned a mixed bag of fighters that were harassing the formation. The swarms of 110s and 109s that used to appear at major targets against the 15th have not shown up lately. We get a little bit of everything. These guys are still dangerous as hell, but seem to lack the expertise and enthusiasm for the kill that was so evident in the 8th, and for a while here in the 15th. From my tunnel vision atop this sub-zero ammo can, I see attrition beginning to take its toll. Fewer front line fighters, fewer combat-proven pilots and more and more 24s and 17s plowing through whatever they toss up at us in the air. Am I a prophet or just a whistler in a flak barrage?

The fighters followed us out of the target area and made some passes at the more isolated and, therefore, more tempting boxes. Some distance off to my right, and gradually losing altitude, was a three-ship formation. One ship had been hit hard, and preparations were under way for bailing out. A bad thing to get hit, but a good thing to have time to jump. The other two ships stuck with them to keep the fighters off until the crew had a chance to get out. We could hear them on the command frequency, and we could all hear the conversation between the crews. It went something like this:

"Joe, you guys better get back and join the group before you get picked off."

"Nuts, Ed, we'll wait 'til you get out."

"All right, then, thanks. Navigator, are we out of Tito's territory?"

"Yeah, it's OK to bail out. Tell the other guys to get a fix on us so maybe they can get us out later on."

"Did you read, Joe?"

"Roger. We have you marked."

"Guys in the rear go first, sound off when you leave."

"Rear turret bailing out, see you, sir."

"Take it easy, Red, and the rest of you get to it. I can't hold it much longer."

"Hey, Joe."

"Right here, Ed."

"I'm leaving. Do me a favor, will you? Send my stuff to my wife. You keep my uniforms. I don't want some friggin' paddle foot to steal my gear."

"Sure thing, Ed, take it easy."

"I got to get going. C'mon, Bill, it's time to go. See you later, fellahs."

This conversation went on for ten minutes or so, and I could not get it down verbatim. The above conversation was interspersed with talk about fighter passes from all these planes. There was just too much action to record accurately, so I put down enough so that you could get a picture profile of the kind of crews that climb into these lumbering box cars every day. They would be asking their buddies to do this or that for them, break off to shoot at a fighter, then resume the conversation as if nothing had interrupted them. I think I get redundant from time to time, but redundancy for the courage of the combat crews should be even more redundant. So, you guys, you are really something.

The other two ships poured it on and caught up with the formation after the last man got out and, although out of sight, we know when the ship went in . . . no more static on the radio.

This was number 44 for this paleface. When I contemplate six more to go, beads of sweat pop out. When I think of the last 44, the stuff comes in rivers. I keep thinking things can't get any worse, but my buddies Finger and Bull are still hanging around to make sure I don't get overconfident and blow it right at the last minute.

The entire 15th flew a mission to Mac's target today. Ploeski. Rhymes with pesky. Pesky Ploeski. Mac would like that. I hope we finished off this target today, but somehow I doubt that. The Jerries have thousands of slave laborers down there, and they get things glued back together in a hurry and keep production moving.

We were on the wrong end of very heavy antiaircraft fire today, and a number of ships went down. Two or three just plain blew up. This is not uncommon, but it is (Thank God!) not a daily occurrence, either. A Colonel just six airplanes in front of us disappeared in a huge red ball, and the concussion shuffled two boxes of four ships like a fast riffle with a deck of cards.

He had just opened his bomb bays and probably took an 88-mm right in the guts. His gas went up, and the bombs may have exploded sympathetically. The two boxes reformed and plowed ahead. I presume we all took some damage (ours was minimal) but the guys closer in must have sustained a great deal more.

I flew today's strike with another crew, and my fears that there were only two safe pilots in the entire Army Air Corps proved to be baseless. Woods and Newton were all a "Nervous Nellie" like me could ask for . . . we got home. The weather continues to be hot, so we wear the leather A-2 flying jackets, which keep us relatively warm. We are glad to sacrifice a little warmth for the vastly improved freedom of movement that the A-2s provide. The gear we <u>had</u> to wear in the 8th because of the cold was so bulky, movement was very restricted. At briefing (upon our return, not before leaving), we were informed that the Air Force has new regulations. No more double credit missions in the 15th. Today's blood bath counts for only one. The missions are not that much easier, and I suspect the rear echelon wants to hang onto the combat experienced crews as long as possible. Five to go . . . I better get to it before they start 1/2 credit missions. If I was Fletcher Christian, the rear echelon "harpies of the sea" would be on their way to Pitcairns Island without fighter's escort, ammunition or Capt. Bligh to navigate for them. Short of gas, too. Mutiny has not raised its ugly head, but bitterness has swept the combat enclave like the "Red Death."

I am fast becoming a case for the meat wagon. Awoke this morning sporting a 102-degree fever and chest pains that just won't quit. I usually have a small temp and some pain, but this was a major league hardball. Went down to the dispensary for pain pills, and the Doc informed me I was for the hospital tomorrow if I'm not any better. Tomorrow I will be better if it kills me! At this stage of the game, no one is putting me away for the cure. Besides, I think I still rank pretty high on the hospital's shit list.

Sat around operations sun bathing and listening to Sally the Berlin Bitch. According to Sally, every gal in the States is shacking up with a draft dodger and nuns are being preyed upon by defrocked priests and, by the time we get home, odd little bastards will be hanging onto every apron string in the country. She has a very sexy voice, but the only effect she has on morale is to cause some heated speculation, pro and con, about her looks and her movements in the sack. She did claim our clock in operations was a little slow, and she was right. Will H.Q. post a guard on the clock? Withdraw .45 automatics at the clock?

Some time ago, Sally warned one of the groups about playing dirty tricks in the air. It seems one smartass dropped his wheels and flaps as a token of surrender and, when a couple of Jerries slid alongside to shepherd them down, our boy gunners salivated the fighters, killing both of them. He then pulled up the flaps and gear and rejoined the formation, laughing his stupid, irresponsible jack-ass head off. Until that time, both sides had an unwritten understanding on this method of surrendering. Saved a lot of lives. Not any more . . . nobody trusts nobody. Well, anyway, Sal always knew when this group was going out and would warn them to look out the next day. Sure enough, the Jerries would pass everybody and work this group to a fare-thee-well. We usually felt pretty good when we got scheduled with that unhappy bunch.

Reported into the dispensary as ordered this A.M., feeling a lot better than yesterday. The doc stuck a thermometer in my mouth and, when he turned his back, I shook it down where it belonged. It was easy to fool the medico because most of his customers are trying to get hospitalized for the rest, food and a peep at a white brassier. I swore up and down that my health was superior in every regard and, with the evidence of the thermometer, the doc let me go. I still have some pain pills left in case it gets real bad again. The only way I go back there is in irons and kicking and screaming the whole way.

Went to Grottaglia in the afternoon and made a small contribution for the construction of a new chapel. The altar in the old chapel is quite beautiful and is covered with a gold-appearing metal and semiprecious stones. The church appears to be solvent, even luxurious, compared to the parishioners who are all barely hanging on by their toenails. Is there something ironic here, or is it just me?

I sent some stuff home for the baby. I hope Shirley does not take the kid out while wearing any of these creations, except maybe at Halloween. It might even be better to bury them in the back yard with the dog's treasures.

Hope to get a day or two to spend in my open air Solarium. I need some heat on the old bone yard to ease the aggravation.

Hopes became reality, and for the next two days I made like a paddle foot. Making like a paddle foot is good duty. Do these guys volunteer for these pension sureties or does the Air Corps, in its infinite capacity to screw the dog, just assign them willy-nilly? I know that support and logistics represent the vast bulk of military manpower, and them that's got it generally wins . . . but I wonder a lot about the individual man who wears a uniform and what motivates him or her. I think a lot of the enlisted people in the rear ranks are there because saving your ass is an American tradition. I think the higher the rank, the more politics to insure promotion and a sinecure of respect. Writing themselves up for decorations is also part of the game. Fool the civilians with the fruit salad, if that is your bag, but every guy pulling that off knows in his hidden gut what part he really played. These bastards must be hollow and self-serving uniformed draft dodgers. My opinion only here. Better face the wrath of the Luftwaffe than a lynch mob of fraudulently decorated officers.

Last night, Buck and I attended an Arabian USO show that was really different. They had a four-piece band that hit all the loud notes and, otherwise, ignored the score altogether. They had a son of the desert who stuck needles in himself in places that made us involuntarily pucker up. The star of the show was a pretty belly dancer. She did things with her hips and hooters that defied gravity and description. There were a lot of calls, too, from the cheap seats to "take it off", but she was an arteest and didn't go for that low brow stuff. There will be a line at the stage door and, if she gives the nod to anybody, his only hope for a future afterwards will be a good chiropractor. We finished off the day at a British cinema, eating some of the locally produced fruit. The fruit is pretty tasty when you consider our mess hall as the alternative. The fruit and mess hall share something in common, however . . . either an immediate onslaught of the green apple two step, or three days wondering when to open the bomb bays and salvo. C'est la vie, c'est la guerre!!!

BITING THE BULLET BILL

P.S. Hoping the Bluebird of Bombardiers drops some more mail off here from you. Shall I finish here or come out there looking for you? Keep me posted.

Sat. 20 July 1944 to
Tues. 25 July 1944

DEAR GUNS—-

No mail from the rim of the world, but in order to remember what's cooking, I'll write from time to time until I hear from you . . . soon, I hope.

We flew a real quickie today. Started to the target as usual, but inclement weather forced us to return after about an hour en route. We ran into a cloud formation that was literally a wall. The base of this mass was about 4,000 feet, and it extended upward to near the 35,000 foot level, extending horizontally for as far as I could see. No going over, under or around. This is the most unusual phenomenon I have ever seen, and it's more than likely I'll never see anything like it again . . . Ma Nature showing us little people what for. Flak showed up in a few desultory bursts, and a couple of fighters looked over the possibility of a free lunch and, as a result, we got credit for the mission. Please, send some more just like this one.

Mac, Buck, and I hopped a truck and went to Taranto today. Taranto is the big Italian naval base. The harbor was fairly active, with a number of ships from here and there.

The Italian Marines fancy themselves as the Italian equivalent of British Commandos or American airborne troops. They dress to the nines and parade around with their lower jaws sticking out like their one-time boss. Mostly show and blow. Six of them disputed the right of way on the sidewalk with us and started the pushing, shoving and shouting routine. Mac, as you know, is quite a large boy of Indian heritage and sensitive to such boorish behavior. He stuck his cigar in the head honcho's eye, followed by a real thumper to his solar plexus. The guy went down, Rogers came in waving his Jim Bowie . . . and I booted one in the jewels. The field was ours, four running, one hobbling,and one still down. M.P.s being what they are, Italian crowds being what they are, suggested withdrawal before having to explain our impromptu behavior. Actually, we ran a little.

We turned into the Allied Officers' club in downtown Taranto. The club had a terrace on the second floor overlooking the street, and we took a table there. The waiter kept bringing bottles of green champaign (?), and we did our best to keep him moving. In the midst of this debacle, some French guys down on the street started shooting at a formation of Italian Marines and M.P.s. What with popping our heads up to see what the action was without getting shot or dropping the champagne, we had a busy, but hazy few minutes.

An American major and a nurse were crossing the street when the festivities commenced. He hit the grit like a footballer going for a fumble. The nurse trotted over to the club and came in without a hair out of place. She had a drink ordered when he showed up, looking somewhat worse for wear. His lonely theater ribbon was barely noticeable among the traces of human, animal and vehicular traffic that he now wore on his heretofore starched and impeccable khakis.

After the shootout at the O.K. Corral, Mac hoisted Buck and me into a supply truck headed for our base. Okies must be weaned on green fire-water . . . Buck and I were not. Rogers and I tossed our cookies for forty minutes, finally collapsing drunk as skunks on our cots, and calling on the Great Spirit to stop the tent from spinning so madly. Taranto is more dangerous than Ploesti.

Speaking of Ploesti, our snotty orderly got us up an hour after we went to bed in order to brief for that target. Buck and I were sucking oxygen before we were airborne, hoping for divine intervention. Intervention came not from a Divine Spirit, but from the clouds of smoke, red flashes and lusty explosions of the flak barrage. Heavier by far than on our previous trips here. This, I had previously believed, was quite impossible. The tonnage we leave behind us here must be approaching the unbelievable, and yet they continue to fight like tigers.

I had my head in the starboard window bubble when some unforgiving hard-nose on the ground shot out my window. I got a face full of plexiglass and a sliver of flak that cut my eyebrow. The oxygen mask and helmet prevented any serious damage, but the eyebrow bled for a few minutes and really only amounted to a deep scratch.

Homeward bound, we were intercepted by some enemy fighters, and they made things miserable for awhile. They put down two B-24s before breaking off the engagement. Tonight, at briefing, we found out that it wasn't that wall of clouds that forced us back on the last mission, but an estimated 150 fighters that were in ambush on the other side of the cloud. This is not the usual tack the planners pursue, but we . . . the almost ambushed . . . sure appreciate their thoughtfulness this time. 150 fighters could have meant disaster. Whoever skeedaddles away from those odds is one damned smart, scared aviator.

An absolutely perfect mission today, even with moderate and very accurate three gun battery flak (reminded me of the Pas de Calais region in France). Twenty-nine minutes to the target with the assist of a powerful tail wind and fifty-one back to base. All ships carried six 1,000 pounders for the Berat Kincae oil works in Albania. I was in the bomb bays looking down for our strike pattern after releasing the bombs when some eagle eye on the ground put three bursts beneath our bomb bays. The noise about scared me to death, and the pitter patter of hunks bouncing around in the bays sent me back to the peace and quiet of my office in the nose . . . where I promptly shut the big doors on the bays. So much for eyeball reporting on the hazards of flak in one's bomb bays.

We were flying the usual four ship diamond-down formation today, and our position was on the right wing of the lead ship (here is a sketch of what this battle-tested grouping looks like). I did one of these in an earlier letter, but thought I would refresh your memory, and give you a picture of the action that follows:

Three planes at same altitude

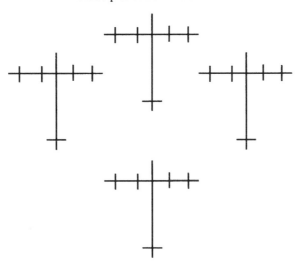

Slot ship behind and below and
in close to avoid prop wash and
provide max cover.

A very effective configuration to provide maximum protection for each other during fighter attacks.

In any event, one of the men in the lead ship had a bad case of diarrhea and was using an empty .50 calibre ammunition can as his airborne chamber pot. After either filling it, or running out of that with which he had been filling it, he tossed it out the camera hatch. As if it had eyes, it impacted against the inboard port engine of the diamond-down airplane. The large steel can, plus the filling, knocked out the engine, causing the pilot to abort the mission and return home. Talk about the doo hittin' the fan! When he was questioned about aborting (wrong description . . . third degreed), he answered in all truth that he had been hit by a bucket of shit and had to abort. Intelligence, always looking for someone to pillory, didn't believe a word of his report. They sent their Major (who was in charge of shit) to check this out, and he verified the pilot's report. As far as I know, this still remains part of the records.

Mac and Lazenby left for Naples today, Lazenby still wearing my hack watch. The rest of the crew finished up today, and I am now the Lonesome Ranger. Two more to go. Kemosabe, old buddy, don't let those damned German palefaces get me now.

I hope to hear from you shortly about the continuing excellence of your health. May it continue another 50 or 60 years. Hang in there, Will, and be ever more cautious every day.

CLIFF HANGER BILL

Wed. 26 July 1944 to
Friday 4 Aug. 1944

DEAR WHEREVER YOU ARE—-

A couple of days or so here did not really amount to much, so on to the meatier stuff that might prove interesting to you . . . or at least give you a diversion from splashing Zeros and hunting for native firewater in the dripping boonies.

Three of our guys, now turned to ground pounders, took off for Naples today. Jake, Duncan, and Ehlers. Sgt. Tietz is still here, due to some monumental SNAFU with his walking papers. Bummed a ride over to Taranto, not looking for any thrills, but merely to pass the time. Visited the Red Cross facility, and as usual, had to pay for everything marked as gifts from an unsuspecting American public to their service men. There were two battleships, several destroyers and a carrier in the harbor. I wonder what's up . . . if they start another war some place, and me with just two to go, I'll be the first P.O.W.

Got home early in the afternoon . . . I couldn't afford the prices at the Red Cross Canteen. A few front line ground troops were there looking as grungy as I did and getting the quivering nostril treatment from the P.X. ladies. I felt right at home with them so, up the misplaced debutantes. Arriving home here, lo and behold, was a ration issue containing real little green bottles of Coke. Frank liberated some more onions, bread and butter, and we ate far too many for the quality of the air surrounding us. Two to go!

Got in another one today . . . Budapest, formerly a double credit mission, but which now leaves me one more to sweat my way through. Our target was an armory and an airplane factory, reportedly the largest in Hungary. From what I could see, a good pattern of our bombs struck in the target perimeters. Some moderate flak and about ten fighters buzzed around, not showing any inclination to mix it up. For the first time in combat, I got back in an airplane that had not been hit by something or other. The unpredictable Boche probably knew I have one more to go at them and are saving everything for a maximum effort to get Bill when he takes off on his last flight. Damn, that was an unfortunate choice of words.

Received a couple of letters from Shirley today, who was ticked off about my attitude toward my first born being of the female gender. She must be referring to the one I wrote after Brunswick. A combination of male ego and combat fatigue. We'll both get over it.

Sat around and chewed my finger nails.

Sat around and bit my toenails.

Je-suis-fini. That is French for I have done done my duty, send for a replacement, shove combat in the wild blue yonder . . . and which boat going West is mine?!

This last mission was a storybook milk run at a cracking plant at Budafusza. There was no opposition from the ground or the air, and we left a towering column of smoke in our wake. After all the finger and toenails I sacrificed worrying about this last ride, it now becomes a mite embarrassing. I am extremely grateful for my enormous good luck and, after all, finger and toenails will grow back.

I began walking our papers through, thus bypassing the time it takes for the Army to send them on a globe circling whistle stopping trip through various interested commands. Our papers meant Frank Tietz' as well. Somehow, his got into a bureaucratic minefield somewhere and have disappeared from view in a cloud of self-serving "I ain't never seen dose papers". Anyway, we went to Bari and back in the now-familiar rear end of a six by six, and another day on an airplane ride to Manduria. The guy driving the Gooney Bird (C-47) had his nomenclature scrambled; he thought he was in a P-47 Thunderbolt. While in Manduria, attended an evening concert featuring Lily Pons, conducted by Andre Kostelonitz. Very soothing and exciting at the same time. There was a 449th truck there, so I hitched a ride home with them. Another bruising experience, but a small sacrifice to avoid a return flight with the Mad Baron and his acrobatic Gooney Bird.

Finished up all the processing at the 449th today, and Frank and I leave for Naples tomorrow. The Colonel gave me some Air medals, a Purple Heart and a pitch on flying ten more for a Captaincy. I took the hardware and declined his offer to continue the fight for Mom and apple pie. A bird in hand is surely better than one in a bush full of flak and fighters. Napoli, here I come!

Frank and I got started off today in great nostalgic style. One of our ships was sent to Naples on official business, and the crew signed us on as observers. I wonder if that is to be my last flight in a combat-rigged B-24? No matter, when I think of this war in the time ahead, the first thing that will pop into my mind will be a mental photograph of this big, ugly and ungainly flying machine, whose crews loved her to a fault. Our course took us over Vesuvius, a bird's eye view that tourists seldom, if ever, find in their itineraries. The tourists are at the base buying filthy post cards and obscene statuettes from the local con-artists. From up here, it could be the pot where Mrs. Murphy found the overalls, and just about as exciting.

Transportation was provided for us out to the Replacement Depot . . . or Repple Depple as it is referred to here by its denizens. Frank took off for five stripe Sergeants quarters, and I to another tent just off the roadway and adjacent to the parade grounds. This depot is located in the crater of an extinct volcano. Extinct, I hope, is the key word here. The depot is huge. The poop from group has it that it will take a couple of weeks to get a berth on a ship bound for the States. Checked out the mess hall and ran into Mac and Buck. They have made the manifest on one of the transports, but their departure date has yet to be announced. I sense an Army-Navy SNAFU in the making here. The logistics must be a nightmare.

I feel just a bit guilty ranting and raving about finishing up and going home while it appears, short of a miracle of some kind, that your theater of operations will continue on into the foreseeable future. I plan on keeping the letters coming your way and hope you'll reciprocate. The way I hear the combat crews talk around here, many of these veterans get 30 days' leave at home and then assignment to a B-29 squadron in the Pacific. I may end up as a friendly contrail over old #628. That is really not my dish of tea . . . more like Hemlock.

In any event, it appears as if I'll be here for some time, so will post this to keep your interest peaked at all the comings and goings at the Repple Depple. More to follow . . . as a matter of fact, I'll begin my next installment tomorrow. Hopefully, my next posting will not be to combat, but something of interest for me to share with you.

Lift that barge, tote that bale, I'll be in touch.

BEMEDALED AND BEMUSED BILL

Sat. 5 August 1944 to
Wed. 16 August 1944

DEAR FORE AND AFT—

The past ten days have not been much to shout about, but I have managed to keep busy doing nothing. A welcome change from some of the hectic scheduling of the past year or two. The two pilots that have adjoining beds in the tent, play cribbage starting after breakfast and continuing until it is too dark to read the spots. Fifteen two, fifteen four, fifteen six and a run of three is nine and the crib is ten. If I knew what was going on, I could live with it, but their fifteens and cribs are driving me up the tent pole. I have determined to learn this game first off when I get home . . . well, not exactly the first thing, but soon at any rate.

Mac and the others left on the 12th for home. Watching them all head for the dock gave me a real feeling of loss. Over the past year or so, we have shared together experiences that we will never have again and that most people will never have or, for that matter, ever conceive of having. The chances are we will not meet again, none of us being particularly demonstrative. It is sad to contemplate, but remembering these days as we grow older will only make us look that much better, and the missions a lot tougher and longer.

"Son, you won't believe this, but one day over Brunswick", or "Ploesti, my boy, we could have climbed out of the airplanes and walked on the flak" or, "Fighters you say, hell, there must have been 300 of the devils shooting cannon shells and machine gun bullets at your old daddy"!

There are troops coming in here to be assigned to combat units that are staging in other locations or merely as replacements for casualties. Having been over that road myself and being able to understand their fears at this time, sweating out a ride home on a boat is a real piece of cake. Latrine rumors about returning ships and replacements for invasion casualties have everyone on their ear constantly. Every new rumor, like a lightning bolt, spooks the herd, and they head for the bulletin board en-masse. This adds up to about 20 stampedes per day. It is easy to tell from the expressions on the faces those who are about to enter The Valley of the Shadow, and those who are leaving The Valley for a sea voyage home, hopefully without U-boat interference.

The depot is a very large one physically and is being staffed by a huge number of support people. People and prisoners going home, support and replacement combat troops coming in and going out. They have a self-contained M.P. force and stockade, logistic planners and Navy people to coordinate ship, train and airplane arrivals and departures. There are large mess facilities, P.X.s and on and on.

A lot of the homeward bound infantry guys are nursing big hates for the German and Italian POWs. All manner of fights and disturbances break out, including not only military, but civilians as well. Rape, murder, bar-busting and knee-smashing keep the M.P.'s hopping. The combat vets are not usually involved in the mayhem, but they do take a toll on mouthy Italians. There are some real bad looking guys looking out of the barbed wire stockades.

The Red Cross in town, or rather the edge of town, is the usual nifty building and facilities, housing a high-priced haven for the local paddle feet. The average Lt., Capt. or even Major coming from combat does look pretty seedy when compared to the starched khakis, creased pants and shining half boots that distinguish the far-to-the-rear guys from us, the great unwashed. These guys wear scarfs instead of neck ties (Keerist!!!). The Red Cross should rethink the priorities and get the cart in back of the horse where it belongs. Paying for cigarettes plainly marked as gifts from home folks still infuriates me. Two visits to Nob Hill was enough. They win this round, but when donation time comes around, the unwashed will arise and get even.

Today, the 15th, another red-hot rumor about a new ship posting got the nervous herd to its feet, and with horns clicking and tails sticking up like cat tails in a slough, we headed balls out to the bulletin boards. My name was first on the list of First Lts., only because my name begins with an "A" and not because of any heroic deeds. We are to hold ourselves in instant readiness for orders to board ship. So, I'm holding myself (one more unfortunate choice of words)!

Embarkation has been scheduled for tomorrow. Scheduled, in the Air Corps, is a rather iffy pronouncement under the best of circumstances. When they say instant embarkation, one knows that it will be a long day in the hot sun waiting for the "poofy scarfs" to get off the dime. Another pronouncement was not so iffy; turn in all firearms and films, or suit up for Siberia. I know I made a mistake by surrendering my films and weapon, but I wanted no wrong impressions about my desire to climb the gang plank. They promised to return the film. Sitting here now, I realize that frisking over 1,000 guys and their baggage would be highly unlikely. Win some, lose some. Bill Boy, you were dumb. Completed another stack of papers and am now officially cleared for the cruise ship.

I paid a last visit to the main Post Office and found a letter from Shirley and . . . one from you of all things. I will answer yours while on the bounding main and mail from the U.S. of A. at the first corner mail box I see.

Maybe our lines of communication might speed up if I get a more permanent posting in the Zone of the Interior. That would be nifty. I start getting a little antsy between letters and wondering what cooks in the jungle paradises.

Ok, Captain, permission granted to start engines and point this bucket in a westerly direction at high, submarine outdistancing speeds.

BARNACLE BILL

Thurs. 17 August 1944 to
Thurs. 30 August 1944

DEAR PARADISE ISLANDER—

 Whilst boiling on the dock for several hours obeying the directive from far above that we should be prepared for instant embarkation, I read your letter # XXV, dated 14 July 1944. A great letter, Bill. I read it several times on the dock . . . and it got better each time I read it. If and when I ever get off this damned dock, I'll begin a reply . . . unless some Lt. J.G. has me chipping paint or sweeping down fore and aft. The voyage, without trouble or inconvenience, is scheduled for about 14 days. I should have time to put down a line or two, as well as perch in the crows nest with an eagle eye looking for torpedo wakes.

 As you can well imagine, the mob of us natives on the deck became increasingly restless and hostile as the day wore endlessly on. Surrendering our firearms now makes sense. The Navy hasn't repelled boarders since the days of John Paul Jones, and this randy bunch was close to seeing if the modern swab jockeys have ever heard the late J.P.'s famous words.

 From time to time, I have expressed some negative feelings about accommodations at Grottaglia . . . never again. Life in the open air with sun, rain and a private privy was Eden with an Italian accent. My quarters in this ship are the Inquisition with a Navy accent. The hold I am to exist in somehow for 14 days is the farthest one forward in the prow of the ship. This hold is also the deepest one down, so deep I get the bends going up on deck for fresh air. The air in the compartment has already been filtered through the colons of 300 other lowly Lts. Knowing I can swim is small comfort when the sides of this ship are so thin you can hear a dolphin fart at 100 yards and torpedo propellers at half a mile. One thousand hours in the nose of a B-24, and I am now a claustrophobic. You may now stop laughing.

 Bunks are stacked six high and end to end with narrow passageways between them. Negotiating these pathways requires the agility of a mountain goat, due to the piles of B-4 bags and duffel bags, six each to each layer of Lts. To add further demands on my already nonexistent spirit of fellowship, the top bunk is mine. Try as I might, avoiding protruding parts belonging to the other guys is impossible on my climb to the top. Reactions are incredibly vulgar and threatening. The clearance between my canvas rack and the overhead is about 18 inches. Once in that thing, turning over means a trip to sick bay for band aids or bandages. The final straw, after avoiding a fate worse than death from my stack of bunk mates, was the ventilator. That sucker is right at the head of my sack and, every five minutes or so, blows a tornado down the length of my bunk and into the hold. That thing could lift a '24 to 1,000 feet. The first time it went off, I like to have contused myself on the overhead. A way out of this ill wind has to be found, and speedily.

 The past few days have been uneventful, peaceful and restful. I prowled the ship after the night of the "Big Wind" and located a spot behind a funnel out of sight of the bridge and, actually, everybody else. A couple of Navy guys, who had the responsibility for keeping people out of off-limit areas, chose to ignore my presence after I got on my knees and cried and cried about the hold. I owe those two swabbies. The weather has been delightful . . . and with a blanket for sleeping under and sunbathing on. I need only sneak below to shave and dine. My suntan is now a deep shade of mahogany, and an all over at that. Speaking of dining, your Navy boys set a marvelous table. Napkins, tablecloths, silverware, glasses and, unlike Army fare, it is tasty, presented in a civilized manner and seconds are available upon request. Bill, are you in a different Navy? Maybe they don't want to get expendables used to the finer things.

 There are several ships in our zigzagging convoy and, among them, a small aircraft carrier. A day or two ago, some sort of a crisis developed and the mast head flags were running up and down the lanyards on most of the ships . . . as well as semaphore signalmen waving their flags with wild precision. Since deserting the hold, the thought of a torpedo staring me in the eye down there had about faded away, but returned in a flash. My fears, as most fears do, proved to be without periscopes or propellers. My two Navy cohorts informed me that a boatload of nurses off our stern quarter had been separated from one of their necessaries . . . Kotex. The recaleritant and pristine nappies were finally located and dispatched to the nurses by cutter. A Navy yeoman, probably married, managed to convey Kotex by navy flags. My friends helped me out of my life jacket and sat with me until I was once again under iron control.

 The second deck of our ship is lined by little cabins occupied by German P.O.W.s The three hundred 1st Lts. in Davy Jones' Locker have taken extreme umbrage at this display of chivalry for troops who were trying to kill them not too long ago. The Jerries are wounded, and the medicos can treat them easier in the cabins, but hate dies hard. The thought crosses my mind that the medics and rear echelon orderlies feel sorry for these Nazis and forget that half the American guys in the hold are wearing Purple Hearts themselves. Compassion seems to be a trait belonging almost exclusively to the people who have never faced the business end of a rifle, bayonet, machine gun or an 88 mm flak battery. How about tossing the Nazis in the bilge? This would screw up the P.O.W. protocol we subscribe to, but at least we would be replying, in kind, to that which they have enthusiastically visited upon countless thousands of helpless people over the length and breadth of Europe and its environs. Don't get mad, get even.

Last night, we lost a man overboard. He was an infantryman suffering from severe combat fatigue. He slipped away from his attendants (somebody screwed off their responsibility) and walked over the side. With the choppy seas and darkness, the destroyer escorts were unable to find him. So close to home, and as it turned out, as far away as you can get. Sad for him, sadder for his folks.

The ship is a floating Monte Carlo with all manner of games of chance operating under cover throughout the vessel. The authorities severely frown on these activities and have a squad searching for law breakers. The law breakers have an inside source among the posse and have, thus far, eluded capture. Many of the hounds that are sent out to apprehend the fox end up in the hen house screaming, "Shut up, damn it, and deal the friggin' cards!".

My Navy babysitters dropped by the funnel today with the welcome news that the American mainland should be within sight tomorrow. They suggested I make a visit to the hold and get my gear together and up to the funnel. They say 300 guys with B-4s and barracks bags create the world's most dangerous back up, as they all try to shinny up one ladder at the same time. The carnage is awesome, according to my two boys. These two obliging sailors saved me from a rotten voyage at the mercy of that wind tunnel, and I am more than a little grateful. Two weeks up here helped, not only the inner man, but physically. I'm rested, gained some weight and burned out the pleurisy while acquiring a great tan.

From the Atlantic to the Pacific instantly via my pen. The jewel of the Pacific, Los Negros, apparently stroked your philosophical button. Admitting to fear, as you point out, is step one in learning to live with it. Fatalism is big with me now and, like you, I don't rattle that chain by being anything but alert and careful. I, too, have to be where I can see events as they develop, change them sometimes if I can, and if it seems the thing to do at the time. You are right, we all get accustomed to our special kinds of dangers. How riflemen, submariners and tankers handle this, I'll never understand. Those guys make my job look easy. I admire them all.

That strange emotion you feel when another guy buys the farm and a pang of guilt shoots through you at your survival and his death, is shared by yours truly. I usually then have a mental chat with the Fickle Finger . . . one of my ways out.

A dirty business everywhere!

Your sustained absence from the finer things of life (white, wholesome women) seems to have become an ongoing psychological aversion to all of that gender. I can only hope that when you return to life, as you formerly knew it, this aberration of yours will gradually fade away as you, from a safe distance, scout the herd. Assimilating, almost by osmosis, the tantalizing hint of Chanel #5, bras barely restraining lavish hooters, long legs making silky noises as they move, undulating hips a firm axe handle wide, Pepsodent teeth, a raised eyebrow and twinkling eyes will gradually restore the lustiness of your youth. Do not worry, you will pull through eventually.

Having Japs around you, unseen except when they shoot or sneak up on you at night, must give you the Willies. We can at least see what's coming at us and take some sort of countermeasures. Your situation would have me bonkers in a week, make that one night, with those slithering sounds coming from the jungle.

I also note you conjure up visions of food, clean mildew-free clothing, rock solid beds and, lo and behold, an English-speaking woman. I told you so. Your proclivity for poong is returning. You will soon be 100% my boy. The bilious, greenish, sick color of old #628 should act as a shield. Not even a Jap would sink her and risk polluting the whole Pacific.

Glad to hear you begin to see some signs of the Japs easing off barrage type small arms and mortar fire. Their logistics problem must be awful, considering the distances involved and the interdiction of their convoys, land and sea, by our forces. The hand writing may be on the wall . . . too bad the Japs don't read more and worry less about losing face. I think there may be more brutal fighting to your north, as well as smaller, but as deadly, actions that you will be engaged in during your supply missions.

Knowing this, even though I am not sure of my ultimate assignment, I shall continue to write as regularly as possible. I hope you will also. The mail will eventually get to us, and writing and receiving is something I look forward to constantly.

True to my spies' info, land was sighted this A.M. The yard birds were estimating our landfall from Nova Scotia south to the Florida Keys. The Captain, however, had a different notion, and drove us past the Statue and into New York Harbor. You would expect a lot of yelling and cheering as we slid past the Statue, but it was strangely quiet. The quiet of guys looking back and, at the same time, forward. Me, too! Fifty missions, Earl Norris, George Sloan, the crew, the terror, the laughs . . . and the great good luck (with a shot of guilt) that I feel standing on the deck as we go past the symbol that put us all here in the first place.

In retrospect, my job and contribution, small in the overall effort. So many more guys gave more. The average guy seems to be the glue, even if he knows the deck is stacked against him, that sticks everything together . . . and he just wades in and does the job. The contemptible ones will be with us forever. Profiteers, draft dodgers, military of all ranks who scheme and plot to remain out of harm's way, and the politicians who use all to grind their own personal axes. Thank God for the average Joe, who is smarter than he looks.

Zigging and zagging around the harbor consumed the rest of the day. The increasingly restless troops wanted the Captain to beach the SOB and drop the boarding ramps. Others had some really bizarre suggestions, but the Captain, and his 5,000 co-pilots, finally got the ship docked. We were then informed that disembarkment will be tomorrow. The average Joe then began to say bad things about the Captain, his crew, Mom and even green apple pie. So much for my theories about Joe.

I shall shut this down now and prepare to disembark on the morrow and shoot this into the nearest mail box at the earliest.

Tomorrow will be the first of September, 1944, an auspicious day to begin my next letter and to, perhaps, discover what will be crouched on my next job, waiting to pounce. Please be careful . . .

PENSIVE & PROUD BILL

Friday 1, Sept. 1944 to
Monday, 4 Sept. 1944

DEAR SLOCUM—-

Now hear this, Army troops, prepare to debark. For two weeks, about every five minutes, some guy with a whistle and a voice like breaking glass advises the crew to sweep down fore and aft, dust overheads, find the nurses necessaries . . . or man overboard, throw out a preserver. This time, it was music to my ears, Bosun's shrill whistle included.

The "Ladies Aid Volunteers" met us at the foot of the gang plank with fresh cold milk, Cokes, cookies and other goodies long-dreamed about and almost forgotten. The ladies, for the most part, were middle-aged, showing a little gray and speaking New York English. They were absolutely beautiful. They smiled and talked to every man who stopped for refreshments. These gals make their younger sisters of the Red Cross look pretty third-rate. The sight and sound of the ladies made the train ride to Camp Shanks, New Jersey, bearable.

They tell me a bus runs between Shanks and New York, but I am also told passes are nonexistent. Inside an hour, everyone had been briefed on a hole in the fence and how to take advantage of this avenue to some R & R. Camp Shanks is home to several hundred Italian P.O.W.s who seem to have the run of the place, as well as passes to the city. The restricted returnees view this with clenched teeth and pungent language directed at the officer staff at Shanks. Coexistence here is on very thin ice and may not survive an irritant of any kind.

Ground hogged under the fence and went to New York with a navigator from Chicago by the name of Petri. We went to some joint, had three overpriced, watered-down drinks and decided Shanks was a better choice. The waiter gave us a bill for twenty bucks, and I tipped him a buck. That brillianteened S.O.B. grabbed me by the shirt and demanded more tip or he would have the bouncer give me what for. A lot of bottled-up resentment roared to the surface. I hit him with everything that had scared me and pissed me off for the past year. Great shot, got him in his pointy nose . . . he and the table went down, and Petri and I beat the bouncer to the door.

In our absence, coexistence with the P.O.W.s hit the skids. A group in New York had made arrangements to hold a dance, with refreshments, for the Italian prisoners. A fleet of buses dropped a couple of hundred women off at the recreation hall to entertain Benitos' former Brownshirts. Their former adversaries got wind of the shindig and a huge crowd of them advanced on the enemy, male and female. The C.O. appeared in time (just) to prevent a brouhaha that would have filled all the hospital beds in the county. The women were put back on the buses, the Italians to their barracks, and the G.I.s dispersed . . . still hot as stove lids. Betcha the Guineas stay in after dark. Hate dies hard. Typical planning by liberal, rear echelon jerks. They'll never understand why it all hit the fan.

The telephone booths have been jammed since we scurried off the ship. Several thousand guys and only a few available phones. More thoughtful planning by the permanent paddle feet. I finally decided to skip a three- or four-hour wait for a phone and just walk in at home and see what happens. Hard not to call, real hard . . . but the surprise at home, hot doggies!

To my complete astonishment, a bunch of us are to board a train for Fort Sheridan, just north of Chicago, tomorrow. I think they were a little uneasy about the behavior of this bunch of short-tempered returnees and goosed their processing people to skip their coffee breaks and move the troops out. This was not much of a letter . . . more to follow, and hopefully more interesting.

BILL OF THE SQUARED CIRCLE

DEAR PERMANENTLY PACIFIC—-

As I waited to board a train this A.M., with the rumored destination of Fort Sheridan, Illinois, I had a little spasm of guilt pop into mind. I'm about 1,000 miles from home, and you are apparently marooned out there until the end of hostilities, slogging your way toward Japan . . . miserable island after miserable island. Somehow, it doesn't seem to be an equitable division of risk and length of time spent under combat conditions. Keep your head out. This will all pass.

We were herded aboard our troop train by a highly starched 2nd John wearing glasses (sun, flying); a piss cutter you could slice meat with, vestiges of acne and the desire to impress the raunchy combat troops with the efficacy of the O.C.S. graduates. He got a mixed bag of comments and suggestions, some of which horrified him and caused him to blush furiously. Felt sorry for the kid.

Our troop train is on the absolute bottom of the railroad's priority list. We were shunted to every siding that exists between New York and Pittsburgh. Trains going by us, in both directions, would blow sardonic sounding whistles at the "Little Engine Who Would If He Could". We had compartments on the train, which was a first for everybody, and there was also a dining car attached. These amenities made our snail-like progress toward Chicago more tolerable than our usual vintage '05 cars.

Pittsburgh finally appeared on the horizon, and even more slowly receded from view behind us. Late in the day on the 7th of September, our Iron Horse putt-putted past 74th and Greenwood on the Illinois Central right of way . . . three blocks from home. I seem to hear fiendish laughter from some sources or other. We arrived at Fort Sheridan after 11:00 P.M. Sixty miles in seven hours left our conservative train driver breathless, and the rest of us with anxiety attacks. At 11:00 P.M., more paper to process. Lord love a duck.

On the 8th, I discovered that getting out, even on temporary leave, is not the cinch getting into this outfit was. The paddle foot in charge here estimates our departure to be in three more days. This E.T.A. was howled down, and he promised us his utmost in speed and efficiency; this may get us away from here in three days, maybe. Good resolutions are made to be broken. I couldn't stand this, so near and yet so far, so called my mother. She is the only one in the family who can keep a secret. She will take a day off from the carbine assembly line to prepare a pork roast, strawberry shortcake and whatever. Ma has been sworn to secrecy. Dad, on the other hand, keeps a secret like a colander holds water. Our zealous processor says maybe tomorrow.

Our continued baying at the moon paid off. We did, indeed, leave Sheridan on the 9th, and I rode into downtown and the I.C. station with Lt. Petre and his parents. I hopped the I.C. train for home . . . and none of the commuters in that damned car even said hello. The returning hero with medals, wings, dirty khakis, beat-up musette bag, shaggy hair and a horny look in his eye, got the end of the car to himself. If I had talked to myself and stared wildly around, I could have had the whole car to myself. So much for an inflated ego.

When the train stopped at the 71st street station, I exited from the rear of the train and walked under the viaduct to Kimbark, hoping not to be spotted. If anyone did see me, they did not rush out spreading rose petals in my path. When I walked in the house, Grandpa was sitting in his chair smoking cigarettes that I had smuggled to him. I waved at him. He waved back. No ticker tape . . . you would think I had been down to the corner for a short beer. Incidentally, Grandpa's ancient cronies, as well as some younger addicts, have been trying to pry out of him the source of his supply and keep wondering at the large variety of brand names.

There was a good deal of commotion from the back bedroom and kitchen, and, as long as Gramps didn't appear ready to dance a hornpipe, I headed that way. Shirley's mother saw me then and seemed about to faint. She did open her mouth, but I held her up with one arm and covered her mouth with my other hand (would not risk that again). She pointed to Uncle Joe's room, from whence the uproar was coming. This raggedy ass soldier was a happy man to meet Dawn Marie for the first time and say hi to Shirley. It was almost as if the last several months had passed in the blink of an eye.

As I had expected, Dad let the cat out of the bag, except for Shirley, her mother, and the rest of them at Kimbark Ave. I do believe I detected the aroma of Jim Beam on his breath, and it is possible he celebrated this August event with a few too many drams. Mom had prepared a real feast over at our place, all of my very favorite specials. I couldn't tell her, of course, but I was forcing myself to eat. My mess hall conditioned innards rebelled at good, rich food, skillfully prepared and served delightfully to both my families. My biggest contribution to the festivities was remembering that I was back in civilization and not to ask Mother to pass the friggin' butter.

A proper time for a sad mental salute for Lt. Earl Norris and Sgt. George Sloan.

I will, once again, hasten this into the care of the Post Office people and hope they find you quickly. More will follow.

IN HOG HEAVEN BILL

16 August, '44

DEAR BEREAVED MAGELLAN—-

Please excuse my shaky handwriting. I am a little excited over a big mail call. I have yours dated May 12 to May 22, and another dated May 23 to May 28. Long time between letters! By that, I mean the delivery for you and me. It is noted that you are writing frequently and are keeping notes on a daily basis. It is difficult, if not impossible, for me to do the same.

Your missions are mounting, and I hope they don't change the rules near the last one. Sorry, but I just don't trust them! It seems wrong to me, too, that you go through all the motions, and take the flak, and fail to get credit if you don't drop the bombs. Perhaps your chaplain could make you feel good about this form of robbery.

I hope the pilot that shot the radio operator can handle it. There are those who won't understand, but I believe you and I do. One ought to be as humane toward his shipmates as he'd be to a faithful dog or cat.

The condolence letter routine is fraught with problems . . . and pain. One can write a wife and not a mother and be in trouble. A letter to whomever is next-of-kin is all we can do, and sometimes it goes on and on. I believe those back home suffer more than we do . . . and perhaps we've become too hard-nosed about it.

Your "revenge" in dropping defanged 50 cal. shells down the smokestack was brilliant and, no doubt, fun . . . for you. A truce to save the nerves also sounds good.

The accidents you describe are, to me, the most difficult to explain to next-of-kin. Somehow, my feeling is that to be killed or hurt in combat is different, and more soothing to relatives, than the same injury or death due to accident. Maybe it's best they didn't know and maybe the old telegram routine is not specific. The letters of condolence bring on the questions. What do you say for a guy that, while drunk, drowned?

Congratulations on your achievement as a navigator! Knowing nothing of that role in a B-24, I would think it might occupy the mind . . . and hopefully pass the time faster. Hope so! Glad you got to stick with your crew.

Be sure and let me know when your offspring arrives. I had forgotten when all that began. It appears that time is moving after all.

Can't imagine your narrow-minded colonel insisting the painted "maidens" on your plane be painted with clothing. Hope they don't send him out here. The paintings we see are true works of art, and it is nice to see at a glance that girls are indeed different from boys. We basically see only B-25s, along with the usual fighters. There appears to be no censorship. I would suggest that you paint the underside of your aluminum box to appear as several butterflies . . . perhaps a flock of black birds. Surely, the German gunners wouldn't waste scarce ammo on such targets.

Your trip near Leipzig sounds terrible. It seems the more missions you run, the more practice you provide for the German gunners. Maybe you need to spend a day per week bombing gunners!

Glad you had some fighter help on the trip to Tutow. It must be a long, slow trip for a fighter if he travels the same distance you do. Then to get home and be strafed seems a bit unsportsmanlike. What a miserable mess all this is.

Your second letter correctly translated "snake's belly" into "lower than ___". I seem to suffer periods of despair and unhappiness followed by a small amount of bravery and willingness to get on with it . . . and end it. I believe, for me, inactivity is the worst. You don't seem to have much of it (inactivity, that is).

Dugout Doug is not well-liked here. He is such an ego maniac and feels he is an immortal. Every appearance is a big show, and cameramen are everywhere. I can assure you that his "wading ashore" on dangerous beaches is just not so. If he ever censors my mail, I'll be in the brig . . . or the Navy, forever!

The Salvation Army ladies must be a most welcome sight at the end of a flight . . . or any other time. Like you, I have a good feeling for them, but am not fond of the Red Cross. I don't know if either of them are out here or not.

Your trip to Brunswick should get you a credit for multiple missions. Glad you got one of Goering's fighters, and especially because it was headed for you. All that, plus three passes in order to drop, must have been tough on the nerves and the underwear. Hope your hand is hurt enough to get you some much needed rest. Hope it isn't bad enough to provide an excuse for your lousy shotgun shooting at a future date. Perhaps you will qualify for an early trip home. Having made these snide remarks, I hope your hand wound was as minor as you indicated.

Watching George Sloan and his crew go down would be most difficult and troubling. On top of that, who were in the three chutes . . . and which seven didn't get out?! It may be forever until you know. Again, I feel your comraderie and closeness makes these things all the more trying. We are not that close.

When we talk with the Army or Marines, we pretty well assume we won't be seeing them again. The relationship is always short, but we do see most of them over and over. With our own crew, it is somewhat different, but I still maintain a distance for that very reason.

So you're going to Italy. Is that good? From here, it would sound good, but I don't really know what your missions will amount to. Take heart in that the move will consume some time. I'll be happy to hear about Italy.

It seems like a long time since I wrote, and I may repeat a bit. We fooled around in places like Namur, Surabaya, and Salamaua, plus Manus and Los Negros. It was fairly easy, and not too risky as far as I could tell. Still, it's hard to relax, and one hates to get hurt because of Piss-Call Charlie or some suicidal dog-face from Nippon. I guess it was as restful as it gets here, and we were able to hear "Drifting & Dreaming" a few hundred more times. I now know where every scratch in the record is, plus all the notes. No one has the guts to throw it over the side because it is our entertainment.

Of course, all that came to an abrupt halt, and we loaded and went into Cape Sansapor, which is north and west of New Guinea. Another small invasion for the expendables in order to shut down (and use) another jungle airstrip. That was, I think, 30 July, and we have been back to find it quiet and relatively peaceful. All the debris has been bulldozed to one side of the airstrip, and it is a rather impressive display for a small invasion. Mostly Jap aircraft…Zeros with a few Betty Bombers. They have a plane very similar to our C-46, but I don't know what it's called. On our second trip, the Army was settled in and said it was only bad for a week or so. I was able to procure an aluminum watchband made by U.S. Army labor from Japanese materials, and the business is good. The G.I. leather watchstraps last about a month before rotting away. On the first day, we were ordered in to the left of the main infantry point, which I thought was great. It didn't turn out that way, in that we were left unprotected when the beachhead was established. We had about 50 feet of water ahead of us when we went aground, and it took some time before Sea Bees could build a sand ramp so we could unload. We therefore became spectators for a while and enjoyed the singing of the various pieces of metal flying around. I picked some shrapnel up and found it is sharp, and some of it almost is like little stars. I tried not to think of the procedure to remove things like that from one's fleshy parts. We had some destroyers offshore quite a distance. They do that so as to lob their shells in at the end of the arc. That way, they fall down on the target rather than breaking up on the trees. Pee-Call Charlie played around one night and was absolutely dissolved by one of the destroyer's guns. Another had a wing shot off and, while afire, circled as he fell. It was beautiful. The tides took out our sand ramp, and our equipment was apparently not a priority, so we were a few days in limbo. It was a little comforting at night to have some water ahead of us, and we doubled and sometimes tripled the watch to warn of infantry approaching. One of our boys was issued a Thompson sub machine gun in the dark of night and, while trying to guess which was single and which was auto fire, he also pressed the trigger and blew away about 20 rounds, which ricocheted off the deck and deck house. He was some 8 feet from where yours truly had just fallen into a deep sleep. I was deeply into a nightmare about a Jap platoon rushing our ship and swinging those damned swords and shouting Banzai. I do not have the word skills to describe how a half-naked coward can move when properly motivated. I tried to dig down through the deck, out through the bulkheads, and finally collected my thoughts and grabbed the .45 and joined some others who were controlling themselves as the poor shipmate lay on the deck shouting, "American, American!". I was tired enough, so I quickly went back to sleep, praying for a dream of a platoon of winsome female beauties threatening my innocence. I was able to sleep two hours before another General Quarters . . . aircraft in the vicinity. They never showed.

I guess things are looking up a bit. We now own Eniwetok and Kwajalein, and Saipan and Guam are supposed to be secured. These are all north of us, but are taking some of the heat off. We are now "resting" before reloading, and I suppose it may be a resupply of Cape Sansapor. With all my bitching, I must say I love the sea and the sailing. I do not love the Navy, but the sailing is beautiful. I note the merchant ships that are in our convoys do not stress themselves with all the chickenshit that we endure. Of course, they are not really armed, and their crews are small. Anyway, the nights at sea are magnificent, and it's a great time to think about the old days and how far away that really is. Here we are, a couple of college boys who used to fish, hunt, swim and sleep in that big north window of the fraternity house with the snow on the blankets. Now you are scaring the hell out of the German military, and the Japanese military is scaring the hell out of me. After careful consideration, I liked it better in the old days. I believe that if I get home, I will try and finish school. It is painfully clear that I will get home only when this is over. No one goes home from here.

So, give 'em hell and protect yourself as best you can. I'm glad I'm not in your shoes, and I'm looking forward to viewing your pheasant shooting exercises once more. If I can't do that, I'll just listen to Bob Hope!

WORN OUT BILL

Sunday, 16 Sept. 1944 to
Tuesday, 26 Sept. 1944

DEAR WORN OUT—

The mailman brought some mail that had been forwarded from the squadron in Grottaglia. Amongst this unexpected booty was yours of 16 August 1944. I wonder if they will send any more here (official Army address) or sit on everything until, somewhere in the morass of Postal people, someone discovers my new duty station. Actually, I think they have done a great job overall, considering the millions of troops and the thousands of places they must reach.

Your comments on the men who get killed, either by misdirected friendly fire accidents or equipment failure, and not actually confronting an enemy in combat, are well taken. My reluctance to write to the Norris family stemmed from my feeling that the unvarnished truth might appear to be a waste of a good man and, thus, hurt more or cause bitterness. I couldn't falsify the truth either. In situations like these, I consider these guys lost to enemy action, regardless of cause and that, when you get down to the nitty gritty, is the real truth.

Your favorite General, Corn Cob Doug, is not enjoying the reputation over here that he seems to work so hard to create. In his many poses for the photographers, if you will look closely, you will see the MGM lion yawning wildly in the background. Some of his aides act as human stepping stones, so the "Great One's" booties remain free of just plain, everyday dirt and grime.

The list of Islands that are beginning to fall, or at least be subdued, is becoming quite impressive. You may regard this as another small step toward your return to life in the land of plenty. The names of all those Islands do not lend themselves to the beaches as you see them during an operation. We have to fly straight and level during a bomb run, which is really scary, but we don't run aground on sandbars and park for a couple of days while the good guys and bad guys exchange heavy fire around and through your rigging. It's no wonder you have nightmares . . . I would be catatonic instantly. Be careful when you pick up shrapnel. The last hunk I picked up on our deck was red hot. As you say, one considers what those things could do to your softer parts . . . and if they are hot, my God! What a way to go!

I am pleased to hear of your increasing respect and love for the sea. The vistas of horizons, calm and angry seas, weather and its volatility, must afford you times of serenity and contemplation that helps to overcome the sheer misery of the rest of the job. We also share the same feelings about our environments. Mine is like yours, without water . . . only the boundlessness of the sky.

My next move to a permanent (?) post will probably be back to Caspar, Wyoming, to work with brand new crews as an instructor. That has an ominous sound to it. New crews, beardless pilots, mountains and violent weather. Another possibility would be me in chains, aboard a B-29 headed for the Pacific to aid you in your efforts to put out the fire of the rising sun. There must be an alternative hiding out somewhere in the less violent of the Army's job categories. How about dog robber to Dugout, or perhaps baggage handler to our much traveled First Lady, Eleanor R.?

The life of a returnee bears no resemblance whatever to that from which he just recently escaped. At the risk of causing you additional pain and suffering, on top of your daily dose of same, I will describe some of the things I must now accommodate myself to. Instead of a Corporal with bad breath shouting to get my ass out of the sack for briefing, a sheer, shorty nightgown breathes gently in my ear wondering if I would like breakfast or, perhaps, wait just awhile. A tough decision, but luckily the clatter of pans from the kitchen suggests that Grandma's hot biscuits need more time in the oven. God bless slow yeast

Breakfast is no longer diarrhea roulette or shrunken gums. Grandma stands by her trusty gas range and will be delighted to take orders for eggs (any style), biscuits (butter, honey or preserve), sausage (patties or links), potatoes (any style), or pancakes and waffles (real maple syrup from Bloomington). Juices, toast, coffee and a variety of preserves are available on the sideboard. This, of course, is repeated at lunchtime, as well as dinner, with appropriate viands calculated to awaken longsuffering taste buds.

I am not trying to rattle your chain, William, but merely to remind you to be the most careful Naval Officer in the annals of naval warfare. These goodies await you, too, so stay out of the line of fire and plan ahead.

Since getting home, I have been doing the usual mundane things you would expect. I now attach a great deal more significance to this mundane routine than ever before; walking over to the lake with Shirley and pushing the stroller with Dawn aboard, taking in a movie, eating frequently with my folks and sisters, and downtown on the I.C. train to shop (actually bought Shirley a new coat and replaced some of my uniforms). Save your money . . . you'll probably need some new gear, and prices have escalated. All the things I here-to-fore took for granted are now gifts to be savored and appreciated.

For a few days, we have been running into other guys who just got back from other assignments and are awaiting new orders and new postings. Jim Fletcher and his wife, along with Harry (Moe) Anderson, are two people you know. Harry is a Lt. of infantry (Combat Infantry Badge) and got machine gunned in Italy, which eliminates his dreams of pro-baseball or basketball. He is thinking of coaching down near Bloomington. Chet Wetterlund was killed on a training flight out of Pensacola Naval Base. We had met Harry downtown at the "Jug", and later at the Hotel Knickerbocker Officer's Club.

Met and renewed friendships with several other old friends and, what with entertaining at home and being entertained elsewhere, we have been busy. Had the baby christened and also opened up a checking account (could these two events be related?).

Took a trip up to our summer cottage at Gravel Lake, near Paw Paw in Michigan. Had a nice, lonely two days. Ate out with longtime friends up there. Incidentally, had dinner with Leo Garrity and his mother in our own neighborhood. Leo, as you remember, was our replacement Nav.

We are scheduled for an R & R in Miami Beach, leaving on the 27th, so I will close this missile and resume on the day of our departure for the land of money and skimpy bathing attire.

BASKING IN BOUNTY BILL

P.S.   Quite seriously, I don't want to rub in my luck in any of your sensitive spots, but thought you would like a report on what's cooking. W.H.A.

30 September, '44

DEAR SITTING BILL—

It has been busy here at the end of the world, and I now have yours dated 29 May to 13 June. I see that you, too, are busy. It would be nice if there were less time between letters, but I don't know how they do as well as they do. From May to the end of September is a long time.

You indicate that the joys of transferring leave something to be desired. I agree, although it has been a long time since I changed stations. I note some nostalgia on your part in leaving your "lucky" airplane to a new crew. I suppose I might feel the same way if I were to leave this battered and rusted tub. It has become "home", but leaving it depends on where one goes from here.

Your days at the seaside resort hotel and on the beach do sound like heaven. The waitresses and chambermaids also sound good. All this and people who speak English is truly a dream.

Your flight sounds a bit like a local commuter train . . . minus the square wheels and coal dust. I'm sure the lack of square wheels was replaced by what is affectionately called turbulence. It's nice to hear about the large collection of fighter planes over there. Sure hope they are for the purpose of escorting you in your future runs against pigs, goats and frightened farmers!

Africa sounds beautiful, and I suppose you left before fully enjoying all the sights, sounds and smells. I note that the cuisine was wanting and that you did not have box springs and mattresses. No chambermaids, either. Have you spoken with the chaplain about this?

I gather that Naples, at least at first, was somewhat of a disappointment. It does sound as though your new chambermaids are friendly and cooperative. Also, the local Natives. I guess that's what pro-stations are all about! If you should happen on an instruction manual regarding what to do with girls, I'd appreciate a copy.

Congratulations on your self-control with the Italian girl who thinks the Italians and Germans are so superior in several respects. That would be hard to take, living among civilian enemies who feel free to shoot off their mouths.

It is noted that you now have double credit for your 8th Air Force missions . . . and you have 28 to go. Take heart in that double credit will leave you about half way toward home. Don't know that I'd like counting down, but there is at least a goal . . . an horizon, a dream. Keep the dobber up . . . you'll make it!

Surely your tepee home brought out the outdoorsman in you! Living close to nature and its creatures can be a wonderful thing . . . I'm told. I have only been a visitor in this type abode, and my only observation has been that the floor is steady and there is no lurching here and there. I was not reminded of home, nor were any fond memories aroused.

Yes, our gunners are terrific. The guys on the 20 mms do a little better job because the guns are more maneuverable, but the 40 mms keep popping away and eventually catch up to a plane if the plane doesn't take evasive action. Seeing them come down is a joy, whether we hit them or someone else does. It's hard to imagine here that we are talking about people as well as aircraft. The Japs are so brutal to their enemies (and civilians) that I feel no emotion, but joy when they go. If we don't get them, they'll get us!

Our jeep cost a mattress and some cigarettes. It fit neatly into our Higgins boat, and we then opened our bow doors and dropped the ramp at anchor. The boat nosed up onto the ramp, and the jeep was driven into the tank deck where slight alterations were performed. It is extremely handy in running for supplies, etc. It is often a long walk to a supply depot, and then one must wait for a truck to take the booty to the boat. It is often a full day's frustration, and then load the supplies aboard in the dark, and maybe with some dangerous rolling seas.

Congratulations to you and Shirley on the motherhood-fatherhood event. I'm sure Shirley would have wished your presence and I'm doubly sure you would have rather been there. Is the offspring male or female? Either way, you now have an additional reason to act with good sense and work toward survivability. Perhaps you've already thought about that.

So, your letter is answered to the best of my ability. We have returned from invasions at Morotai and Halmahera. These well-known places, as you undoubtedly know, lie between Chicago and Tokyo and are not likely ever to become tourist attractions. Unfortunately, we drew a bad beach area at Morotai, and Halmahera was no dream either. The scuttlebutt has it that about 17 Japs were taken prisoner (all wounded), and the rest were killed or were suicides. They know they've been abandoned and have no hope, but they will not surrender. They did a job on us we won't soon forget. We are now licking our wounds and repairing and trying to get supplies. We know the next one is not far off.

Meanwhile, our boys have been busy north of here and I dare say they've had it rougher than we. Guam and Tinian, Eniwetok, Kwajalein and Tarawa are all ours. The tales of Tarawa are bloodcurdling. We are seeing some new muscle around, but it's a big place and I do not see any mammoth concentrations on either side. We still wonder where the Jap Navy is and when and where they'll hit us.

I've avoided Malaria . . . and the Jungle-Itch is treatable, but keeps growing back. Uncomfortable, but not life-threatening. The eyes and skin are yellow, and the weight disappears and cannot seem to be replaced. I don't imply there isn't any food . . . it's that for days, we live on coffee and sandwiches and, at times, these calories are thrown away or left for quieter times. For a long time, we were worn out with false alarms about subs or aircraft in the area. Now it seems that the alarms are not false, and we get nasty surprises. I haven't figured out which way is best, but my choice would be to have neither. Truly, my real aptitude would have placed me at the Pentagon shuffling papers from 9 to 5. My present attitude would suggest any duty as a civilian in charge of nothing!

Now I have some info designed to make you feel better on your fights over the garden spots of Europe. You, very likely, have no idea of the AA fire a group of ships can throw up. An approaching enemy plane can fly broadside, head on, or any way it pleases, and when it comes within range, it must come through a nearly solid curtain of steel. This, along with the shell bursts, can blacken the sky and spray the water in a concentrated area. Obviously, there is a depth-perception problem here, but I have watched the scene many times and wondered how in the hell a plane can survive all this. Nevertheless, they often do and they'll turn and come back and do it again. We are primarily firing on Zeros, which are not at all durable. When really hit, they drop engines or wings and flame up quickly. So . . . my point is that your B-24 <u>is</u> durable and sturdy and, although seeing the flak from the wrong end is bound to curl your hair, it can be beat. You already know that. I know the German 88 is a better gun than we have, but our heavier ships have good guns and are accurate. Hope you can keep this in mind the next time the urine freezes around your ankles and your heart keeps bumping the back of your tongue.

Our little pause at the moment is, I suppose, somewhat refreshing, but I can't erase a feeling of foreboding about the immediate future. We'll be going several places for replenishing supplies and also for reloading. I've hated the small invasions with little support, and everything figured on a shoestring basis. I've assumed they were more dangerous, but I'm not sure of that. It seems ridiculous to be in the Navy and develop a fear of mortars, rifle fire and possible infantry infiltration. The bodies look like so many clumps of soiled laundry . . . and a day in the equatorial sun blows them up like balloons. They look to me like the boy next door . . . I only glance and move on.

We'll be expected where we're going next. I guess it doesn't make much difference. For all I know, we were expected all those other places. Still, it's an eerie feeling, and I need to grab the bootstraps and pull like hell.

Keep 'em coming. Give my best to Shirley and offspring. We'll meet again . . . but it will never be the same!

DISPOSABLE BILL

Wed. 27 Sept., 1944 to
Sat. 14 Oct., 1944

DEAR DISPOSABLE—

When we arrived back home from our R & R in sunny Florida on the 14th. Miraculously, yours of 30 Sept. '44 (#XXVII), was waiting for me. I'll hold off answering your letter until I cover the trip to Florida and give you a chance to gnash your teeth and wish you, too, were a member of the elite flying corps.

Left Chicago at 3:30 P.M. and arrived in Pittsburgh about 12:30 A.M. I called my Aunt Jane and Uncle Hobson, and we stayed up until 4:30 catching up on the news. Later on toward evening, went out to the old family house in Mt. Lebanon for a bite to eat and for Shirley to meet some of the Aldersons. My aunts were disappointed that there were only about 30 of them that could join us. The Alderson women are as large in stature as they are in numbers. Shirley was a little overwhelmed by the sheer volume of flesh and physical enthusiasm of their welcome.

Took in the sights in Washington, D.C., and stayed the night due to overcrowded trains. Got to ride the cane seats all night the 30th, behind a coal-burning locomotive, and all day the 1st of October. The closer to Miami, the warmer it got, and soon all the windows in the car were open and soot and the lung-killing coal fumes rendered visibility and breathing next to nil. Checked into the Lord Tarleton and laid in the tub for an hour, breathing deeply.

Over the next few days, did a lot of poolside sitting, eating out and playing tourist. Ran into all kinds of people we knew from the Army and from home. Sgt. Tietz and his wife, McGlasson, Harry Anderson and his wife, Mrs. Clancy and Florence, Zane Grey Hall and wife . . . and a couple of others from Caspar and our crew. Went deep sea fishing, golfing and a couple of boat trips through the maze of waterways hereabouts. At the Tarleton, one dollar a day covered our room, and meals were super at one dollar each. The menus overflowed with selections, and service was top drawer. Returned home Sat. 14 October, fat and suntanned . . . and quite unwilling to pin on bars and wings and return to the fray.

With the amount of exposed flesh, bouncing buttocks and heavenly hooters at the swimming ponds, you surely would have ended up in the intensive care unit at the local hospital with a critical case of hyperventilation. I was caught by Shirley ogling one such edible morsel and was informed that a little ogling was permitted, but if my mouth remained hanging open, she would stuff a beach chair in it. Strange critters, womenfolk!

Pleased to hear you liberated a jeep. Let me suggest, with all the paint you have on board, that you apply enough of the stuff to the jeep to give it a new appearance. Maybe mount a .50 caliber on it to discourage snipers and former owners.

The major invasions we hear about; Tarawa, Tinian, Kwajalein and the Canal . . . but there never is even a squib in the major newspapers about the little ones. The casualties on those big ones were horrific, but a guy is just as scared and just as dead on a small one. I do not feel the press is doing an even adequate job of reporting. Looks like they take press releases from the services and add their own swivel chair quarterbacking to the stories. Your experiences should be an item for the front pages. "Navy men dodge mortars and infiltrators in dozens of small invasions". "Navy men fight side by side with soldiers and Marines during bitterly contested small invasions". Until now, I didn't realize that the entire scope of the loading and unloading procedure also includes some deadly exchanges of fire over, around and at "Ole 628".

Your feeling of foreboding about the immediate future is not abnormal. When I looked at the number of missions I had left to fly, foreboding came easily. You have to expunge foreboding from your thinking. We have survived so far, so luck is on our side. Feeling lucky makes the adrenaline move faster when needed, sharpens the eye, improves reaction time and is not nearly as depressing as looking at the hole in the doughnut. Think positively . . . go kill a Jap or two . . . and I'll take out an orphanage and a hospital. C'est La Guerre!!!

I think when you signed off your last letter, "Disposable Bill", that your git up and go was sputtering a little. How about "Buoyant Bill" or "Sterling Burling"; they have a more permanent ring to them. Hang in there, the Germans know to the inch where we are on the bomb run, but some of us continue to fox the bastards. I have a friend in the Injun spirit world; a Shaman called "Rabbit With Twelve Feet"!!! He is one very, very lucky Redskin. He will thump his many feets in your burrow, should you believe that you, too, will return with your brass balls clanking and your lucky feets ready to depart Dodge City instantly.

Should you write before you get my newest address, mail to 7042 Kimbark Ave, and they will forward. I will probably be instructing green crews preparing for combat. This does not figure as a picnic in the park. I will stand ready at a second's notice to have Feets burn rubber.

It is very difficult to live with a patio chair in one's mouth! Women?!

BUG-EYED BILL

Sunday 15 Oct., 1944 to
Friday 20 Oct. 1944

DEAR SURVIVING—-

Just a sentence or two, mailing my new addresses quickly as possible.
Lt. W.H.A.
2nd AF, 211 AAF, BG
Casper, Wyoming

W.H.A.—SRA
231 South Grant St.   don't move in here until Nov.
Casper, Wyoming

Always write to me at Air Base, not apt. More to follow.
Be brutal and brave, Bill Burling,

REAR ECHELON BILL

7 Oct. '44

DEAR QUICK DRAW BILL—

A real surprise to receive your letter dated 14 June to 23 June . . . along with a small change in our orders. I just wrote very recently, but will answer yours and tell what I can. I <u>think</u> I'll get a chance to mail this soon.

Your stories of the bomb runs cause chills up and down my spine and are somewhat offset by the mention of the Red Cross girls and others who inhabit your new home. It sounds as though you are making your canvas abode downright comfortable. The lizards and snails should make good pets and prevent loneliness. It is with some mirth that I hear of your semi-private outhouse. We, conversely have flush toilets and have acquired the skill to stay put in heavy seas. There are only seven or eight people per toilet, so it is luxurious. The natives relieve themselves when the notion strikes, but apparently it is written that one must move to the edge of a path or road. The native shanties have a hole in the floor, and one learns not to walk beneath their homes. They are naked and unashamed, and maybe smarter than we "civilized" people.

Congrats on your 2nd Wedding Anniversary. How time flies! It has been a busy year, and poor Shirley has been alone a lot. You, too, of course!

Sorry to hear of your pleurisy. I understand it is very painful. I'm surprised you snapped out of it as quickly as you did. Perhaps your well-directed anger at the Major was a partial cure!

Your run over Trieste sounds very successful and, better still, a little hair-raising. I note that upon your return, you were fed by pretty American girls. I wonder if they'll ever send some of those girls out here. When I have time, I must figure how long since I saw a white woman . . . or any woman, except for these natives.

Obviously, Munich was well-defended and your trip there must have been pure excitement. The flak you took sounds large to me, and I'm sure you feel as I do . . . that ragged, sharp steel would be extremely unhealthy in soft body parts. Hurray for your pilot for deviating from a plan in order to survive and fight another day. Then, with an easier run over Yugoslavia, you are building up an impressive number of missions.

It would appear that if you guys should find yourselves on the ground, you have a scrambled political situation to face. I do hope you learn all you can; especially how to tell friend from foe. So far here, our natives are friendly (thanks to brutal treatment by the Japs) and "normal" for them would be to have British or Dutch around. I believe we are considered as liberators, and we do not fear the natives. Now that you are armed with two pistols, a knife or bayonet and Lord knows what else, will your aluminum box still get off the ground?

I have a great feeling of glee for you. I really believe I may soon mail letters to you in Chicago. Keep up the good work!

We are now involved in some shuttling around. We sometimes travel empty, or nearly so, and deliver this and take on that. Can't be more specific. This particular area is winding down. We (others) took Pelilew recently and, in our taking leave of New Guinea, we ventured close to Borneo, where I could see signs for Shell Oil Co. . . . and fires. All I know about Borneo is that there used to be a wild man from there. Now that I have glimpsed it, I suspect it is more civilized than any place I've been in a long time.

I'm sure you're aware that, when you join the Navy, you see the world . . . have free medical attention. I can now verify that the dental attention is also free, and worth every penny of it! With a jaw swollen to the size of a small ham, I sought and found a genuine, licensed, educated, tooth jockey. He explained that two wisdom teeth needed removal <u>now</u>. A friendly sort, he poured a drink of whiskey and then another . . . and still another. Eventually, he quietly mentioned that he had no novocaine, but it wasn't really necessary anyway. We had a discussion regarding "necessary", and he conceded he could pull a tooth just as well without any pain killer. I slyly asked for another drink, with the idea I would then bolt from his tent and suffer in solitude. He had obviously dealt with cowards such as me before, and his accomplice arrived on the scene to steady me on my chair. In short, the teeth are gone . . . as is the bulk of the swelling . . . and I am on the mend. He gave me six aspirin as he opened the fly of his tent and pointed my way out. With compassionate humanitarians like this, one has a tendency to stay well if it kills one!

So, I am not feeling very chipper and am allowed to lie in my rack for a little while. The diesel exhaust enters my port as we slowly roll from side to side. An ice pack would be nice, but there is no ice, and the water temperature is somewhat less than 100 degrees. The diesel fumes have never been pleasant, but today they have me close to losing my lunch of hydraulic milk and soggy bread. Wish I were home! Again, it is clear that the Navy brings us to the boiling point in the hope we'll take out our wrath on the enemy!

The sea is smooth, with some medium ground swells that are comfortable. Like being rocked to sleep. It is not now very dangerous here, so it's a perfect time to feel like hell. I have requested round-the-clock nurses to bathe my fevered brow, only to hear someone say I was delirious. He is wrong . . . I am desirous!

An unexpected chance to mail this. It will be awhile before I can write again. Take good care of yourself.

THE SEAGOING GUINEA PIG

Saturday, 21 Oct. 1944 to
Sunday, 31 Dec. 1944

DEAR GUINEA PIG—

Yours of 7 Oct., 1944, arrived here at Casper on the 15th of November, after a rather convoluted journey. I'll go back to Sat. 21, October, and begin a recap of my activities here at Casper and leave the reply to your letter until I have covered the mundane day-to-day here.

Shirley and I got a nice train (can you believe that one?) out of Chicago to Casper, got in around 6:30 and put up at the Townsend Hotel on the 19th. Fortunately, we were tired, so the regular patrons, sheepherders and their cronies disturbed us not with their revelries.

Went out to the field and signed in, and am now an instructor. It is a good thing that the war seems to be going our way because I instruct mostly in how to protect your ass and just toss the bombs out any old place. Shirley found some ladies she knew, including one of her school friends from Kimbark Ave. who is married to one of the aspiring combat crew trainees. Ed Dumas and wife are still here, and he still loses two pounds every time he climbs aboard a B-24. He is thin. Ate antelope at his place this evening and then to the Officers Club for a dance. Ed could have danced with a clarinet and made a nice couple.

Walked around town looking for an apartment and got a lead on one for the end of the month. We have moved to an auto court in the hope our money will last until the next check. In the meantime we ate at the field, or with anybody who invites us. I am starting regular, irregular hours. I fly nights, days and afternoons. The mountains, weather and inexperienced pilots take their toll on my easily disturbed nerve network. I have to find a way out of this before one of these guys mistakes a mountain for a large cloud.

We bought a 1938 Packard, formerly the pride and joy of a sheepherder who had moved the gas tank into the trunk so the high-centered prairie roads wouldn't rip off the regular tank. The car also has a gasoline-fired heater in the front, and it puts out heat . . . big heat, right now. Being warm is great out here in the big wind, but that heater has to be watched like a coiled diamondback. This flying at night is beginning to wear me down . . . out to the field about 3:00 P.M. and back home about 3:00 A.M. Took a quick trip to the mountains . . . terrific scenery, but those suckers are twice as hard and awesome on the ground as they appear to me from the nose compartment in the "24." Wings, don't quit near those hills.

Got an apartment in same building with Dumas. Newly redecorated and new furniture . . . we are ecstatic. Broke a bone in my hand and am playing this for all it's worth with the flight surgeon. He has grounded me . . . what a relief . . . I was in the air every day or night for quite a spell. We have met a lot of returned officers and their ladies, and we now play cards, eat at one another's places and attend all the functions at the O. Club. Real nice people, and mostly our peers in age, viewpoint and a tendency to kick up their heels from time to time. One of the couples, Zane Hall and Charlie, lost their baby and we all felt rotten with them . . . they had a support base of some 40 officers and their wives and this, I'm sure, was a help to them at this very sad time. The Dumas' had a baby boy. All OK, except for a hare lip, which is being repaired in the hospital's body and fender facility. Ed and wife were pretty distraught about the boy's lip, but the group talked them out of the doldrums.

Attended a small bash at one of the officers' apartments for poker and drinks. They had a new puppy who got into everything, including my hat. We put our plastic rain covers in the crown of the hat (when not in use) and the puppy peed in the hat . . . the rain cover worked as advertised. When I left, I put on my hat. Everyone else thought this was hilarious . . . I did not.

Took a day and went sleighing up in the mountains. You and your crew would have loved the snow, cool weather, and sparkling mountain air. A day or two later, went out on an antelope hunt and failed to bag one of the elusive speedsters. The antelope post sentries so nobody gets real close before the sentries spook the herd and, man, those little devils are speedy and also bound up in the air every few strides to further complicate drawing a bead on them.

You mention taking on this or that and delivering it here and there and were reluctant to be more specific. You sure know how to get my curiosity bug in a tizzie. I'll bet there is a good story or two behind those modest words. Did you, when you coasted past Borneo, think of all the Dutch girls that probably inhabit that big island? Now you know why that guy on the island is called the "Wild Man of Borneo". He needs help. Had you advised your Captain of this lopsided mix of boys and girls? I'm sure he would have anchored and sent you ashore to even up the odds.

The experience you had with the "Tooth Fairy" is similar to my occasional brush with the medical mafia who forget the Hippocratic oath as quickly as it is administered. After three shots of booze to lower your guard, he brought in muscle to render you immobile in the chair and removed the offending wisdom teeth with an old and rusty pair of pliers. Though crude, his operating methods worked, and I am relieved that you are on the road to recovery and will soon sic your choppers at the steaks customarily provided by the Navy at dinnertime. It also gives you a chance to rest and enjoy the comforting breeze of fumes coming through your port.

When the excavation in your jaw bone heals up, for Pete's sake, brush your teeth after every meal, no matter what's going on on deck. The war can oblige you that small comfort.

I don't recall telling you, but I have applied for pilot training. Flying with fledgling aviators just out of four-engine training does not tend to give me confidence in my immediate future. Another alternative would be to volunteer for B-29s, and missions with veteran crews. This, too, leaves my retirement plans somewhat iffy. If I am going to buy the farm, I would rather be driving than sweating in the back seat. Will keep you advised.

Keep your ivories polished and your head turning 360 degrees so you can duck when necessary.

BARON BILL

24 November, '44

DEAR BOMBER MAN—-

It seems my last letter to you was eons ago. I remember it wasn't really completed when I got word a mail boat was coming alongside, and it was my last chance . . . I thought. At that time, we were partly loaded and thought we were just keeping busy. We made one more trip and unloaded and then reloaded combat equipment and Army troops. We were greeted at Leyte on 20 Oct. at dawn. Most of our other invasions haven't been real early in the morning, but the time has partly to do with tides and reefs and water depth in general. We arrived in one of several convoys and passed by the ships, shelling the beach and the transports and the hospital ships . . . and rammed the beach right in front of a short strip of sand and then jungle. In short order, there were LSTs, lined up side by side for a couple of hundred yards, and it was pretty impressive. The ships that had been working up north of us had joined us a night or two ago. We felt strong and invincible for awhile. The rains fell and we got some tanks ashore, but they were held up . . . nowhere to go. None of the other gear could move because tanks blocked the short beach area. Meanwhile, it was fairly quiet, but we nervously watched the jungle for infantry. Down to our left, Navy planes were bombing and strafing a short distance inland, and before long, the tanks moved away along the beach where the jungle petered out a bit. We were on the east side of the island, which is fairly large, and were anxious to unload and back out so another ship could come in. There was some confusion on the beach as they were trying to take units in order, and some of the ships were aground short of the beach and couldn't unload. Our efforts to find the beach master were a waste of time and, as suspected, before long the jungle came alive to our right and left. Troops coming ashore were destined to join other units, but found themselves under fire. After some very hectic moments (or hours), the troops set up Mortars (105s) and machine guns, and riddled the jungle immediately ahead of us. All fell quiet, and we began unloading heavy trucks, only to have them stopped in their tracks by someone. We raised our ramp so the Japs couldn't come aboard and manned rifles and pistols in case they tried. Some Army was still aboard and wanted to go, but were ordered to stay with the supplies. It soon became apparent that all was not well. There wasn't enough room to off-load the equipment on the ships, and the Army had moved into a hornet's nest just beyond the beach and in all sectors. We were forbidden to fire ashore, even when we could plainly see targets. It was confusing.

Through the day, Navy planes worked feverishly, answering calls to attack a machine gun, a native hut . . . a sound in the jungle. Twice a destroyer came close in and fired into the hills, fortunately missing our mast. We had reports of subs, but saw none. A few Zeros showed up and ran across all the LST's in a line, showering us with whatever they had aboard.

It seemed that we hit the beach and all hell broke loose. I had hardly chewed off my last fingernail when dusk arrived with more rain and some thunder and lightning. Now the destroyers fired parachute flares (like I made at Tipp City, Ohio, so long ago) and the night turned to day briefly. Still, the trucks sat in the oozy sand and rifle fire from the jungle made one wonder if he should sit tight or move. I have no idea what time it was when some wounded were brought down and loaded in the Higgins boats for the trip out to the hospital ships. We were told by an Army Captain that the Army was about to be driven off the island. It was our understanding that there were about 130,000 Japs there and, obviously, we didn't have that kind of power ashore yet. We were all fairly well concentrated on the beaches.

I thought many times you had received your last letter from me. I was as well armed as you with your .32 and .45, and a knife or two. Like you, I wondered what good it would do.

We survived the night and the rain, but fear took on new dimensions. In the morning, the big ships were gone . . . the Navy air, too. Another day of confusion and waiting . . . but the Army had held. I believe it was the 2nd or 3rd night that we heard Dugout Doug on the radio . . . his troops had met moderate resistance on the beach, but were driving inland and creating havoc with the Japanese forces. Allied casualties were light. Following his heroic speech, we heard the news that John L. Lewis had ordered his union out of the mines and a strike would take place until the miners received decent pay and working conditions. In my emotional state, I was so angry at MacArthur, John L. Lewis, the Navy and the Japanese that I could have easily committed mayhem. Everyone listening to the radio shouted obscenities and the radio was shut off.

I believe it was 23 or 24 October when word came down that the Japanese fleet was closing in on us. To the north of us is San Bernadino Strait, and to the south of us is Surigao Strait. A Jap fleet is headed through each strait from the west, having come in out of the South China Sea. We were to be in the middle of a pincer movement. Having furnished that bit of cheery news, the radio cut back to local fighter control, along with some Army field conversations. I can't describe how I felt. I thought I was used to fear . . . but not so. I determined that somehow I was going to see to it that I went down like a man.

You may or may not know that when the Japs came through those straits, our Navy sailed across in front of them in a classic crossing of the "T" . . . and the Jap Navy was shattered. The group up north badly outnumbered the U.S. ships, but took a bad beating, turned and left. Another large battle took place up north near Formosa, and the Japs were badly beaten there. So that is why our big ships left us in the lurch.

Meanwhile, Marines were put ashore and the situation is now in hand. Mac's chestnuts have been pulled from the fire once again. Meanwhile, the taking of this island is deemed unnecessary by everyone but Mac. What a horrible waste! What a hellish experience! His personal war continues.

We finally unloaded and took on a load of spent brass and left. We returned twice under somewhat better conditions with miscellaneous supplies, and we are now at rest . . . briefly.

Another fairly new experience at Leyte was the arrival of genuine, bona fide, suicide planes. Also, suicide boats and swimmers dragging mines against ships at anchor. They're crazy! On watch, day and night, we fired rifles at anything that floated near us. We got two more Zeros, and I believe we hit several more. The infantry still has a way to go, but barring surprises, Leyte should be quiet before too much longer.

There are probably thousands of islands here in the Philippines. Several languages are spoken, and most based on Spanish. It's a short swim from one island to another, and we wonder what the Japs in the north and south will do about their buddies here. They have no Navy now, and I guess they'll just wait their turn. The local people are more handsome and civilized than we've seen for God knows when. We expect they'll remain friendly, but some of them look like Japanese and one can't relax too much. They suffered at the hands of the Japs, and they have nothing left. The town of Tacloban is up north on Leyte, and I expect to get there soon. Across just a little water is the island of Samar, and it, too, is being taken.

All my fear, grief and fatigue are somewhat wiped away when I realize I am alive. It seems impossible. We are all a bunch of zombies with no expression, no emotion . . . no nothing. No complaints about coffee and sandwiches, no complaints period! Is this good? I don't know.

Much more to tell, but not now. I fervently hope you've completed your missions and are home. I do believe your war is way ahead of ours, but we are stronger now. I had no idea what a big, worldwide operation this damned war has been.

I'll write as I can. Surely, for a while, it will be somewhat easier to eat and sleep.

SHADOW BILL

Monday 1, Jan. 1945 to
Thursday 1, Feb. 1945

DEAR SHADOW—

I have read yours of 24 November, '44, three times and find something new each time I go through the letter. Leyte was in the news here a time or two, but their reporting seemed to be a press release from Dugout's H.Q. Your on-site reporting made my hair curl, which I had considered impossible, since it has been standing on end for six months. Who was commanding the Navy task force when they crossed the "T" on the Japs? Brilliant maneuver. Word of the engagement made the papers here, but your explanation of the "T" told the real story of the success of the mission and the unsung guys on the beach.

The press doesn't cover what any of you invasion participants are thinking or enduring. Two or three days of that kind of combat would turn anyone into a zombie. The after battle letdown is worse to overcome than the fighting itself. Adrenaline sustains you during the action and then the aftermath of fatigue and the astonishment of still being in one piece sets in. It is a wonder to me that you overcame the confusion and got anything on the beach at all, while trying to unload with tanks and trucks stuck in the sand, planes strafing and that new wrinkle they're tossing at you . . . suicide planes. Add small boats and suicide swimmers . . . unbelievable! I can imagine one of those suicide planes hitting an LST. It would be absolute carnage. By the way, splashing two more Zeros is quite a feat, congratulations!

Strangely enough, as I look back on those 50 missions, they don't look as tough now as they did at the time. Hearing what you are going through makes my contribution to the war effort seem to be a rather modest one. I am not too thrilled with being an instructor or ending up in B-29s beating up on the Jap mainland. My application for pilot training is somewhere in the bureaucratic hopper. I hope they OK it. I have acquired a six-foot white silk scarf to stream behind me as I soar into the wide blue and don't want it to go to waste.

Like you, my attitude toward union strikers, draft dodgers, etc., borders on the edge of homicide . . . justifiable of course. We have both seen the lengths our rear echelon support troops will go to remain far from the sights and sounds of the actual fighting. The majority of the politicians and mobs of the civilian population also work the same side of the street. It will ever be so. What really gets my nanny goat are the guys who have never been shot at, yet sport combat award ribbons.

The sound of those big naval shells passing so close overhead must have raised a goose bump or two, along with the hope that they know you are in the same Navy they are. The departure of those ships during the hard fighting on the beach must have prompted some pretty pungent language from the expendables on the beach, and a wish to hear them roaring through your rigging again. The rumors from the front lines about how badly goes the battle must have added to your already overflowing cup. I don't know how you take the stress and still manage to do your jobs, invasion after invasion. The prospect of riding a B-29 over the Nip homeland is not nearly as discomforting as the thought of riding your LST up onto a beach and undergoing that kind of abuse.

Word has come down that I will be going to pilot training, and orders will follow. Shirley will go on home to Chicago until such time as I get settled in somewhere for more than 15 minutes. Shirley spent a few days visiting and saying goodbye to new friends and old ones. She was scheduled to fly to Cheyenne the 16th, but we had a bear of a snow storm, so she left the next day. Trained from Cheyenne to Chicago and was lucky to get a seat. I finished up clearing the base on the 20th and took off in our vintage Packard the same day. I ran into a blizzard and all I could see was the back end of a semi going east. The storm was so bad I was afraid to lose sight of the truck, so stayed behind him for some 20 hours . . . at ten or fifteen mph. Visibility was a little improved when dawn came, and I continued on to Chicago. All in all, it took 50 hours and damn near killed me. Barely spoke to anyone when I got home . . . just fell into bed. A lot of the 50 hours I don't remember.

Hopped one more train on the 27th bound for San Antonio, and, as usual, the train was not concerned about a record-setting dash to destination. We did finally crawl into San Antone on the 30th of January, and I find myself in the exact same place I was in at the end of my first train ride with the Army. My progress in the military seems to be very slow at the very best.

My new address: 1Lt. W.H.A.
        Sqdn. 111 Flight H
        Section MM
        S.A.A.C.C. San Antonio, Texas

Being forever the optimist, I hope this does not screw up our continuing chain of letters and that we both will continue being lucky.

RUNNING IN PLACE BILL

27 December, '44

DEAR BELIEVING BILL—

Can you believe I have your letter written 24 June to 1 July? It has been a bit rumpled and has mildew and dried salt on it, but is legible . . . and enjoyable.

I note that you have sampled some cheap wine and noticed your limits for same. Your quaint Italian village sounds great, although somewhat lacking in privacy for the inescapable human necessity of relieving one's bladder, etc.

Perhaps your tail gunner is as valuable as your pilot in that he used his head to down the persistent JU-88. He, and you, should be proud . . . and thankful. Nice to have people around that think.

Ploesti does, indeed, sound like bad news. I must confess, I am not totally acquainted with the place, but it must be very important to Germany . . . and your fellow wild blue yonder wanderers. It is perhaps most fortunate that Ploesti is often cloud-covered. Tell your CO. that you are allergic to Ploesti and that you'd rather journey to Chicago.

Good Lord! Parachute trouble again?! Sounds like sabotage. I believe I'd take mine with me to chow, the latrine and everywhere else. One's last chance should be in impeccable shape. Your story about the guy's chute catching fire caused my imagination to send chills up the yellow streak down my back! What a damned shame!

Your story about the photographer is funny, although I'm sure the humor was somewhat tempered for you. I hope the photog has, by now, been to the laundry and is requesting his transfer to the Red Cross. Sounds like a hell of a trip to Ploesti, and I'm sure glad you made it back. Keep up the good work. One day soon there will be no Ploesti. I have joked in the past about the chaplains, but have changed my mind. At least here, their job is rather sober in that they give the blessings before the landings, and then the last rites to anyone who can still hear. Their days are not joyful. Meanwhile, they, too, are exposed to most of it.

You have complained about your loose formations and the attending danger before. Apparently, nothing is being done. It would be <u>bad</u> <u>enough</u> if everyone would pitch in and do right.

Yes, the hormones may as well be on vacation . . . wish they were. Not much time to think about it though.

And so . . . your letter is answered . . . sort of! It has been so long since I wrote and there is so much to tell that this letter cannot do it. Since D-day at Leyte, we have been here and there and all over hell bringing things back to Leyte and taking things away from there. We have been to Guam (very nice . . . white sand), the Gilberts and a beautiful place called Ulithi. Ulithi is about 1 foot above sea level at high tide. Barges have been anchored there and we tie up to the barges in a seaway. The weather is a little rougher up north, and one wonders all night if we'll still be there in the morning or swept away by currents or wind. It would be safe to say I don't like Ulithi. Guam I liked, although it's a bit torn up. I suppose, because it was good, our time there was limited.

Meanwhile, on 15 Dec., we went into Mindoro, which is another Philippine island up north. No great resistance, but the presence of four Jap destroyers running north in the South China Sea sure caught our attention. They were in a hurry, but took time to fire a few rounds as they headed home. We were on the beach and were not hit.

Meanwhile, we have seen some of the island of Samar and the town of Tacloban on Leyte, along with Dulag, and have visited Ormac Bay. Ormac is on the west side of Leyte. I was pleased as punch to see Zamboanga . . . another fine South seas tourist spot. Tacloban, in our dreams, was a city filled with libraries, culture of all sorts, beautiful lonely women and perhaps a place serving liquid refreshment. A local, hoping to build a tourist trade, probably described the town to someone who passed it on to us . . . with some dramatic additions.

We found Tacloban to be a series of grass huts with streets serving also as sewers, and with assorted naked children and/or chickens running amok. The people are beautiful, as compared to the Natives we've grown accustomed to . . . but perhaps we are suffering from too many dreams too long ago. As is usual, if one puts his mind to it, there is entertainment of sorts nearly everywhere. A friend from Midshipman's School (ages ago) and I located a source of beverages, and we had two choices. One was fermented coconut milk dispensed from a douche/enema bag. One merely put the tube in his mouth and released the snap to alleviate the dry mouth problem. This was not especially tasty, and I had some objection to the vessel in which it was fermented. The "bartender's" wife on the porch looked as though she had never given up the douche bag. In addition to this libation, we found that the man's cousin down the road a piece was brewing some very fine corn whiskey. We found this product in bantam beer bottles and guaranteed to be several hours old. At $1.00 per bottle, we could afford more than one . . . and did. It was both terrible tasting and strong. We were well aware that corn is not a big crop in the area, but who cares?

It was after consuming our fair share of their delightful repast that we met the two girls. They were very young and looked clean and were pretty. They were urinating at the side of the road as we introduced ourselves. They wiped away the last trickle with their cotton skirts and agreed to walk with us awhile, although their parents had warned them to stay away from sailors. They led the way with us, breathlessly, alongside and in no time we were at their parents' home. It was a nice house with framed walls and a grass roof. And it was sizeable and clean. We were invited to supper, which I discovered was fish heads and rice. The fish heads are actually small minnows seized from a nearby ditch. The concoction is not likely to grace many cookbooks in the U.S.A. I knew that we were having baloney and cheese "back home" on the ship, and it suddenly sounded good. I was trying for an excuse to miss supper when all hell broke loose outside, simply because my friend had made an indecent proposal . . . probably in an indecent manner. The girl pretended shock, and her sister moved away from me. I explained to the mother that, since my friend was such an idiot, it would be necessary that we move along. She agreed it was time to go, but told me a nice man like me should not be in the company of so crude an individual. I agreed and advised it would not happen again. And so it was we escaped eating supper and anything else that might have happened. We did purchase some very small eggs for $1.00 each, and they were delicious with baloney and cheese. The Filipinos may get rich at these prices.

In the rush of loading and handling all the other things that need doing, we nearly overlooked Christmas a couple of days ago. I thank God I am a year older. It is my third or fourth Christmas away from home. Three or four of us tried to make a tree on the beach out of palm fronds or anything else, but it didn't really work. We were there in the dark trying our damnedest to get the spirit, but it never came. We tried a few carols, but that didn't help. So, Christmas has come and gone!

We are now a "Flagship", and I report this without knowing whether it's good or bad. The "Flag" is a commander and his retinue of reporters, communicators and God knows what. Their ship blew up in the night when a Jap swam under with a mine. They were blown out of the sack and some were wounded. The purple hearts were passed out last week. None were hurt bad enough to go home. We are now a bit crowded and, as usual, some of these people are delightful . . . and some not. I am guessing that the plot will soon thicken.

We are nearly loaded now and it is a heavy combat load. Army personnel will be coming aboard soon and we have fuel, water and ammo. I've about lost count of the number of these things so far, and each impending invasion seems worse than the last. We have a long way to go, and there is little doubt that a surrender of the enemy is, at least, highly unlikely. As we get closer to Japan, the air raids grow in intensity, and their do or die tactics keep one on his toes. They are good sailors, soldiers and flyers, but it is hard to understand their tenacity when it is clear that all is lost. I believe they have hauled their best to the home islands for a last ditch defense. Of course, I know little.

We have been to a rear area where a crew welded cleats along both sides and a crane hoisted a long barge on either side. The barge or pontoon rests on the cleats and is turnbuckled down to our deck at the top. We appear even more ugly and unwieldy. Maybe they'll serve as a weak armor plate!

The mailboat is on its way, and this must go. I shall do my damnedest to mail another letter when possible. Meanwhile, keep alert and check the parachute often. Get the axis out of this so you can go home, and some of those other guys can come over here. We're tired, and I know you are, too. War is mostly work and lack of sleep. The danger is almost secondary. The loneliness is an adjustment.

FILIPINO BILL

Friday 2 Feb. 1945 to
Thursday 1 March 1945

DEAR FILIPINO—

Got your letter of 27 December, '44, and will comment on your ongoing trials and tribulations after I cover the further indignities your hero of the Air War over Europe must up with put.

After the usual obstacle course of sign-in paperwork and the supercilious attitude of the jerks shuffling papers behind their desks, got bedding and a bunk in a barracks. My memories of good food here vanished when I ate lunch and then dinner at the Officers' Mess. The cuisine has gone downhill and now ranks with Flukies at 63rd and Stony Island where waitresses line up eight hotdogs on one hairy arm and then add mustard, piccalilli and onions, then plop the dog down on the table. It takes courage to eat one of those dogs, particularly after it gets hot and the girls begin to sweat.

Here at SAACC, we'll do the same things we did when we arrived here as cadets. If we can get through this again, we move across the road to pre-flight school for classwork, etc. The Air Corps has begun shutting down some primary and basic schools, and judging from this, I suspect that the brass must figure the war is winding down. That reflects on their attitude about the schooling . . . pass or else. The advantage of being an officer shows up here in that we usually outrank the tactical officers, and the medals and wings intimidate them a little. They are usually polite, a change from cadet days.

We had our first P.T., and for the most of us, it was the first time in a year and a half that we did anything in the way of a workout. The whole barracks is disabled to some extent and moaning about being mistreated. A couple of days should iron out the cramps and charley horses. I rather enjoyed the P.T., and am actually looking forward to tomorrow's session. The P.T. is now about four hours daily, just to keep us busy.

We want to get out of classification and into pre-flight. In pre-flight, you need grades of at least 80% to continue on. The Morse code is my only problem. Sending and receiving 40 words a minute doesn't sound like much, but I find it difficult. I am spending extra time at the keyboard.

Had a birthday on the 9th of February. I am not wild about getting older, but considering the past few months, I am delighted to have made it to 23. I look forward to the next 50 with the same delight (I may have to eat those words should my skill as a pilot prove to be a myth). In any event, press onwards.

I qualified for Pilot Training and have moved to Pre-flight school . . . new address, Lt. W.H.A., class 235-Flt 1, SOG-AAFPS, San Antonio, Texas. Lucked in real good on quarters. One of the guys I've been running around with grabbed a room for three in the new barracks and invited two of us to share it with him. We did. Our classwork will be math, physics, theory of flight, ship and plane ID, code and others. Providing I can hack my way through all this, will go to primary flight school to learn to fly . . . probably by the end of March.

I ran into a couple of fellows from my bombardier school and also heard from McGlasson, who is at Kelly Field, just a short distance down the road from here. I hope to get over there for a visit. I probably have been boring you stiff with all this chitchat about nothing in particular, so I'll switch to some comments on your letter.

By now, I thought you would have run out of islands and atolls to invade, and yet each new letter I get from you has another list of places you have been. These never-ending engagements you are involved in must lead you to believe that there will never be an end to this fighting. Wrong, we're going to whip the Japs and the Germans, and I think they will cave in before the end of the year. My prognostications in the past have been notable for how far wrong they were . . . but this one has a nice ring to it.

In order to preserve your liver and kidneys from native distilling, I hope my guess on the war's end comes to pass. I also hope that you develop a more fastidious selection of what you drink when you get home. After all, customers in American saloons are not accustomed to guys wearing cod pieces, bones through their noses and shouting for a head hunter's special in pidgin English.

In a more serious vein, I continue to read your letters with my mouth hanging open. It is just unbelievable to me what you guys are contending with out there. I am sure that the people here at home haven't the faintest notion what our men are enduring in these seemingly unending invasions. Outside of a few big ones that the media exploited, I'm sure they have no idea of the extent of the casualties being taken almost daily in your theater of operations. Someone in Washington should grow some balls and let everyone know what their men are accomplishing, and at what cost.

I find myself getting pissed off at the backfield brass and complacent civilians, so I'll change my subject matter before the tack officer suggests that shining my belt buckle is a big part of the war effort, and I tear off one of his arms.

I noticed that you, too, were delighted to be a year older and wondering a little bit how you managed to reach that plateau in one piece. Now that you are a "Flag Ship", maybe your exposure to the shot and shell will recede. On the other hand, the "Flag" and all those correspondents might be a more tempting target than just your run-of-the-mill pigeons, so continue to be alert and ready to duck. Your remarks about the air raids increasing in intensity sounds ominous; if you can reason with "Flags", tell him to stay out of bunches of ships, so speaks the retired bombardier, we never could hit a single.

I hope the mail brings something more from you so that I can recount to you my fledgling attempts to coax a heavier than air machine into the air . . . and hopefully keeping it there. Let us both try for the next age group.

KITTYHAWK "45"

23 January, '45

DEAR BUZZARD BILL—

Just got back from another invasion and your letter dated 2 July to 11 July was here. Two reasons to celebrate, plus I have some time to answer.

Thanks for the note that Harry Anderson is in Italy and that Ernie Jarke survived his carrier sinking. I can add little, except the rumor that Johnnie Rodino is in Italy and Chuck Correll is still alive in the merchant marine. He's been on the north Atlantic run, which I understand is terrible.

Your trip to Schweicat sounds chilling as usual, and I'm glad you made it back. I believe just the take off in one of those boxes would chill me.

I do hope your accidental strikes that go wild don't bother you. There will be more people killed or maimed by accident than on purpose before this is over. We have been lucky in that when we're in a crowd, the gunners have to cease fire before their sights cross a friendly ship. This takes experience and alertness. In the excitement of it all, mistakes are made. What a way to go!

Eight (double) missions to go. The end is in sight . . . and that was mid-July. Good Lord, I may be writing you in Italy and you may be basking in Chicago! Hope that's the case.

It sounds as though your food is less than the gourmet variety of former days. Take heart, one can survive on lousy food, but the weight does fall away. I don't know what your schedule is, but we cannot eat before an invasion . . . the doctors don't like working on full stomachs!

The ladies of your vicinity must ride round-trip on their Toonerville trolley in order to point and shout as they pass your limited-privacy latrine. Nice that you can entertain them!

I hope they show us the color V.D. film you mentioned. They assumed (correctly) that no one would engage in off-limits exercises in the Solomons or New Guinea. The Philippines are an improvement, so I suppose our day will come.

Your outing over Budapest sounds terrible. Hair trigger bombs hung up and you trying to kick them out while on a catwalk. Perhaps when you get home, you will qualify for a job walking tightwire over Michigan Ave. Who loads those things?

It must be very emotional to see Leo Garrity go home when you are so close. I'll bet he was as happy as he'll ever be!

Your trip over Rumania reduces your time in Italy by two, but what an experience. One would be filled with anger to see fighters firing on the parachutes. Out here, we have long since given up any thought of civilized rules of conduct. The Japs fire on men in the water after a ship-sinking and kill or torture (or both) any prisoners.

Your Pleurisy certainly made your venture to Toulon a hair-raiser. I've never had that, but those who have are impressed with the pain. Glad you had time to soak up some sun and get well.

And now an engine knocked out over Ploesti. Good Lord! Your description of the trip "home" is nerve-wracking. You should get credit for all your remaining missions for that one. Ten guys and a B-24 saved by the skin of your teeth! Hang tough! The good news is that you are nearing the end of all that. Before long, you can complain about those square-wheeled antique trains as you drink your way to Chicago. May it be soon!

I was going to say more about Leyte, but now it seems like so long ago. We carried a small ship on our deck, and I didn't want to mention it when I wrote. Upon our arrival, we listed our ship and kicked the little ship over the side. I expected it to bounce back and damage us, but no such luck. It and its small crew went elsewhere, and who knows where they are now.

We then reloaded, and I wrote before we left for D-day at Lingayen Gulf. This is up north on Luzon and is the same spot the Japs chose when they invaded. The trip was about 11 days, as I remember, and the weather was beautiful. We ran the gauntlet all the way up the South China Sea in a large convoy. We even had destroyers with us and their carriers along, but out of sight. We had been told enough about the place to keep us on edge, and we were bypassing Jap territory most of the way. One night, on my watch, I saw what looked like colored ping-pong balls arching across the sky about a mile ahead and to our right. We sounded General Quarters and maintained course and speed, and no one knew what was going on. Soon, we got the word that a Jap destroyer had sneaked into and among our convoy. The ping-pong balls were one of our destroyers firing on the Jap. Never heard another word about it and don't know what happened. We were kept awake and at General Quarters most of the last several days and nights because of "Bogies", which seldom materialized. On 1 January, we hit the beach, or rather on the way into the beach. We then waited for Sea Bees to push a sand ramp out to us. Then the air raids began, and they were the suicide planes. One could see the Zeroes hanging in the distance while the pilot chose a target or said his last prayer. Then the last Zero would head for the target and fly straight as an arrow until he was either blown up or hit his target. A few did chicken out, it seems, but were usually shot down anyway. Meanwhile, Japanese artillery was working over the LST's on the beaches. The Army had a reasonably easy time of it at first, and we waited breathlessly for them to find the Jap artillery and stop the firing. It seemed like a long wait. We were not hit. Unloading was slow with all this going on. One night, we were warned of enemy aircraft in the area, and we had moved off the beach and were at anchor. We could hear a Zero or two idling around at slow speed, but had no way to see them. One of our boats was dispatched to lay out smoke pots . . . square floating boxes with a pull-out igniter. The boxes generate a great volume of thick white smoke and are designed to make a ship invisible. We had battled suicide boats and swimmers, and going out in a boat could be very dangerous. Our boat did not position the smoke pots properly, and I was ordered to go with the boat and see that the ship was covered with smoke. We did it and then wondered how we'd get back to the ship without being fired on . . . if we got close to another ship. A Zero idled around overhead and seemed to just circle us. I was waiting for the smoke to thin so we could get back to the ship. Suddenly, the Zero flew right into the ship next to us. It hit the port boat deck and wiped out a gun tub and its crew. Fire broke out and now we were really visible. In no time, the fire was put out, and after what seemed like all night, we made it back to the ship. The next day, the adjacent ship was cleaning up the mess and burying its dead.

The following day or so, we shot down a Jap bomber at long range. It caught fire and went down slowly and crashed ashore. We hit it with our twin 40 mm gun at the bow, and I had a front row seat. That is my station for General Quarters, and I am among four 20 mm's and the twin 40 mm. The noise is deafening and painful. My little ear plugs don't help much, and my helmet bounces up and down, pulling on my chin strap while I'm trying to keep my mouth open. The pain in the ears is sharp , , , and strong.

Must get this mailed ashore. We're leaving again. My guess is back to Lingayen Gulf. It's a big island and much supply is needed. Hope you're home, but I'll keep writing anyway.

HOMESICK BILL

Lieutenants Hawkins and Burling (l-r).

Friday, 2 March 1945 to
Tuesday, 3 April 1945

DEAR HOMESICK—

Picked up yours of 23 Jan. '45, on my last stop before I left San Antonio. Will read and answer as soon as possible.

I am writing from the lobby of the New Chickasha Hotel, Chickasha, Oklahoma. When you write, address me here until I can get more adequate quarters. The "New Chickasha Hotel" . . . I wonder what the old one looked like? I think the new one might have hosted Jim Bridger, the mountain man, on the way west to the mountains on his first trip.

Getting here proved to be an exercise in futility and aggravation. Five of us hitched a ride with an oldster who chawed "baccy", sipped white lightnin' out of a Coke bottle and drove about 90 mph, mostly in the wrong lane. Got to Dallas around 7:30 P.M. and discovered trains and buses would take 15 hours to negotiate the remaining 250 miles. I opted for a plane that left at 11:30, but got bumped by a priority passenger. I think priority is now used by ribbon clerks flexing their puny muscles. Spent what remained of the night in an Army B.O. Q. Next morning, after a three-hour delay, we flew to Oklahoma City (150 miles from here), and it was socked in, so we pressed on to Wichita Falls, where I was now 250 miles from my destination. The airline got tickets for me on the 4:30 train, which departed, finally, at 7:30. At Oklahoma City, the last bus had just left for Chickasha. At 2:00 A.M., I found myself on the road hitchhiking for Chickasha. It was raining, so traffic was thin. Finally got a lift and got a room here a little before 5:00 A.M., wrung myself out and hit the sack.

Quite incidentally, the manager of the hotel is a Mr. Alderson Mole. I never did get a chance to visit with him and inquire into his family tree. Considering his last name, it is perhaps best that I didn't.

That business of carrying a small ship to the Leyte invasion sure must have jostled your curiosity, as it did mine. I can envision all sorts of hairy assignments those guys might have been sent on, and I can only wish them luck and be glad I'm not on that lonesome little boat.

D-day at Linguyen Gulf . . . you do get around, don't you? Linguyen has made all the news reports here, and it gives me the willies to see those reports. Then, to get a combattant's hands-on summary leaves me again wondering where you guys get your reserves of strength and courage. Getting stuck on a sandbar short of the beach seems to be one of your hangups. You must stick out like a sore thumb perched out there on a sand pile. This, I am sure, does nothing for your desire for another candle on your birthday cake. As you might well imagine, the suicide planes interest me, and I wonder how their commanders get men to throw themselves away in such a fashion. It must be religious, or something rooted in their Samurai traditions.

I have warned you about being visible to your captain when someone screws the pooch, but you were apparently looking heroic and in plain sight when the smoke pots failed to hide your ship from a variety of Jap shooters intent on sinking your butt. Dashing about in a small boat in all that flying metal is not making your retirement look like a sure thing. For God's sake, be careful and try and fade into the woodwork at the first sign of a need for Sir Lancelot.

Your station at General Quarters may be great for viewing the action during air raids and exchanges between you and land based artillery, but going deaf and being a choice target must cross your mind from time to time. However, shooting a Jap bomber down and being able to see the whole action does, in a way, make it worthwhile. That must be the fifth or sixth aircraft you guys splashed. I should have had you and your 40 mm's with me in my little greenhouse . . . you would have had a ball. Congratulations, great shooting!

The action here, of course, does not compare with what you are still going through . . . but it is the only action I got, so here goes. The 15th was Shirley's birthday and my first flight in the airplane that hopefully I will be able to pilot after about 12 weeks of actual flying and some more concentrated ground school. The instructors here are civilians with thousands of hours in these Stearman bi-wing airplanes. The Army refers to them as PT-17s (Primary Trainers). Two open cockpits and no frills . . . actually they remind me of the Spads and Fokkers of WWI. In any event, Mr. Guth (my instructor) took me up for a half an hour and did some things that I did not think were possible. Snap rolls, slow rolls, spins, stalls and on and on. I got to drive for a few minutes and am rather ashamed of my performance. This, at this time, is not as easy as it appears to be. I hope Mr. Guth is a real patient man.

We are working pretty much 7:00 A.M. to 6:00 P.M. Ground school (theory of flight, D.R. navigating, basic engineering, flight instruments, etc.) occupies several hours per day and usually we fly twice, weather permitting. Today, we were doing stalls, spins and S-turns down a highway. I'm enjoying the whole flying experience immensely. Driving one of these things sure beats riding as a crew member.

Shirley, her mother and Dawn arrived in Oklahoma City about 8:00 Tuesday, 27 March, '45. My dad drove them down in our old beat-up Packard. I couldn't believe that car when I saw it. Tires, baby furniture, boxes, suitcases, etc., were on top and around and inside. Grandma was jammed into the back seat while Dawn, Shirley and Grandad had the front. They had five or six flats on the way here, as well as mechanical problems, and they were all tired and crabby as hell. There was a train leaving for Chicago at the station (I met them there . . . easy to find), and Dad got on that thing and waved a thankful goodbye to his passengers. He got the hell out of Dodge as fast as he could. They were on the road since very early A.M. on the 25th. Can't blame Dad for cuttin' and runnin'.

We had two rooms in the hotel until the 31st, when we got a bedroom with kitchen privileges in a private home; Mr. and Mrs. Crews and two small girls. The Crews are about 50% Choctaw Indian. More on this later. Grandma trained and bussed back home on the 3rd of April. During these days, I was flying and attending class and coming into town to eat and sleep. A little hectic, but you can make anything work if you try.

Will write again first chance I get and hope to hear from you in the meantime.

ACE ALDERSON

3 February, '45

DEAR HOMEWARD BOUND BILL—-

At least I hope I'm correct. No mail lately . . . we've hardly stopped long enough for anything but to clean-up, load and go.

I awoke in the middle of the night recently and, I believe I wrote that we invaded Luzon on 1 January. It was 9 January . . . just to be accurate! I hardly know what year it is, and keeping track of the days is a waste of time.

On our second trip to Lingayen Gulf (Luzon), I had an infected large toe and refused to submit to any treatment by our "shanker mechanic", as the medics are called. Running to General Quarters in the dark, I stepped lengthwise on a hawser and badly sprained the ankle connected to the sore toe. I could barely walk, but taped the ankle and took aspirin. When we reached Lingayen and were unloading during an air raid, I got a piece of shrapnel in my sore ankle. I believe it may have been one of our own shells coming down on us. I kept quiet about it for fear of being left on the island, and then Lord knows what. When we were unloaded and cleaning up, I hitchhiked to the nearest field hospital to see what could be done. It was hot as hades and humid, and the "Hospital" was the usual tent with a lot of activity. Men were on stretchers or sitting in the sand, and many were very badly wounded. I felt like an ass with my tiny piece of shrapnel sitting with all these guys who were really badly hurt. Furthermore, the sights, sounds and smells were getting to me. I soon discovered that the few doctors were trying to decide who should be saved, and who was hopeless. Meanwhile, the less seriously hurt were fanning the badly hurt and mopping foreheads and, in general, trying to be useful. A chaplain was busy talking to the men and ambulances continued to arrive and unload a couple of men at a time. A medic gave me a shot and an aspirin and told me to watch for infection. I hitchhiked back to the ship and thanked my stars that I was better off than anyone I'd seen all morning.

All is going well on Luzon, but the terrain is new to most of the troops . . . and us. Up until now, it's been thick, dark jungles with a civilized place being one with palm trees planted in rows. What I've seen of the Philippines is some jungle, but also rice paddies and rolling hills. The people are much better looking, and CLEAN. They are friendly and many speak English. The old sailors tell me Manila is a nice city, as are other cities like Subic on Subic Bay. Wonder if we'll ever get there.

We're getting closer to Japan now, which means more air raids . . . at least more frequently. They are nothing like you are putting out over there, but the suicide-type attacks are hard to stop. It is the carriers that catch it the worst, and I don't believe I'd like that duty. At first, I prayed to be near carriers so they could protect us. Common sense and observation soon taught me that they protect themselves . . . otherwise, no place to land. Of course, their planes are off in the distance knocking down Jap planes, so that is protection. Also, if an air raid comes along, the Japs will go for the carriers, and we are a low priority. So there's both good and bad news wherever one is.

We've been so busy, the time has really flown. I'm a year older now . . . never knew I'd get this old. I am now a Lt. (Jg), which is a step up in pay. I haven't drawn any pay since New Orleans . . . nothing to spend it on. I understand I now will make about $17.00 more dollars per month which, with sea pay, brings me up to about $171.00 per month. I've come a long way from $21.00 per month, less insurance and laundry. If I get hit, my mother will have my $10,000 insurance, plus whatever the back-pay amounts to . . . she'll be rich! She deserves it. Being a Lt. (Jg) is a ho-hum thing for me . . . I want to be a civilian.

In spite of all the frantic movement and the sheer terror day and night, we've also had some fun. We "borrowed" a pretty good sized sailboat for an afternoon of relaxation. It was a real yacht with mahogany paneling below deck and teakwood decks and rails. We weren't the best sailors in the Bay, but we got back and put the yacht back where we found it. Hope the owner didn't mind.

Another afternoon was one of those beach parties where each man gets two cans of warm beer. As usual, the nondrinkers were the victims of much bargaining. It was a nice day, and I was able to relax very well with just a few more than my own allotment. When I returned to the ship, some of the flag officer's retinue decorated me with a colorful crayon decorated paper medal they called the "Beer Suds Star". I tried to be humble, and I also wondered what in hell brought that on because I thought I had behaved in a gentlemanly manner. Who cares?!

And so it is that Dugout Doug has nearly accomplished his personal goal of retrieving the Philippines he lost awhile back. It has been very expensive. On our first trip to Lingayen Gulf, he came wading ashore behind a platoon of cameramen. He was about fifty yards from our ship. I was on the beach with about four of the crew and all was quiet. Suddenly, there was a lot of commotion, and a Sea Bee on a bulldozer was rushing at us. He had the blade raised high and was half-standing to see over it. He approached a tree right ahead of us and lowered the blade and knocked the tree down, piling sand all over it. Then he ran over it before piling on more sand. A soldier told me a Jap sniper had been hidden in the tree roots and was visible from the side opposite us. He was now buried alive. I still wonder how long he'd been there and if his target was Dugout Doug. We had been on the beach over a day and had walked near the tree, but not the side where he was somewhat visible. Strange, but wonderful.

I often think about you and those B-24s and all the hell you are surviving. It appears that your base in Italy is somewhat less wonderful than England, but the flights are just as bad. With all the time since I last heard from you, I suspect you may be home by now . . . sure hope so. It's been a long, long time since college and the trials and tribulations of tests, tuition, fees and books. I think if I make it, I'll go back and finish.

Most of our talk and thoughts has to do with speculation about what's next for us. It was obvious to us (and the Japs) that, with MacArthur in charge, we would be involved in the Philippines. Now it is not obvious what's next. It's still a long way from Japan and no one thinks they'll ever give up. They have to know their war is lost and everyone that dies now will be a total waste. One might wonder if they could have suspected that before they started this miserable war.

The Army is living better . . . and they deserve it. As you may have noticed, the combat troops are always combat troops. If they take a decent place, they are ordered to move on and the reserves move into the decent place. We haven't really been involved with any decent places, but we're hopeful that we will. Meanwhile, the Army we're seeing is in nice tents, and food and supplies are stacked high. They have their guitars, pet monkeys and parrots and are resting before moving on. There are a few young ladies that make a little money sweeping out the tents and various other odd jobs and, for the moment, all seems well. One must enjoy these short times to the fullest, and everyone here knows it. The Philippines have taken an awful licking, but most have handled it well. I recently was on the beach and a young woman, carrying a baby, walked aimlessly along the water toward me. Her eyes were dull and she was thin and her dress was all she wore, which was full of holes and patches. As she passed, I said hello and she nodded a little, but never hesitated in her walk. She seemed to be crying, but there were no tears. It shook me a little. I did feel that maybe I complain too much! I doubt I'll ever forget that woman. With a little food and rest, and a decent dress, she would be very pretty. I'll bet she could write a book that would have us all thanking our lucky stars!

The watch calls. I hope to have some time to write a bit more frequently. Hope the letters are finding you. If you're in Chicago, please tell me in detail how fresh meat, vegetables, eggs, milk and anything else tastes. I'm sick of Australian cheese and mutton. We're getting a lot of liver, and I cannot eat it. I have lost 25 pounds since San Diego. I wonder if my yellow skin and eyes will ever return to white.

STUDENT OF THE PHILIPPINES

Wed. 4 April 1945 to
Mon. 30 April 1945

DEAR FILIPINO STUDENT—-

The hand that holds the "stick" of my mighty PT-17 holds your latest letter bearing the date of 3 February 1945. The problems you had with your ankle and toe remind me of the pleurisy that about finished me in Italy. You were hurting pretty good and afraid to go on sick-call for fear of being left behind to fend for yourself, or maybe getting assigned to underwater demolition or some equally expendable occupation. Going to the field hospital was a good move when you picked up that flak fragment. Did you go on record as being wounded? A Purple Heart is worth points toward rotation. After seeing the guys in the field hospital with horrific wounds, I'm sure you would be reluctant to get the P.H. for a scratch. I was, but took one anyway, scratch or no scratch. It was points to me in case I needed them. Every time I wear the damned thing, I think about Norris and Georgie Sloan and others and am embarrassed. I reckon it would be the same with you. I have not been in a field hospital and will avoid strenuously going to one . . . no guts.

Congratulations on making Lt. (Jg). A nice birthday present with a modest (puny) raise in pay. You would think the Navy would be a little more generous to its combat men. I didn't realize you had been rat-holing your pay since New Orleans. Should the war continue for a while, you will be able to hit the Polar Grill and not come out for a couple of months.

Your story about Dugout Doug coming ashore and uttering his famous "I have returned" line was fascinating. Strange that the sniper didn't take Dugout out. Also a little unusual was you and your ship being just a few feet away and having the opportunity to see and hear a bit of history. Doug's picture that day made all the papers worldwide. Your cynic button must have gone berserk.

The question about where you are going next must be kind of worrisome. If the Japs don't toss in the towel soon, you might be faced with the nasty proposition of hitting the beaches on the Japanese homeland. Fanatical as they are, this could prove to be the biggest bloodletting of all time. Every civilian would be attempting to stop the Foreign Devils from gaining a foothold. I have heard that one million people could be killed. I would not like to be on the cutting edge of our sword and have to cut down on women and kids defending their homes. Let us hope that we and they don't have to go through something like that. Saner heads may yet ignore "saving face" and stop this craziness before it gets to that extreme.

Your request for a description of the various foods and drinks here and how they taste are going to go unanswered. I am afraid, after hearing of your 25-pound loss of weight and the color of your eyes and skin, that a discussion like that might run you over the edge. You must look like a giant sized yellow "Crayola", and I do not want to be responsible for a further remission of your health or your psyche. I will not describe sex to you either. A Crayola with a pump handle would be just too much.

The flying at Chickasha becomes better by the day. After about six or seven hours of dual instruction, I managed to solo. We were up practicing stalls and loops, and when we returned to the field, Guth got out and told me to take it around the traffic pattern and land. This landmark in aviation history was accomplished on the 5th of April 1945 and lasted some 30 minutes. My first landing was actually three. The first time my wheels hit the ground, I was sixty feet from the perimeter fence. No matter, I bounced thirty feet in the air and cleared the fence easily. This time, as I skillfully bounced the airplane again, I only soared back into the blue about ten feet and, when next the wheels touched, I managed to remain earthbound. My instructor, a heartbeat away from apoplexy, sent me around three or four more circuits, during which I managed to land and take off without mashing myself or the airplane. Since then, I grease that baby landing and taking off. I'll tell you, that first bounce over the fence was a real barn burner, and I could see me and my trusty flying machine in a big pile of arms, legs and airplane parts.

Classwork is not that hard anymore, and I seem to be learning the basics of flight and the hundred other things that hopefully will permit me to survive this phase of training and move on to the next phase, basic training.

Life in our home away from home is pretty good. We have the run of the house and often babysit for the Crews' children when they go out on the town. Grandma Crews, the Choctaw, and Shirley are hitting it off nicely. One problem did arise, but has been solved to everyone's satisfaction. Unbeknown to us, Grandma's five-foot black snake lived under our bed and came out one day to meet Shirley. Needless to say, Shirley like to have leaped out of her bloomers. She and Bre'r Snake took each other's measure, and Shirley lost the round. She and Dawn then retreated, and old Nokomis calmed everyone down. The five-foot mouse trap now lives under Grandma's bed, and we keep our door shut.

There are other strange things that are part of life in the Crews' household. I'll skip them for now so that I don't bore you out of your socks. Those strange things, as well as news from the field and wide blue yonder, will keep until my next installment.

    This combat that you continue to chase all over the Pacific keeps me continually on edge and hoping for your continued well-being. Keep writing as you find the time . . . and energy to do so.

REGARDS, KANGAROO BILL

1 March, '45

DEAR WILD BLUE BILL—-

It had been a long dry spell as far as incoming mail goes. We've been back to Lingayen Gulf a few times, as well as Guam . . . and, my very favorite, Ulithi Atoll.

The Army moved away from the Gulf and went south toward Manila at a pretty good pace . . . all things considered. They had some "mountains", as well as rice paddies and flat areas, and the Japs chose the times and places to defend their retreat. As usual, the Japs love to counterattack at night, but the soldiers I talked with said it sure was better than the jungles of New Guinea on the other side of the equator.

Although the war had moved away from Lingayen Gulf, it was our main supply point until recently. We are getting closer to Japan and are more concentrated as we move north, and their air raids are more frequent and more intense. They seem determined to lose their air force, and we are helping all we can. There have been warnings of Jap subs in the area, but we haven't seen any, and we doubt they would waste a torpedo on us.

We were recently at Subic Bay, and the captain allowed my roommate and me to take the jeep and go on "rehabilitation leave." Manila was about 140 kilometers away, and we understood it was secure, so we grabbed some clean clothes and unwrapped the jeep. Unfortunately, the battery was dead and my friend, who had never before cranked a vehicle, got a fractured wrist when the engine kicked back. It was painful but, with a cast, tolerable and we set out on a journey to get the hell away from it all. We figured we could borrow a battery along the way and travel in style. We were fortified with some sandwiches and a few cans of that delicious Spam. My friend drove first in his best left-handed manner, and we had covered a few miles when the transmission became stuck in low gear. I knew how to fix it, but we had no screwdriver. The cleaning tool in the M-1 Garand wouldn't budge it, so we drove the rest of the way through the hills and valleys in low gear. We saw no one until we reached the city and, in no time, we were on Dewey Blvd., at which time we realized we were there a bit early. The streets were empty, and the Japs were holed up in the walled city. Our fighters were bombing and strafing the walled city (or anything close to it), and the Japs were throwing out whatever they had in the way of mortars and cannon fire.

Nobody in the Army had a screwdriver . . . nor did they seem much interested in the problem. They wondered what the hell a couple of sailors were doing there, and nearly died laughing when we announced we were on Rehabilitation Leave. We did discover that the Japs were surrounded and that the battle was local. We had the choice of attacking the Japs with the Army, or seeking out a more quiet spot. We chose a bamboo building with a thatched roof, chameleons on the walls and ceilings, rot-gut booze, dancing girls and a three-piece band that had never before played together. They were pretty good on "San Antonio Rose", which is known as the National Anthem of the Philippines, but on their other attempts it was difficult to tell if they were playing the same song. All was saved by an old man who pounded out a beat on an old drum, thus providing a rhythm for the tenuous gyrations of the dancing girls. One girl was about 8 months pregnant and another needed several good meals and a small anchor to bring her up to about 90 pounds. A third girl, who seemed rather comely, left before dancing at the request of an Army sergeant who likely offered more than dancing pay. A replacement girl came out of the woodwork, and she was another thin one. On the way to the dancing platform, a soldier accidentally caught her bandanatop in his fingers and revealed the chest of the average 12-year old boy. She danced anyway.

The booze was mostly grain alcohol with some coloring and possibly some flavor added. It's effects were sudden and devastating and caused us to leave before the place closed. We found our jeep and instantly fell asleep, despite a torrential downpour. We agreed that the next jeep we steal must have a top. I believe it was about 0200 that a soldier offered to share a tent with us . . . we declined because it would have required a walk of nearly 20 feet and we were already wet.

Heavy equipment moved up in the morning and the ground shook. My friend was lucky he was with me. Had he been on the ground, they would have taken one look and buried him. I'm sure I looked better than that, but I could not bring myself to a breakfast of Spam. The Army advised that the Japs still held out, but an assault would take place soon, after a good shelling, and that could mean that Manila would be secured as MacArthur had announced a week ago. An invitation by the Army to join in the upcoming assault was declined because we held very important posts about 100 miles away. Also, we were wet, tired and afraid of getting hurt.

And so it was that our Rehabilitation Leave came to an end. We fixed the jeep, got some gas and drove off into another tropical downpour. Moving into high gear was like a vacation itself, and the rain trickling into the ears and down the spine made me think a great deal of home and steaks and potatoes, perhaps a beer and my girlfriend. I remember when it rained, one used to don a raincoat or stay inside . . . that was a long time ago.

On the way "home", we laughed at our eagerness to again board that rusty, beatup hulk, the USS LST 628. But it has carried us this far and, scars or not, it is home.

Upon arrival, we stowed the jeep and fell into our bunks. I suppose everyone thought we'd had one hell of a leave. Upon some reflection, I guess it was . . . we survived!

I wonder about you. It has been a long time between mail calls and you seemed on the brink of going home. The lack of letters is from everyone, and perhaps a ship was sunk or a plane went down. Too, we have been on the move. There are a lot of ships out here now, and I don't know how they ever get mail delivered.

You may or may not know that Iwo Jima was invaded recently, apparently because we needed it for an air strip. All our information comes from the wounded, but the stories curl the hair and may very well portend the future. A lot of fresh Marines went in there, and it was devastating . . . but it will be all ours!

It's a long way ahead for us. The fanatical nature of the enemy is very hard to understand but, having understood it, all we can do is press on. We learned early that there was no going home and now, at this stage of the war, it is clear that we are here until it's over. Everybody goes about his job and is seemingly oblivious to all the noise and distraction. Thoughts of home have pretty well faded now, and we are like machines that work, eat and fall asleep.

We are loading for the next one. Always a little exciting and always a little frightening. Where or when, we do not yet know.

I'm glad I'm not in one of those flying aluminum boxes, so I guess there's always something worse than this. Now that I've seen what war is like, I don't like it and cannot recommend it!

BLUE BILL

DEAR CHICAGO RESIDENT (I hope!)——

My last letter from you was dated 11 July, 1944. At that time, you were approaching your last few missions, and I am therefore assuming that you may be home or at least Stateside. I am not getting mail from anyone else, so I am blaming the Navy Postal Service, while realizing that they have their problems. Activity out here has been on the increase, and the war below the equator appears to be tapering off. As we move north, we now see ships that have been involved here, and some of the anchorages now bristle with masts and hulls. It's a beautiful sight to anyone but a Japanese, and it is very comforting to be with so many "friends". We are seeing some big ships, and the few Zeros that attack don't last long in the air. Sure wish I was allowed a movie camera. Watching the air attacks from a distance is much more fun than being one of a few targets.

Some day you will receive my last letter, which related some of my experiences in Manila while on a rehabilitation leave to rest my weary bones and shattered nervous system. There is much to be said for staying with the work because the play times can be devastating.

Upon my return from the "rest" period, we loaded and went into Mindanao, which is south of Leyte and had been bypassed. It was not heavily defended and, for us, was kind of a ho-hum trip. For others, of course, it was as bad as it gets. Another one under our belts and it is good to be at a relatively peaceful spot again. Although this is not the north Pacific, there are differences in water temperature, tides, winds and the terrain of the islands. It is like a new experience, and therefore somewhat interesting, but not much. In the first few days here, we cleaned up the ship and set out to find supplies (always interesting) and did some repairs. It is not the usual frantic situation, and we discovered a large store of Army uniforms ashore and helped ourselves. Navy uniforms are not generally available, and I have been wearing Army wool socks and heavy shoes and shirts for a long time. Now I have some shirts and some new green underwear and a new pair of shoes. Pure luxury!

Recently, I returned to our ship after a brief absence and found that my boss is gone, as is the old boatswain's mate and five of the division. The old boatswain's mate (probably about 30) and my boss had been out here before and were showing some signs of stress. I'm glad for them, but it puts me in charge, and it is a bit frightening. The other men were apparently reviewed by Army psychologists and deemed ready for some rest. This leaves me with some damned good sailors who know their jobs, but I fear that there are many things I do not know and hope I'm never tested with something new and strange. So be it!

Our ship has been loaded, and we have some up-to-date modern and mammoth equipment. The tanks are huge, as are some of the trucks and the trucks are on the top deck and are heavily loaded. The tanks are down below on the tank deck, and they are a sight to behold. They have flotation tanks welded to them and are equipped to move in the water and blast off their flotation tanks on the beach. Interspersed on the top deck are weapons carriers and trailers. It's a mess and difficult to secure all this stuff when we get underway. The various equipment is Marine Corps gear, and tank crews will be aboard soon. A tank commander is now one of my roommates, and he is a great guy.

We are ready to go, but are standing by and will probably leave on rather short notice. We have been briefed, and it is frightening. More details than usual, which I could have done without. I have learned still more from the Marine Lt. and am searching frantically for whomever it may be that can quickly raise the amount of my insurance. I fear this one.

Meanwhile, one of my men learned that his brother had been killed, and he was pretty upset. I told him he could do as he pleased for awhile, but I felt he would do well to keep busy and keep on the job. He followed my advice, but apparently there are two boys in the family and, in my opinion, he should be sent ashore at the very least. My opinion doesn't carry a hell of a lot of weight out here! I guess he's more concerned with his mother's grief than with anything else. What a way to live!

We long ago thought we could be "rotated" out of here, based on promises made by people who didn't know what they were talking about. I now, after this period of time, have the authority to send one man home. I chose a section leader who rightfully deserved a much higher rate and who is clean-cut and the father of four children. He is about 2nd or 3rd in command at this point, but he is the only one with children. I can't tell you how happy I was to find him and tell him he was going home and that he should be ready to leave in the boat in short order. In no time, he was at the quarterdeck with all his gear and the biggest smile I've seen since San Diego. His buddies were with him, and it was a very short and emotional goodbye. I believe he stowed his gear in 5 minutes or less. If ever a guy deserved a break, it was he.

Of course, several others wondered why they weren't chosen, and I told the leading boatswain's mate it would have been him if the other man had not had four children. Not very comforting, but true. We have already lost six men who were not replaced, and one more won't hurt. It may very well have saved the one man's life.

Now I have time to reflect a bit before we leave, and I'd rather write than wander around and look at all the dour and frightened faces. The Marines are now aboard, and there are a lot of them. No room to put all of them, so they'll be sleeping on deck . . . as usually happens. There is no cheer among them, either.

I am hoping against hope that you finished your allotted missions without undue incident, and endured the cold shower before leaving for Kimbark Ave. in Chicago, USA. I suppose we all think, when we can, about the "good old days" and have forgotten that they weren't all that great. Still, there can be no question that they were a hell of a lot better than you and I have now. I chuckled a bit when one of our officers made Lt. (j.g.) and seemed proud of it, and I thought that an Ensign shuffling papers in Washington, D.C., got the same promotion. It's a question of how much time in grade, and has nothing to do with capability or experience. If this goes on long enough, we'll advance again. And if it doesn't, we'll be discharged and forgotten. I guess it has been ever thus and that, in any war, a few give it all and the rest are allowed to march in a parade once a year on Armistice Day.

Enough of this drivel! The mail boat approaches, and this must go. Hope I hear from you when I get back . . . and I am determined to come back.

SCARED SILLY BILL

30 April, '45

DEAR WILD BLUE BOY——

Still no mail! I guess it's understandable because we, and no one else out here, have been standing still. I can't tell you how happy I am to be writing.

I persist in the idea that you have finished your allotted missions and gone home. I do hope your mail will be forwarded and that you can remember my simple FPO address.

We put to sea and joined up with a huge convoy after my last letter. We had a lot of Liberty ships and other merchant and cargo ships along with numerous LST's and some carriers. We had several destroyers and destroyer escorts, all of which made me feel somewhat better about a trip that we were told would be pure hell. It was the understatement of the century! Our goal was Okinawa, which is north and west of Iwo Jima and fairly near Foochow on the China coast. We were to arrive on 1 April (April Fool's Day) . . . from now on, I'll call it Navy Fool's Day.

All went well for the first few days of a rather long trip, and then the weather kicked up. I'm glad I went through that hurricane on Shakedown Cruise, and we've seen some heavy seas since . . . but here we ran into a full-fledged typhoon. All these storms are the same, only the names are different. This one was BAD! The LST has a rather blunt bow, which does not cut through the water, but just smashes into it. In standing watch 52 feet above the waterline, I believe I looked up another 50 feet at the top of the oncoming seas. The wind blew the water horizontally and one about had to turn his back on the wind to get a breath of air. The seas came at us off our port bow and threw the ship a quarter of the way off course. There were times we had to use the engines to get back on course. My own real problem was the heavily loaded trucks on our top deck. They were chained down from their frames, which is the only way we could secure them, but the beds and bodies of the trucks rolled violently as if they might break the springs. Marines were everywhere . . . in trucks, under trucks, under trailers and simply on deck with a poncho over them. Our crew checked the chains constantly to keep them tight. If we lost a truck in the center, we'd likely lose them all. When the bow hit the oncoming seas, the ship shuddered and shook, and the bow would bend up and then down and one wondered if we'd break in half. When we topped out on a wave, the screws came out of the water and ran wild. I could barely see freighters 500 yards away, and when they rolled away from us, we could damned near see the whole bottom. All this in the afternoon with night approaching, but it was already dark as night and getting worse. The lifejackets were little comfort.

Sometime in the night, I was awakened with the news that the tanks down below had broken loose, and I went down to see all the tanks sliding from side to side and banging into the bulkheads and tank flotation tanks. We usually put dunnage (wood planks) under tanks or anything else with steel treads so they won't slide, but none had been available. The chains holding them were heavy chains, but they had broken. Our efforts to crawl under to retrieve chains proved too dangerous, and it seemed that the tanks would soon punch holes in the bulkheads. The problem was solved by placing timbers between the tanks so they couldn't move, and then we chained them again. Then the flotation tanks had to be welded up as best we could. By then, the night was over.

I think it was two days later, we entered the eye of the storm and had complete and sinister calm. We knew it wouldn't last long and repaired what we could before the onslaught returned. Meanwhile, we had to change course, which would put us right in the trough . . . the seas would be hitting us broadside. Everyone was alerted because it seemed we might roll over. I was so tired, I didn't give a damn. For some reason I'll never figure out, our new course wasn't much worse than the original one. A couple more days and the seas began to moderate and the wind dropped . . . and so did I. I vaguely remember lying on deck asleep and being awakened to go on watch, and I just went back to sleep. I lay there for a few hours and stumbled up to relieve the watch and was told to forget it.

It may have been a day or two later that we got the word from destroyers up ahead that we should keep a sharp lookout for floating mines. Whether the storm broke them loose or whether the Japs had sowed them from the air was not really important. The destroyers could not blow all of them, and we counted nineteen that day that floated by us and went down the columns of the ships. We could not fire on them. Then came the night, and we couldn't see them. Everyone was moved away from the bow, but the man on bow watch had to stay there in the 40mm gun tub and he was to shout it out if he saw a mine. He didn't see any, and we didn't hit any . . . another miracle.

We arrived right on time, 1 April, at Okinawa, and the sea was moderate. Nobody had been fed the previous night, and the chaplains were holding services in the dark before dawn. The boatswain's mate could not get the bottom turnbuckle off our bow doors, and he had to get boats ready to launch, so I went down the ladder into the darkness and into the water and removed the turnbuckle. When I came back up, the sky was clearing and it looked as though the sun might shine.

We didn't wait long for our turn to come up, and the Marines started their engines and we ran at the beach, but came up a little short on a sand bar . . . as expected. Except for ships firing over our heads, all was an eery quiet.

The first tank went down the ramp and nearly swamped as its nose went under briefly and then moved a short distance before moving onto the sand. The second tank sank, but two got out. The commander of the third tank had the jitters (and who wouldn't?), but moved off and was successful. About three tanks would not start and others could not leave because the way was blocked. After what seemed like a long, long time, they did start and we unloaded the entire lower deck, except for boxes of supplies that were not critical. Then we had to wait for bulldozers to build a sand ramp so the trucks could get off, and the bulldozers were on another group of ships and having trouble with deep water. Meanwhile, the tanks joined others in their unit and began moving inland without any resistance that we could see.

By afternoon, we had been able to unload all the boxes of rations, etc., and that was moving along well, and then all hell broke loose in the form of suicide planes. They came in strength like a bunch of hornets and simply dove on the first ship they saw. It seemed that ships were afire in all directions . . . and still the planes came. All ships firing in every direction, and some of it coming close to us. I could see for miles in every direction, and it was the same everywhere. I was certain that this was to be my very last day on earth. The sky was filled with black smoke from burning ships and flak bursts . . . and the hot, sharp shrapnel fell like rain. We are pretty close to Japan now and are told that some of their flyers are teenagers as young as 14. They are taught to take off and given fuel for a one-way trip.

Between air raids, we can clean up a bit and renew ammo supplies near the guns and have a cup of coffee or a sandwich. Everyone is very, very tired.

Before night fell, we were warned that Japs were taking debris, such as boxes, and swimming under them out to the ships, where they would either force a mine into a ship or tie it to the screws so that it would explode later. So we had our trusty Springfield rifles in the hands of shooters whose job was to shoot at floating debris. I had obtained my very own M-1 Garand from my Marine roommate, and I also fired on floating debris. This went on during our entire stay , which seemed like eons.

Okinawa has been owned by the Japanese for many years, and we were advised that the natives might well be as dangerous as the Jap soldiers. The island contains a couple of bona fide cities, and the hills are terraced and cultivated. There are numerous concrete burial vaults and rocky caves which have been fortified and stocked with the necessities for holding out over a long period of time. The shoreline is such that landing ships can only beach in certain areas and so are badly concentrated. One might suspect that the Jap soldiers are aware that they now are the last stronghold and that the home islands are next. I frankly doubt that they can be any more suicidal than they have already proven themselves to be. In any event, it was a true nightmare!

The watch calls. I expect to be here awhile and will complete my tales of Okinawa in the next few days. Meanwhile, I hope to hear from you.

WHITE-HAIRED BILL

DEAR SCARED SILLY, AND BLUE AS WELL—

As you can plainly see, I have received a couple of letters from where all the action is taking place. Yours dated 1 March and 14 March have finally reached me after a long, hard and circuitous journey. I say that because of the less than pristine condition they were in. They also smelled like a shower room that has not been cleaned for many a moon.

Aside from your R & R leave to Manila, I was happy to hear you have not been shot at or bombed for a few days. It is hard for me to understand why you didn't join the Army in their assault on the walled city; after all, you did earlier on profess a desire to get a piece of the action. This was a golden opportunity to show the Army why you and your one-armed companion showed up instead of a battalion of Marines. It would have made history if you had charged the walls of Jericho in first gear, waving a jug of spirits and a broken arm and have the ramparts come tumbling down.

Despite the many setbacks of your R & R, it must have been a real lift to get away from #628 for awhile and experience something besides your watch on watch, the Zeros, mortars and rifle fire that seems to accompany you like leeches on a vein. Returning home to the old rust bucket is almost like returning home to see old friends and familiar surroundings. It ain't altogether peachy, but it's still home for the moment, and usually better than the surrounding countryside.

Mindanao might have been ho-hum for you, but it got written up pretty big-time in the newspapers. Maybe the Army and Marines bore the brunt of the action. Your personal invasion of the Army's menswear and haberdashery sounds like a successful action. On leave, do not remove your pants while entertaining a young lady . . . the color of your GI green skivvies will send her home screaming for mommy.

Don't fret about command. You have been doing it on a small scale right along.

Your responsibility only increased a little when the boatswain and his mate departed for a "rest", but the function of command is about the same. For you, a piece of cake. With command, there are some perks. You discovered one when you selected a man for rotation. Makes you feel eight feet tall. Listen to the gyrene Lt. and be ready to watch your butt on this next landing. A commander does not have to stand on the bow and shout obscenities to draw fire away from his men.

The new tanks and heavy trucks, etc., might make it easier for the Marines to survive another beach and another campaign to clean out the enemy. I am waiting anxiously for your next letter and am as worried as you are, but still have the gut feeling we are both going to walk away from this in one contiguous piece.

Speaking of walking away in one piece, I find driving airplanes is not for the faint at heart, nor the mistake-prone novice. During April, got about 40 hours in the air, of which about 14 hours was solo. I was playing things close to the vest and trying to get the feel of things. This month, dual flying, timewise, is greater than solo, and so it should be. I need all the instruction I can get. Some of these acrobatic maneuvers are hard to do (correctly) and require coordination of feet, hands and eyes. I am getting an enormous kick out of the whole thing. I've done a few loops, snap rolls, spins, immelmans, slow rolls, stalls and a host of other maneuvers. Some of the guys have had trouble landing. Ground loops (airplane does a 360 or two after landing) are embarrassing and sometimes damage the airplane if it tips over on a wing. We have not had any bad accidents, but a hell of a bunch of close calls. Hurrah for our instructors. Classwork continues, but is actually rather easy, at least for me.

Back at the tepee, the kitchen window remains open all the time to allow Grandma's pet crow and a couple of squirrels easy access to the leftovers the little Crews girls leave on their plates. For breakfast, one girl eats the whites of eggs only and the other only the yellow. Makes the plates look a little weird, but the critters don't care. The crow has a five or six word vocabulary, which surprises people who have not visited the Crews before. Fortunately, most people do not understand Choctaw cuss words and praise the crow for his vocabulary.

I am going to hustle this into the mail and hope it will give you a few minutes away from the awful burden of command.

Be careful continually.

BARON BILL

2 May, '45

DEAR HOMEBODY (I hope)——

Again no mail. Again we are lying more or less idle and awaiting our next move. Meanwhile, I shall bring you up to date on the forgotten war. To show that we are now in touch, somewhat, with the outside world, I know that Italy is out of the war. We have also heard that allied troops are advancing well on all fronts. This is great news and, of particular interest to us is the idea of seeing more muscle here.

On our way to Okinawa, my Marine roommate gave me some details about the terrain and the fortifications we all were to face. He had been warned that the civilians should be considered as unfriendly and as fanatic as the Japs. The word had it that all civilians had been told to do whatever they could to kill the American invaders. His orders were to shoot anything that moved . . . and he was considerably upset by that. On D-day, he told me he would be wearing his "lucky" red socks and that he hoped we could get together later and exchange stories.

On our second trip to Okinawa, I sought out members of his unit and was told that his tank was discovered burning and damaged and that someone saw a body partly covered with sand . . . and the body was wearing red socks. He was very badly hurt . . . but alive. He was flown out for treatment and, presumably, back to the States. He was the absolute epitome of the intelligent, strong, good-looking people who are bearing the brunt of all this. I wish him the very best.

I recall horrendous air raids on 6, 11 and 21 April. I'm sure there were many more when we were away. We made three trips and will likely make more. On our second trip, we were chastised for careless firing during an air raid . . . we deserved it. In following a Zero down, some of our guns fired very closely to another ship. As punishment, we were ordered to sail alone to Ie Shima, which is a very small island north of Okinawa. It was scary. The weather turned sour and dark, and we were still very much in awe of the typhoon on the first trip. Thoughts of the demise of the Spanish Armada were on my mind. Nothing in the way of really bad weather developed, and we arrived at Ie Shima . . . and we were alone. Sunken ships were everywhere, and we tied up to an LST that had its stern underwater, but was stable. Nearby was a Jap freighter with its upper deck visible at low tide. What the hell we were doing there, I've never known. I do know that I saw to it that we took several wash bowls, one for my compartment . . . and all the 20mm guns we could squeeze in on our ship. The whole place was a disaster scene, and you may read someday that a reporter named Ernie Pyle was killed here in recent weeks. Now the communications officer and I can wash our faces in our own room!

Upon our return to Okinawa, we anchored offshore in a spot where the big ships were firing over our heads again. Close by were carriers . . . bad news. A sixteen gun fires a hell of a shell with deadly accuracy out to 20 miles, and the sound of the shell going over is like a Zero diving with his engine shut down. At night, the shells are visible with different colored tracers . . . after they've gone by. The battleships and cruisers laid off quite a distance in order to arc the fire so that the shells came down on the target. It was peaceful until another air raid the following day. On that day, we watched Admiral Spruance change flagships twice as suicide planes crashed into his carriers. We got a good workout with our guns, but it was obvious that the carriers were the targets. We now have taken credit for seven Jap planes, and I have to laugh when I think of that. Often a plane comes down with several ships firing on it, and who knows which round brought it down? We have been very honest in our tally, which often has been a case of being alone or being the final ship to fire. I'm guessing that the number of planes shot down (as claimed) is about 100 times more planes than the Japs had on their best day.

The rest of our second trip, and all of our third trip, were just a repetition of what I've already written. The Marines moved well inland with heavy losses, and civilian women and little kids would hide grenades in their clothing and approach any American for water or food . . . and then pull the pin and blow up anyone close. The capital city of Naha was left in bad shape, and the whole place is a mess. On one of our trips, an LST moved into a river (I believe the Hagushi) and were attacked and boarded in the night by Jap infiltrators. Good God, when will this end?!

When we came back after our first trip, the ships about to go there had heard about the storm and the air raids, and they were on edge. We helped a few of them with ideas about how to double secure their loads, but I don't think they ran into any bad weather.

So, now I think things will be easier for awhile. We've had some sleep and some hot meals and have licked our wounds and rested. It is amazing how much some rest helps. I believe we will make more runs to Okinawa, but the Japs are about out of airplanes and their infantry there is about gone and they have no Navy to replenish it. Obviously, we are nearing the end of the line, and the only place left is Japan itself. We are constantly told what a fiasco that will be and, yet, there seems no other way to conclude this massacre.

Must quit for now. Duty calls.

I WANT TO GO HOME BILL

7 May, '45

DEAR BOMBARDIER—

I am bombarding you with mail because, for the first time since who knows when, I have some time to myself and there are no sirens, bells, whistles or explosions to distract me. I love it! I shall bring you up to date on some things I could not tell about in my earlier letters.

Not too long after D-day at Linguyen Gulf in the Philippines, an interesting event took place. The Japanese have an airplane that looks very much like our C-46. They approached a landing strip in the night with emergency lights on, and the AA batteries held their fire and let the plane land. Out of it poured Jap soldiers with their damned swords swinging, and they spread out and raised all kinds of hell for what seemed a long time. The guards on the perimeter of the strip were sacked out in jungle hammocks (which have to be unzipped to get out of), and the Japs had a ball for a short time. Nobody knew who was who and one couldn't fire a shot in the midst of the fiasco. Several Japs were killed, and several ran into the hitherlands, and there was not much sleep the rest of the night. Just an example of the fanaticism here!

For the first time at Linguyen, we saw LCIs with rocket racks full of rockets firing inland at the beach. A lot of fire and noise, and a tremendous amount of power, as they launched hundreds of rockets. It was a real show of force, but I doubt they can do much but blanket an area and scare hell out of the Japs.

About that time or later (my memory is slipping), our doctor, who was very much liked, diagnosed himself with appendicitis, and we were under way in some fairly rough water. He declined surgery at the hands of our very own Shanker Mechanics, and a large ship with a doctor aboard came alongside to take him (our doctor) aboard. So we ran alongside each other and, as we rolled, I wondered if the masts would hit each other. We rigged a line around our deckhouse and passed it to the other ship, and then we hung a block on that line and hung the doctor in a basket stretcher on the block. The other crew hauled him over, and both crews had to keep the slack out of the lines as we rolled. It was pretty hairy, and I'll never see the doctor again, but I wonder how he felt about it.

We were pretty well aware of Roosevelt's death when it took place. We were glad the war was well along when that happened.

On our trip to Ie Shima, which I mentioned recently, we stopped by Iwo Jima on the way back. It was bought at one hell of a price. We had never seen an island like that, all a fine black sand and a mountain or volcano at one end. There was still a lot of junk on the beach . . . a great many Higgins boats were destroyed there. The entire place had sulphur fumes coming out of the sand, and it looked like one big volcano ready to blow. Some Marines said it was the first time the M-1 Garand was a problem . . . the fine sand fouled it.

At Okinawa, we were able to get radio news and we listened, when we could, to the Fighter Control Unit. The Marine pilots had to wait their turn to report their kills, and it was interesting. I remember one pilot reporting, "Splash one" and then almost immediately, "Splash two". They were having a real field day with the Jap suicide pilots, who were intent on hitting a ship. The destroyers out on the "picket line" reported incoming Jap aircraft and took a real licking in the process.

I believe it was our second trip to Okinawa (the whole thing is almost a blur) that we got the "all clear" after the umpteenth air raid, and the crew just walked away from the guns to collapse somewhere or grab a sandwich. We were about 50 feet from the LST on our starboard side, and I went to the Wardroom (dining room, meeting room and operating room) for a cup of coffee. All was quiet, and suddenly the nearby LST opened fire. I ran out just in time to see a Zero pancake into the drink between the two ships, and I saw the pilot push his goggles up and try to move his canopy open. The Zero slowly sank, and the pilot never came up. When the water cleared, we could see the plane on the bottom and one wing was dislodged, and the pilot was still there. I don't know if the other ship hit the Zero or if he just missed his mark. A guy can't even get a relaxing cup of coffee!

Can't tell where we are now. We'll be involved with Okinawa for a long time. Equipment from all over the place is gradually being moved up.

Before the Philippine campaign, we had to overhaul our main engines. We did it at sea, in a convoy, one at a time. It was a bit scary at first, but worked out fine. We couldn't outrun a native canoe, so speed wasn't the problem . . . it was being able to turn and keep station with ships that had both engines. There were a lot of hours on those GM engines.

HAPPY DAY! Just heard scuttlebutt that your war is either over or will be in a day or so. Even if you are home, this should be great news. I knew that France, or most of it, had been liberated, but this comes as a wonderful, wonderful shock! I'll bet that our ex-friend, Hirohito, is biting his nails and wondering why the hell he ever started this mess. I don't believe I've been this happy except, perhaps, in my dreams. Now there is some hope that the Japs will give serious consideration to reality.

If for some unfortunate reason you are not yet home, please tell your General to send the 8th Air Force and any other Air Force out here. They should be able to make it in a few days, and we will welcome them with open arms. They will have all expenses paid at the local bars, dining rooms, hotels, pools and brothels . . . if they can find any of the above. Good Lord, I am happy!

I just took a little break from my letter writing and everyone is dancing in the passageways and talking about going home. I'm afraid that's a bit optimistic. In fact, reality is somewhat sobering, but necessary. Having stayed alive all this time, and through all this hell, it would be a shame to get hit now with the end actually in sight. I'm just not going to think about it. They predict that at least a million of us will die in the invasion of Japan.

One can't be sure, but perhaps they have so many ships here now that they can only handle so many on the beaches at Okinawa. To have big convoys lying at anchor and waiting their turn to unload would subject them to all their air raids and the resulting losses. I may be giving someone credit for some long-range planning, but at least we are living a relatively leisurely existence now.

Our boat is to return with supplies and, among them, will be two sheets of 1/4" steel (4'x8'), which is a real bear to bring on board with our little crawler crane. Very dangerous. Must go and tend to this and then the watch calls. Hope to hear from you soon.

ANXIETY BILL

10 May, '45

DEAR CLIFFHANGER BILL—-

Mail at last! I have yours of 13 to 18 July, '44, and another of 20 July to 25 July, '44. They have been wet, and a slight mildew covers part of your tales of woe . . . but they are most welcome. It is a bit difficult to piece things together when our mail is nearly 10 months lagging. Anyway, it is sure better than no mail. The dates on your letters, and even the signatures, are blurred, but I'm guessing the above is correct.

Your description of the bomb flights sends chills up and down my pale yellow spine. Particularly difficult, for me, would be to take off and run through some flak and fighters and then be scrubbed and get no credit for a mission. Obviously, this has to do with the word "fair", and I guess that word has been stricken from our vocabulary.

Seeing other planes go down, and being unable to help them, must be traumatic, too. The pilots who fell 10,000 feet before pulling it out deserve the Flying Cross . . . and a trip home!

Interesting that your observance of the Ma and Pa business with the daughter being the product for sale was followed by the lengthy VD color movie regarding some of the pitfalls faced by the customers. Very timely! There is no need to show those movies here because that type of ribald behavior is not possible . . . and, of course, we would eradicate it if we knew about it.

Sorry to hear of your heated experience in your family latrine. All this, followed by your flight with the hung-up frag bombs and your frightening experience in kicking the bombs out sans parachute while some distance above the hard, unforgiving earth. I would not enjoy that! It seems that you continue having trouble with loose formations on your runs since arriving in Italy. Sounds dangerous and hard to understand. Hope you and yours get some changes made.

Your missions continue and you are nearing a trip home (in your letters). I can imagine your emotion in seeing the firing on the guys in parachutes. I have heard stories here about Japs firing on sinking survivors, but have not seen anything myself. It appears the Golden Rule is on hold.

Your pleurisy sounds terrible. You seem to be stricken at intervals and hate to give up and rest for fear of losing out on missions, or ending up with another crew. I guess as long as you do recover, it is a good decision. Hope so. I'm sure glad you did get a chance to recover before the next action.

Ploesti has always sounded like bad news, and I see that it nearly got to you recently. The whole thing, from the hit in the engine until you got home, sounds like pure terror to me. Five hundred feet of altitude doesn't sound like much to me, but it's still a hell of a fall. How much can a guy stand?

Your attack on the rat in your tent discloses that all your small arms training in the Army Air Force has not brought about any improvement in your marksmanship. Take heart in the fact that you did hit the sentry box, even though you missed the rat. It was not your usual clean miss of everything! You can also salivate a bit in the knowledge that the rat probably expired from uncontrollable mirth. I hope Goering appreciates the fact that you are a bomber and not a gunner!

Your most recently penned letter describes the strange cloud-wall that aborted your mission to somewhere. All that, and credit too, is great news, and I'm sure you and your crew were delighted.

Your trip to Taranto and the meeting with the Italian Marines sounds interesting. I'm glad you showed them what for and also that you avoided any MP's who are not always noted for their understanding. I have little experience with living among former enemies who throw their weight around, but would feel as you do. Out here, the first we saw of it was Okinawa, where the locals were either sympathetic to Japan or were told we were cannibals. If they acted like an enemy, they were treated like an enemy.

I note that your next relaxation was in observing a skirmish in the street between French and Italians. All this while imbibing green champagne (whatever that is) and hiding behind a wall. I would have enjoyed seeing the nurse and the starched Major crossing the street with her early arrival at your vantage point and his late arrival in his soiled and wrinkled khakis. I trust that his Good Conduct Medal was not scratched and wonder if he will be decorated for bravery above and beyond. It seems that your iron nerves and weak stomach were not compatible with the Italian green champagne, and I do hope that, by now, your tent has stopped spinning. Perhaps I can be somewhat of a guiding light for you in becoming more temperate in your intake.

Ploesti again, and this time they nearly got you. Glad to hear it was not worse and that your eyebrow took the main punishment. Mighty close to an eye, though, and scary. You'll have to stay away from those damned windows . . . in fact, find a way to stay out of that aluminum box.

I'm still laughing about the guy who used the ammo can as a latrine and then threw it out, knocking out an engine on another plane, which then had to abort. I suppose headquarters has heard a million reasons for aborting, but this may be a new one. Hope the Germans don't hear of this method of damaging U.S. aircraft. Your last letter, which I believe is dated 20 to 25 July, '45, states that you have two more missions to go and you sign it "Cliffhanger Bill." I would think so! It is both wonderful and unsettling. I believe I can imagine, to some extent, how you feel and yet, maybe not. I've never been comfortable with a specific number of missions being necessary, although your tougher ones, in another's view, did count double. Now that you are down to the wire, it has to be tough on the fingernails . . . if indeed you have any left! It is clear that this letter can be of no help. I am confident that you are going to make it, and I am extremely happy for you. You and your crew have done a great job and deserve the best. It goes without saying that I'll be most anxious to receive your next letter and learn that you are on your way home. Sweat it out . . . one or two more times in the air and you can relax and enjoy life with the rear echelon!

I can't report much from here now. I do hope to get more mail and will keep answering, even though we have a hell of a time lapse in our correspondence.

We are enjoying some relative safety, and I am going to write all I can while I can. Several of us went swimming the other day, but it was not much like old times. We had men with rifles watching for sharks, but I was a bit uneasy, and the salt water was not real clean. Still, it was different and a break in the routine. This place is pretty, and the sand looks like Lake Michigan . . . truly a step up from those miserable islands south of the equator. If I had to stay permanently anywhere, I would choose this.

The watch calls! Can't wait for your next letter. Please tell me about American women, real food, a full night's sleep and whatever else I may have forgotten.

ANXIOUS BILL

Mail again! This is unbelievable and wonderful. I guess if one waits ten months or so, he can hope for gobs of mail. I have two letters from you, and they are both in bad shape. Must have been in some dark, dank ship's hold for awhile. On one, the date is illegible, but it is signed "Biting the Bullet Bill" and was clearly written prior to the one which is dated 26 July to 4 August, '44.

As I suspected, the news of our activities is not getting home, and that isn't all bad. I feel a little badly that we are the forgotten ones, but am not anxious for my mother or girlfriend to be reading about all these small invasions (which now seem a long time ago). The small ones still cost a few thousand Americans, and often 15,000 Japs. Not chicken feed by any account, and the worst is that there was often little support, and supplies were always short.

Bob Campbell is in the Merchant Marine, but I have no idea where or how he is.

You are correct in that collecting souvenirs can be a trifle dangerous. I am well aware of the booby traps, but have been able to collect 3 Jap rifles, bayonets and a helmet. The rifles are all of different types (and two calibers), and the bayonets are long and mean looking. What I will be able to do with all this booty remains to be seen.

You mention bombing a bridge at Var, France, and actually hitting it. You then mention flying as bombardier and gunner on another plane. I breathed a sigh of relief when I read that you had no need to fire the guns. Goering's boys missed a chance for safety and hilarity all at the same time.

Sorry to hear of your itching at the terminal end of your digestive tract. If you cannot desist from scratching, perhaps you should stay away from polite society until healed. It is my understanding that you can scrub the area with a stiff brush and aviation gasoline, and the itch will disappear.

So you dunked Garrity again and started him home with messages for kin! Surely there are strong, mixed feelings in seeing someone go home. You're close, so hang on.

Your tale of the rain and problems with the tent sounded a good deal like what the Army has lived with (prior to now) in that they would be wet several times per day, but the sun would steam them dry in between rains. It is great for growing mildew.

You mention the raid on Budapest and the seeming lack of grit and skill in the enemy fighters. It does sound as though attrition may have hurt them. We are seeing that, too. The matter-of-fact radio conversations as one crew bailed out are interesting, and we sometimes hear similar conversations either from ships or aircraft. And so McGlasson and Lazenby finished their tour and start home!

Ploeski again with the usual flak and some direct hits near you. All this, followed by a raid with another crew. I know that it bothers you to be with "strangers" and am glad you were able to mail the letter.

The news of no more double missions has to be a hard and low blow. With your war seemingly winding down, surely there are some eager recruits somewhere who would like to see some action, and thereby provide some relief. It has crossed my mind that a damned small percentage are bearing the brunt of all this. Nobody listens to me, either!

"Sally the Berlin Bitch" sounds a good deal like "Tokyo Rose". It shows how much information gets out in spite of the efforts for secrecy. Rose provides entertainment, and her tales of what is going on at home don't cause a lot of thought. Sally's news of the U.S. plane pretending surrender, only to shoot down the escorting fighters, sure could be bad news. Hope it doesn't cost any lives, but it does seem that the crew who deviated from the agreement may pay a price. We have no such gentlemanly rules here . . . we expect nothing, and we give nothing.

I see you again beat the hospital and the medics with your chest pains and high temperature. Hope you don't pay a price for that. I, too, would not want to miss any missions at your stage of events. You go on to say that you did get time to rest . . . Lady Luck strikes again!

I understand your feelings about the non-combat people and the rear echelon officers who write up decorations for each other. I really don't see much of that here. Our rear areas are still dangerous, and it is sometimes totally difficult to tell an officer from anyone else. We do run into some smart asses in seeking our supplies, but we generally tell them to their faces what we think of them. I really have seen very few people of high rank here.

It is with great envy that I read of you and Buck visiting the USO show and the dancing girls, all of which was followed by the British cinema and gulping fresh fruit. Actually, we can have all the fresh coconuts and breadfruit we want. Movies are available out here, but I don't know where. Bob Hope and his retinue have been available once, but we were loading and could not go. It is nice of the actors and entertainers to come this far, and I'm sure they are good for morale. Frankly, I have a feeling about being teased by the females and then sent back to my lonely rack. So I suffer alone!

Now your letter dated 26 July to 4 August, '44, which you signed "Bemedaled and Bemused Bill." I note you visited the Red Cross and investigated Taranto and found that the Red Cross still is aiding "Our Boys" . . . but at a price. I haven't seen any Red Cross here yet, but will be on guard. I note your observance of some heavy Navy ships there . . . send them over.

Budapest again, and you and yours ruined an armory and an airplane factory. Good for you! One more to go and then you tell of a milk run to Budafusque (wherever that is). I'll bet you didn't care where it was as long as it was a milk run. Congratulations! I'm so happy for you and hope that now you can avoid red tape and confusion the rest of the way to a well-deserved rest.

Your ride in the C-47 sounds a bit exciting, and I assume you told the pilot to go slow and low. A concert and then back home. Then receiving Air Medals and the Purple Heart from the Colonel. I'm sure glad you passed up the offer of ten more missions for a lousy Captain's Rank. Good thinking! Very soon, General or PFC will have equal value and either one, plus a nickel, will get you a cup of coffee anywhere but the Red Cross.

Now a ride as an observer on the B-24 en route to Naples. I understand your nostalgia for the airplane . . . it always brought you back and was the scene of some of the most hair-raising episodes you'll see if you live to be 200. I don't know that I'll feel that strongly about the LST 628, but the same nostalgia would apply. It must have been wonderful to be on a flight without flak and fighters bothering you.

It's nice that you ran into Mac and Buck at the Replacement Depot, but I imagine that awaiting a berth on a ship will be like a kid waiting for Christmas. I hope it happens soon for you and that, meanwhile, you can partake of the scenery and entertainment in the city.

Let's do keep writing and keep in touch. You mention that the scuttlebutt has to do with 30 days' leave and then possible B-29 squadrons. Please use all your skills and experience and whatever else you can muster and do not allow them to put you in B-29s. There are several reasons I say this, and one of them is that you damned well might end up out here. Much as I'd like to see you, I'd rather it be anywhere but here. You've done your bit and run the risks, and now put your mind to staying alive. You have Shirley and the baby and a whole life ahead of you. Don't allow it!

Not much here that I can report. We are away from radios and are ignorant of any news from the outside world. We are involved with short trips here and there, but are never far from one or another rear area. Scuttlebutt has it that we'll be moving out soon, but I'll believe it when I see it.

Sometime back, on one of the trips to Okinawa, my girlfriend wrote and inquired whether I felt inclined toward marriage. She is one fine person, and I felt badly, but had to tell her the truth. I am dreaming, first of all, to stay alive . . . and then I want my freedom from the Navy. I'll not gain my freedom from the Navy and then get involved in a marriage. I was as diplomatic as I could be . . . and the fact may be that she has found someone else. So be it!

With all my complaining about the busy times and lack of sleep, I must say that being in limbo is not getting us anywhere. I can understand the monotony of which the Army complains so much. We know very well what's coming and I, for one, would like to get it over with.

Must quit for now. Maybe our correspondence will catch up a bit in the near future . . . hope so.

HAPPY FOR YOU BILL

17 May, '45

DEAR BARNACLE, ETC., BILL—

Now the mail pours in . . . I love it! I wonder if it was slow in getting here or if nobody volunteered to take it to Okinawa. Anyway, I now have a total of three letters from you. They are dated 5 Aug. to 16 Aug.,'44, 17 Aug. to 30 Aug.,'44, and 1 Sept. to 4 Sept., '44. We may, someday, catch up to a near normal correspondence.

We learned several days ago that your war is over for sure. I was afraid to put much stock in the scuttlebutt until I got it from the horse's mouth. Congratulations! You beat them and survived! Of course, your letter preceded the end of it by some eight months, but congratulations anyway because I am assuming you are getting my mail, but yours is coming very slowly.

You said goodbye to some friends who left on a ship and felt some pains for some newly-arrived troops that were wondering what the future held for them.

You mention some strong feelings between our combat troops and POWs, along with some physical encounters. I suppose it was ever thus, but we have seen little of that. We did see some of our people come out of Billibid Prison in the Philippines, and they were a sad sight. They were whisked away quickly, but the sight of them was impressive. There are extremely few Jap prisoners, and they are well treated, but are not living in luxury. They keep their mouths shut.

At the end of your first letter, you boarded ship after giving up your firearms and films. Of course they'll give them back to you!

Then you received letter of 14 July, '44. Good God! At the rate of 14 days to get home, you must be zig-zagging or moving in a convoy with ships even slower than we. It will be a chance to rest and relax and think about how much time would be involved if you were cruising in a B-24 with a choice of wines, along with roast pheasant or a standing rib roast.

It appears that you did not draw VIP quarters on your transport home. From what you describe, your berth was way forward . . . and way down. Wish I had been able to communicate with you at that time so as to point out that you could have done worse. Space aboard ship is indeed limited, and it appears the designers did, at the very least, allow a little for the people. I note you abandoned your rack for a fresh-air spot above decks. Glad you enjoyed good food (probably reserved for the Air Force) and note that the nurses got their necessities due to the signal flags that had you featuring your life jacket and water wings.

I can imagine your feelings at finding German POWs in cabins and receiving good care. Chances are that it will take awhile before you, or I, will cool off a bit.

Sorry to hear about the soldier overboard. One never knows about that. We saw a couple of instances like that when men jumped off ships ahead of us. Never knew what it was all about. We never had a man overboard, but we did have one fall in rough water while getting out of a boat. He was a non-swimmer and was saved by my friend from Plattsburg who lives in Evansville, Indiana. He was lucky.

Your trip into New York Harbor brings almost as much emotion to me now as it did for you then. Home at last . . . but at what a cost? Why not the others . . . why me?! Always remember that they had several chances at you and did their best to ruin your chances, but you made it in spite of them.

In your last letter (of these three), you relate disembarking and being met by the Ladies Aid Volunteers with real milk, cookies and Cokes, and the ladies were greeting you and talking with you as though you were a genuine human being. Makes it all worth while! Then you were off to Camp Shanks in New Jersey, which proves to be as little as I guessed it would be. Your trip to New York with Petri was probably an eye-opener. High prices and snotty, condescending people out for a buck. Sorry you only hit the waiter once, but it appears you got his attention, and later in the evening someone may have received courteous service. My only real exposure to gouging took place in the Philippines, and we were happy to spend the money and realized the people had lost everything. What you ran into will live in one's memory.

I can't believe the dance and refreshments for the POWs and with the women bussed in so as to make their stay in the USA pleasant. Our homebased troops should have enough sense not to flaunt all this in sight of returning combat people. It crosses my mind that the time and money spent trying to make the POWs happy would be very well-received out here in the forgotten paradises. I must not think about it.

Your letter ends with the info that you will enjoy a train ride to Ft. Sheridan shortly. New Jersey (and you) will part without a tear!

It is truly great to hear of your homecoming. I'll admit to worrying about you . . . especially these last several months when the mail was fouled up. I knew nobody was receiving mail, but it seemed pretty eerie.

We have been at Guam or Saipan or the Philippines for some time now and have enjoyed the relative quiet. We are under way now for Okinawa, and I am going to try to catch up with some mail we got just as we left. All incoming mail is old letters and is most welcome.

We are carrying miscellaneous supplies and, as usual, there is a certain amount of anxiety over how Okinawa will be at this stage. Unofficial news is always suspect, but we understand the air activity continues, but on a lesser scale. The Navy has taken one hell of a licking there, but there are now so many ships available that the outcome of all this is clear. We have heard a great deal about the invasion at Normandy (and particularly Omaha Beach) and I suppose that invasion will be the biggest and best, but it's hard to imagine anything worse than Okinawa. Still, Tarawa and Iwo Jima have to rate at the top for smaller, but pure fury. It matters not! The thought has crossed my mind that the big-time war reporters would rather report from their hotel rooms in London or Paris than to dig a foxhole in the sand and report from here.

We expect a rather quiet cruise this time. If one expects nothing, he is seldom disappointed, but I'll take a chance this time. We hear reports of submarines, but we have always heard that, so we put it in the back of the mind.

I can't help but think of the enormous job of bringing food, clothing and all manner of supplies out here for all these people. It's no wonder the mail has to take a back seat once in awhile. It would be great to correspond in a more timely fashion, but I guess what we have is better than nothing. One might think of a Jap on some island, like Bougainville, who probably hasn't had a letter from home in some three or four years. Also no food, clothes, ammo or visits by girlfriends. Well, they started it!

It is time for me to do something constructive. I shall try and devote as much time as possible to answering mail . . . and we have a long trip ahead.

Tell me about Chicago!

SHORT FINGERNAIL BILL

20 May, '45

DEAR HOG HEAVEN BILL—-

Getting mail is a little like seeing a little action . . . it comes in bunches . . . but the letters are more welcome. I wrote recently and will continue to write as often as possible. Someday you will get my mail in bunches . . . and then maybe we can finally catch up and correspond in the present instead of the past.

Your letter of 5 Sept. to 9 Sept., '44, relates your arrival at home and the difficulty you had in making it a total surprise. I can say that it makes great reading and arouses the emotions.

The rather shabby treatment you all visited on the poor, young OCS 2nd Lt. reminded me how I felt at New Orleans, at the age of 20 and facing men up to age 40 as their Division Officer (who knew little or nothing). It is embarrassing. I don't feel that way anymore and will have your same attitude if and when I return home. It sounds like you got the usual "local" train, but the compartment and the dining car should have made the trip comfortable, except for your urge to speed homeward. I have never experienced a compartment, but will if the chance ever comes about.

What a sensation to be within 3 blocks of your house and keep going to Ft. Sheridan! Couldn't you get the window open? Surely there was one of those ropes to pull for an emergency stop. Sixty miles in seven hours sounds like old times, so it seems that winning your war has not yet affected rail travel . . . for Military personnel. I well remember bitching about the lousy trains we both rode at the beginning of our adventure, but I'd give anything for another ride on one now! Then paperwork and delay and no passes from Ft. Sheridan, and you a short distance from home. Finally, you did get on the way home. Your ride on the I.C. train and the attitude of the other passengers toward you is probably only the beginning of reality for the homecoming combat serviceman. I am scratching your thoughts deeply in my memory so that I won't be expecting any thanks or kindness from those I encounter . . . if I return.

Your meeting with the family sounds wonderful, and seeing your daughter must have been the realization of many a wish. I'm quite surprised that the good home-cooked food was hard to assimilate, but am guessing that will change. It was thoughtful of you not to demand that food be passed to you in the usual Army vernacular . . . it may have resulted in the lack of an invitation to ever eat there again.

Your letter dated 10 Sept. to 26 Sept., '44, states that you had received my letter of 16 August, '44. That's a whole lot better delivery than we're getting now.

You write now of the possibility of a return to Casper, Wyoming, and training new crews. Another possibility may be B-29s, which I truly hope you will avoid like the plague. You've had enough, and flying in those monsters is all over water with loads so heavy they need long, long runways to get off. They, plus B-24s, are setting fire to a lot of paper and bamboo houses, but the flights are long and there are no friendly places to ditch in an emergency.

You spent some time and effort in relating your schedule . . . with the wakeup call, followed by gorging yourself with real food and, perhaps, a walk to the Lake in the sunshine. I can envision you at about 300 pounds and looking like Herman Goering . . . and too large to fit into an airplane. Perhaps you have gained a good deal of wisdom in the months away from home, and a certain amount of devious behavior. In any event, I have reread your tale regarding the food to the point that I have lost my appetite for dinner tonight . . . and we are having one of our better meals, s__t on a shingle. I must recover by tomorrow because we will dine on gourmet Spam browned in Australian mutton tallow with genuine hydraulic potatoes. Yum, yum!

I'm sorry to hear of the death of Chet Wetterlund . . . and the wounding of Moe Anderson. Glad you were able to meet with Moe and Jim Fletcher. Incidentally, I have stayed many times at the Knickerbocker Hotel . . . but, of course, did not know they now have an Officer's Club. Your eating out and having people in sounds great, and the trip to Gravel Lake sounds like fun, along with dinner with Leo Garrity and his mother.

All this, and now the impending R & R in Miami? It is my very fond hope that the upcoming trip will prove some better than my R & R in Manila. At least the booze should be better quality, but I suppose the cost will also be somewhat higher. Best of luck.

Don't worry about putting me on a bit about the great food, etc. I'll admit it does cause me to drool a bit on my shirt front but, actually, I have drooled very little for awhile now, and it is not a bad experience. We are not really super neat here anyway.

Your letter dated 27 Sept. to 14 Oct., '44, relates the sheer hardships of Miami, along with the receipt of my letter of 30 Sept., '44.

I didn't realize you had relatives in the Pittsburgh area and wonder at your visit to Washington, D.C., before entraining to Miami. The old cane seats again and a little coal dust en route probably made you wish you were in the wild blue yonder smelling cordite, oil and gasoline fumes instead. I note you met new and old friends, sat by the pool, went deep sea fishing, golfing and boat riding, but you had to spend a dollar every day for you hotel room and top notch meals cost another dollar. Good God, William, are you related to Harry Truman? Please check and advise where I should send the bill for my Manila trip. I believe I spent four or four-fifty and have never been reimbursed. Maybe, upon my return home, they will offer me R & R on a South Seas Island. I bet I can count on it.

I just glanced over your description of the heavenly bodies at the pool but have, I admit, compared what you ogled with the ones I last ogled . . . and yours are the winners by a light year or more. I do remember the dark-skinned lasses, about five feet tall, with the boobs bouncing off the knees, the flies swarming around the grass skirts and with the yaws and other open sores decorating the legs, arms, faces . . . and likely other parts. Those females probably had great personalities and were good to their mothers, but they were the greatest enticement to abstinence known to man. I can understand why you signed off as "Bugeyed".

You are probably correct in that our story is not being told by the press. It may be that they recognize MacArthur for what he is, but the end result is that <u>he</u> will write the history of his part in this fiasco. Furthermore, it is not a comfortable place for newsmen to visit and write stories. There are no hotels, restaurants, bars or brothels.

Now comes your letter of 21 Oct., '44, to 31 Dec., '44, and you were indeed at Casper after a nice train ride. You and Shirley are again lucky on housing and friends. It is understandable that your already overworked nervous system has a little trouble with the day and night flying in bad weather and near mountains.

Your '38 Packard sounds good and should get you away when the opportunity knocks. Getting away from it all should help preserve the nerves and keep you going. I note that you broke your hand, and now the Surgeon won't let you fly. I absorbed this information with some devious thoughts, but realize that it will take more than a broken hand for me. In fact, it will take so much, that I believe I will just forget it. Hope your hand healed well and that you can now hold a glass of scotch without spilling it.

You failed to shoot an antelope. I can only assume that it was because none presented himself in a satisfactory manner. Surely, had one been close enough, even though bounding up and down or doing multiple twists in the air, you could have drawn a bead and fired a bullet through one eye or the other . . . and called the shot. Smart, those antelope!

Now you have applied for Pilot Training, and I hope you get it . . . if that's what you want. Hopefully, it will take a long time and you will be involved with "Entering Cockpit 101" when the war concludes. Think William, think!

You sign off as "Baron Bill," and I suppose that means a long silk scarf flying in the breeze, rather than a reward from the Queen at the sight of your 8th Air Force missions. DON'T TIE THE SCARF TOO TIGHT!

Not much to report from Paradise! Everyone is goofing off a bit, and I am happy to be an example. The sea is reasonably smooth, with some large rollers that are pleasant, and the sky is loaded with clouds moving in a pretty good wind. We are able to sleep our usual allotted four hours at night, and the work . . . the hell with it! Soon enough, all this will end and we will get another crack at those yellow bastards! I am taking it one day at a time and enjoying it as best I can. I still have more letters to answer from you and will get to it as time is available.

In your flights, ask your brand new pilots to stay away from the mountains. Unless you have thought of bailing out and practicing survival tactics, I see no reason to push your luck. Keep those letters coming.

GUNG-NO BILL

23 May, '45

DEAR KITTYHAWK BILL—-

Today, with luck, I'll answer your remaining two letters while underway. Yours of 1 Jan., '45 to 1 Feb., '45, and 2 Feb. to 1 March, '45, are in my hot little hands. While everyone else plays poker or shoots dice, I'll reply to your letters.

You had just received my story of Leyte. It was Vice Admiral Kinkaid who battled the Japs in the Philippines . . . Admiral Halsey was drawn north by a Jap trick, but it worked out well for our side with the Japs taking a real licking in both places. There was a goodly amount of luck involved also. Early reports from the corn-cob pipe immortal merely stated that, due to intellectual planning, the Japs were divided and conquered quickly at a small cost. When it was over, the figures were: American casualties, about 11,000 . . . Jap casualties, about 113,000. Navy casualties were not announced, but several ships were sunk or damaged, and several people were lost.

It is good to hear from you that the 50 missions now seem a little less frightening. It does appear that the mind remembers the good things and somehow covers or forgets the bad ones. I sure hope so!

We sure agree on the attitudes toward the shirkers, but we must adjust because, when this is over, they will be just as much veterans as we are . . . and their stories will likely be more lurid and bloody than ours. I note that you find the rear echelon wearing combat ribbons, and that would make me angry. Here, of course, nobody has any ribbons to wear.

Congratulations on getting pilot training, but it does mean a separation from Shirley . . . though apparently brief. Your trip in the Packard through the snow for 50 hours sounds terrible, and it was followed by another train ride to San Antonio. Now you are back where you started after making the mistake of enlisting. Do you ever feel you are moving in circles?

Thanks for your new address. It may well screw up our contact, but not for long.

Your second letter relates a certain disappointment with San Antonio regarding the usual paperwork routine, less than gourmet food and about the same treatment you experienced as a cadet. I find it interesting that they are shutting down primary and basic schools. Please tell your Congressman, and anyone else who will listen, that there is another war going on and it is not over. Maybe they will just wind everything down and forget us out here!

I note that you have some difficulty with morse code . . . so did I. The keyboard itself was not learned well (except for SOS), and reading the light wasn't much better. The way our guys send the semaphore with flags turns me numb. I sometimes pretend to get part of it (and sometimes do), but I'm lucky I don't really have to be an expert.

Congratulations on your birthday! I keep forgetting that you are much older than I am. Work hard to celebrate the next birthday, and I'll do the same. I hate to sound morbid, but we both are very lucky to be here at all.

Your move across the street and into Pilot Training requires a new and lengthy address. Hope that doesn't foul up our correspondence again. You seem lucky on obtaining living quarters, and I hope that Shirley can join you soon.

Your prediction of the end of the war by the end of the year is good news . . . even from a prognosticator who is questionable! I love to hear it and hope to believe it , but reality tells me the end of the year is a hell of a long way off. I'm going to take it as you took your 50 missions . . . one day at a time. No need to worry about my health being affected by the corn whiskey. That was a temporary joy before the rear echelon arrived and shut down the home distilleries. Since then, it has been all clean living with no vices or joys of any kind.

Our Flag Ship status has worked out rather well. It has not changed our routine very much, and the "Flag" is not important enough to single us out as a target. In fact, the "Flag" is as interested in keeping his abode secret as we are in having him do so. I don't really know what the hell they do all day, but I know they sleep at night and are not available for watches because whatever they do takes all their time and energy.

Take heart in that soon you will be skilled in guiding a few tons of aluminum through the air with takeoffs and landings a humdrum affair that could be accomplished in your sleep. After several "successful" takeoffs and landings, you will be elevated to Colonel and shipped to Washington to direct strategic air strikes. You may well elect to make the Air Force a career and retire at age 40 with money like Midas. If so, don't forget your old friends!

We continue plowing our way toward Okinawa in moderate seas and with some intensity in the adrenaline. Reports disclose that the land battle is moving slowly, but surely . . . the casualties are high. We believe that the major damage to their Navy has been done and that it should be easier now. We hope so. It is the Japs' last chance to keep us off their home islands, and it is our last chance to show them that they should give up before we visit in force. I am in no uncertain terms hoping this can somehow end before we actually go to Japan. It will be a terrible waste of people on both sides, and the outcome is clear.

B-29s are working over the Home Islands, almost on a daily basis, and it should be very impressive. Japan doesn't have all that big a manufacturing base, and they must surely feel the results of all that bombing. The 8th Air Force is coming out here, and Japan is going to learn that what they have faced so far is only a small part of what is now available. Hope they are impressed!

When back in the Philippines, after Leyte. Another LST Captain brought Joe Foss aboard our ship. Foss is one of the aces in the Air Force from the early times when things were a bit tougher. I did not talk with him, but he was an impressive individual, and I have wondered what happened to him since. I hope he went home. Someday, you may read about the Bunker Hill and the Franklin . . . carriers that survived recently from suicide hits. Grisly facts and much heroics.

In thinking, as I often do, about the "forgotten war", I wonder if the folks at home ever heard about the CBI. The China-Burma-India theater is a quiet topic with some real shirt tail supplies and jungle living (and dying) going on. We don't hear much of it, either, but will, now and then, meet someone who has been there and expresses some bitterness.

I'm in hopes that there will be some mail at Okinawa and that I can mail what I've written during this trip. After a long, dry spell, we are about to enter the present with our correspondence. I have never been able to write on a more or less daily basis, as you sometimes can, but at least we have pretty well kept track of each other through all this mayhem.

Think about your future and don't speed unnecessarily through Pilot Training. Maybe you can get a borderline grade and take it all over again.

Our ETA is a few days away, and we shall tighten up our habits a bit as some enemy activity is predicted. This is not a good time to get hurt. I'll hope to write when we get there, but in any event, will write as soon as possible.

END OF THE ROPE BILL

DEAR WHITEY LOCKS, ANXIETY, AND TO GO HOME—-

As you can plainly see, the Post Office people had delivery diarrhea to the tune of three letters, dated 30 April, 2 May, and 7 May, 1945. Needless to say, I was plumb delighted until I began reading about your voyage and anchorage at Okinawa. I got a few sympathetic white hairs merely by reading your account of those days and wonder again how you guys can go through such extremes and still function.

That typhoon must have been the mother of all typhoons. Your description of Mama Typhoon left me on the edge of my seat. I compliment you on your skill as a writer, and your equally skillful professionalism as a deep sea sailor and fighting man. I now understand what a "loose cannon on the deck" really means. The wooden sailing ships of earlier days dealt with cannons a great deal smaller than the steel behemoths that were loose in your holds. Those tanks could have sunk you, Willum. The storm's dying down must have been an enormous relief to all aboard, and the rest of the convoy as well . . . only to be replaced by floating mines. If you counted 19 in one day, I wonder how many the rest of the convoy saw and how many bobbed by at night? They must have been like flies on a road apple.

You have apparently disregarded my advice about volunteering, and next I find you swimming upstream like a spawning salmon to open the bow doors. Out of 300 guys, are you the only sailor on board who can swim? At this point, I was almost afraid to read any further for fear you may have commandeered a tank and were leading the charge against the Jap positions.

I was right, except it was suicide planes for which you did not volunteer. Now I feel badly for smart mouthing about the tank. In any event, I can understand the terror those planes can create. I've seen enough of them blow up to know the havoc they would cause hitting a ship with oil, high test gasoline, explosives and other combustibles packed into one rather small space. That must be pure, unadulterated hell to be on a ship that, in the space of seconds, is turned into an inferno. I can feel the agony, and I'm sitting in Oklahoma . . . relatively safe. Damn, the thought makes me twitch!

That floating debris thing was a sneaky little trick. I'm glad the shooters, and I loosely include you and your trusty Garand in that group, must have had a ball. Finally shooting back and, hopefully, a little round Japanese head under all the floating junk. I am not there, of course, and have no desire in any event to be there, but I would not hesitate to shoot floating junk on the water or a civilian on the shore. The civilians can kill you as easily as a soldier. Don't give anyone a chance to put out your lights. If he's around the neighborhood, he's up to no good. Shoot first, wrestle with your conscience later on.

I wrote that bit about shooting civilians before I read your letter of 2 May, and I'm glad your Marine roomie verified my attitude about civilians (even women and kids) being dangerous to your continued longevity. However, stick to your ship and you may not have that problem to contend with now and, perhaps, later on. The fortunate part of my job was not being able to see the results on human beings that my bombs hit. Still, it sometimes niggles at me a little . . . less as time goes on.

More air raids, and your tally of enemy aircraft at seven. I feel like we had a walk in the park after some of the stuff you have endured. The death of Ernie Pyle was big news back here. Unlike most of the "fourth estate", he got down, dirty and scared with the troops. He makes the others look exactly like what they are. How come your "Flag" parks near a carrier or carriers? Is he brown-nosing the Admiral or was it orders? The passage of the 16-inch shells over your ship back at Okinawa must have been intimidating, as well as somewhat comforting. You are definitely on the attack . . . and winning.

Your next visit to Linguyen turned out to be pretty hairy, despite your hearing no sirens, bells or whistles. Rocket fire from LCI's must have been a sight to see. The return trip to Okinawa and a suicide plane hitting the drink between your LST and another, 50 or so feet away, must have made you a believer. Your luck is going to hold, Wm. "Prognosticator" Alderson has spoken. Be careful anyway . . . do not volunteer. I will not be responsible; my prognosticating does not cover volunteering.

Since last writing, I have successfully completed the primary course of training at Chickasha and am now a basic student at Perrin Field in Sherman, Texas. The airplane we fly here is an AT-6, a low-winged airplane a little like a P-51 in appearance, not in performance. Before leaving Chickasha, I came to the conclusion that I was not a hot pilot and capable of violent acrobatic flight. This came about when, on a solo flight in the PT-17, I dropped the nose at 4,000 feet and started downward with the idea in mind of a loop and an immelman at the top of the loop in order to come out right-side up. When I pulled up out of the dive, the G-forces were rather significant. In fact, significant enough for me to pass out temporarily. When I came to, I was pointed straight up at an altitude of 800 feet with the propeller turning so slowly that I could see the grains of wood. My airspeed was almost nonexistent. When I looked over the side and saw the ground as close as it was, I thought I was about to become a blot on the landscape, as well as on the family and Air Corps coat of arms. I rammed the stick and throttle forward and pulled out seconds before I bought the farm. I have concluded that I cannot take too much in the way of G-forces and, thus, will go for multi-engine planes, providing I don't exceed my own limits again in another balls-out loop.

We have a fairly nice place to live; kitchen, bedroom, etc. The only problem is big, he-man sized mice. They run around behind the molding in the ceiling, and when they want to peek down at us, they gnaw a hole right through the molding. Shirley won't let me shoot them, so when they make a hole, I nail an orange crate slat over the hole. They then gnaw another one, and I nail up another slat. I hope the landlord doesn't come on a surprise visit.

You can send your letters either to the field, usual name and class number at Sherman, Texas, Perrin Field, or if you prefer, 302 W. Moore St., Sherman, Texas.

The AT-6 turned out to be quite a machine the first time I hopped into it. Two cockpits covered by a canopy and a mess of instruments and handles that I thought I'd never figure out. After a few days, however, I was lowering and retracting the gear and flaps, and pretty much understood the many instruments on the panel. The AT-6 is a lot trickier to handle than the PT-17. Turning in on the final approach, one must be careful not to cross the controls and end up headfirst into the ground.

Army 2nd Lt.'s and Ist Lt.'s are the instructors here and are a lot less forgiving than our civilian instructors at Chickasha. They ride pretty rough-shod over the cadets, but treat us hoary combat veterans, if not very friendly, at least politely. A lot of them I'm sure wish they could get out of here and into a P-51 or P-47 operational unit, so a certain amount of pique is understandable. So far, I'm not having any problems and am having a great thrill driving these things around the skies (particularly soloing).

My inhibitions come to the fore when an instructor is present . . . and pissing and moaning about the sloppy figure eights or slow rolls I am trying to perfect.

The Link trainer is a simulated airplane that the student pilots fly by the instruments only. The trainer has a solid canopy, so you cannot get a visual reference on anything and must learn to rely 100% on your instruments and not on the seat of your pants or instinct. The trainer also moves as if it were an airplane in flight. It is taking me a while to get the hang of this thing. I'd better . . . in advanced twin-engine school, they are real big on the trainer.

In the meantime, we do acrobatics, cross countries day and night, and whatever other maneuvers we should learn in order to become "old pilots." The saying is that there are bold pilots, but very few old, bold pilots. I believe in that pearl of wisdom wholeheartedly, having once tested the bold part of it and luckily walked away.

There is more hum-drum to weary you with, but I'll save it for when next I take pen in hand, which should be pretty quickly before you forget my admonitions about volunteering above and beyond.

Keep your head out . . .

LOOPY BILL

DEAR ACE, KANGAROO, AND BARON—

I now have your letters dated 2 March, 4 April to 30 April, and 1 May to 1 June . . . all of the current year. We are making progress! I have been here at Okinawa awhile and have been busy, but shall now reply as best I can.

Your trip from San Antonio to Chickasha, Oklahoma, sounds like a real nightmare. You apparently tried every method of travel but donkey cart and, in the end, the donkey cart may have been the fastest way to go. Having arrived in Chickasha, your comments indicated it was not a place to which you might wish to retire.

You mention an interest in the suicide pilots and wonder how their commanders get them to do their duty. We also wonder and, of course, it is a matter of discipline, rigid training, religion and fanaticism. It may also have to do with a few shots of Saki and fuel for only a one-way trip. In any event, it is still unbelievable and frightening (to us), but it is not going to win their war.

You relate that on Shirley's birthday, you took your first flight in a Stearman. I trust you celebrated the birthday first. Even though you have experienced many hours in your bomber missions, I would feel that, after a few snap rolls, slow rolls, spins, stalls and landings, the birthday celebration would have to wait a week or so. Guess I was not cut out for that kind of insanity, but glad you enjoy it. I note that you are back in the classroom, and I know how tough that can be. Sweat it out!

Your dad's trip in the Packard with the women and packages must have been much shorter than it seemed. I'm sure it is good to have Shirley there and note that you are housed in a private home. You do seem lucky in finding housing, in spite of the shortages.

No, there is no record of my being wounded. The field hospital was so busy, and my injury so minor, that it was just forgotten. I did not know it would help on points toward rotation. There is no such thing as rotation here anyway, so I guess I haven't lost anything.

Congratulations on your solo flight! That is quite an accomplishment, and I'm happy for you . . . and I also wish to suggest that you give some thought to screwing up somewhere along the line in order to prevent assignment to someplace where single engine pilots fly toward Japan. You have had enough.

Your landing at the end of your solo sounds somewhat hair-raising to me, and it is good to note that you have acquired the skill of hitting the ground just once, and gently. Glad the classwork is not as difficult now.

Your landlady and the black snake mouse catcher should make for some interesting days and nights. At least you are able to climb into the friendly skies during the day. I imagine the first time Shirley saw the snake, she very nearly joined you in the wild blue yonder.

It is good to hear that you are enjoying the flying, in spite of the difficulties and the danger. I am somewhat acquainted with the Stearman and believe that flying it would be fun. However, it is not World War I, and the more sleek, high-powered planes seem to leave little room for error. Perhaps you have thought about this and will develop a mysterious malady that requires rest and good food for a year or two. Think about it.

Just the word Okinawa sends chills up and down my yellow spine, but I believe it's about all over here . . . at least unofficially. We arrived shortly after Naha (the Capitol) fell along with Shuri Castle. These are the only outstanding places. Naha was not much of a town, and Shuri was an important shrine to the locals, but was fortified and heavily defended by the Japs. Both Naha and Shuri are simply gone now, although the rubble discloses that something was there. The stone burial vaults, so precious to the locals, were held to the end by the Japs and they, too, are simply gone or badly burned by the flame throwers. The place was different because of the many terraces, and some substantial buildings, but it doesn't look very good now. The civilians were afraid of the Americans, and several were herded out of caves by the Marines as things settled down a bit. Unfortunately, Jap soldiers often joined the civilians in the caves, so they all suffered from flame throwers, white phosphorous or satchel charges. It was unpleasant. More recently, we were able to see both soldiers and civilians leaping to their deaths from cliffs on the south end of the island. Marines tell us they had to handle about 4,000 Jap prisoners, most of whom were shocked out of their minds by shelling. Some 90,000 Japs were killed. Only God knows how many Okinawans died. All in all, with the horrible losses of the Navy, it has been a necessary, but dreadful invasion. It is difficult to imagine anything being worse than this for all concerned, but the predictions are that the worst is yet to come.

There is good news, and one must strain to enjoy any that comes along! Your 8th Air Force has arrived and is in action with a vengeance. They do not especially like their quarters, the Spam, or the lack of hotels and night clubs, and they seem determined to get this over with as soon as possible. They are taking the B-24s off bumper to bumper in the early mornings, and they return about 16:00. It is a wonderful sight to see, and most all are coming back undamaged. They have little to worry about from the Jap Air Force, and they are literally tearing the hell out of Japan. B-29s are operating from Tinian and, I believe, Saipan, and we are told that entire Jap cities are left in flames. It is no secret that our Navy is operating very close to Japan, and it should be clear to any and all Japanese that the jig is up. I pray they get the messages . . . and soon.

Some LST's are taking Okinawans to new villages on the north of the island, and I hope we don't draw that duty. It's hard to know if they are trustworthy.

Saw my first P-51, which I assume came over with the 8th Air Force. It made a strafing run along the beach, and it was a beautiful sight to see. Wish we had had some of them before. It is supposed to be very fast and able to go a long distance.

It is pretty quiet here now, and we must fight being lulled into a feeling of security. There is still some danger, but it is so much better than formerly that one almost feels like it's a vacation. I believe one's spirits are automatically raised by seeing the new power, and knowing that the enemy is taking a licking he richly deserves. In the general scheme, we have been sucking hind teat here from day one. Short of equipment of all kinds and making invasions sometimes without adequate shelling in advance, plus the same people moving inch by inch from one hellish island to another, with little rest and almost no hope.

Some joke about the Marines having platoons of about 50 men, 30 of which are cameramen. I do not joke about any of the other services because we're all in the same boat, but the point is that the newsmen and their cameras seem not to be interested in our little war. The living is not easy out here, and there is no after-hours revelry. To my knowledge, only Ernie Pyle came out here . . . and he did not last very long. In talking with others, the general feeling is that Europe was important, but here is not, and that everyone (but us) would just as soon forget it.

Sorry about my lapse into perhaps some bitterness and despair. That was yesterday, and today is a new challenge, and I shall approach it with a better frame of mind. There is much to be thankful for.

We are taking on spent brass, which is an absolute puzzle to lash down, and will soon leave for who knows where. I hope it is not a long or rough trip. I've always wondered who takes this stuff where, and if it is reworked and sent back in a short time. There is a good deal of it, and it looks as though you had fired at a pheasant, or maybe two, with the usual result. Perhaps if you upgraded from the 12-gauge to a 155 mm filled with #6 shot, you would wipe the laughter from the faces of those pheasants. I hope I live to see it.

One tries not to think too far ahead. Someone else is doing the thinking for us, but the conclusion is obvious . . . we will have to go to Japan. It is just as easy to be optimistic as pessimistic, and a lot easier on the nerves. The predictions about the casualties could be wrong. One could draw an undefended beach. One could face a division of cowardly Japanese troops. Possibly, we could charge into a whole Japanese army that was out of ammunition. Our Navy might inspect its sailors and weed out the cowards, in which case I could be at the Polar Grille within 30 days. I think it's only 7,000 miles or so, and I'll hitchhike if necessary.

Duty calls, and I'd better mail this today, because I don't know how soon we're leaving. Keep your airplane right-side up (the cockpit is on top), and I'll regale you with more misery at my earliest opportunity.

URGENT CIVILIAN BILL

Sunday 1, July 1945 to
Wednesday 1, Aug. 1945

DEAR ANXIOUS—-

The mailman, in the swift completion of his appointed rounds through the ice, snow and blizzards of July in Oklahoma, staggered by and left yours of 10 May 1945. You did not have much to report, except doing a little swimming in the azure blue of the Pacific and lounging on the golden sands of same. I am really happy that you are able to get some time off from the maelstrom in relative safety. Again, I must decline to discuss women, food, sleep or sex. Your long-term denial of these God-given rights has put you on the edge of mutiny, and I want no part of your mutinizing and the Navy losing the war as a result. When you return home, you may wallow to your heart's content in all of the above. If you expire at that point, it is on your own head. What a way to go!

I got so wrapped up in your activities and my own that I didn't comment on some events of world-wide portent that directly affect both of us. As you undoubtedly know by now, the C.I.C President Roosevelt died on the 12th of April and Harry Truman succeeded him in that office. We were saddened by FDR's passing and are waiting to see if Harry can cut the mustard. I know very little about him, nor do I suspect does anyone else. With Germany sagging against the ropes and the Japs throwing the kitchen sink at you guys, Harry has a real plateful.

The Germans finally surrendered on May 7th, and official V.E. day was proclaimed on Monday, the 9th of April. You, of course, are aware of all this by now . . . I hope. I am curious to know what your reaction has been to these changes. I have a wait-and-see attitude about Harry, and the surrender of Germany did not find me in the streets dancing a hornpipe, or even a jig. This thing is not over until the Japs accept the inevitable and throw in the towel. I'll celebrate when all of the fighting is over and the casualty reports stop being calculated. After this whole thing is over, it will be interesting to see the hidden secrets that come oozing to the surface and where the fingers will point. Surely, all is not like it has been made to appear. My suspicions and cynical bones tell me there are some nasty things under the rug.

Back to the mundane. Flying, of course, occupies most of the day and some nights as well. I am now into acrobatics and formation flying and am enjoying everything, even link trainer, which I haven't whipped, but manage to stay even. The periods of solo flying are longer and more fun each time. We arrange rendezvous with fellow students and do a little dog-fighting and other forbidden tactics. Buzzing cattle, flying under bridges, etc. These maneuvers are done at a very comfortable distance from our own field. Graduation was on the 27th of July, so the next move is to advanced school. Since graduation, we have been flying daily, but all solo. The final check ride before graduation was a pistol. A captain was my check rider and was a real perfectionist. The toughest part of the whole test was doing an eight-point slow roll. That involves rolling the airplane completely around a longitudinal line and stopping the roll at eight different degrees of roll. Holding that airplane with the nose on the horizon at all times is a real pistol. Upside down is particularly difficult. I barely managed, but did to my own amazement.

On the 1st of August, we flew in the morning and in the P.M., we celebrated Air Corps Day by watching a variety of airplanes do a fly-by. A jet fighter buzzed the runway and scared the hell out of most of the watchers . . . the speed and noise were awesome. Rumor has it that we move again on the 3rd. I will advise you of my new location. In the meantime, keep
your baby-blues wide open.

STRAIGHT AND LEVEL BILL

17 July, '45

DEAR LOOPY BILL—-

Received your rather lengthy epistle dated 2 June to 30 June, 1945, just before getting underway and leaving beautiful Okinawa. Our tears at leaving were few and brief, and we experienced the joy of watching some of Japan's last pilots throw themselves and their planes away. A relatively small part of the action was close enough for us to fire on them, and we blew some ammo with no hits. All the bogies we saw went down, and only one was able to hit a ship.

We are now underway in calm seas and hoping for a pleasant trip to a place I cannot name at this time. It should make for some more quiet time, and we'll appreciate that. We are with about eight other ships.

Your letter is in answer to mine, which relayed some information about our trials and tribulations enroute Okinawa and D-Day there. It was my most miserable experience yet . . . and I had thought I'd learned to control fear. I guess one does control it, but it sure as hell does stay around. The entire crew held up very well, and I'm guessing that perhaps being totally worn out by the time we got there may have helped to some degree. I'm sure you know what I'm talking about.

There was no swimming involved in removing the turnbuckles from our bow doors. There are several of them that hold the doors closed, and all had been released but the lower two, which were underwater. One merely climbs down a ladder welded on one door and fishes for the turnbuckles and releases them. This is done for every beaching and is routine . . . not dangerous, but a little scary in the dark.

Shooting at the floating boxes and debris was fun, and all the LST's enjoyed it. We only fired close to our own ship, so as not to skip bullets into another ship. We had no encounters with civilians, and I'm thankful for that. The Marines had a hard time with the orders regarding civilians, and some suffered as a result. They learned fast. In all the invasions I've seen, the infantry always orders a Jap soldier to completely disrobe before getting close to him.

I'm surprised that Ernie Pyle's death was heavily reported back home. It probably shocked the fourth estate and will cause them to think twice before reporting first-hand about the life and woes of the combat rifleman. Actually, anyone who did not have to be near the heat and noise would be stark raving mad to go there.

I have no idea why we anchored near the big ships. It was a first. The joy of seeing them in action was exceeded only by the joy of moving elsewhere.

Good Lord! You survive 50 missions with all that entails and then fool around with a loop and an immelman (whatever that is) and risk smashing the grass on the parade ground because of passing out. What would the taxpayers think about shattering their airplane? Surely there is a safer way to find out how one responds to G-forces . . . like riding the local ferris wheel or diving from the bar stool to a mattress on the floor. On the other hand, perhaps the Alderson brain is still superactive, and I note that you have switched to twin engine craft. Perhaps, after some time, you can switch to four engine machines. Just kidding, but think about it!

You state that you have a fairly nice apartment, except for a few mice that peek at you through the moldings. I certainly can understand that Shirley does not want you to shoot them. Living in an apartment full of spent casings AND mice engaged in hysterical laughter would not be an improvement. And Shirley has never even seen you shoot at pheasants!

The AT-6 sounds somewhat interesting, and I note you figured it out rather quickly and love flying it. I can understand your sentiments in having picky instructors, and I believe they would be less strict if they were not riding with you. Riding with a student doing slow rolls, figure eights and perhaps immelmans could bring on what we affectionately call nervous explosion. I doubt I could be a driver's training instructor, let alone fly in one of those airplanes with a novice.

So it is that you are perfecting your operation of the Link trainer, plus flying cross country, acrobatics and other maneuvers . . . and apparently loving it. To each his own, William. I'm truly glad you enjoy that kind of adventure. I'll stick to my life jacket, First Aid kit, sunburn grease and prayers.

The sea is beautiful, and I have had a little fun firing my trusty Jap 6.5 mm rifle at flying fish. The cartridge has a long, thin bullet and the velocity is high. The sights are crude, so I do not hit the flying fish every time. In all honesty, I do not really come very close, but it's the only target I have. It is a pleasant rifle to shoot. We few ships are in our own little world now and just plowing along and enjoying it. The signalmen "talk" to each other with semaphore, and we all put up our guess as to our location at noon or so. It's always interesting to note the ship that goofed and did not figure his position. The flags go up slowly as the signalman reads the position on the flags of the other ships. It happens to all of us, especially when we are in a group.

Sailing with merchant ships is also interesting. They do not have the endless rules and regulations we must follow, and it seems they do the job real well without all the stress. Their crews are smaller, and the men are older and more experienced . . . they just seem to take it easy and enjoy life. Although I have not tried it, I can imagine their life as a pretty good one (in peacetime), and I understand the pay is good. Something to remember.

The LST 628 is showing signs of wear. The starboard bow door is sprung a bit, and there are spots in the deck that are thin to the point that we dare not load anything really heavy in those spots. It is interesting, when heading into a pretty good sea and the hull is bending up and down in the middle, to wonder about metal fatigue and how much is too much. It is best to take the attitude that the Chicago Bridge and Iron Works did a good job and that this vessel will go on and on.

The news has reached me that two more of my high school classmates are dead, and one is missing. No details, but I guess one of them was in Italy. Can't help but feel badly for their families and friends.

I trust that, in your zeal to be a hot pilot, you will remember that your craft is a heavier-than-air craft, and subject to the law of gravity. As you say, there are no old AND bold pilots, and those I've talked with out here say that flying low and slow does not contribute to longevity, either. Obviously, you should switch to administration or run for Congress. If you are elected to Congress, you may need an aide to shuffle papers. You already have my name and address, and I am an applicant. As they say in the Navy, "Expedite!".

The Captain thinks the deck should be painted. My protest that we have no paint went down in flames when he advised that he had obtained some paint. I explained that it was my plan to paint the deck ocean blue with some whitecaps to make us look like only a piece of water. I explained that I was searching for the proper colors for this camouflage. We paint the deck starting at 0800 tomorrow, and the color is an outstanding dark green. I guess I showed him a thing or two!

I'll write next in port. Looks like I'll be busy the rest of this trip.

EXTERIOR DECORATOR BILL

24 July, '45

DEAR AIRBORNE ACROBAT—

It has been a bit busy since I last wrote. The lack of mail when we reached the end of our pleasant voyage was a disappointment, but I guess disappointment is a rather widespread and frequent thing. I shall, nevertheless, pen a few lines to let you know you still have a pen-pal.

It seems strange, but I grow even more cautious at this point in the war. It seems an especially bad time to get hurt, and I believe most of this crew feels the same. Our recent trip took place in beautiful weather and could well have been a peacetime cruise to a vacation spot, but all aboard seemed to feel it was just TOO quiet. It is frightening to wonder if one can't live with peace and quiet without fear of what is coming next . . . and in what form. We know there are submarines and fanatic Jap soldiers nearly everywhere, and we suspect the soldiers have no word as to how the war is going. We guess the Japs would still swim a mile to kill, even if they knew the war is lost. At the same time, we realize that we are winning and are nearing the end . . . but that the worst is still to come. It is not a comforting situation.

When you finally got to a place of safety, did you still have the constant jitters about what comes next?

We have unloaded and reloaded, are again underway and will arrive very soon at our destination, which must remain nameless at this point. Our last stop was at a small island down south, and it was totally lacking in anything interesting. I got ashore enough to fire my trusty Carbine at targets, and I found it to be nice and light to carry, but not terribly accurate, and I prefer a bit more power. We did again put up with the local Piss Call Charlie, who didn't always drop a bomb . . . perhaps they are rationing bombs, which is good news. The Army made half-hearted attempts to shoot him down . . . perhaps because he is their only entertainment. The Army suffers greatly from boredom and card games (with worn-out cards), and the pet parrots and monkeys occupy much of their time. Laundry is still done in 52-gallon drums with a crude windmill and shaft to churn the milky water. They were interested in news from Okinawa and seem glad they are not there. Some of these guys have been through the mill in several campaigns over a few years, and they act almost like emotionless beings with their yellow skin and eyes and worn fatigues. Some of them we have seen many times, and we always exchange news and the latest action that we know about. I hope that, somehow, these people can avoid the inevitable trip to Japan. They've done enough.

I am having to write this in bits and pieces between watches and work, and one loses his train of thought. This trip started out pleasant enough, but we are nearing our destination and reality has set in again in the form of air activity. Nothing really hair-raising, but food for thought. Damn, but I'm tired of this. Wonder what ever happened to my request for duty entertaining WAVES or WACS. I should have had a reply sometime in the last two years!

We're going on the beach. I'll mail this as soon as possible and hope there's a letter here from you.

BARNACLE BILL

Thursday 2 Aug. 1945 to
Sunday 12 Aug. 1945

DEAR SHORT FINGERNAILS—-

We left Sherman, Texas, for Enid, Oklahoma, on the 3rd at midnight and arrived in Enid around 7:00 in the morning. Shirley and Dawn rode with another Enid-bound student pilot and his wife while I brought up the rear with all our junk. Shirley found a place to stay, two adjoining rooms and a kitchen across the hall. One bathroom services about 18 people, plus "Clarence". More on the bathroom in a minute.

Checked the mail before leaving and found two of your letters dated 14 May and 17 May, 1945. These two were nice, newsy epistles, fun to read . . . particularly when you were enjoying a combat-free few days and a chance to get your nerves under control and, second-handedly, mine ,too. We are both hoping, I'm sure, that this hiatus from shot, shell and suicide pilots will become permanent in the near future.

The schedule for my tenure at Enid has a large dose of ground school with advanced navigation and the other usual courses . . . and now familiarizing sessions on the B-25. The "25" is the Billy Mitchell bomber that Doolittle flew off carriers earlier in the war. A real nice airplane . . . twin engines and a sexy twin-tailed rear end. For a medium bomber, it carries a comforting number of 50 calibers for self-defense. As you are aware, self-defense is very big on my wish list. As long as I will be driving and unable to protect our formations with my vaunted skills as a shooter, I am looking for the best instructors for our tenderfeet gunners. Would your crew from #628 (Old Ironsides) like to TDY to Enid to instruct our boys for a couple of weeks? I'll try and work this out with General Arnold. You, of course, are invited to accompany them as chaperon. Your crew has a reputation as "Zero Killers" that has spread through the armed forces like green gooseberries through a goose. Finally got to fly one for 30 minutes, and it's a lot different than AT-6's or PT-17's. First of all, you sit up very high in the cockpit. We had become accustomed to seeing the ground about four feet from our fannies and the nose slanting upward, obscuring the view directly ahead. We always taxied in an S-pattern, but the "25" has tricycle landing gear and the visual effect sitting on the runway and landing comes as a bit of a surprise. The "25" has a wheel instead of a stick, and that is hard to get used to. Instruments all over the place, and you wonder if you will ever be able to learn them all! I'm not really concerned but ,initially, it is a little overwhelming. The airplane flies real nice.

In the midst of all this, one of our B-29's dropped an atomic bomb on Hiroshima on 6 August, followed by another on Nagasaki on the 9th. I'm sure you are aware of these significant strikes, as well as the fact of the Jap surrender on Wednesday the tenth. Hopefully, this will mean that USS-LST-628 will wend its way homeward in the very, very near future. With the Navy as thoughtless and perverse as it normally is, I hope they don't send you all over the Pacific collecting men and equipment that they somehow mislaid. Please let me know what is now in store for you. My early comment in this letter hoped for a hiatus from combat . . . the Lord moves in mysterious ways, and that wish became fact a lot quicker than I thought was possible. Invading Japan will now be taken over by the non-combatants. Most importantly, however, you won't have to look at Mt. Fuji over the barrel of your gun.

The rooms we have here are in a private home and come complete with ants, scorpions and cockroaches numbering in the thousands. We have the furniture standing in cans of kerosine (ant prevention), shake shoes in the morning (scorpion abatement) and, for roaches, my own personal brand of warfare. At night when I hear the little devils scampering around on the copper sink, I sneak out in the dark with a rolled up newspaper, stand in front of the sink, turn on the light (string hanging from ceiling) and lay into them with great gusto. I get as many as twenty at a swat. All I have accomplished, thus far, is to titillate their desire to reproduce replacements for their fallen comrades . . . and they apply themselves with great, great gusto to that end. Roaches ten, Bill zip, on a scale of one to ten.

I mentioned Clarence earlier on, and Clarence deserves his place in the about-to-be-written history of the Army Air Corps in WWII. Never have so many owed so much to one 15-year old (apologies to Winston C.), acne-stricken youth. Two officers and six enlisted men wait in line, while Clarence occupies the john each morning. The line of jiggling people increases as wives and kids join the anxious line awaiting deliverance. Clarence's mother is, at the top of her voice, demanding to know "What the hell are you doing in there, Clarence?!" No one has, as yet, informed her what the majority opinion is regarding his extended visits to the growler. The natives are getting restless, and Clarence might need both hands to defend himself from his irate fellow lodgers if he does not soon alter his schedule for morning ablutions, or whatever.

There are 108 student officers in this class at Enid, and the word has come down that, now that hostilities are at an end, we have two options available to us: . . . resign and go home . . . or finish the course and face assignment anywhere they need pilots. I would dearly love to get my wings, but this veiled threat of assignments has spooked me. I can't ask Shirley to continue this gypsy way of life and the continued aggravation of moving from one lousy environment to another, or to go home while I end up in Germany or Japan as part of the occupation forces. I believe, too, that in order to progress in rank in the civilian Air Corps, politics will play a big part . . . as well as kissing a lot of butt. Shirley doesn't go along with the wives of high-ranking officers wearing their husbands' rank at the end of their tongues and in their demeanor. I'm also afraid of losing my aplomb in dealing with some of the twits wearing higher-rank insignia than my own. I have concluded I'm better off as a civilian. Of the 108 in our class, 100 chose to quit. After signing the papers, the Air Corps gave the remaining eight students their choice of any base of their choice that flew B-25s after their graduation. Now that's a typical SNAFU on the part of the powers that be. They lost what could have been good pilots who probably would have joined the reserve forces. I depart the Air Corps wondering how we got anything done at all with so many short-sighted thinkers to our rear.

May I suggest you direct your future letters to 7042 Kimbark, in Chicago. I hope we will continue informing one another about affairs in the Pacific and in Chicago until we can once again prowl around a cornfield. It will be a thrill to count on you as my birddog and gun-bearer.

Particularly now, be very careful——-

FORMER FLYING FOOL BILL

14 August, '45

DEAR STRAIGHT AND LEVEL BILL—

We are catching up in our correspondence. I now have yours dated 1 July to 1 August, '45. Your letter made here in less than two weeks . . . hooray!

I cannot remember when I heard about Roosevelt's death, but it was pretty soon after the fact. In fact, I may have written you that I knew. Yes, it was somewhat sobering in the middle of all this to take on a new President.

I also was aware that the war in Europe ended, but cannot now remember when the word got to us. I hope others felt as you did that we should also end it out here. Yes, there will be some fingers pointed and some accusations made when hindsight sets in, but I also believe that a good many secrets will be kept for many years. It will be interesting to see how history is written . . . and if anyone is interested in the truth.

You seem to be more reckless and careless as the weeks go by. All your solo flights and dogfighting and flying under bridges is rattling my nerves in spite of the distance between us. Please stop and think about saving yourself for tomorrow. Congratulations on your graduation . . . and now on to advanced school. I can hardly wait for your next letter to see what the Army Air Corps does now that the war appears to be over.

We arrived here, at Okinawa, at the time I mailed my last letter. I was surprised at the amount of air activity because I thought the Japs had run out of airplanes. Not so! There were a lot of ships here, and the land battle had wound down near the end, but it was still pretty rough with the suicide attacks. We heard rather quickly about the atomic bombs (and cheered mightily) and rumors about a Jap surrender. On 9 August (our time), we got the news that the Japs had surrendered. It was hard to believe, and the idea that it might be a trick was on everyone's mind. Nevertheless, all hands on ships and ashore began firing guns in the air in one wild celebration. It was brought under control rather quickly, but what goes up must come down. It was reported that 42 men died in that celebration. What a sobering and sad situation! What a shame! We all fell quiet and felt true sorrow. It was like a bunch of kids on the loose, and I hope the next of kin never knows how their man died in the last minutes. I feel terrible. I feel happy. I feel like this is one hell of an anticlimax to all the work, sweat, lack of sleep and ever-present fear. We so wanted it all to end, and now it is here . . . and there is little joy in Mudville.

As with all the other low points in this miserable war, we will have to collect ourselves and get on with it. None of our crew was hurt, but I believe they all feel as I do.

The big scuttlebutt now has to do with what comes next for us. Of course, we want to go home . . . NOW. Of course, we will have to wait and see. There are a lot of possibilities ahead, and I can hardly wait to know what's in store for us. Meanwhile, the work goes on and we should be leaving for somewhere before long.

Perhaps at this time, our Flag Officer may be worth his weight in gold . . . I hope so. He is only a Commander, but surely he can speak for us in places we cannot speak. We'll see.

I'm sure my mother, sisters and friends are happy to know the war is over. It is about 7,000 miles to home, but I'll swim if necessary. I'll write again when I settle down a bit.

SURVIVOR BILL

29 August, '45

DEAR FORMER FLYING FOOL——

Your signing off (letter dated 2 Aug. to 30 Aug., '45) pretty well told the story before I read your letter. I don't always read letters in backward fashion . . . it was the way it was folded! It is delightful to now send and receive letters while we can still remember what we last wrote about. The Postal Service people are doing a great job.

I'm at a loss to describe my emotions at learning that you are going home and will become a civilian. Your choice of the alternatives is the same as mine would have been . . . and for the exact same reasons. Your letter was lengthy and newsy, with your usual expertise and humor. But, for me, it all revolved around going home . . . and as a civilian. At least soon a civilian. Congratulations! You sure earned it the hard way, and I hope you never entertain any second thoughts. There is Air Corps out here to the point that the sky is crowded, and it is high time some of the newcomers got their chance. Please keep writing, and I'll do the same until I can see you in good old Chicago. May it be soon!

Other than the above, you relate a move to Enid and a verbal picture of another apartment, including various vermin and crawling companions. Your efforts at elimination of the cockroaches must have kept Shirley in a state of mirth. I do hope she was able to take some photos to show the varied skills and accomplishments of the Air Force personnel.

I note that you were set up for B-25s . . . with which we are familiar. They have been around for awhile and are apparently reasonably airworthy and durable, and I'm glad to hear you enjoyed moving around the skies in them. Your difficulty with a wheel, instead of a stick, is perfectly understandable . . . you, as I recall, had trouble with the steering wheel in a car. But I digress.

Your offer to use our gunners and assist as chaperon so as to provide you with safety struck me just right, but the end of this miserable war will prevent your close association with General Arnold (or anyone else in a position of authority). Nevertheless, it is really interesting to hear some information about the B-25, or any other operational aircraft. We see them, but know little about them. I, of course, would live in total fear of knowing very much about any heavier-than-air vehicles because of the possibility that I might be asked to ride in one. For me, they are not yet perfected and are not to be used by those of us with the broad yellow stripe down the back. A little known fact has it that that is why the Air Force was formed.

You informed me of the end of our war, and my last letter did the same for you. The difference in dates in your letter and mine has to do with the idea that we are on the wrong side of the international date line.

Your tale about 15-year old Clarence is amusing to me, if not to the cross-legged people grimacing in the hallway. Is Clarence still alive?

It is noted that, out of 108 trainees, the magnificent number of eight will continue training on the promise that they can choose their very own base. It seems to me that there are key words here, one being "promise" and the other being "choice." I wish them luck and congratulate you on your common sense! All the reasons you list for going home seem sound to me, and the same thoughts would cross my mind of the Navy if they were to offer me the same choice. Of course, you have enjoyed your flight training and liked the B-25, and it is tough to leave before your silver wings arrived. However, you do have a family and have been through hell and, as you mention, Shirley has lived as a gypsy. Don't look back!

Yes, I shall look forward to our next journey through the cornfields in search of the running pheasants (and laughing pheasants), and in my most diplomatic manner I suggest that you buy a case or two of shotgun shells and practice under the guiding eye of a coach. For starters, I suggest that the wooden part of the shotgun is the part that one places at the shoulder. This basic point will make things go much more smoothly, and you can work on accuracy later. Our meeting will not take place in the foreseeable future, however. There are three reasons, and they are: the Navy, the Navy, and the Navy.

My last letter to you was mailed very shortly before we left Okinawa. The end of our war had come, and the emotions were mixed. We had the deaths because of a silly, spur-of-the-moment celebration, and that was very sobering. Of course, a million of us may now get home because of the atom bombs, and we can forget about invading Japan. We straggled back to Luzon in the Philippines in a convoy that was, perhaps, a little loose compared to the strict station-keeping we had become accustomed to.

What happens to us now has been decided. Someone had the idea that we could pick Jap soldiers on the various bypassed Islands and take them home. I believe our Flag officer explained that Jap soldiers might not be in perfect safety aboard our ship, and also mentioned that popular opinion pointed toward taking American soldiers home and then the Japs. The upshot of it is that we are loading tanks and excess equipment and taking it to Japan as soon as we can load and get underway. The Army people we are taking are encamped near the beach, as their equipment is loaded and they are an outfit we have seen more than once in the past. They, like we, want to go home, but a trip to Japan could be interesting . . . so all of us are not complaining too much.

We still wonder if all this is a dream or a dirty trick. We can't help but wonder about our reception in Japan and if the civilians will be as murderous as their soldiers. Still, they are a disciplined people accustomed to obeying the Emperor, and they should be glad the war is over, even though the outcome, for them, has been defeat. We are already in the process of passing the word as to how to treat the Japanese, and it's for sure they will be treated a hell of a lot better than they would treat us had they won the war. I have no real problem in treating them in a civil manner and am looking forward to seeing them and meeting some of them. One of our old regular Navy sailors has advised some of the more naive in the crew that the Oriental women have an important body part in a horizontal position, as opposed to the same part which is in a vertical position on our occidental women. Some of my men have asked my opinion on this anatomical detail, and I usually reply that I am surprised to hear that our conventional women at home are of the vertical variety. It is clear that this matter will have to be determined by personal observation upon our arrival. I am already searching for a trustworthy man to determine the truth and relay the information to me.

It is still lights out at night, and it is hard to imagine how it will be to turn the lights on again. We have lived in the dark so long it will seem strange. Perhaps our vision may be bothered by lights at sea. We shall find out before long.

You may or may not have heard of Admiral Halsey's message to all ships after Japan surrendered. In effect, he said the war was over and that there would be no Jap planes in the air. He added that if anyone saw a Jap plane in the air, he was to shoot it down in "a friendly fashion". Admiral Halsey has a reputation here as one tough character, and it is nice to hear some humor from him . . . or anyone else.

Now, we are both in a position to write about things that, some time ago, would have been censored. Strangely enough, this freedom, along with all the recent good news, leaves me blank as to what I may have wanted to tell, but couldn't. Maybe later.

Loading seems to be going slowly. Some of this equipment has been to hell and back, but I suppose the numbers will be impressive. The men don't look much better, and they have said the same about us. We hear remarks such as, "Will this thing hold together for one more trip?" We tell them there are no certainties and to bring their water wings. Everyone is pretty jovial, considering that a short time ago there was no joy and the future looked bleak. Reviewing one's will or life insurance beneficiaries does not induce much levity. Now the men talk of home and wives or girlfriends and their favorite food and drink. A short time ago, it seemed really silly to talk of these things. There was no realistic hope until now.

I don't know how much of a trip it will be to Japan, or where we will unload. I'm looking forward to it. Having come this far, it will be a geography lesson at the very least.

Your letters from Chicago will be interesting. I can picture several places I know there, and I can't wait to see the buildings, streets, restaurants and lights. It sure seems like a long, long time ago.

It appears that my presence is desired elsewhere. I've rambled on and on and said little. Keep them coming, and I'll do the same.

BANZAI BILL

Friday, Aug. 31, 1945 to
Thursday, Sept. 20, 1945

DEAR GUNG-NO—-

You nearly dealt my funny bone a mortal blow when you signed off your letter of 20 May with the above nom-de-plume. I darn near died laughing. I regret not thinking of that one as a most appropriate moniker for our combat-bashful B-24 and its trembling occupants. If you will recall, we were all "Ho" and no "No" for the first hour of our first mission. From then on it was all downhill and "Ho" became "No" in the blink of an eye, simultaneously with the appearance of a Fock-Wolf shooting real bullets at us. Shortly thereafter, the "No" became "No, help us, Dear Lord!!!" and remained, ever thus, for the rest of our missions.

I got this far replying to yours of 20 May when yours of 23 May (a minor miracle) appeared on the scene. I will take a break to read your latest news and then press on with my reply to your two fat epistles. If I may steal one of the General's one-liners, "I shall return".

Returning took a little longer than anticipated, due to the exigencies of the service. Exigencies, for non-flying former student pilots, is Air Corps talk for "chicken shit" details . . . such as Officers of the Day, four-hour tours as Guardian of the Gate and chaperon for visiting pin-up girls (a detail I am sure I could sell to a sailor or two from USS-628 at whatever price such delectables would bring at an auction on your fantail).

You were plowing your way towards Okinawa in your letter of 23 May, and I am replying long after you had arrived there. The reports we received about Okinawa, the fighting and the weather, were horrendous . . . the beaches chaotic and the terrain extremely difficult to move in because of the volcanic ash, which afforded no cover for the ground troops . . . the harbor alive with ships, which afforded the Kamikazes' targets they could hardly miss . . . and Mt. Subiachi alive with dug-in and fanatical Jap soldiers. The weather, I am told, was a real S.O.B. for you naval people. I am looking forward to your descriptions of the action in your next letter. You will note that I am confident about receiving one . . . do not disappoint me. What you guys are going through out there (all of you) defies description, and only somebody who has survived horrors like that can really describe what it was like. Most correspondents write from a safe vantage point and I don't believe they can really write about the "down and dirty" that the fighting men endure. Hang in there . . . you have the wily pheasant, the fleet rabbit, the shy deer and, best of all, Dead Eye Bill to return home to.

The reports you mentioned emanating from the Throne Room about Leyte and the Philippines cite 11,000 Americans as casualties. "A small cost", and that's only because of inspired planning by J.C. and his prophets. I wonder what the 11,000 would have to say about that? The occupants of the Throne Room in the security of Hqtrs. have, in their inane and uncaring attitude, forgotten what every 2nd Lt. knows . . . one casualty is not a small cost, let alone 11,000.

You mentioned that the 8th Air Force will be joining your Pacific Pacifiers. I am glad I opted for pilot training. That would be the biggest Gung-No of them all if I had ended up soaring over the wide Pacific and peering through the bomb sight at Fujiama.

When things have settled down and histories are being written about this war, it will, from a cat bird's perch, make fascinating reading. We were encapsulated, as it were, in our own little theaters of operations and unaware of so many really big and small events that changed the course of this war. Some of the individual experiences will undoubtedly prove to be astonishing (and maybe inexplicable), but always beyond the call of duty.

Currently, far from all the action, aside from C.S. details, we dine frequently at the base . . . lunch mostly after a protracted dip in the pool. If I'm busy, Shirley and Dawn come out with a gaggle of other wives and kids and I try and make lunch with them. In the evenings, we sometimes come out to the base for a movie or dinner and hobnob with others of our ilk. Dawn is finally walking, after a slow start, which really was not backwardness on her part, but a surrender to the fire ants. We dared not put her down in the house because the ants would bite the hell out of her. Hence, soup cans with kerosine for all the furniture legs to keep them out of beds and off the tables.

The people here play a lot of bridge, so we join them from time to time to make up a foursome. This, of course, probably ruins the day for our partners. They are long suffering, I'm sure, but Christian enough not to scream and lose their tempers when I trump my partner's ace.

Word has come down that we shall soon be leaving here for Kimbark Ave., so packing up our plunder for shipment by train is going on intermittently. I am not leaping for joy or Gung-Ho-ing about the train ride home. Dawn will probably wet her pants and shriek all the way home . . . well, better her than Shirley.

By now, or at least when you get this letter, you should have some notion of what lies in store for you in the immediate future. Hopefully, your prow will be aimed at San Francisco. If you are required to visit Japan, please continue to write until you do return to the land of plenty. If you do make Japan, beware of the Mama-sans, and if hormones prevail over your aversion to beautiful Oriental ladies, please let me know if what is whispered about those ladies is really true.

WONDERING WILLIAM

Friday, 21 Sept., 1945 to
Sunday, 21 Oct. 1945

DEAR URGENT DECORATOR—

It is indeed fortunate for the success of the Air Arm's agenda that I avoided duty in the Pacific. In my last letter to you, I put volcanic ash and Mt. Surabachi on Okinawa. So much for the resplendent certificate of navigational excellence that I was awarded upon completion of my longitudinal and latitudinal studies. I hope my dead reckoning has not died completely and that enough of a spark of life remains to get us on the train for Chicago next Monday. It would be embarrassing as hell to end up in San Antonio where all this madness began.

Two of your letters have arrived dated 26 June and 3 July. I will answer probably from Chicago, providing, of course, that I manage to mount the right train. I know if I can find my way to the right train, all the guy has to do that is driving is follow the rails. That gives me a feeling of confidence that I seldom enjoyed at 20,000 feet, staring at a map and wondering if I could hit England; anywhere on the island would have been welcome, as well as astonishing.

Back again. We departed Enid on the 3:00 A.M. train, a conveyance which in its youth transported forty doughboys and eight horses to the point of embarkation. Our bridge playing friends provided us with a chicken dinner, a hand of bridge and transportation to the R.R. Station. These kinds of small kindnesses have become commonplace in the many different stations we have lived in over the last two or three years. We met and became friends with scores of people from all over this country with differing backgrounds, religious beliefs and interests. It is with a sense of loss that I have arrived home and probably will never see or hear from any of these fine Americans again. Their motto, if there had been one, would probably be that of the Three Musketeers and their protegee D'Artagnan, "All for one and one for all". In our nomadic way of life, with frequent separations and the ever-present danger, these friendships made tolerable, even enjoyable, the often intolerable circumstances. This may come as a surprise to you as it did to me, but I rather miss the whole shebang. Flying, narrow squeaks, camaraderie and parades with the band bashing out Sousa's Stars and Stripes. I was also hooked on retreat. I have the feeling that when my thoughts wander through this whole experience, the 50 missions will take a back seat to the many, many good things that came my way during my active duty tour. Experiences, such as you and I have had (or endured), will provide the fodder for years of reminiscing and BS'ing with our kids, grandkids, friends, neighbors and guys on adjacent bar stools. We survived, William, and from 7042 Kimbark, it doesn't now seem to have been all that bad.

The ride home on the 40 and 8 was not all that comfy, but accustomed as we were to less than opulent accommodations, we endured the twenty hours (two in a B-25) and were met at 11:00 P.M. by Shirley's Uncle Joe and her mother. Dawn was quite good on the train and prowled the aisle talking to anyone who could understand her fractured phonics. Shirley, as usual, was a worrywart about where the kid was every minute. She felt everyone in the car was a kidnapper in disguise. On a train??!

Right at the moment, we are solvent. A circumstance which has not prevailed since our nuptials. I had about three months leave accrued, plus current pay and the travel allowances for the trip home. Hopefully this should tide us over until I get gainful employment. Not knowing what I want to do is one hurdle, and my resume is another. Three years of college and three years of riding around in airplanes bombing schools, convents and orphanages does not inspire a lot of enthusiasm when I prefer to start at the vice-presidential level. Many times I have heard the sounds of laughter behind me. Next interview, I will remove my medals from my newly purchased three-piece suit.

In the interim, between surly and unimaginative personnel flunkies, I am painting (you have had a lot of experience with paint; bear it in mind when you apply for unemployment benefits) and also wallpapering and laying linoleum. At one time, over Brunswick, this was a consummation devoutly wished for, but . . . come to think of it . . . Brunswick wasn't too bad. Shirley's room at 7042 is tiny. One 3/4 bed and a dresser fills the whole room. I can stand the claustrophobia, and sleeping in a 3/4-size bed does have its good points. Unfortunately, all I hear is, "Bill, stop that! Not now! You will wake Dawn, and my mother can hear a mouse pass wind at a hundred paces!". Out of gas over the Adriatic was a great deal more thrilling.

Your news came at a good time. I am awash in paint, wallpaper and negatives from personnel moguls . . . and a much too modest bride. You arrived at a good time at Okinawa, most of the fighting was over. I am certainly happy to hear that. The losses were awful on both sides. You mentioned seeing soldiers and civilians leap to their deaths from the cliffs on the south side of the island. You spoke almost casually, after a while, about how some of these real sad events became rather matter-of-fact. I found that to be true also . . . it's probably a psychological trick our minds used to keep us from going completely bonkers.

I can readily understand your being bitter about the fourth estate and its plethora of cameramen and prognosticators, barely within the sound range of the fighting and, thus, unable to describe what is really happening. They can't really understand or envision the real world out there because they have only been lurking around on the perimeters. The soldiers, sailors, marines and flying men in the Pacific deserve to be bitter. I do not subscribe, however, to your lapsing into despair. You are a survivor; survivors don't despair . . . they dig a deeper fox hole and survive to have at 'em again. You probably had a belly ache from gorging on your daily ration of gourmet chow.

In yours of 3 July, you are leaving Okinawa after seeing some of the Emperor's boys get splashed attempting to ram your ships. I have had a similar feeling more than once. It doesn't make either of us kinfolk to Ghengus Kahn. Just a couple of average combat men with a grudge against a guy who's trying to kill you. Your Jap 6.5 rifle sounds like fun to shoot, and I consider your remarks about the crude sights being responsible for allowing the flying fish to soar through the air with the greatest of ease to be unworthy of a true marksman. A shot gun doesn't have sights, and your kill ratio is about the same with both firearms. It must be that both flying fish and pheasants zig when you had figured they would zag. In any event, I will be happy to coach you when next we get afield, and you will reap the harvest of the many hours I spent hunched over a 50 caliber wondering why that bastard in the 109 zagged when he should have zigged.

I went down to Chanute Field to be discharged officially on a Friday. They were too busy to get to me, so home I went, arriving there at 5:00 A.M. This kind of made me rethink all those nice thoughts I had about life in the military. Left again for Chanute at 6:00 P.M. on Sunday. They discharged me very damned slowly, and with the usual ten pounds of paper to go with their snail-like pace and persnickety adherence to details. Arrived home late Tuesday night.

A fellow bombardier, John Albanese, and I had dinner downtown and talked about where we had been and what we had done. Some of my old friends are beginning to show up: Warren Nilsen from Sea Bees and Jim Clancy from the Coast Guards. He was on an LCI, and hit Sicily and Salerno. A couple of Phi Gams also appeared, Nelly Nettleton and Bill Treerweiler. Harry Anderson and wife joined us again downtown for eats and drinks.

Write again soon—be careful wherever you are!!!

JOB HUNTER BILL

9 October, '45

DEAR WONDERING WILLIAM—-

It seems like a long time since I was able to write or get anything in the mail, but the delay at least has furnished me with your letter dated 31 August to 20 Sept., '45. If my feeble memory serves me correctly, I believe I last wrote from Lingayen Gulf at Luzon as we tried, with some difficulties, to load quickly and get on our way to Japan. My activities since then will be covered when I have answered your recent letter.

I'm happy to have tickled your funny-bone by merely butchering Gung-Ho to Gung-No. The interesting part is that you understand just exactly how I felt because you have felt the same way. I wonder if, from now on, those of us who have "been there" can communicate only with each other. Hope not. We both have seen strong, young guys who made no claims to bravery and had no shame about their fears, but just did their job no matter what. It certainly is in contrast to the Hollywood war heroes who have no fears and who seek out "another crack" at the enemy.

It is interesting that your present duty (in your letter) has some of the usual incidental duties, such as Officer of the Day, Guardian of the Gate and chaperon for visiting pin-up girls. Now not all of these extra duties seem all that bad and, in fact, could provide a pleasant interlude from your reckless and dangerous airborne playing. After careful review, it appears to me that your very most important duty is not in any way related to flying, but rather is a sly development of outwardly courteous behavior, which hides one's basic thoughts and dreams. I speak of chaperoning visiting pin-up girls and all the while behaving in civilized fashion. I trust that as you develop this devious and dishonest manner and polish it to a science, you will soon consider running for Congress where you can behave in any manner you choose . . . and with impunity. You will, of course, need an aide to interview the girls and select those with the best personalities. You already have my address, and I shall give up my present career as soon as you can get me out of the Navy.

Your letter then carries on at some interesting length regarding your lunches at the pool, surrounded by women and children, or dinner out . . . and also the joys of fire ants and other creepy insects. It would be hard to see little Dawn suffering from the bites, and I know nothing personal about fire ants.

The games of Bridge have to be a real challenge, and I note you seem to feel somewhat less than an expert. I fall into the category of Bridge skill that precludes me playing the game with anyone who can tell a Queen from an Ace. I not only am not wanted in a game, I suffer verbal referrals to my lack of skill that have damaged my ego and brought about depression and loss of self-esteem. Gambling is not allowed in the U.S. Navy so, of course, no one does. Most of the games I see here revolve around poker and there are prizes for the winner, but no gambling. I'm sure you've noticed that there are some people in all branches of the service who possess extraordinary skill in the game called Poker. My attempts to pursue the position called "winner" have been devastating failures and, inasmuch as I have still not drawn any pay since leaving San Diego, I elect to sleep or engage in pleasant dreams or stare into space and save my money.

Incidentally, your letter contained a paragraph about Iwo Jima, which may have to do with a letter from someone else. I have been there after it was quiet and it was truly a terrible place and a terrible invasion. I lost at least one longtime friend there. You then state that you are packing for the train ride home, and there may be some misgivings about the journey with child, etc. I will greatly appreciate it if you will relate details of the train itself when your journey is completed. My interest lies toward whether or not government travel is now allowed on World War I trains rather than the Civil War variety, with which you and I became so enamored at the beginning of our subsistence on the Government Dole. Are the seats still covered with skillfully hidden needles, mixed with the aged cane weavings? Do the inoperable windows still provide a view of soiled glass covered heavily with coal dust? Do the conductors still roam through the cars mumbling names of cities and stops in a foreign language? Do these trains still stop endlessly on sidings so that a handcar can proceed on its way? Does a one-ounce bottle of whiskey still cost an arm and a leg . . . and is it still available while passing through a dry State if one treats the porter in the manner to which he is accustomed? My questions are endless, and my curiosity is bottomless.

And so your very interesting and well-written letter is now answered to the best of my ability. Your letter arrived in pretty good time, but was back here at Luzon . . . not Japan. Perhaps the mail will be delivered soon in Japan.

We arrived in Tokyo Bay on 12 September and found that, other than major ships, we were in pretty early . . . along with a galaxy of freighters and LST's. It was late in the day that we nosed up at the side of a roadway along the Bay and, along with Lord knows how many other LST's, began to disgorge our tanks and heavy trucks, along with some pieces of heavy construction equipment. It was impressive as a seemingly endless line of tanks rumbled along the road. The ground shook and the noise was indicative of power. Having unloaded, we anchored in the Bay and, the following day, I went ashore with about half of my division for a sightseeing tour. It was clear, and Mt. Fujiami looked just like the grade school geography book pictures. We were afoot and in the uniform of the day, wandering through the hills outside the city. We saw no people, but did see some Shinto Shrines and beautiful scenery and gardens. Out of nowhere came a jeep with a 2nd Lt. driving and a pudgy Army Captain in his starched uniform sporting a campaign ribbon for the American Theater and the Asiatic Theater. I greeted them cheerfully, and the Captain was red-faced and approaching apoplexy as he screamed, "You are under arrest!" Before he spoke, I already disliked him, and I sure as hell was not afraid of him. I couldn't imagine what the problem was, but eventually he said we were in an area that was off limits. I tried to explain that we were following to the letter the directions we had received and that it was obviously one more communication foul-up. One thing led to another and my men gathered around me and it became obvious, even to this Cretin, that we did not take kindly to threats from a fat Captain, newly-arrived, from the safety of the rear echelon. He seemed to digest the logic that some 40 of us could not ride his jeep to the Brig (unless he and his Aide walked) and, furthermore, that we simply were not going. Soon he moved away and, I daresay, it was none too soon. We took our time and I wondered if we would have some surprises in store for us upon our return, but there was no way he could tell who we were. We had no trouble.

This is absolutely my first brush with some wise-ass Stateside malcontent with a little authority . . . and I am somewhat ashamed at my lack of self-control. I have feared the Japanese, but I have never hated them with the passion this idiot released in me. What has happened to me through these years that caused me to think the things I thought and nearly do the things I wanted so much to do? Have you felt this rage? My God, I came close to ruining the rest of my life . . . as well as his.

I have paused awhile since my last paragraph and have cooled down. Somehow, remembering my disgust with the whole thing was as bad as my original anger. I'm sure both you and I could go on and on, but I won't. I do wonder who conceived the idea of sending these pampered stuffed shirts out here to play chicken-shit games with those of us who have pulled the triggers . . . and buried our dead friends. Those SOBs are not dealing with raw recruits, and I fear for their lives if they don't get the picture quickly. And so I guess the war with Japan is over, and the war between the combat people and the non-combat people has just begun.

A couple of days later, while at anchor, we got a warning of an approaching typhoon. The clouds and winds had already told us that trouble was ahead. The harbor is large, and the tides are much higher than those we are accustomed to. The harbor, at least near us, has very high walls of fieldstones and concrete. We lengthened our anchor chain and battened down, awaiting the onslaught. We had a boat out, and when it returned the seas were already heavy. We had a really bad and dangerous time picking it up with its crew and load of shipmates coming back from a short Liberty. Quickly, the weather became a monster intent on levelling everything in its path. For what it's worth, a harbor is not a place to wait out a storm and, as miserable as going outside may be, it is a lot less chaotic.

A Destroyer ahead and off our port bow dragged anchor, which became fouled in our anchor, which then began to drag. Due to the fortunate warning, most ships had warmed engines, and I have no idea how many ships dragged anchors and suffered minor collisions as they tried to maintain, or gain, positions of safety. A man could not stand in the wind, and rain felt like ice or needles in the face. After Lord knows how long, it all moderated. The Destroyer came back for its anchor, which we had lost as we weighed our own. They were not happy. Following the storm, the weather cleared somewhat and we took a jeep ride through the center of Tokyo . . . which was once a beautiful city, but now needs extensive repairs thanks to B-29's plus the 8th Air Force. Later, a couple of us braved a train ride and went to Yokohama and found that Yokohama was simply gone. We saw some Japs searching through all the rubble and that was it. The Jap trains are clean, fast and wonderful, but the people are packed in like sardines in a can. I just cannot tell you everything or my letter will be even longer.

The Japanese people are clean, courteous, hard working and disciplined to do as the Emperor says and as tradition dictates. They have looked upon Hirohito as a descendant of God. Now they have had a chance to meet and obey, not a descendant, but the real God . . . Dugout Doug MacArthur of the corncob pipe and wet pants. They seem to accept it all and go about their business. I like them.

I am again at Luzon. The trip north was somewhat cold, and the Japan current was cold. It was interesting and educational, and I noted they have crows just like ours . . .and trees and bushes. The latitude is similar, and the sight of a "civilized" city was a wonder to behold. We are now "promised" that, after another trip to Japan, we will go home. The "promise" part must be discounted totally, but the part about going back to Japan is real. We have nearly unloaded, and all the gear which is to come aboard is in sight and waiting. We are in a hurry, but no one else is. I don't know if we should expect one of those typhoons or not. I guess we'll take what we get.

I hope you are home and dressed in the most comfortable garb of YOUR choice and doing what you want to do. I shall work toward that goal and will write when I can.

RELUCTANT WANDERER BILL

DEAR BARNACLE BILL BURLING—

A threesome to be reckoned with. Yours of 24 July in hand, and beau-coup welcome as usual. This indeed would be a bad time to get hurt. Be as cautious as possible, short of hiding out in the chain locker, and I suggest you stay away from firearms during this cautious period. I note that you have been firing your trusty carbine and finding it inaccurate. My myopic and frail mother has been on the line testing carbines and reports that she finds them quite responsive and accurate. Are you using both sights, front and back? Are you afflicted with ague and tremble a lot? Do the targets resemble Japs and frighten you? Has war dampened your enthusiasm for the smell of cordite and the sharp crack of the gun as your bullet leaves the barrel on its way to someplace in the vicinity? My enthusiasm for a stroll down the corn rows, without a flak jacket, declines measurably each time I hear about your latest practice shoots. The long trip home across the Pacific should provide enough time and targets of opportunity to hone your hand and eye to marginal safety standards.

The Army guys you spoke of will not have to be concerned any more about landing on the Jap mainland. I am very happy for these troops who have had their necks stretched out for so many landings and assaults. Let us all hope that the few remaining Japanese soldiers on scattered islands have been informed that hostilities have ended. This would be a real lousy time to get shot for soldiers on either side.

Writing a reply to your concern about "the worst is yet to come" when I already know the worst is over is somewhat awkward. I work on the presumption that you have made it through the time span between your writing and my receiving, so don't disappoint me.

Civilian life takes some getting used to. I enjoy it, of course, but I can still hear the thundering of a couple hundred Pratt & Whitney's being run up at three in the morning prior to a mission. I would not care to repeat those many mornings, but the memories linger on, and not unpleasantly so. I guess when you are a survivor, the real bad times fade away and nostalgia creates its own scenario of what you really want to remember.

I will hang up my dish towel, change the baby's pants and return to hanging wallpaper and painting.

Love the roar of those big engines.

THE HOUSEMAID'S KNEE

17 November, '45

DEAR JOB HUNTER BILL—-

I must confess to having received yours dated 21 Sept. to 21 Oct., '45 sometime in the recent past. Duty and confusion have delayed my answer until now . . . mostly confusion.

Congratulations on your return to Chicago! You did accomplish the often difficult task of boarding the right train. I note that you all did not draw one of the most modern trains, but the trip home probably would have been pleasant in a caboose.

You are likely right that the friends one meets and the experience with all the people from different places may be what we think about in the future. I wouldn't go through all this again for a million dollars, but I'm sure glad for the experience and the memories. I already think of the Stateside places and the characters I've met—and I think of it a lot now that I really can believe I'll be back there one of these days.

Your job hunting sounds sobering. I would have thought there would be jobs aplenty and employers eager to hire a returning fly-boy. True, your experience is mainly in dropping bombs on chickens, meadows, perhaps a German farmer, or even a truck. Don't give up!

You write of painting, papering, laying linoleum and other equally exciting homebody tasks. Sounds like you better step up the job search. I would also suggest a larger bedroom with a spare room for children so as to forestall frustration.

Your remarks regarding my marksmanship on flying fish fail to take into account my attitude about conservation. It would have been a shame for me to demolish all the flying fish in the Pacific. Perhaps you have never witnessed the face of a flying fish stricken with stark fear. These things caused me to ease up, with the result that we still have flying fish out here.

Your trips to Chanute Field for discharge sound like the same old "hurry up and wait". Can't they get anything right? Of course the snail's pace and the lost days, plus the transportation, are still worth it. Congratulations again!

It would sure be great to meet several friends, as you recently did. Say hello for me to the ones I know.

My trip to Tokyo was described in my last letter, but did not contain everything. We took our trusty jeep into the Hinterlands, which were mostly fishing villages with squid drying on clotheslines and perfuming the air for miles around. I shall never eat squid. There is a great variety of people among the Japanese, with some being pretty dark-complected and others very light-skinned. Most of them went about their work as though we weren't there, but none were either friendly or unfriendly. None, that is, but one older man who read us the riot act and then seemed to expect to be shot. We did not understand a word he said, but it surely was not complementary. We took it in stride.

My Japanese-English dictionary (prepared for the Army) is not terribly helpful with the questions I had in mind. I could instruct someone to put his hands up or throw down his weapon, or I could ask where the bathroom was, but a soulful discussion with a female about philosophy was not possible. Next best was pantomime, and I learned that when the Japanese hold their head steady and move their hand back and forth and say "Ie", it means no. I can also count to ten in Japanese in the highly unlikely event I ever need to.

We learned before leaving Tokyo Bay that the typhoon blew with winds of 172 knots. I hope I never see another one like that.

Right after I mailed my last letter, we headed back to Japan, and this trip was longer and more pleasant. Our destination was Aomori, which is close to Hakodate on the northern tip of Honshu. To the north, we can see the northernmost island of Hokkaido. Our latitude is right at 45 degrees north, which is somewhat north of your home and mine. The weather is about the same as it would be at home, with a little snow and slush and generally disagreeable. Many Japanese walk around barefoot or with the shoes you and I might wear into a shower. This isn't much of a town, and it seems its claim to fame arose from a pottery factory that manufactured those blue and white dishes with flowers and/or dragons. Unfortunately, someone in our Air Force dropped a bomb dead-center on the factory. Now the blue and white shards of table settings cover a circle about a half mile wide. Hopefully, the local citizens have paper plates.

We are at a dock built to handle small coal luggers, and we have lined the rail to watch the coal unloading process. The coal comes over from Hokkaido early in the morning until dark, and is unloaded by men with steel hooks that hook the burlap bags containing the coal. They then place the bag of coal on a backboard carried by a woman, and she walks to the end of the dock and unloads it on a cart. The women form a line like a bucket brigade and do this all day. Some of them are very pretty and stay reasonably clean, in spite of their work. We laugh and joke with them, but nobody knows what anyone else is saying. A stroke of luck!

Good fortune struck when we ran into some newly-arrived Army troops and found that we had carried them more than once in the past. They are a loose knit bunch and, like us, putting in their time before going home. I visited some of them in their large pyramid tent and warmed my bones near their stove, which burned red cedar and smelled great. It was then I learned they had discovered a local brewery and had fired the local workers and set up their own guard on the building. The beer is bottled in liter bottles and is stacked 20 feet high in a large building. It is very tasty, and I could recommend it to anyone, but it must remain a secret known only to this infantry outfit and the LST 628. It takes away some of the cold and homesickness and brings on a slight hope of lingering awhile.

The Executive Officer and I took the jeep to a nearby town named Asamushi. It is a tourist town in the summers (in peacetime), and we were welcomed by a skeletal staff at the Hotel To Kan. We were able to communicate somewhat with the desk clerk, who is also the bellboy, cook, waiter and general maintenance man. We told him what we would like to eat and asked if there were any virtuous ladies with whom we could perhaps discuss art or poetry. In short, we had crabmeat and Saki, served by two charming ladies named Hiroko and Medoti. As time drew near to leave for the ship, it became abundantly clear that the desk clerk had taken us literally in our request for virtuous ladies.

You will be surprised to learn that we made several more trips to the Hotel To Kan, and before everyone on the planet learned about it . . . we had a good time and learned a little Japanese in the process. It is with modest pride that we brought a certain culture to a large group of females by teaching them to dance (and perhaps make money) in the high art known as stripteasing.

Our Captain had some difficulty in operating without us on board and had the gall to ask if we could possibly show up once in awhile. He seemed somewhat distressed, so we had to take him to the To Kan. Now the ship is under the command of whomever is on board.

All things must come to an end, and so it is that we could loaf no longer. Ever-present in our minds is the trip home, and to screw up now might mean a little rest back at Olongopo . . . or worse. The rear echelon is arriving and setting up rules and regulations and doing all sorts of important things in their well-pressed uniforms. Our cold weather uniforms are stored somewhere, but we are wearing part Army, part Marine Corps, part Navy and part native. We are leaving just in time.

We have been well-received in Japan. The people seem to know that they lost and that we will be just and generous. The U.S. combat people have behaved beautifully in spite of their experiences, and I would guess the Japanese will, perhaps, like the combat people better than the incoming rear echelon. My real guess is that Dugout Doug will get great credit for organizing and administrating the occupation. He can have it!

In a short time, we leave. We can't make it all the way, and our hope is a stop at Pearl Harbor. It would be nice to see Honolulu with lights on and no curfew. And it will be a lot nicer to see the good old USA. Good Lord but it has been a long time, and a lot of miles.

It is hard to explain what this stay has meant to all of us. I know that some of the others feel as I do, and it is as if we had received a shot in the arm. Good food, streets, buildings, trains, trees with leaves, a cup or two of beer and a dram or so of Saki. We have been living like real human beings . . . and we love it. I'm not real sure I can take all this and going home, too. But you can bet I'm going to give it a try!

I'll mail this now. Our trip will be about 30 days, and we sure won't go home empty. That means a stop in one of those damnable islands and loading whatever someone thinks is worth taking home.

Check and see if they have room for one more person in Chicago.

INCHING ALONG HOME BILL

23 November, '45

DEAR DOMESTICATED BILL——

I wrote shortly before leaving Aomori, but have some time and shall write again. It is a long road from Aomori to Pearl Harbor, and we are taking the great circle route and using lights at night. The lights seem strange, but it does help to keep station in a convoy at night. Many a night in the past we just could not see well and kept station with radar, which was a bit tricky because radar was busy watching for aircraft. We still maintain all the watches, but it is relaxed by comparison. I can't help but hope that ALL the Jap submarine Commanders have been informed that the war is over.

Our Supply Officer and his trusty Division discovered our cold weather gear, and we need it. It is wintry and choppy in the North Pacific, and the wind cuts the face and hands. On watch, we have hooded, full-length, fur-lined coats and, during the day, the fur-lined jackets feel good. Our convoy is small and contains many of the ships we have sailed with for what seems like a long, long time. The messages between ships are casual and pleasant, and it is a whole new ballgame. Still, a lot of the old habits seem to be ingrained and real, genuine relaxation will hopefully come some time later.

We still scrape, paint and repair lines and keep things neat and clean, but the workload is purposely kept light. During the days, the radio shack still plays our only record . . . Guy Lombardo's "Drifting and Dreaming." The record has not improved with the years, but it now brings back some nostalgic thoughts and some painful memories. It is a song I'll always remember, and I wonder what songs are popular now. I wonder if Johnny Long is still in the Blue Room at the Roosevelt Hotel. I wonder where we'll land in the USA. I wonder about a lot of things.

There are some things I can tell you now, but I'm not sure they are of any great interest. At Guam we saw the Indianapolis, a true beauty of a cruiser, as she left at high speed, we assumed, for home. She had just come out and looked brand new, and we wondered how to get duty like that. We learned some time later that she had headed for Leyte and was torpedoed and went down with most of her crew. I believe we were at Leyte when we saw the carrier Hornet all decked out in "going home" pennants. Her forward deck was all bent downward and corners curled under from a typhoon. We saw one of her hot pilots buzz everyone in the anchorage, and then crash as he landed. Later, we were near the Calloway, a Coast Guard transport, when she was hit by a suicide plane. She survived, but many were killed and hurt. I can't now remember all the things I wanted to tell you, but could not at the time.

Japan was a combination of very modern and also pretty primitive. The train I rode would put ours to shame for punctuality and speed, although it was very crowded. The restrooms are for both boys and girls, which can be disconcerting. At least in Ashamushi, the restrooms were little more than inside outhouses, and the buckets were carried out periodically by some lucky soul and dumped on a vegetable garden. While in Tokyo, I was able to find one of the fabled public baths and discovered my friend, the Executive Officer, cavorting with some of the local men and women. It was there that I hoped to solve the biological question as to the construction of Oriental women (as related by the old sailors). I stayed as long as I could, but neither the Executive Officer nor I were able to reach a conclusion. It was at the Hotel To Kan in Ashamushi that we learned of some Oriental dancing girls and attempted to teach them the bare rudiments of the classic striptease. At that point, I was able to determine, in a clinical manner, the answer to the long-suffering question. I shall not bore you with the details, inasmuch as you are married and settled in Chicago and shall never really need to know about the parts of Oriental women.

Today the sky is gray, the sea is black and choppy, and the dolphins are running ahead of us by the hour. They seem to be happy creatures, and they swim with the greatest of ease. They do this for hours at a time, and we are making about 11 knots (we may burn up our engines on the way home). At the end of the day, we have moved about an inch on our chart and there are many inches to go. It's a little like a prisoner marking each day off his calendar during his 20-year sentence.

I suppose I just need more patience. Going home has been my goal since leaving home, and it seems like a lifetime has passed in between. There are so many things I want to see and do, but I admit that I wonder how it can possibly be as good as my dreams. The fact is that it likely will not be as good as my dreams, but staying in the Navy is not the answer for me. Much as I like ships and sailing, I do not like the Navy. I think I'll go back and finish school and hope I can decide what I want to do and get at it. I have wasted a good percentage of my young life, as have you, fooling around with this war.

After several interruptions, I am going to give up and go do my job. I should be able to write more before we see and smell that beautiful Hawaii . . . and we are all counting the minutes.

WAYFARING STRANGER BILL

Saturday, 1 Dec. 1945 to
Thursday, 20 Dec. 1945

DEAR BANZAI BILL—

The Bluebird of Happiness flew over Kimbark Ave. and dropped, not guano, but two letters from you. One dated 14 August, and the other 16 August, all in the same year, 1945. The P.O. Dept. seems to be learning how to do their thing in a much speedier time frame.

I am delighted to hear that you are catching up on the world's latest news. It was not so delightful to hear that 42 guys lost their lives while celebrating Japan's surrender. I am sure the armed forces have their ways of advising next of kin about a man losing his life due to accidental means. Sparing families the truth in a situation such as that seems to me to be the kindest thing to do. The unvarnished truth can hurt in more ways than just the finality of death. To carry the knowledge that it (death) was in vain could destroy a lot of people. Our navigator's mother inadvertently learned that an accident had claimed E.J., and it nearly put her over the edge.

The many doubts you have regarding your reception by the Japanese civilian population have no doubt been answered by now. I would think that, as you point out, they are a disciplined people and will conduct themselves as their Emperor commands. If this is difficult for them, the thought of another bomb or two should encourage cooperation and humility.

The big question facing you, however, is whether the ladies are constructed from east to west or from north to south. I am most anxious to know the answer to this geographic puzzlement. I have a lot of bets laid on at the local grog shop. Immediately after dropping the hook, rush ashore and ask the first pretty lady you see to open her kimono. If she is reluctant, offer her candy, which is dandy of course, but failing with this ploy you will discover that liquor is quicker. A word to the wise, beware of Japanese bearing Sumari shives with a yen to carve a round eye (no pun intended). As an afterthought, try to get a couple of snapshots . . . the boys in the back room may want proof! Reply ASAP, as I have a vested interest in the outcome of this investigation.

Shirley's Uncle Herb wants me to enter the tire business . . . recapping. I feel I should start with the keys to the executive washroom, but have been assigned to a delivery truck. If I have the need for a washroom, we pull over to the side of the road. I have not learned much about tire recapping, except that truck tires weigh a ton apiece and have minds of their own if they start to roll. The heaviest thing I have lifted in a couple of years is a fork, and every bone in my body is begging me to seek other gainful employment. The head honcho on the truck is a 6'4" colored guy called King. I, of course, call him Kong when I'm sure he can't hear me. Kong handles two or three of those tires at a time. He should pose for Michelin Tires, with two tires on each arm instead of the little guy they use now holding a candle and in what appears to be a doughnut. My heart is not 100% into tires, but I owe my soul to the company store and will continue with Kong The Lord of The Jungle until I find another way to wrap Shirley in mink. I must get something with a little more tread on it and less wear and tear on my sidewalls.

I trust you are playing this last hand close to your vest and not trying for a CMH. I will write again before civilian life swallows me whole and spits me out as a leaky inner-tube.

BLOWOUT BILL

Anchor detail - Dec. 22, 1945, Pearl Harbor. (l-r) Rosiek, WIlliams, Botkin, Kamp, Spangler, Burling, Waters, Pearman.

Friday, 21 Dec. 1945 to
Monday, 31 Dec. 1945

DEAR RELUCTANT WANDERER—

It was with mixed emotions that I carefully read and then re-read yours of 9 October '45. You had dropped anchor in Tokyo Bay and proceeded ashore with a glint in your eye and lust in your heart, only to waste all that adrenaline tangling assholes with a rear echelon Captain. He must have mistaken that glint in your eye, and that of your forty mild-mannered associates, as a long immersed and ferocious hatred of all things Army . . . and paunchy captains in particular. It is well that he was bright enough to recognize his vulnerability and left the field to the Navy. It is also well that you contained your (deservedly so) inclination to separate him limb from tree. The services frown on Lt.'s removing the stuffing from stuffed-shirt Captains. I can now understand why you did not get to the exploration of the physiognomy of a mama-san, although I had hoped that that would be number one on your list of things to be done. As long as you will return to Japan shortly, I am again forced to wait and endure the jibes and skepticism of the grog shop gambling aficionados.

That typhoon you guys endured in the harbor sounded like the mother of all typhoons. If it ain't the Japs or the Germans shooting at you, it's God and Mother Nature letting you know who really is the boss. I'm glad you survived again, and you now have another tale to tell posterity, embellished each time you tell it until you have to include your own death in the maelstrom. I can harden my heart to the lost anchor of the Destroyer. It would seem to me that losing something that big and heavy would not be easy to do, even for a cocky destroyer crew.

You wrote from Luzon and have been assured, not only of going to Japan, but of beginning the long, but happy cruise back to San Fran or Diego, or whatever. Let us hope that this is one promise, out of the many that have not been kept, that will bear stateside fruit. Complete your assigned mission (regarding Mama-Sans) before embarking for home . . . two of us wondering for the next 50 years is too painful to even consider.

I departed the tire business with no backward glance and embarked on a career in the publishing arena. Little did I know when signing on with R.R. Donnelly & Sons that they, too, believe that executive aspirants should begin on the ground floor and learn executing on the way to the top floor. In Donnelly's case, the ground floor turned out to be the loading dock. I have leaped from the fry pan into the fire. "Hoist on my own petard," as another damn fool once said. Tires were heavy, but not mortally dangerous. Paper rolls, unlike the variety commonly found in the average bathroom, are enormous, hard as rocks and in the confines of a box car and as unpredictable and dangerous as a bull with his family jewels caught in the barbed wire. I have not yet figured out how they get these 700 to 1,800 pound rolls neatly stacked in the box cars. They are not stacked on end, but sideways, so a false move gets the whole bunch moving. My footwork now would put Joe Louis and Jess Owens to shame. You have seen pictures of loggers twirling logs with their feet; we do a lot of that just to stay alive. The Germans just shot at me, R.R. Donnelly & Sons are trying to squash me like a bug. Take me back to Ploesti.

There are good sides to this precarious way to earn a living. I get paid, even if it is a niggardly amount. Like the village smithy, I got arms like iron bands, but he was a lot smarter. He stood under a chestnut tree. Shirley goes by the loading dock on the Illinois Central every evening and gives me the razzberry. It is nice to see her and realize I escaped, for another day, being reduced to the shape and size of a garbage can lid. Up with this, I cannot put. I will begin seeking employment again, forthwith.

Christmas came and went here and, because of the presence of Dawn and all the hoopla connected with a child's X-mas, it was a festive occasion for all of us. Thoughts of friends lost, of friends homeward bound and of friends returned were part of the X-mas spirit . . . I'm sure not only on Kimbark Ave., but throughout our country, and perhaps the world.

I just feel in my bones, still all connected as the song says and not withstanding any occupation, that you are nearing the shores of the Land of Liberty, and my hopes that, indeed, it will be Liberty are quite positive.

Should I get any more mail from you, I will address it in the usual fashion and leave it up to the P.O. to deliver wherever you are.

TOTE THAT BALE BILL

23 December, '45

DEAR RETURNEE BILL—-

It has been some time since I wrote, but there was not much to write about. I doubt any real interest on your part in our daily schedules or the antics of flying fish or the weather. It has been one slow, but pleasant, trip and we are back in warm weather, and the breezes are balmy and the sea is beautiful. We are seeing birds now and should make Pearl Harbor tomorrow in the early morning. At that point, I shall mail a couple of letters and hope to pick up mail from all my pen pals. My pen pals may fall away now that the war is over.

We expect to lose some of our crew to points. We have several older men, and many are married. Most of the Officers are older, and most are married. We have all been counting points and all are in good shape and raring to go . . . out. Still, we many hang together until we reach the USA because they probably want this ship back. Why, I don't know?! It is only in fair shape.

Everyone is cheerful and the talk is all of home and greeting wives and girlfriends. Some of the expectations are going to result in disappointment for many, but it's fun to dream. Wherever we go from here, it will still be a long way from "home" and, for my part, I am actually happy to ride another of our antique trains, no matter how long it takes or how dirty I get. In my dreams, I walk down the gangway and onto a fast train and sleep all the way home. A really disturbing fact is that I don't really have a home now. I guess I'll see you and Chicago first, and then on to Bloomington, where I've spent most of my previous life. All this is a little premature, of course, but one has to let his mind wander now and then. I do hope that you will be able to break away, if only briefly, from your domesticity for a cup of beer or a dram of wine so that we can regale each other with our various experiences and the sights we have seen. Our letters have been hindered by censorship, and even the time to write was short because both the Air Force and the Navy seemed to feel we were not there for the purpose of letter writing. Good Lord, but it has been a long time!

We are, and have been, working on our "Flag", the Commander, to make our stay in Hawaii as short as possible. We'll need fuel, water and some food, but other than that, we want to be on the move. How much influence he will have remains to be seen. We are carrying a load of trucks and trailers and some heavy construction type equipment . . . but no Army or Marines. It is not to be unloaded at Pearl Harbor.

I have been weeding out my personal belongings with the idea that I will have to carry what I own on my back or in my hand, and I want the load to be light. Much of my junk is souvenirs for my kids, if I ever have any, or for me to peruse in my old age. It will go in seabags through the Postal Department if I can figure out where to send it. My sister and her husband have left Ft. Riley, Kansas, and perhaps I can mail it all to her in Illinois. At a time like this, it is interesting all the thoughts that pass through one's mind. I'm almost sure you had the same thoughts because the men aboard here all seem to have the same thoughts. Here we are, finally on the way home, and having lived together for so long in circumstances that were debilitating at best, and the thrill is tempered somewhat. Why us and not the others? Why should we feel guilt? Survival is what we all wanted, but only some of us got it. Will the mother of a dead son look upon me as a shirker? My mother's best friend lost her son in the Philippines . . . what will she feel when I come home unscathed? She'll be happy for me and for my mother, but maybe she'll cry a little. The mothers and wives who have written me about the loss of their sons and husbands want to know more. What more can I tell them?!

I never really was able to contemplate all this before. You have been through it, and I hope we can talk about it someday. It sure throws a damper on coming home. I don't feel I could have done more than I did but, at this point, I feel a little guilty because I'm alive. Good God!

The night has passed quickly, partly due to a midnight to 0400 watch and then coffee and talk. Nearly all hands were on deck at dawn, and Hawaii was a dim shadow ahead. It is not the end of the rainbow, but it is close to it. As time dragged by we could see lights, and the outline of the island became more clear. We haven't seen it before from this direction but, frankly, it looks like a score of other less friendly islands in our past. This is where it all began in this same month a little over four years ago. Another hour or so, and our small convoy will form a single line and enter Pearl Harbor, the "Crossroads of the Pacific". I wonder how many men came through here on the way out and how many will come through on the way home. The people of Pearl Harbor saw the loss of some proud fighting ships that one morning, and on this morning, they'll see some proud, if ugly, throw-away ships of the amphibious Navy that carried the anger right to the shores of Japan. Somehow, I wonder if we'll be noticed. In any event, I hope we don't stay long.

As suspected, we'll anchor, and I must get on station for that little chore. Will get this off as soon as possible and will keep in touch.

CHOKED UP BILL

27 December, '45

DEAR HOUSEMAID'S KNEE BILL—

Yours of 22 October to 30 November, 1945, is in my sweaty little hands, and I now have time to write. You must realize that the necessity of checking some things out in Honolulu has delayed my correspondence somewhat. The big Banyan tree is still in the courtyard of the Moana Hotel, and the Air Corps still reserves the Royal Hawaiian Hotel. The drinks cost as much as they used to, but the girls are much prettier and sexier. It is unfortunate that, when the girls have a few hundred thousand men from whom to choose, I remain a cull. It was ever thus and, at least, I'll avoid a trip to Sick Bay for any treatments due to social experiments. How's that for rationalization? We are on our way to San Francisco, and whomever wants to be first had better be on the dock.

Your snide remarks about the accuracy of my shooting, as you compare it to your mother who builds these carbines, is noted and taken in stride. My reasoning is that, like everything else, what nobody else wanted, we got. My carbine will spout bullets into a bushel basket at about 50 feet . . . beyond that, who knows. You need not fear my shooting, except for the usual problem in that I down the pheasants before you raise your gun.

I have no idea what has happened to our Army and Marine troops. It is hoped they have all gone home or are en route. I guess that Jap soldiers will have to go to some of those islands to pass the word the war is over. Frankly, I'm guessing that Jap soldiers will come out of the jungles very slowly. They feel it was their duty to die for the Emperor, and being alive and hiding out may be difficult for them. So be it!

I note that your life as a civilian includes thoughts of the sound of Pratt & Whitneys warming up at 0300, and that those thoughts are relatively pleasant. I am particularly happy to hear that the bad times fade away and the good times are remembered. I have given this some thought, but can't imagine how I'll react to all that. I love ships and the sea, and some of our time has been very pleasant. I sometimes wonder how I'd like the Merchant Marine, but I know it is not a life for me over the long haul. I guess I'll wait and see.

You sign off by hanging up your dish towel, changing the baby's pants and getting back to hanging wallpaper. It seems that you are thoroughly domesticated, but it is obviously less exciting than your flights through the wild blue yonder and the dropping of heavy bombs on German chickens or a bicycle.

Our letters through the war have helped me a great deal and, I hope, you too. It is, and has always been, great to look forward to mail from you, and there have been many, many times that I wondered if each letter might be your last one. I was nearly as happy as you must have been to learn that you were finally home. Your letters were better organized than mine in that you seemed to keep notes and write more frequently. I, on the other hand, suffered from long delays in the receipt of mail, and then had to write from my poor, failing memory. In any event, it has been rewarding, and I hope we can keep it up a little while longer.

We are underway for San Francisco, which will be a relatively short trip. We shall move as fast as this tub can handle, and we all are like kids before Christmas. Speaking of that . . . Merry Christmas! Another one under the belt, and a birthday, too! My ambition for all these years has been to see another birthday, but now it seems rather routine. I forgot it, and also Christmas, in my zeal to get moving again. We did pretty well in our plans to get in and out of Pearl Harbor quickly, and we did get a little taste of what may be in store for us at our next stop. We were received a little better than the average bum with the plague. Obviously, people are tired of thousands of servicemen tramping through their towns and fouling up their lives and crowding their places of relaxation. Many have come home before us, and all the war stories have already been told. I guess we are not especially desirable with our yellow eyes, gaunt frames and "salty" uniforms. I weighed 172 pounds when I left New York and I now top out at 143, so the uniforms fit like the average raw recruit. When I get the chance, I shall eat like a pig and sleep like a log and get back to some semblance of my former self. More likely, you and I will never get back to our former selves.

So now it's back to the routine. The sea is pretty calm and the weather is clear and warm and, frankly, I would not trade this weather for yours in Chicago. It is great to sleep at night knowing there will be no Piss-Call Charlies or other interruptions except for the inevitable watches. The watches are even pleasant now, and we talk more to each other than formerly. The talk, of course, is of home and each man's dreams are similar. There will be a lot of disappointment, I'm afraid. Many of these men forgot that they have been gone a few years and things will not be the same. Still, one listens, but says little.

My excess belongings are packed and ready to mail to somewhere, and I have no plans to buy uniforms to fit. I intend to eat and grow into what I have.

You'll hear from me when I get in!

HOMEWARD BOUND BILL

Tuesday, 1 Jan. 1946 to
Wednesday, 2 Jan. 1946

DEAR INCHWORM—

This is in answer to your letter of 17 November '45, and I shall forgo mailing this until, as I suspect, I hear from you when your feet once again are firmly planted on the land of your birth. I would hope that you would call or drop a quickie as soon as possible, with your address and phone number so that I can mail this, and perhaps exchange an awkward word or two with you. This is anti-climactic, at the least, and I am struggling for something to say . . . and like a bridegroom, am wondering what to do or say next. However, something will occur and I'll put it down.

In the meanwhile, your visit to Japan sounded like a real great experience. I personally have no expertise in coaching or, for that matter, in viewing striptease artists doing their thing. My mind boggles as I picture you doffing your T-shirt and tossing it to a rapt gaggle of geishas (play on words there, in case you missed it) and departing the stage throwing a fingertip kiss and snapping the waist band of your G.I. skivvies for your audience of awe-struck and salivating mama-sans.

I gather that, regarding the main exploratory mission, you choose to remain tight-lipped (another play on words) about the true slant of the Oriental honey pot. I may have to fight my way out of the back room at the saloon when I announce the results of your investigation. These guys take this very seriously, and it scares me a bit. Your Captain, bless his little scrambled egg hat, has finally learned that there is more to war than Honor, Duty and Country. Did he catch your version of the bump and grind, or were your students causing his lustful gaze?

It was indeed a stroke of good fortune to run into some troops you had previously carried. It was a lightning bolt of luck that the fortunes of war yielded a brewery in operating condition to these dehydrated veterans. Your sixth sense for the smell of hops at exceedingly long distances has presumably stocked Old 628 with enough brew to last the trip home. A lusty brew or two at every change of watch will seem to make the voyage a much shorter one. With the Captain, fresh from To Kan and now one of the boys, you can hook your heels over the rungs of his chair and hoist a couple to the memory of To Kan and its Nimble Nips.

Perhaps you can complete the mission. Instead of beating an ignominious retreat when they holler "Ie", lay a little of the vaunted Burling charisma on them. What is "how about a little" in Japanese? That may result in a little bloodletting, but on average, may be worth the loss of a few red corpuscles from time to time.

No inspirational light bulb came on to light my way to what may be my last wartime letter to you. I want to be sure, however, that I am on record as applauding your last letter and its tantalizing undercurrents. Like the day you slid inexorably down that frail sapling into the raging waters of a babbling brook, To Kan will remain one of my fondest memories of WWII. The vision of you in your undies coaching the varsity squad of geishas will help see me through the transition to civilian life. After a martini or two, it appears to be the lynch-pin that assured the success of the occupation of Japan; Dugout Doug not withstanding.

I await your call . . . or letter . . . with bated breath.

SCRIVENER BILL

7 January, '46

DEAR TOTE-THAT-BALE BILL——

I now have yours dated 1 to 20 December, 1945 and 21 to 31 December, 1945. Pretty good mail service!

In your first letter, you mention receiving mine from mid-August,, '45. Wonder where they have been. We agree about the next-of-kin and the accidental deaths and how to handle it. Actually, the number of accidental deaths and deaths due to friendly fire must be astounding. We have been responsible for some of those fatalities and I, for one, will forever grieve and feel guilty, even though I recognize that these things were bound to happen.

You refer to the "big question" regarding the construction of important parts of Oriental ladies, and state that you have laid bets at some watering hole and require specific facts, NOW. It is with some shyness that I admit to knowledge in this regard, in spite of my efforts to remain pure as the driven snow. Several visits to various public baths (in order to remain clean of body), plus our attempts to make the ladies knowledgeable regarding the dance known as the striptease, resulted in the scientific observance that the Oriental ladies are constructed in the conventional manner. Upon learning this, I was neither shocked nor disappointed inasmuch as it was a purely scientific study and very educational. So it is that neither of us must constantly wonder about this important fact. As a clinical observer, I can state that there are some differences, but none of any great consequence. Should you have any interest in this subject, perhaps you should plan to ply me with liquor when we next meet. Snapshots I do not have.

I laughed as I enjoyed your tale of executive training in the tire business. Your decision to search for another job sounds like one that may have well been made the first day on the job. Good luck.

Your second letter is in reply to mine written from Tokyo. Yes, the tangle with the Army Captain turned out well for all concerned. I can still get a bit angry when I think of it.

The main thrust of your letter was that question regarding the vertical or horizontal nature of the Oriental woman's second set of lips. That question has been answered for the most part, and any details will be furnished slowly and grudgingly as you ply me with liquor or food.

Yes, the typhoon in Tokyo Bay was a thriller and likely was as bad or worse than the one on the way to Okinawa. I am not fond of typhoons or hurricanes, or any other type of revenge from Mother Nature, and tolerate them only because of the lack of alternatives.

Now I see that you left the muscle-building area of the tire business, only to engage in executive training in the publishing business. The rolls of paper you describe sound downright dangerous, but the bright side is the improvement in your footwork. Perhaps when you next get lucky and wound a pheasant, you can run it down with more speed and grace than you have yet displayed. It appears that your job search will be activated early on.

Your Christmas sounds enjoyable, and I'm happy for that and the thoughts that went with it. Maybe next year for me . . . I laugh now as I remember some of us trying to make a Christmas tree out of palm branches and with no ornaments. At least it kept us busy.

My address will remain the same for some time. San Francisco appears somewhat overawed with the volume of returning ships and what to do with them. I don't care what they do with the ship, but it is obvious they can get rid of me by sending me home and by first discharging me from Naval Service. My wishes have been stated and universally ignored, but I shall persist.

We arrived early in the morning of 31 December, 1945 and found that we were among many ships of all descriptions lying dead in the water and covered with a fog so thick one needed gills to breathe. One could not see a ship 50 yards away, and the fog horns moaned, the ships rang their bells and everyone hoped against hope that we could escape being rammed and sunk at the brink of the Golden Gate. We wondered if we could launch a boat or swim in and be the greeter at the dock. As time passed, the fog began to burn away in the sun and we noted the presence of Carriers and Cruisers, which gave us a clue as to who would go in first. We also noted that an LST had nosed into the side of a small Carrier and impaled a Carrier lifeboat on its forward twin 40mms. The Carrier had released the boat, and the LST would later enter the harbor carrying the lifeboat on its forward guns. Probably a large demerit for the LST Skipper, who likely cares not one whit about a promotion anyway.

After endless delays, we were allowed in and were greeted by a fireboat with streams of water shooting skyward and all hands waving in our direction. It was a nice greeting, and I discovered the next day that some enterprising soul had been aboard the fireboat and taken our picture . . . and the picture would be available to each and every one of us for a dollar a copy. I already know what we look like, but out of sheer recklessness, I spent the dollar.

Our dreams of surging onto the dock and greeting the thousands of beautiful girls that had come to welcome us were somewhat shot down when we were assigned an anchorage in about ten feet of muddy water near San Quentin and Tiburon and Sausalito. We found it is either one long boat ride to San Francisco or a somewhat shorter trip to Sausalito, and then take the A-train over the bridge.

My next bit of luck was in the form of an announcement that I was needed for unloading and that I would miss New Year's Eve in the city. All of a sudden, it seemed that nearly everyone was gone but me. I dutifully found the man in charge of unloading and asked him, in my very best sarcasm, how in the hell we were to unload at an anchorage. Our conversation was by radio, and I learned that we would be unloaded at a dock as soon as dockspace was available. The next afternoon, we did dock and were able to be unloaded largely by stevedores, who do these things the easy way . . . with cranes. After darkness fell, I was free and clear, but not free for Liberty. I strolled down the dock a bit, where I was told some Red Cross girls were serving coffee. Having found them, I accepted a cup of coffee and tried to engage some of the "girls" in conversation. They were pretty busy stacking their paper cups and talking with each other, but they did find time to tell me that the coffee would be 25 cents. I was somewhat embarrassed, and also angry, because I assumed this was a little gesture financed by people who gave money so the Red Cross could provide a little comfort for our boys in the Service. I paid the quarter, but discussed it a bit, and they agreed that coffee was still a nickel in many places, but not on a dock on a cold night in the dark. I quietly walked away, realizing that these women did not make the rules or set the prices, but had I been in their shoes, I would have told the boss to shove it.

Further down the dock, in the other direction, was a fisherman's wife selling cooked Dungenous Crabs. I don't know how to spell the word, but that's how it sounds. The only crabs I've ever heard of are the ones for which the old blue ointment was invented. Such is the case for a boy from the midwest. The crabs were absolutely great, and I soon learned how to eat them. They are large (about ten or eleven inches across) with big claws and legs.

Liberty finally arrived for me, and three of us set out to see the various places we'd been told about by the lucky ones who had been ashore. An early stop, and a very quick one at that, was the My-O-My Club, which featured dancing boys pretending to be women and those who relish entertainment of this type. There were no women present, and we left in great haste, lest we be seen in that place. Then it was from one grog shop to the next where we all found that our capacities were not up to snuff. I had great difficulty in restraining my friends when we were approached by a gunner's mate who knew where we could engage in intimate behavior with a female friend of his. The price was 20 dollars, and I told the gunner my friends only had a short rental in mind . . . not ownership. He left in a huff.

San Francisco is a beautiful city with about everything to offer. The food is equal to New Orleans, but different, and it is fairly easy to get around. It is also expensive, but I have drawn some of my back pay and shall spend it as I please . . . which is eating real food (about five times per day) with something to wash it down. It is like being in Heaven, except for the cost.

We are now on Liberty every other day for close to 20 hours. We take the boat to the foot of Market Street and work our way up the hill to the Mark Hopkins Hotel. There is a revolving room atop the building where one can pay a week's wages for a drink, and largely look out the windows and see fog. It seems to be the place to be, and is a great hotel. Downstairs is a sort of canteen for Officers, with several volunteer hostesses who are apparently told to be friendly, but not too friendly. My efforts to strike up a platonic, long-lasting, meaningful relationship have fallen on bad times. It is clear that these girls are mind readers. They have heard all the war stories and look with suspicion on anyone who says he's just arrived. They point out that all the boys who have spent the war at Treasure Island have at least four rows of campaign ribbons. I have no ribbons and have no idea which I may be entitled to. May have to buy some to keep up with the rear echelon!

Back out at anchor now in the general vicinity of the first place. Now it is a boat trip to Tiburon or Sausalito, and then the train across the bridge. It's a long way to San Francisco, and a seemingly much longer way home in the morning. I love the fog horns, the food and the wonderful scenery when the sun shines. It is COLD. The nights fall to about 30 degrees, and we have no heat. There is some suspicion ashore that our crew purposely damaged our evaps or boiler, and the decision as to where and when we go to where is delayed. I have no idea what happened, but we had heat in Japan and sure could use some now. 30 degrees in a damp steel box is extremely unpleasant, and I am glad I experience it only every other day. My second home is now the Mark Hopkins Hotel. Aboard ship, we are doing little except keeping it clean and dreaming of getting off. The initial joy of arriving and seeing the city has diminished somewhat. We are home, but we are not in our homes, and there is a big difference.

On our way here, we learned of a big volcanic eruption near Hawaii and were warned by radio to be alert for a large tidal wave. It was supposed to be about 60 feet high, which is bad news coming up on one's stern. We did see it coming, but it was no more than a big ground swell at that point.

Must take to the boat to continue my pig-like eating habit. So far, I haven't gained much weight. Climbing too many hills, I guess! It now seems clear that I am not flying to Chicago or anywhere else soon. I'll write again and, hopefully, have some news.

FRISCO DERELICT BILL

Saturday, 12 Jan. 1946

DEAR CHOKED UP WAYFARER—

Just received your last two letters and have decided to mail my previous letter, and this one as well, hoping the P.O. is aware of your next Port of Call and will hold your mail until you can pick it up. This presumably will be San Francisco, or possibly San Diego. In any event, if you are rich, call me; otherwise, drop a quick note when you hit the Good Earth.

Your synopsis of some of the events that you didn't cover in your letters (security measures) was fascinating and gave me further evidence that I was indeed right in going the Air Corps route. I am not entirely sure my nerves would have held up under the adversities you guys had to face on an almost daily basis. However, all things eventually pass, and you are home . . . all in one contiguous piece. We're both luckier than hell.

I must confess that your last letter of 23 November contained a sentence or two that were vastly disappointing. Merely because I'm married and settled down is not sufficient reason to keep me from knowing the answer to the question regarding the physiognomy of our sisters from the far east. This question will niggle at me now until I meet St. Peter at The Gate. He will probably repeat your reasoning that I have no real need to know any more, and that inquiries along those lines are forbidden behind The Pearly Gates. I now plan on getting you in your cups, hoping that you will have a slip of the tongue as you recount your days and nights at To Kan. If that is pronounced "Two Can," I am hot on the trail.

Welcome home, Wandering William. Get in touch when you are able to spare time from shouting Hallelujahs and Hosannas!!!

WELCOME WAGON WILLIAM

DEAR WELCOME WAGON WILLIAM—

I am the lucky recipient of your letters dated 1 to 2 January and 12 January, both of 1946. The quick mail service makes it easy to keep up and your letters are still appreciated very much.

Your first letter is in answer to one of mine from Asamushi, Japan, and I note that you have erroneously interpreted some of my statements. The teaching of the fine art of striptease dancing was a lesson in western culture and involved no demonstrations on the part of the teacher. The girls were merely taught how to artfully remove clothing in the prescribed fashion. You may already have surmised that there was a certain tiny amount of deceit in this procedure, but due to your urging, it was necessary in order to determine the slant of things normally concealed.

Yes, the sharing of the brewery by the Army was a stroke of luck, and the consensus was that the Japanese make beer even better than they make war. At least it was far more enjoyable. However, no beer ever went back to the ship. Booze aboard ship is a strict negative, and a little experience way back in the Russell Islands taught us that.

My Army English-Japanese dictionary was about totally useless for ordinary conversation, but it is amazing how people can make their wishes known without language. A negative response can be picked up immediately.

You may have noticed that I have not called. People are arriving here by the thousands, and finding a telephone that is not in use seems impossible. I have phoned no one, but have written notes to family and friends to announce that I made it home.

Shortly after my arrival, our radio man advised that, in my absence, a message (garbled) had been received from a woman. He was sorry, but just could not hear the message. It was a day or two later that I got a note from my girlfriend telling me she had married and would be in San Francisco on her honeymoon and would try and call if I was in by then. Ships arrivals were printed in all the papers, so she went to some trouble to make the call. She is a fine person and will be remembered. And I am glad she married because that's what she wanted. I, on the other hand, want freedom. My attitude is that things worked out for both of us.

Your second letter gives us credit for surviving in our little world, and modestly states that you may have had it better. I doubt that any of us would have traded places with anyone other than the rear echelon. I also doubt that neither you nor I would have settled for the rear echelon. After a little experience, yes, but not through the whole war. In my view, the ones who really had it tough were the combat riflemen. The CB's have my very great respect and, of course, there were numerous people involved in risky jobs we don't even know about. The fact is, as you say, we are both lucky as hell.

Your letter then turns, again, to questions regarding the female Oriental physiognomy. Since you wrote, you have certainly received my clinical report in that regard, and I trust that the boys in the back room at your entertainment center can now relax and get on with their lives. Having learned the answer to a titillating riddle (a whole new question, William) perpetrated by old seamen on the inexperienced, now one can relax and go about the more mundane. However, if an opportunity for further study on this subject should arise, I shall do my best and you shall be the first to know. All you will need is an explanation as to how you came to know these facts.

Most of our crew is gone. We who started as supernumeraries are now in charge, and we search in vain for the news we want to hear. We are still freezing at night and sitting around doing little. All we want is to go home and get on with our lives. Those ashore who are trying to figure out what to do with all these ships and men are having their problems. We are short of men, and ones we have are totally inexperienced. On the other hand, we are not at sea and are not standing wartime watches. I am making an absolute SOB of myself by standing at the quarterdeck and seeing to it that these raw recruits, just out of boot camp, do not go on liberty wearing three and four rows of ribbons. I suppose it is a petty thing to do, but it rankles me to have them pose as someone they are not. My efforts are merely displaying my attitude because I know full well they carry their ribbons off and don them when they are out of sight. My prediction long ago is now fulfilled . . . no matter what we did or where we were, we are all equal now. I accept it, but am not thrilled about it.

We have now pressed the powers-that-be enough that we got an answer. I feel we should press someone else in hope of a different answer. We are going to sea somewhere near the end of the month, without repairs and with our green crew. Our orders are to go through the canal and report at Charleston, South Carolina, where we will decommission this ship. That means an inventory against issued equipment and disposal of same to the proper authorities. It also means a hell of a lot of time. I read in the papers that those who joined the Navy recently are being sent home. There is no joy in Mudville! No chance for a few days at home; no nothing.

I have purposely paused in this letter in order to write something other than profanity. I am shocked, saddened, depressed and angry as hell. I have experienced the depths and the heights of emotions over these past years and, without doubt, this is better than most, but it is still a terrible surprise. I must remember that I am number 360031, a Junior Officer and one of several thousand. I did not mind the not asking why, just do or die . . . but somehow I view this as shabby treatment. I know I'm not alone.

So, one does what one must, and my feelings will be curbed and cured. The new crew members are anxious to go to sea, and we must teach them what they need to know. We were once in their shoes and know there is much to learn. I pray for good weather.

The money goes like water here, and I must settle down a bit. Eating is still high on my list because I need to gain weight, and because it is so good. It is the search for companionship, and the time and money spent at the watering holes that must suffer. There is much to do aboard ship now, and we can run various drills to help the new personnel get the picture. Boat drills and anchor drills must wait.

Another tidbit of information is to the new effect that, when possible, men will be discharged in the Naval District at which they enlisted. This means that at some time in the future, I will be at Chicago rather than Borneo (unless I let my feelings be known), and at that point I'll be in touch. There is also a very cute and charming member of the female race who resides in Chicago and who has been very kind to me over several years, in spite of some shortcomings on my part. Whom I call first is as yet undecided, but it is now a long way off, and I'll be thinking about it. Right now, she gets the nod!

So, our wartime letters have overrun the war a little, but we both are now in the USA, and you are struggling with a living for a family and I am in the last throes of my military service. Your letters, over these years, have been a Godsend, and I thank you for the time and effort. I daresay I worried more about you than me. I'll keep in touch and hope you do the same, and one of these days we shall meet again. It is my hope that we can have, perhaps, a dram or two of something liquid and discuss some of the many, many things we could not write about. I would like to know Shirley better and have a great feeling for her and the way she has sacrificed in order to be with you at some of those awful spots. I still believe we had it better and easier than the women who had to wait long periods of time to know whether they had received their last letter or not. It truly has been hell . . . but it is over.

This letter is building in bits and pieces, and I add a little now and then and may not mail it until we leave. Life here now is dragging. We have seen what we want to see and want to get on with it. There are so many men here that it is nearly hopeless to think of having a date or a conversation. I have given up.

The end of the month nears, and we are taking on fuel, water and provisions. They are still trying to get rid of wartime food, so my weight-gaining project will be on hold. Our new sailors now know the bow from the stern and can find the chow line. They will be all right!

3 February, '46. We leave at 0800 tomorrow . . . not a minute too soon. San Francisco will be fondly remembered, but it will be good to get to sea again. Port duty has its special problems. Again, I pray for good weather and an uneventful trip. The old ship has been a good one, and I can see how old sailors love their ships.

As far as I'm concerned, Chicago is my next real stop. Can't wait to see you and the entire brood. Thanks again for your letters.

RELUCTANT SEAFARER BILL

12 April, '46

DEAR BILL—

You are doubtless involved with such elementary things as family, a job, taxes, etc. The purpose of this letter is to keep in touch, and to advise of the latest news from your nautical traveler. The end here is nearly in sight and I can look forward to my trip to Chicago and, hopefully, a visit with you.

Our trip to and through the Canal was uneventful, as was the remainder of the trip here to Charleston. Since arriving we have tried to work around the clock in order to complete the Decommissioning process . . . and go home. You will not be surprised to learn that nobody seems to know how to go about this process. We are lined up with several other LSTs in the river and beached near a street where we can off load.

The Navy has several categories of equipment which range all the way from "throw away" to "don't dare lose it". Due to our diligence in trading this for that with the Army and Marines, we have some items that do not fit on the official inventory lists. The people ashore who are to aid us in this miserable task do not wish to take any responsibility for the warehousing of non-Navy items. Even the offer of a drink or a bouquet of flowers cannot elicit any advice. Consequently, all of the LST Skippers put their heads together and the disposal of inventory proceeds, but not necessarilly in the manner set out in the incessant memos we receive.

My mother and younger sister visited from Florida, but we had time only for a dinner and small talk before they had to return. It was good to see them, but I had wished for more time and, perhaps, some sightseeing. Charleston is a beautiful old city with a lot of history, but it is difficult to get around for those on a low budget. We can walk through a mess of taverns and peep shows to a section of downtown, but there is little there. The reckless spending in San Francisco has moderated considerably here.

Sometime back a part of our crew was returning to the ship, in high spirits, when they clashed with some men at the taverns area who insulted and assaulted. They quietly made it to the ship where they picked up their souvenier weapons. They then cleaned out the tavern area, fortunately without using the weapons. The local police caught most of them, which meant a trip downtown to spring the men from the dungeon . . . and to remind them that they are now "home" and must change their ways.

On another day, a wind of gale force blew a freighter through a neaby bridge, taking out a section of the bridge. It was an exciting day, but the LSTs appear to be stuck in the mud and did not move an inch. I supect we'll need a tug to get off the beach.

Charleston has an Azelia Festival in the spring and I hope to see some of it. We really haven't seen much of the people here, nor have we had the free time to find out where they gather. My guess is that they go where the sailors do not go.

We are disposing, on a piecemeal basis, of our medical booze . . . which is largely sour mash whiskey. The shorebound people thought it should be inventoried and turned in first, but we explained that we had suffered a good deal of illness over the past couple of years and had never been able to replace the supply. How dumb do they think we are?!

Our Captain, formerly the Communications Officer (and my roommate), offered to make me Captain for a day when the ship goes up the river for mothballing. He and I will be going to Chicago together and he will then go to his home on the west coast. I declined the Captain thing because I must get our train tickets and finish the last minute details. I will not go upriver with the skeleton crew.

At the moment it appears that I will be able to leave here the first week in May, and I hope I can hear from you and know if your address is still the same . . . and if you can break free for a lunch and some conversation. In the event that I do not hear from you, I'll try to reach you by phone in Chicago. The days are flying now and I shall soon experience my first train ride in a compartment; hopefully, on a train built since the Civil War.

I am experiencing some of the anticlimax you indicated when you went home. It has dawned on me that I do not have a home! I've decided to go back and finish school, but will have to get civilian clothes, find a place to live and find the money for all this, plus tuition, fees and books. I have no idea how this can be done, but I know it will be done.

Please direct your reply to LST #628 at the Charleston Naval Base as listed on the envelope.

SOON A CIVILIAN BILL

17 April, '46

DEAR SOON—

Decommissioning, I presume, refers not only to the stationary target ("Ole 628"), but to Lt. (Jg) Burling, as well. I am sure that, as these notable milestones are reached, you will view them with a mixed bag of conflicting emotions. Nostalgia for the ship, shipmates and some hairy, never to be duplicated, experiences . . . then casting your eye forward, wondering what kind of hand you will be dealt in the future.

I think returning to school is a great idea, and some of the other guys will undoubtedly be there, as well. When you do get back to Bloomington and Illinois Wesleyan you can arrange with our numerous farming brothers for reservations in their corn fields for the upcoming bird and bunny seasons. In light of my three-year absence, the pheasant population has probably exploded. This will be your golden opportunity. Shoot into a large bunch as they break cover, and maybe one (with a weak heart) will fall.

Shirley's Uncle Herb lives in deer country in Wisconsin. He as extended an open invitation to us to join him in the timber swamps for a try at the wily whitetail. Herb lives in a shotgun county, so you will be shooting one projectile from your trusty 12 bore, and not a handful of shot. This puts you at a serious disadvantage, particularly since deer can run at a very fast clip through the brush. Do practice beforehand . . . a lot.

I can well understand your unfriendly feelings toward the heroic shore clerks and their inability to use some common horse sense, instead of their manuals, when dealing with ships and equipment that have been three or four years at sea under some downright nasty conditions. A year or two ago, a whole ship could have disappeared with all hands and not caused a ripple on the nit-pickers ocean of paper and forms. The absence of your medicinal booze probably caused a tidal wave of raised eyebrows and veiled threats. Keep a poker face as you lie unashamedly! After all, they can hardly send you to a combat zone anymore.

I was relieved to hear that #628 will be moth balled as opposed to facing the acetylene torches of the ghouls in the scrap yards. You, no doubt, felt even greater relief than I did upon hearing that #628 will be retired intact and, perhaps, may even someday become a "lucky ship" for another bewildered young crew on their first shakedown cruise.

We remain at 7042 S. Kimbark Ave., and our phone will ring if you dial DOR (Dorchester) 4364. It is not necessary for reply to this letter, unless you re-enlist and head for Pago Pago . . . just come on by. We can hardly wait to see you in the flesh (or whatever remains of your flesh). I know you are anxious to get on with things, but please plan to stay long enough to recap the last three or four years.

I am stocking the pantry, the meat locker and, most importantly, the potables from the vineyards of California, the stills of the mountains of Kentucky and the breweries of Messrs. Anheiser and Busch.

Hurry . . . I am not to be trusted, surrounded as I am by all these goodies.

BACCHUS BILL

AFTERWORD

While reading "Thunderbolt", a book written by Robert S. Johnson, the leading P-47 ace in the 8th Air Force, I was struck by his description of a mission he had flown on 9 April, 1944. He and his wingman, Sam Hamilton, broke up a large gaggle of FW-190s who were intent on killing a group of B-24s south of Sweden over the North Sea.

This was <u>our</u> first mission and our first encounter with the Luftwaffe. On their first pass, the Germans shot down a B-24. Then, as they were forming up for a second pass, two P-47s tore into them and scattered them.

I wrote in my diary then that, someday, I would like to thank our "Little Friends" for saving our virginal butts.

Bob Johnson replied to a letter from me on 10 April, 1990. A wish came true, and 46 years later I was finally able to thank him for his timely intervention.

In his reply, Bob clearly remembered taking on the 190s and breaking up their attack. He also discovered at a later date, that the lone B-24 that went down had as a crew member a young man he grew up with in Oklahoma, Bebe Skaggs.

Two very strange quirks of fate. Out of the thousands of missions flown, to be involved in one where a friend goes down in the only ship lost, and then to hear a grateful thank you from a surviving crewman in one of the other ships . . . forty years and one day later.

As Mr. Ripley says, "Believe it or not."

BILL ALDERSON
10 APRIL 1990

Ball of Fire Quarterly Express
Newsletter of The 93rd Bb. Gp.
2nd Air Division, 8th Air Force, Hardwick, England

The 1995 spring issue of the above 93rd Bomb Group newsletter contained an article written by Gordon Reynolds and Douglas Howeld . . . a wonderfully meticulous accounting of a midair collision of two B-24s over Henham, England, on 29 March, 1944.

Our navigator, Earl J. Norris, was killed in that accident. Prior to reading their story, "Tragedy Over Henham", I had been privy to only the bare bones version the Air Force had given us as the time of the crash. Huge kudos to Gordon and Douglas, for they have satisfied 50 years of wondering what really happened that terrible day.

On that morning, seventy-seven B-24 Liberators of the 20th Combat Wing assembled in spotty overcast for missions against German V weapons at Watten and sub pens at St. Nazaere. One B-24 suddenly dropped out of formation and collided with another B-24, severing the tail section from the fuselage. Three men escaped the airplanes by chute and survived. Two other men got out; one was found in his chute in an oak tree, but apparently had been hit by debris and killed . . . the other was found with an unopened chute.

Debris, including bombs, propellers, engines and large and small pieces of fuselage, fell over a large area. Two or three bombs (1,000 or 2,000 pounders) exploded upon hitting the ground. Another exploded as firemen and medical personnel from the AAF attempted rescue operations. Nineteen men were killed and more than 30 injured. Fourteen other casualties (minor injuries and shock) were suffered by English servicemen and women. All in all, the casualties totaled 89; 36 dead and 53 injured.

Even after 51 years, as I think of the crewmen, the heroic rescuers and all of their families, I am uncommonly saddened and chastened.

BILL ALDERSON
20 JUNE, 1995

EPILOGUE

Early in May, 1946, Lt. (Jg) Burling stopped by Kimbark Avenue during his delayed-travel time before reporting to Great Lakes Naval Station for discharge. The long-awaited, and frequently despaired of, reunion took place, and became a story to tell all by itself. This get-together marked the end of the wartime letters, but became the beginning of another series of letters which, along with some legend-making hunting, fishing and luncheon experiences, have continued for almost fifty years.

Bill Burling and his wife, Dorothy, now live on North Twin Lake near Howe, Indiana. Bill spends summers and winters out on the lake, hopefully dangling a variety of tempting lures to a lake full of suspicious and neurotic fish. He is widely known locally for his fish stories. Dorothy is very talented in art work, antiquing and gourmet cooking. This tends to have a civilizing effect on her erstwhile Isaac Walton. They have four grandchildren.

Bill Alderson and Shirley live on the shores of Lake Michigan in New Buffalo, Michigan, a short drive from the Burlings at North Twin Lake. Congress decreed, again, that Bill Alderson take to the wild blue yonder, and he flew as a bomb-Nav aboard a B-26 (Nearer My God To Thee) for eighteen panic-stricken months during the Korean conflict. He and Shirley are in the 55th year of their marriage and have four children, six grandchildren and a couple of great grandchildren. Shirley knits, sews, crochets, does needlepoint and makes beautiful afghans. Bill sits in his rocking chair, contemplating the ever-changing face of Lake Michigan and wondering if the Postman will ring a third time bringing "Greetings" from the War Department.

Printed in the USA
CPSIA information can be obtained
at www.ICGtesting.com
JSHW060053150824
68134JS00032B/2720

9 781681 622743